Adaptive Learning of Polynomial Networks

Genetic Programming, Backpropagation and Bayesian Methods

GENETIC AND EVOLUTIONARY COMPUTATION SERIES

Series Editors

David E. Goldberg
University of Illinois at Urbana-Champaign

John R. Koza
Stanford University

Selected titles from the Series:

THE DESIGN OF INNOVATION: Lessons from and for Competent Genetic Algorithms, *David E. Goldberg;* ISBN: 1-4020-7098-5

GENETIC PROGRAMMING IV: Routine Human-Computer Machine Intelligence, *John R. Koza, Martin A. Keane, Matthew J. Streeter, William Mydlowec, Jessen Yu, Guido Lanza;* ISBN: 1-4020-7446-8; softcover ISBN: 0-387-25067-0

EVOLUTIONARY ALGORITHMS FOR SOLVING MULTI-OBJECTIVE PROBLEMS, *Carlos A. Coello Coello, David A. Van Veldhuizen, and Gary B. Lamont;* ISBN: 0-306-46762-3

AUTOMATIC QUANTUM COMPUTER PROGRAMMING: A Genetic Programming Approach, *Lee Spector*; ISBN: 1-4020-7894-3

GENETIC PROGRAMMING AND DATA STRUCTURES: Genetic Programming + Data Structures = Automatic Programming! *William B. Langdon*; ISBN: 0-7923-8135-1

For a complete listing of books in this series, go to http://www.springer.com

Adaptive Learning of Polynomial Networks

Genetic Programming, Backpropagation and Bayesian Methods

Nikolay Y. Nikolaev
University of London

Hitoshi Iba
The University of Tokyo

Springer

Nikolay Y. Nikolaev
University of London

Hitoshi Iba
The University of Tokyo

ISBN -13: 978-1-4419-4060-5

e-ISBN-10: 0-387-31240-4
e-ISBN-13: 978-0387-31240-8

Softcover reprint of the hardcover 1st edition 2006

9 8 7 6 5 4 3 2 1

springer.com

Contents

Preface

This book provides theoretical and practical knowledge for development of algorithms that infer linear and nonlinear models. It offers a methodology for inductive learning of polynomial neural network models from data. The design of such tools contributes to better statistical data modelling when addressing tasks from various areas like system identification, chaotic time-series prediction, financial forecasting and data mining. The main claim is that the model identification process involves several equally important steps: finding the model structure, estimating the model weight parameters, and tuning these weights with respect to the adopted assumptions about the underlying data distribution. When the learning process is organized according to these steps, performed together one after the other or separately, one may expect to discover models that generalize well (that is, predict well).

The book offers statisticians a shift in focus from the standard linear models toward highly nonlinear models that can be found by contemporary learning approaches. Specialists in statistical learning will read about alternative probabilistic search algorithms that discover the model architecture, and neural network training techniques that identify accurate polynomial weights. They will be pleased to find out that the discovered models can be easily interpreted, and these models assume statistical diagnosis by standard statistical means.

Covering the three fields of: evolutionary computation, neural networks and Bayesian inference, orients the book to a large audience of researchers and practitioners. Researchers in genetic programming will study how to elaborate model representations, how to make learning operators that sample the search space efficiently, how to navigate the search process through the design of objective fitness functions, and how to examine the search performance of the evolutionary system. The possibility to use reliable means for observing the search behavior of genetic programming is one of its essential advantages.

Practitioners in artificial neural networks will study how to determine automatically the network structure prior to applying the weight training algorithm. They will realize what are the steps of the global search mechanisms that allow identification of relevant network topologies from data. Searching for the optimal network structure is essential for adjusting the network to the concrete application task. Even if one knows how to make the weight training algorithm, there is a need to determine in advance the network architecture. In addition to this, the book gives various activation and basis functions for elaborating different neural network mappings, such as kernels, harmonics, Gaussians etc., which extend their descriptive power.

Specialists in Bayesian inference will read about applications of the principles of probabilistic learning to polynomial networks. The Bayesian training of polynomial networks makes them practical tools for solving difficult real-world problems from various fields. This book demonstrates that polynomial networks can be trained probabilistically not only in offline mode, but also in recursive mode. Novel Bayesian techniques for reliable recursive training of polynomial networks are offered. Practitioners in econometrics will especially find interesting the fact that polynomial networks can be trained using sampling methods, which makes them attractive for financial forecasting.

Students will find this book useful for studying genetic programming, neural networks, and probabilistic learning. There is teaching material from the courses that we taught the last few years to our students in artificial intelligence, machine learning, evolutionary computation and neural networks. The material is self-contained and includes: definitions of the main inductive tasks, formulations of the basic approaches to addressing these tasks, introduction to the fundamentals of genetic programming, review of backpropagation training, and presentations of the basics of Bayesian learning. Undergraduate students will learn how to design and implement the basic mechanisms of a genetic programming system, including the selection scheme, and the crossover and mutation learning operators. Postgraduate students will study advanced topics such as improving the search control of genetic programming systems, and tools for examination of their search performance. In order to facilitate the understanding and easy memorization of the algorithms, they are summarized in tables at the end of each subsection.

The inspiration to write this book came after a long period of conducting research in inductive problem solving. The authors experience started with work on inductive tasks using machine learning algorithms.

The work in this area lead to disappointment due to the many fundamental inabilities of the typical machine learning algorithms. First, they seem to be quite conservative, dealing mainly with inexpressive propositional concept description languages. Even advanced inductive programming systems cannot directly manipulate well-known nonlinear models from the statistical analysis. Second, they lack flexible learning operators that can efficiently sample the search space, as for each representation language they require specific learning operators. Third, they do not allow for observation of their performance, while the learning proceeds, which hinders tuning of the parameters.

Genetic programming offered interesting and challenging ideas for making innovative computational algorithms. This research showed that it is possible to devise domain independent model representations; it is possible to make general learning operators that need not be changed when changing some representation details; it is possible to organize both global and local searches for induction of good models; it is possible to navigate the search using reliable formulae from statistics and numerical optimization; and it is possible to validate the results with standard statistical tools. Above all, the results were better than those produced by machine learning algorithms. In addition to this, the genetic programming paradigm allowed incorporation of the most recent achievements in artificial neural networks and generation of well-performing models from benchmark and real-world data.

An enormous number of experiments on various data sets were conducted during the last several years by both authors. Most of the experiments were successful, which was considered convincing evidence for the potential of genetic programming. The idea of further improving the best results by neural network training and Bayesian algorithms was suggested later by several researchers who expressed scepticism that genetic programming alone could discover optimal models from data. Specialized backpropagation and Bayesian techniques for training polynomial networks were further developed and tested. It was found that on some tasks they really could achieve considerable improvements, and so were worth investigation and special attention.

The developments in this book aim to facilitate the inference of polynomial models for time-series prediction. The orientation toward time-series forecasting comes from the inherent difficulty in many scientific areas to find models that describe, sufficiently well, unknown dynamical systems that have generated the series. The interest in such natural problems is that many everyday tasks actually fall in this category. The presented successful experimental results suggest that, in general, the proposed methodology can be useful in practical inductive modelling.

Acknowledgments. The material in this book matured with our experience. The first author, Dr. Nikolaev, developed his doctoral thesis under the supervision of Professor N. Kasabov who currently works at the University of Auckland. After that he was a postdoctoral fellow in the lab of Professor D.T. Pham at University of Cardiff. During the years Dr. Nikolaev enjoyed working with his colleague and best friend Dr. Evgeny Smirnov, University of Maastricht, who inspired him to work on machine learning algorithms. He also conducted research with Dr. Vanyo Slavov from New Bulgarian University, Sofia on immune network algorithms and Dr. Lilian de Menezes from City University, London on statistical model diagnostics. Dr. Peter Tino from the University of Birmingham thought him to do Bayesian inference. He thanks especially to his colleagues from The American University in Bulgaria and Goldsmiths College for providing him with a pleasant working atmosphere. He is particularly grateful to his dear girlfriend, Dr. Snezhana Dimitrova, for her inspiration, encouragement, and tolerance while writing this book. Nikolay is extremely grateful to his parents for their love and support. They have always helped him, shaped his thinking and made him a scientist.

The second author, Dr. Hitoshi Iba, acknowledges the pleasant research atmosphere created by his colleagues and students from the research laboratory associated with Graduate School of Frontier Sciences at the University of Tokyo. He is also grateful to his previous group and colleagues at Electro-Technical Laboratory, where he used to work for ten years. Particular thanks are due to Dr. Hirochika Inoue and Dr. Taisuke Sato for their providing precious comments and advice on numerous occasions. And last, but not least, he would like to thank his wife Yumiko and his sons and daughter Kohki, Hirono, and Hiroto, for their patience and assistance.

Both authors are grateful to Professor Alexey G. Ivakhnenko and his son Gregory Ivakhnenko for the invaluable discussions on the multilayer and harmonic GMDH algorithms. These discussions reinforced our enthusiasm to work in this area.

Chapter 1

INTRODUCTION

Polynomial neural networks (PNN) are global function models whose parameters, once learned from given data, can be used for generating predictions without the need to infer additional versions for the separate neighborhoods in the data. PNN provide opportunities to reach accuracy superior to many global models such as nonlinear functions, statistical learning networks, multilayer perceptrons, and other feed-forward neural networks on multivariate nonlinear regression, time-series forecasting and classification problems. Inferring PNN models from data is an inductive computation problem that requires development of corresponding learning algorithms.

This book develops a methodological framework for induction of multilayer PNN. It involves several steps: 1) elaboration of neural network representations of polynomials; 2) search for the proper network structure (architecture) using the evolutionary genetic programming paradigm; 3) adjustment of the polynomial coefficients (referred to further as weights) by gradient descent search using backpropagation training techniques; 4) enhancement of the network generalization potential using Bayesian inference; and 5) model validation with diagnostic methods. These five steps make a coherent and integrated methodology for identification of well-performing polynomial models. The rationale is in the tight coupling of the second, third and fourth learning steps which suggest to further adapt the evolved polynomial network and its coefficients by backpropagation and Bayesian techniques.

The difficulties in this polynomial learning methodology are what kind of representation to choose, how to organize evolutionary search with it, whether it can enable neural network training, and whether its prediction can be improved by assumptions about the underlying distribution of the data. What this book emphasizes is that the model representation is essential for the development of inductive learning algorithms. This is the representation which allows us to employ efficient search methods, to derive neural network training algorithms, to tune the coefficient's variance with respect to the target density, and to perform reliable analysis of the results. The key idea is to make tree-structured polynomial networks that can be flexibly tailored to the data. When equipped with neural network and Bayesian methods for weight training and pruning, these polynomial networks become PNN, and thus alternative methods for statistical data analysis.

The PNN are multilayer perceptrons of neuron-like units which produce high-order polynomials [Barron, 1988, Elder and Brown, 2000, Farlow, 1984, Gosh and Shin, 1992, Ivakhnenko, 1971, Müller and Lemke, 2000, Marmarelis and Zhao, 1997, Pao, 1989, Pham and Liu, 1995, Tenorio and Lee, 1990, Wray and Green, 1994, Zhang and Mühlenbein, 1995]. Their distinctive advantage is the ability to find optimal higher-order term weights. PNN inherit some good features from their predecessors, the multilayer perceptron networks, while often showing better accuracy of fit and forecasting. Such an important feature is that they assume gradient descent training by error backpropagation.

The multistep inductive learning of polynomials from data became possible with the recent progress in biologically inspired computation. Search for optimal tree-like topologies can be organized using genetic programming. Search in the weight space can be implemented using both backpropagation and Bayesian techniques for neural networks. Research in artificial neural networks demonstrates that they have the capacity to carry out reliable learning despite discrepancies in the data. A serious criticism to most connectionist models is that they require us to predefine their structure. There are algorithms that construct the network architectures but they do this with an inefficient topological search. A better search may be conducted using the evolutionary paradigms, such as evolution strategies, genetic algorithms, and genetic programming. They perform global exploration as well as local exploitation of the neural network shape spaces, which helps to locate good solutions. Most of the neural network strategies, however, assume that the data are fixed and produce point predictions. Such predictions are unrealistic in practical situations where it is necessary to exploit the data together with uncertainties in them. This directs the attention toward investigating Bayesian methods for proper treatment of the data with their inherent noise. Also proposed are Bayesian inference algorithms that adjust the weights along with their variances, and so enable us to make more reliable probabilistic predictions.

This book integrates the strengths of evolutionary paradigms, artificial neural networks, and the probabilistic methods for efficient simulation of inductive computation processes. The existing multilayer polynomial networks have a flexible structure that allows adaptation of the polynomials to the data. Applying evolutionary algorithms to them helps to discover the relevant explanatory variables and their interrelationships. Multilayer polynomial networks typically use conventional methods to find the values of the weights, such as least squares fitting methods. While ordinary least squares fitting methods are optimal for linear models, it is not clear at all whether they are optimal for nonlinear models. The problem of using least squares fitting for learning the weights of composed nonlinear models is that they do not guarantee reaching sufficiently good accuracy. When nonlinear models are built, the relationships between the variables in them are complex and need sophisticated treatment. This is the rationale for applying specialized connectionist algorithms to polynomial networks.

Even equipped with such specialized weight training algorithms, the polynomial networks assume further adaptation with regard to the underlying assumptions about the noise in the data. During the weight training process, the possible noise in the data distribution has to be considered so as to tune the model better. This involves updating the belief in the amount of noise in order to adjust the belief in the uncertainty of the weights. Having inferred the degree of certainty in the network weights, probabilistic predictions can be made which are more reliable as they reflect the characteristics of the data generating function with a computable level of confidence.

1.1 Inductive Learning

The problem with inductive learning is to identify a model that optimally describes the characteristics of provided data, usually collected from observations of natural, real-world phenomena. The necessary tools for dealing with such a problem include [Vapnik, 1995, Vapnik, 1998]: a generator of example input data, a teacher that associates each input with a corresponding desired output, and a learning device that implements the model. The learning device maps the given input vectors to estimated outputs. Since the desired outputs are known, this formulation is commonly named supervised inductive learning. The objective is to find a model whose estimated output is maximally close to the desired output. The search for the parameters of the learning device that best describes the given data is organized by a machinery for inductive computation. Inductive learning is essentially a search problem guided by proper criteria for closeness with the data.

The data generator draws independently random example (input) vectors $\mathbf{x}$ from some probability density $\Pr(\mathbf{x})$. The teacher assigns to each example a corresponding desired (target) output y according to a probability distribution $\Pr(y|\mathbf{x})$. The joint probability density function of these independent and identically distributed data is: $\Pr(\mathbf{x}, y) = \Pr(\mathbf{x})\Pr(y|\mathbf{x})$. Having collected a set of data $D = \{(\mathbf{x}_n, y_n)\}_{n=1}^{N}$, the goal is to find a mapping $P(\mathbf{x}) \rightarrow y$ as close as possible to the true unknown mapping $P^*(\mathbf{x})$. The mapping is parameterized by a set of weights $\mathbf{w} = (w_1, w_2, ...)$, that is we have functions of the kind $P(\mathbf{x}, \mathbf{w})$. Having an estimate of the error only on the available data, the intention is to achieve high generalization on modelling unseen data. The learning criterion is given by the *total generalization error*:

$$E = \int L(y, P(\mathbf{x}, \mathbf{w})) \Pr(\mathbf{x}, y) d\mathbf{x} dy \tag{1.1}$$

where $L(y, P(\mathbf{x}, \mathbf{w}))$ is a loss estimate (a measure of the training error).

The difficulty in solving this learning problem arises from the unknown probability density, but from another point of view this motivates the need to construct special inductive computation machinery. This computation machinery should be powerful enough to learn from finite data, which is known to be an ill-posed problem that requires apriori assumptions about the complexity of the learning device. The learning device is typically a function, such as a non-linear function, a polynomial, a radial-basis function, a spline function, a neural network function, etc.. This is why the learning device is simply called a function or model. Function models are suitable for addressing many inductive tasks such as density estimation, classification, regression, etc..

1.1.1 Learning and Regression

Inductive learning can be formulated as a regression task as follows: given an example set of input vectors $D = \{(\mathbf{x}_n, y_n)\}_{n=1}^{N}$ that are measurements of explanatory variables $\mathbf{x}_n = [x_{n1}, x_{n2}, ..., x_{nd}]$, $\mathbf{x} \in \mathcal{R}^d$, and corresponding desired values of the dependent variable $y_n \in \mathcal{R}$, the goal is to find a function P that describes the mapping $y = P(\mathbf{x}) + \varepsilon$, where ε is a zero mean normally distributed noise and $P \in L_2$, which on average converges to the true unknown mapping $P^*(\mathbf{x})$. The linear space L_2 contains functions with integrable squares, i.e. is the integral $\int P^2(\mathbf{x})d\xi$, where ξ is the space metric, it exists and it is finite [Kolmogorov and Fomin, 1999]. The function models the conditional mean of the data:

$$P(\mathbf{x}, \mathbf{w}) = \int y \Pr(y|\mathbf{x}) dy \tag{1.2}$$

where $\Pr(y|\mathbf{x})$ is the probability density of the given outputs.

The learning criterion in the Euclidean space is the following quadratic *empirical loss*:

$$L(y, P(\mathbf{x}, \mathbf{w})) = (y - P(\mathbf{x}, \mathbf{w}))^2 \tag{1.3}$$

The objective of inductive computation is to discover a model that minimizes the risk functional applied with this empirical loss, which is the error on the provided training data. Although the search is guided by the empirical loss, the expectation is that the best solution will also have low prediction risk, that is low error on unseen data.

1.1.2 Polynomial Models

The presented investigations adopt polynomials as universal function models. The rationale for choosing polynomials comes from the Stone-Weierstrass approximation theorem [Davis, 1975]. It states that polynomials are a universal approximation format with which there could be described any continuous function on a compact set. The polynomials provide sufficient expressive power for accurate data modelling; in other words they are reliable descriptive tools. Polynomial models can be built, e.g. like algebraic polynomials, orthogonal polynomials, trigonometric polynomials, rational polynomials, local basis polynomials, etc.. Such models can be represented as multilayer neural networks in order to facilitate the structure selection, the coefficient estimation, and the complexity tuning (including term pruning).

This book offers approaches to design and implementation of computational micromechanisms for inductive learning and specializes them for automated discovery of polynomial neural network models.

1.1.3 Inductive Computation Machinery

The development of inductive computation machinery for a chosen function model, like polynomials for example, involves: 1) choosing a search paradigm for model selection; 2) elaborating model representations suitable for manipulation by the operators offered by this paradigm; 3) organizing search navigation with relevant selection criteria; 4) designing parameter training algorithms for their fine-tuning to the data; 5) implementing probabilistic inference tools for enhancing the generalization performance; and 6) carrying out model validation using diagnostic methods and tools.

The Model Search Paradigm. The search paradigm serves to find the most adequate model structure for the data. When working with polynomials, the objective is to find PNN with complexity relevant to the training data in the sense of terms and order. The search paradigm should be powerful enough to perform exploration of large, distant areas on the search landscape as well as to perform exploitation of small, neighborhood areas. Among the different paradigms such as heuristic search, simulated annealing, random search and others, the genetic programming paradigm is preferred. Genetic programming offers learning operators and micromechanisms inspired from biology that have abilities to conduct guided stochastic search in large spaces. Genetic programming is a general search paradigm which operates on tree-structured model representations.

The Model Representation. A search paradigm is equipped with learning operators to manipulate the concrete structures that implement the adopted model representation. The genetic programming evolves tree-like model representations that are processed by evolutionary learning operators. This book develops different polynomials in the form of tree-structured networks, including algebraic network polynomials, kernel network polynomials, orthogonal network polynomials, trigonometric network polynomials, rational network polynomials, and dynamic network polynomials. The approximation characteristics of the models in evolutionary computation are traditionally referred to as their fitness.

Search Navigation. The model search process may be envisioned as flowing on a landscape surface built from the fitnesses of all possible models of the selected kind. The learning apparatus has to efficiently navigate the search on the landscape in order to examine it thoroughly and to locate a good solution. The search is guided by inductive principles which tell us how to define model selection criteria. One advantage of choosing polynomials is that they enable us to directly apply well-known principles for automated induction. Such inductive principles that can be built in the learning machinery are the statistical inference principle, the Bayesian inference principle, the maximum likelihood principle, the minimum description length principle, the structural risk minimization principle, and the regularization principle.

Considered for learning polynomials these principles become criteria that helps to find models that trade off between the accuracy and the generalization capacity. This is necessary because the provided training samples in practice are finite, which requires us to adapt the model well to the data. Complex models exhibit high accuracy on the training data but they are poor predictors, while simple models may tend to predict well but fail to reach a satisfactory training accuracy.

Weight Training. The inductive learning paradigms usually identify the model structure by search, and during the search they estimate the model parameters. The genetic programming conducts evolutionary search for the most relevant polynomial network tree-like structure from the data using the least squares fitting method for coefficient estimation. However, there is no guarantee that only parameter estimation is sufficient to obtain a good solution with optimal coefficients. This book claims that evolved polynomial networks assume further improvement by connectionist training algorithms. Backpropagation techniques for gradient descent search are derived especially for high-order neural networks with polynomial activation functions.

Generalization Enhancement. Having a promising network model structure is not sufficient in most cases to achieve good generalization. The polynomial network model may not exhibit good predictive performance if its weights do not reflect the underlying assumptions about the noise in the data. There could be normally distributed noise, or heavy tail noise, or other noise distributions that affect the model performance on unseen data. If the characteristics of the output noise are not taken into account in training, the weights will not be able to well capture the characteristics of the true data generation process. Probabilistic learning algorithms are presented and specialized here for PNN training. It is shown how the learning algorithm updates the belief in the weights along with the arrival of the data with respect to the preliminary assumptions about the probability distribution of the data.

Model Validation. After inductive inference of a promising model structure and its parameters, this model has to be validated. It has to be measured as to what degree the model is an adequate description of the data. The polynomials can be easily validated using standard statistical diagnosis tools. In addition to this, when polynomials are made as networks they can also be tested using approaches designed for neural network and Bayesian diagnosis. Statistical diagnosis can be performed by residual sampling methods, which can be used to measure confidence and prediction intervals of the polynomial neural networks. The possibility to test polynomials with both kinds of methods increases the certainty in their approximation characteristics.

1.2 Why Polynomial Networks?

Multilayer polynomial networks are a class of power series function models constructed using hierarchical networks of first-order and second-order processing units. These are higher-order neural networks with multiplicative activation functions, sparse connectivity, and parsimonious structure. There are three conjectures that motivate the representation of polynomials as neural networks [Marmarelis, 1994]. First, polynomials can be related to multilayer perceptron networks as universal approximators, so it is worth building polynomials as neural networks in order to use the achievements in connectionist learning.

Second, the modelling of a function requires, in general, a polynomial network of smaller size than the corresponding neural network required for the same function. The polynomial networks produce more compact and accurate models than multilayer perceptrons. This expressive difference is mainly due to the restriction of the activation functions of the multilayer perceptron to a specific squashing nonlinearity, typically the sigmoidal or tangential functions. This leads to increasing the number of hidden units necessary to achieve satisfactory performance.

Third, polynomial networks can be designed with bounded as well as unbounded activation polynomials in the hidden network nodes. There is a long debate on whether or not to use bounding of the activation polynomials through some squashing functions. It is traditionally considered that unbounded activations will enable faster convergence and will also help to reach more accurate results.

A polynomial can show anomalous behavior when applied to inputs outside of its definition domain [Matthews and Moschytz, 1994]. The main reason for such a pathological performance is that polynomials are extremely sensitive to the inputs. Such problems can be avoided by allocating polynomial models onto neural network architectures using bounded activations. Bounding the activation polynomials through squashing functions filters the inputs and diminishes the unexpected deteriorating effects from the high-order terms. Using networks with bounded activations can improve the usefulness of polynomials, especially when backpropagation training is applied. The estimation of the weights by least squares techniques, however, may lose accuracy [Marmarelis and Zhao, 1997, Wray and Green, 1994].

Although bounding of the activation polynomials in multilayer PNN is not explicitly shown in the presented research, it can be applied with minor modifications of the given formulae.

1.2.1 Advantages of Polynomial Networks

Polynomial networks are attractive modelling tools from a theoretical, as well as from a practical, point of view. Theoretically, they are: 1) universal approximators with which one may approximate any continuous function on a compact set to an arbitrary precision if there are sufficiently large numbers of terms; 2) mathematically tractable since they assume manipulations, like decompositions and reformulations, which make them flexible for structural identification; 3) probabilistically tractable with specific assumptions for normal and heavy tail distributions; and 4) statistically tractable as they assume standard statistical analysis including testing of their residuals, the covariances between the variables, and the sensitivity to the data sampling.

Practically, the polynomial networks are: 1) computationally tractable, as their training often proceeds on unimodal error surfaces that enable fast and reliable convergence by well-known algorithms, such as ordinary least squares fitting; 2) open-box transparent models which are amenable to easy comprehension and understanding.

1.2.2 Multilayer Polynomial Networks

The subjects of interest here are the multilayer networks with transfer (activation) polynomials in the nodes [Barron, 1988, Elder and Pregibon, 1996, Farlow, 1984, Ivakhnenko, 1971, Müller and Lemke, 2000]. The transfer polynomials are selected according to some predefined criteria from a pool of candidate basis polynomials, and are cascaded hierarchically. The connection scheme suggests that the transfer polynomial outcomes feed-forward to their parent nodes where partial models are composed of received outcomes from the polynomials below and/or input variables. The network output is a high-order polynomial.

The polynomials are discrete analogs of the Volterra series, known as Kolmogorov-Gabor *polynomials* [Kolmogorov, 1957, Gabor et al., 1961]:

$$P(\mathbf{x}) = a_0 + \sum_{i=1}^{S} a_i x_i + \sum_{i=1}^{S}\sum_{j=i}^{S} a_{ij} x_i x_j + \sum_{i=1}^{S}\sum_{j=i}^{S}\sum_{k=j}^{S} a_{ijk} x_i x_j x_k + \ldots \quad (1.4)$$

where a_i are the polynomial coefficients or weights, and x_i, x_j, x_k are the components of the input vector $\mathbf{x} = [x_1, x_2, \ldots]$.

Popular are the multilayer polynomial networks constructed using the algorithms from the Group Method of Data Handling (GMDH) [Ivakhnenko, 1971, Madala and Ivakhnenko, 1994], which influenced research into similar approaches such as the Polynomial NETwork TRaining algorithm (PNETTR) [Barron, 1988] and the Algorithm for Synthesis of Polynomial Networks (ASPN) [Elder and Pregibon, 1996, Elder and Brown, 2000]. Being familiar with their characteristics gives ideas as to how they work and how they can be improved.

Group Method of Data Handling. The GMDH pioneered the development of network algorithms using polynomials as a concept description language. These are constructive algorithms that grow networks of polynomial node functions layer by layer in a bottom-up manner. In this sense, these algorithms perform hill-climbing search in the space of network structures by adding successively to the network nodes with smallest output error [Barron, 1988, Elder and Brown, 2000, Farlow, 1984, Green et al, 1988, Ivakhnenko, 1971, Madala and Ivakhnenko, 1994, Müller and Lemke, 2000, Ng and Lippmann, 1991, Pham and Liu, 1995]. As well as synthesizing the network architecture, they also find the weights. An important advantage of GMDH is that it infers complex high-order polynomials by cascading hierarchically simple low-order polynomials. This strategy allows us to alleviate to a great degree the fundamental learning problem known as the curse of dimensionality.

Having selected polynomials, one needs to know that the number of terms increases exponentially with the number of inputs. When GMDH grows polynomial networks vertically from the lowest to the highest layer there is no combinatorial explosion of the number of nodes with the increase of the input dimension. For example, a function of maximum degree S can be realized by a GMDH network with quadratic transfer polynomials using $\lceil log_2 S \rceil$ hidden layers (where $\lceil . \rceil$ is the ceiling function). This efficacy is due to the original representation which keeps the polynomials as compact compositions of simple transfer models. The weights that accommodate the higher-order correlations between the variables appear when the model is expanded, while during processing they are virtual. Whereas the complete multinomial (1.4) of degree S in m variables theoretically has $(S+m)!/(S!m!)$ terms, the GMDH polynomial network is an unexpanded multinomial that practically contains only a small number of these terms. The number of terms is restricted by predefining the network width K and depth S parameters.

The GMDH family contains a wide spectrum of constructive network algorithms [Madala and Ivakhnenko, 1994]: multilayer, combinatorial, recursive, orthogonal, harmonic, etc.. Most popular among them is the *multilayer GMDH* which iteratively builds strictly layered networks with regular topology. Strictly layered means that the network consists of nodes whose distance from the inputs at any particular layer is the same. Regular means that the outputs of each layer feed directly only the next layer nodes. When the polynomial outcomes feed forward their parent nodes, partial models are composed hierarchically from the received outcomes. An example GMDH network is shown in Figure 1.1.

The complete *second-order bivariate transfer (activation) polynomial* is used in every network node:

$$p(x_i, x_j) = w_0 + w_1 x_i + w_2 x_j + w_3 x_i x_j + w_4 x_i^2 + w_5 x_j^2 \qquad (1.5)$$

where x_i and x_j are variables from the input vector $x_i \in \mathbf{x}, x_j \in \mathbf{x}$, $i \neq j$, whose indices range up to the preselected dimension $1 \leq i, j \leq d$.

The weights of the polynomial $p(x_i, x_j)$ (1.5) are estimated so as to minimize the sum-squared error:

$$SSE = \sum_{n=1}^{N} (y_n - p(x_{ni}, x_{nj}))^2 \qquad (1.6)$$

where the index n in x_{ni} and x_{nj} enumerates the data.

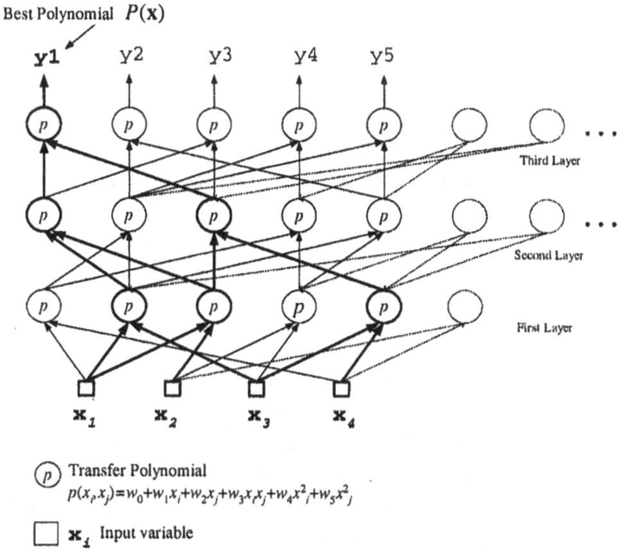

Figure 1.1. Polynomial network of width $K = 5$ constructed by the multilayer GMDH algorithm. The best polynomial model is derived from the leftmost output y1 which makes the model $P(\mathbf{x}) = p(p(p(x_1, x_3), p(x_1, x_2)), p(p(x_1, x_2), p(x_3, x_4)))$.

The minimum of this sum-squared error function is found by *ordinary least squares* (OLS) fitting using the matrix equation:

$$\mathbf{w} = (\mathbf{\Phi}^T\mathbf{\Phi})^{-1}\mathbf{\Phi}^T\mathbf{y} \tag{1.7}$$

where $\mathbf{w}$ is the column vector of weights $\mathbf{w} = [w_0, w_1, ..., w_m]^T$ whose size is $m + 1$, $\mathbf{\Phi}$ is the $N \times (m + 1)$ design matrix of vectors produced by the transfer functions applied to pairs of input variables (x_{ni}, x_{nj}), $1 \leq n \leq N$, and $\mathbf{y}$ is the $N \times 1$ output column vector.

The design matrix $\mathbf{\Phi}$ is made from the data as follows:

$$\mathbf{\Phi} = \begin{bmatrix} \phi_0(x_{1i}, x_{1j}) & \phi_1(x_{1i}, x_{1j}) & ... & \phi_m(x_{1i}, x_{1j}) \\ \phi_0(x_{2i}, x_{2j}) & \phi_1(x_{2i}, x_{2j}) & ... & \phi_m(x_{2i}, x_{2j}) \\ \vdots & \vdots & \vdots & \vdots \\ \phi_0(x_{Ni}, x_{Nj}) & \phi_1(x_{Ni}, x_{Nj}) & ... & \phi_m(x_{Ni}, x_{Nj}) \end{bmatrix} \tag{1.8}$$

where (x_i, x_j) is the pair of the i-th and the j-th input variables, and ϕ_i are basis functions introduced for notational convenience.

This design matrix $\mathbf{\Phi}$ can be assumed as built of row vectors:

$$\boldsymbol{\phi}(x_{ni}, x_{nj}) = [\phi_0(x_{ni}, x_{nj}), \phi_1(x_{ni}, x_{nj}), ..., \phi_m(x_{ni}, x_{nj})] \qquad (1.9)$$

or alternatively it can be represented using a short notation as follows: $\mathbf{\Phi} = \{\phi_l(x_{ni}, x_{nj})\}$, where $1 \leq l \leq m$, $1 \leq n \leq N$, and $1 \leq i, j \leq m$.

Typically, there are considered the following six bivariate basis functions : $\phi_0(x_i, x_j) = 1$, $\phi_1(x_i, x_j) = x_i$, $\phi_2(x_i, x_j) = x_j$, $\phi_3(x_i, x_j) = x_i x_j$, $\phi_4(x_i, x_j) = x_i^2$, and $\phi_5(x_i, x_j) = x_j^2$. Using these basis functions, the transfer polynomial (1.5) can be expressed as follows:

$$p(x_i, x_j) = \boldsymbol{\phi}(x_i, x_j)\mathbf{w} \qquad (1.10)$$

where $\boldsymbol{\phi}(x_i, x_j)$ is the $1 \times (m + 1)$ basis vector.

Since bivariate transfer polynomials are used, there are only two connections feeding each node. The weights do not correspond exactly to the connections, rather one may envision that each connection is multiplied to feed a particular transfer polynomial term. That is why the network connectivity is sparse. The number of nodes in each layer, which is the network width, is determined in advance to limit the possibility of a combinatorial explosion of terms. This is part of the greedy search strategy according to which once a node is added to a layer it remains fixed there and cannot be removed anymore. The network width is chosen less than the number of combinations from input variables. At the highest layer there are several results which are sorted, and the best polynomial is obtained from the leftmost node.

The multilayer GMDH algorithm (Table 1.1) starts with the generation of all combinations $c = d(d-1)/2$ of input variables (x_i, x_j), $x_i \in \mathbf{x}$, $x_j \in \mathbf{x}$, $\mathbf{x} = [x_1, x_2, ..., x_d]$. These combinations of variables are passed to enter the transfer polynomials $p_c^{(1)}(x_i, x_j)$, $1 \leq i, j \leq k = d$, in the first, lowest network layer. Their weights are estimated by OLS fitting (1.7), and the outputs z_c from all K nodes in the first layer are computed $z_c \equiv p_c^{(1)}(x_i, x_j) = \boldsymbol{\phi}(x_i, x_j)\mathbf{w}_c$. Next, these candidate nodes are ranked according to the selection criterion, and only the best $k < c$, $1 \leq k \leq K$ of them are retained in the first layer.

The outputs of the first layer activation polynomials are passed forward as pairs of intermediate variables $(z_r = p_r^{(1)}, z_s = p_s^{(1)})$ to feed the second layer nodes $p^{(2)}(z_r, z_s) = \boldsymbol{\phi}(z_r, z_s)\mathbf{w}$, $1 \leq r, s \leq K$, where the subscript $^{(2)}$ shows the layer number. All $c = K(K-1)/2$ combinations of such variables (z_r, z_s), $r \neq s$, are generated and used to estimate the transfer polynomials in the second layer, again by OLS fitting (1.7). This iterative network growing continues until the error stops to decrease.

Table 1.1. Summary of the multilayer GMDH algorithm.

Multilayer GMDH Algorithm

step	*Algorithmic sequence*
1. Initialization	Data $\mathcal{D} = \{(\mathbf{x}_n, y_n)\}_{n=1}^{N}$ as d-dimensional input vectors $\mathbf{x}$. Let the current variables be $x_i \in \mathbf{x}$, $1 \leq i \leq d$, and $k = d$. Let the network width be K, $K < c = d(d-1)/2$. Let the layer be $(h) = 1$, and the error is $\varepsilon = MaxInt$. Let the transfer polynomials be: $p(x_i, x_j) = \boldsymbol{\phi}(x_i, x_j)\mathbf{w}$ or $p(x_i, x_j) = w_0 + w_1 x_i + w_2 x_j + w_3 x_i x_j + w_4 x_i^2 + w_5 x_j^2$ and also: $\mathbf{\Phi} = \{\phi_l(x_{ni}, x_{nj})\}$, where: $1 \leq l \leq m$.
2. Network building and training	a) Generate all c combinations (x_i, x_j), $1 \leq i, j \leq k$. b) Make a polynomial $p_c^{(h)}(x_i, x_j)$ from each combination; - estimate the polynomial weights $\mathbf{w}_c$ by OLS fitting $\mathbf{w}_c = (\mathbf{\Phi}^T\mathbf{\Phi})^{-1}\mathbf{\Phi}^T\mathbf{y}$ - evaluate the error $p_c^{(h)}(x_i, x_j) = \boldsymbol{\phi}^T(x_i, x_j)\mathbf{w}_c$ $MSE = (1/N)\sum_{n=1}^{N}(y_n - p_c^{(h)}(x_{ni}, x_{nj}))^2$ - compute the model selection criterion $f_c^{(h)} = func(S_c)$. c) Order the polynomials according to their $f_c^{(h)}$, and choose these $k < c$, $1 \leq k \leq K$, with lower values. d) Take the lowest error from this layer: $\varepsilon^{(h+1)} = \min\{f_c^{(h)}\}$. e) If the lowest layer criterion is $\varepsilon^{(h+1)} > \varepsilon$ then terminate; else set the overall error $\varepsilon = \varepsilon^{(l+1)}$ and continue. f) The polynomial outputs become current variables: $x_c \equiv p_c^{(h)}$, $1 \leq c \leq k = K$, and $c = K(K-1)/2$. g) Repeat network building and training with $(h) = (h+1)$.

This GMDH framework is general as it helps to study not only many of the algorithms from the family, but it also describes the basics of the other popular multilayer polynomial network algorithms such as PNETTR [Barron, 1988] and ASPN [Elder and Pregibon, 1996, Elder and Brown, 2000]. These algorithms differ mainly in the chosen transfer polynomials and in the model selection criteria. They consider similar network growing and weight training approaches to construct high-order multivariate polynomial models (1.4).

GMDH Design Issues. There are several GMDH algorithmic decisions which seriously affect its performance. Polynomial networks are inferred when addressing inductive tasks where the goal is to learn models that generalize beyond the provided data sample. The critical requirement of the discovered models is that they should approximate the general trends in the data and should not overfit the training data. Polynomials that generalize well are accurate and simple, i.e. they have parsimonious structure. In order to avoid overfitting, there are several design issues that have to be investigated in order to attain good results: 1) what kind of transfer polynomials to use; 2) what model selection criteria to choose; 3) what data assimilation strategy to follow; and 4) whether complexity tuning can be applied.

The generalization performance depends on the polynomial structure and weights. When the complete quadratic bivariate polynomial is used in all nodes, the GMDH networks tend to overfit the data because the order of the polynomial rapidly increases, and its curvature attempts to pass through all data, thus trying to fit the particularities in them. The early experiments suggested to consider linear bivariate polynomials or incomplete bivariate polynomials, which help to produce more sparse models [Ivakhnenko, 1971, Madala and Ivakhnenko, 1994]. Some elaborated versions even use three-input and cubic transfer polynomials [Elder and Brown, 2000]. There are improvements by passing some inputs directly to higher layer nodes [Barron, 1988]. Section 2.1 offers a set of transfer polynomials for making flexible polynomial networks.

Using different transfer polynomials requires precise tools for analysis of the results, that is there is a need for model selection criteria. The aim is to account more precisely for the contribution to the fit of each polynomial term which is actually a weighted monomial of variables. There exist model criteria that measure not only the approximation error but also other model features like the magnitudes of the weights, the number of the weights when different transfer polynomials are used, the degree of smoothness, etc.. These additional features serve as explicit complexity penalties which help to navigate the search toward parsimonious and smooth polynomials with better forecasting potential. The current research provides various statistical functions [Moody, 1992, Akaike, 1970, Barron, 1988, Barron and Xiao, 1991, Craven and Wahba, 1979], probabilistic functions [Schwartz, 1978, MacKay, 1992a], information-theoretic functions [Mallows, 1973, Akaike, 1973, Rissanen, 1989], risk minimizing functions [Vapnik and Chervonenkis, 1971, Vapnik, 1995, Cherkassky et al., 1999], and dynamic functions [DeBoer and Hogeweg, 1989], that may serve as model selection criteria. Model selection criteria for polynomial networks are investigated in Section 4.1.

The original multilayered GMDH uses a model selection formula that relies on splitting the training set into two nonoverlapping subsets: a training subset which is used for learning of the polynomial weights, and a testing subset which is used for model selection. This data splitting strategy is reasonable when the mean squared error is taken as a model selection criterion. This reduces the risk of overfitting the training examples. However, when the data are split, not all of the information in the training set is used for learning. There are model selection criteria available which do not require data spliting to achieve overfitting avoidance. The polynomial networks developed here identify their structure and weights from all the data.

The GMDH-type algorithms do not attempt additional reduction of the network complexity to prevent overfitting. Recent empirical investigations show that during network construction and weight training, the polynomial term structure can be reduced in order to derive parsimonious models. Several complexity tuning techniques are explored in the book, including shrinking by regularization of the weights while learning and pruning of insignificant weights. The regularization techniques not only help to make the polynomials smoother, but also help to avoid numerical instabilities in training with imprecise real data. Advanced network pruning algorithms that rely on first-order and second-order derivatives of the network error with respect to the weights, are given in Chapters 6 and 7, while Bayesian pruning is explained in Chapter 8.

Advantages and Disadvantages of GMDH. The multilayer polynomial networks from the GMDH family influence the contemporary artificial neural network algorithms with several advantages.

First, they offer adaptive network representations that can be tailored to the given task. They enable us to customize the polynomial network to the problem domain. The network structures are flexible and amenable to topological search. Seeking to discover the most appropriate architecture for the task, these qualities allow us to develop network search algorithms not only using hill-climbing mechanisms, but also using simulated annealing, evolutionary search, etc..

Second, they pioneered the idea of finding the weights in a single step by standard ordinary least squares fitting which eliminates the need to search for their values. This overcomes training problems due to the inability of the learning algorithm to sufficiently identify accurate network weights. The success of least squares fitting guarantees learning at least locally good weights for the transfer polynomials in the network.

Third, these polynomial networks feature relatively sparse connectivity which means that the best discovered networks can be trained fast by backpropagation techniques for artificial neural networks. This implies that if one needs globally optimal weights within the polynomial network, backpropagation can be applied to further improve the weights previously estimated by least squares fitting.

A disadvantage of the GMDH-type algorithms is that they carry out greedy hill-climbing search for the polynomial network structure, and thus only perform exploitation of small neighborhoods from the space of possible topologies. Alternative nodes are discarded early when growing the network and they do not participate in the later stages of the learning process. These algorithms are not sophisticated enough, and even their improvements (for example, by increasing the number of transfer polynomials, and redefinition of the error criterion and complexity tuning) are not enough to adapt the network sufficiently well to the data.

The GMDH polynomial networks can be further improved in three ways: 1) by conducting global evolutionary search for the proper model architecture; 2) by better coordinating the magnitudes of the weights within the model; and 3) by improving the structure through balancing the model bias and variance with Bayesian techniques.

1.3 Evolutionary Search

The evolutionary computation provides approaches for doing global and local search simultaneously. The main evolutionary paradigms are: evolution strategies [Bäck, 1996, Schwefel, 1995, Bäck et al., 2000, Eiben and Smith, 2003, Yao, 1999], evolutionary programming [Fogel et al., 1966, Fogel, 1999], genetic algorithms [Holland, 1975, Goldberg, 1989], and genetic programming (GP) [Koza, 1992, Koza, 1994, Koza et al., 1999, Koza et al., 2003, Riolo and Worzel, 2003]. They conduct probabilistic population-based search which is a powerful tool for broad exploration and local exploitation of the model space. The population-based strategy is an advantage over other global search algorithms such as simulated annealing [Kirkpatrick et al., 1983] and tabu search [Glover, 1989], which works with only one hypothesis at a time, and over algorithms for local search [Atkeson et al., 1997] that perform only narrow examination of the search space. Their stochastic character is an advantage over the heuristic AI [Nilsson, 1980] and machine learning algorithms [Mitchell, 1997, Smirnov, 2001] that also search with one hypothesis.

The research into learning GMDH polynomial networks using evolutionary computation techniques has already developed: genetic algorithms which produce GMDH networks [Kargupta and Smith, 1991], GP systems which learn GMDH networks [Iba and Sato, 1992, Iba and de Garis, 1994, Iba et.al, 1996b, Nikolaev and Iba, 2001a], and evolutionary systems which discover neural trees [Zhang and Mühlenbein, 1995, Zhang et al., 1997]. The genetic algorithms that manipulate GMDH networks can be criticized for the inefficient fixed length genome representation of the polynomials. The fixed size network implementation restricts the topological network manipulations and requires specific operators to preserve the structural relationships in the model. Thus, the fixed length network representation limits the possibility to examine the network structure space well.

There are evolutionary systems that evolve sigma-pi neural trees [Zhang and Mühlenbein, 1995, Zhang et al., 1997], which compose polynomials from sigmoidal and multiplicative activation functions allocated in their nodes. These systems attempt to locate the relevant topology of the neural trees by means of genetic programming. During the population-based search for the polynomial structure, they also conduct a search for the weights by a genetic algorithm. This unfortunately leads not only to slow computations, but to inefficient weights because of the limited capacity of the genetic algorithm to perform numerical search. Another problem is that both evolutionary computation techniques depend on too many parameters which are difficult to tune. The GMDH-type polynomial networks are preferred so as to facilitate not only global structural learning, but also local weight learning.

The sparse connectivity of the GMDH networks makes them resilient and amenable to topological search. The target polynomials produced at the outputs exist within the tree-structured network topology. A single GMDH polynomial is a binary tree-like network which is suitable for tree transformations by classical algorithms. The tree-like polynomial networks have irregular topology; they are not strictly layered because higher layer nodes may be fed directly with input variables. Such tree-like polynomial networks are flexible and assume efficient processing by genetic learning operators. This enables the search engine to detect and discard insignificant terms. Learning by GP allows us to find good tree-like networks, in the sense of terms and maximal order (degree). The first GP system that initiated the research into evolutionary learning of GMDH-type polynomial networks is STROGANOFF [Iba et al,1993, Iba and de Garis, 1994, Iba et.al, 1996].

This reasoning motivates the research into genetic programming with PNN whose principles are established in Chapter 2. The emphasis is on design and implementation of various polynomials represented as tree-structured networks, including algebraic polynomials, orthogonal polynomials, trigonometric polynomials, rational polynomials, local basis polynomials, and dynamic polynomials.

1.3.1 STROGANOFF and its Variants

The research conducted by one of the authors [Iba et al,1993, Iba et.al, 1996] proposed STROGANOFF (Structured Representation On Genetic Algorithms for NOn-linear Function Fitting), which integrates GP-based adaptive processes with the GMDH process. STROGANOFF was very successful in solving system identification problems and lead to the development of a whole family of related algorithms.

Table 1.2. Algorithmic framework of the STROGANOFF approach to IGP.

Original STROGANOFF Algorithm

step	*Algorithmic sequence*
1. Initialization	Initialize a population of tree-like polynomial expressions $\mathcal{P}(\tau) = [g_1(\tau), g_2(\tau), ..., g_n(\tau)]$ $F(\tau) = Evaluate(\mathcal{P}(\tau), \lambda)$ using an MDL function and order the population according to $F(\tau)$.
2. Perform evolutionary learning	a) Select parents from $\mathcal{P}(\tau)$ $\mathcal{P}'(\tau) = Select(\mathcal{P}(\tau), F(\tau), n/2)$.
	b) Perform crossover of $\mathcal{P}'(\tau)$ $\mathcal{P}''(\tau) = CrossTrees(\mathcal{P}'(\tau), \kappa)$.
	c) Perform mutation of $\mathcal{P}'(\tau)$ $\mathcal{P}''(\tau) = MutateTrees(\mathcal{P}'(\tau), \mu)$.
	d) Execute GMDH to estimate the coefficients of the offspring expressions, and next compute their fitnesses with the MDL function $F''(\tau) = Evaluate(\mathcal{P}''(\tau), \lambda)$.
	e) Rank the population according to $F(\tau + 1)$ $g_0(\tau + 1) \leq g_1(\tau + 1) \leq ... \leq g_n(\tau + 1)$.
	g) Continue evolutionary learning (*step* 2) until the termination condition is satisfied.

Table 1.2 presents the original framework of the STROGANOFF approach. A close look at the STROGANOFF algorithm in Table 1.2 shows that its algorithmic structure organizes overall traditional GP search with one essential different and original step, 2.d, which actually carries out a new local hill-climbing procedure for local improvement of the evolved individuals. In step 2.d the coefficients (weights) of the child trees are recalculated using the strategy offered by the GMDH process [Ivakhnenko, 1971]. The application of GMDH here is very efficient because re-calculation of polynomial coefficients is performed only on intermediate nodes upon whose descendants crossover or mutation operators were applied. Therefore, the computational burden is largely reduced as the generations proceed when the crossover and mutation points are usually in the lower layers of the processed trees.

The system STROGANOFF evolves tree-like feed-forward networks of polynomial activations that yield at the root node a nonlinear output function $\overline{f}$. The activation functions are simple (e.g. quadratic) polynomials of the two input variables as in GMDH, whose parameters are obtained using an ordinary regression technique. Usually these are the complete bivariate polynomials of second-order.

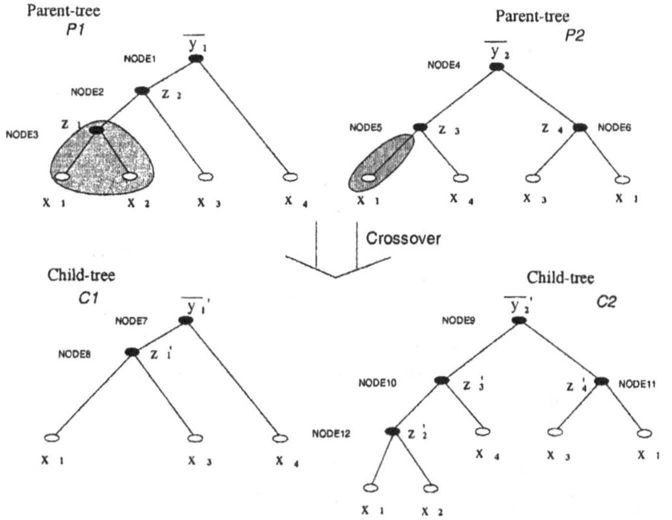

Figure 1.2. Crossover operation in STROGANOFF.

An example of a binary tree generated by STROGANOFF is shown in Figure 1.2. For instance, the upper left parent tree P_1 can be written as a (Lisp) S-expression as follows:

(NODE1
  (NODE2
    (NODE3 (x_1) (x_2))
    (x_3)
  (x_4)))

where x_1, x_2, x_3, x_4 are the input variables. Intermediate nodes represent simple polynomial relationships between two descendant nodes.

Thus each node records the information derived by the equations:

$$NODE3 \; : \; z_1 = a_0 + a_1x_1 + a_2x_2 + a_3x_1x_2 + a_4x_1^2 + a_5x_2^2 \qquad (1.11)$$

$$NODE2 \; : \; z_2 = b_0 + b_1z_1 + b_2x_3 + b_3z_1x_3 + b_4z_1^2 + b_5x_3^2 \qquad (1.12)$$

$$NODE1 \; : \; \overline{y_1} = c_0 + c_1z_2 + c_2x_4 + c_3z_2x_4 + c_4z_2^2 + c_5x_4^2 \qquad (1.13)$$

where z_1 and z_2 are intermediate variables, and $\overline{y_1}$ is the generated approximation of the output.

The coefficients $[a_0, a_1, \cdots, c_5]$, also called weights in connectionist parlance, of the neural network are obtained by the ordinary least squares fitting method (1.7).

For instance, the coefficients a_i in equation (1.11) are estimated after forming the design matrix (1.8) from the provided training data, which (assuming that N data triples (x_1, x_2, y) are available) is:

$$\begin{matrix} x_{11} & x_{21} & y_1 \\ x_{12} & x_{22} & y_2 \\ & \cdots & \\ x_{1N} & x_{2N} & y_N \end{matrix}$$

From these triples, the $\mathbf{\Phi}$ matrix adopting the complete bivariate activation polynomial is constructed as follows:

$$\mathbf{\Phi} = \begin{pmatrix} 1 & x_{11} & x_{21} & x_{11}x_{21} & x_{11}^2 & x_{21}^2 \\ 1 & x_{12} & x_{22} & x_{12}x_{22} & x_{12}^2 & x_{22}^2 \\ & & \cdots & & & \\ 1 & x_{1N} & x_{2N} & x_{1N}x_{2N} & x_{1N}^2 & x_{2N}^2 \end{pmatrix} \quad (1.14)$$

which after solving the normal least squares fitting equations produces the coefficient vector $\mathbf{w}$ (1.7).

Note that all node coefficients are derived locally. For instance, consider b_i's of NODE2. When applying the regression analysis to the equation for node 2 (1.12), these b_i's are calculated from the values of z_1 and x_3 (i.e. the two lower nodes), not from x_4 or $\overline{y_1}$ (i.e. the upper nodes). Therefore, the GMDH process in STROGANOFF can be regarded as a local-hill climbing search, in the sense that the coefficients of a node are dependent only on its two descendent (lower) nodes.

STROGANOFF uses a Minimum Description Length (MDL)-based fitness function for evaluating the tree structures. This fitness definition involves a trade off between certain structural details of the tree, and its fitting (or classification) errors:

$$\text{MDL fitness} = (Tree\_Coding\_Length) + (Exception\_Coding\_Length). \quad (1.15)$$

where these components for binary trees are [Tenorio and Lee, 1990]:

$$Tree\_Coding\_Length = 0.5k \log N, \quad (1.16)$$

$$Exception\_Coding\_Length = 0.5N \log S_N^2, \quad (1.17)$$

where N is the number of input-output data pairs, and the error is:

$$S_N^2 = \frac{1}{N} \sum_{i=1}^{N} |\, \overline{y_i} - y_i, |^2 \quad (1.18)$$

and k is the number of parameters of the tree (e.g. the k-value for the tree P_1 in Figure 1.2 is $6 + 6 + 6 = 18$ because each internal node has six parameters ($a_0, \cdots, a_5$ for $NODE3$ etc.)).

The advantages of STROGANOFF are summarized as follows: 1) the GP search is effectively supplemented with the tuning of node coefficients by regression; 2) analog (i.e. polynomial) expressions complement the digital (symbolic) semantics[Iba et.al, 1996b]; 3) MDL-based fitness evaluation works well for the tree-like structures in STROGANOFF, which controls GP-based tree search; and 4) the GP operation (i.e., crossover and mutation) is guided adaptively [Iba et.al, 1996].

1.4 Neural Network Training

The polynomial network growing algorithms usually learn the weights during forward propagation of the inputs, and once the network is built, they stop and do not improve the weights further. That is why the weights are not sufficiently tuned to be in tight mutual interplay within the concrete neural network architecture. This inability of constructive polynomial networks to discover sufficiently optimal model weights, has unfortunately only been studied slightly.

A remedy to this problem is to apply training approaches for multilayer perceptron (MLP) neural networks, i.e. the backpropagation techniques [Werbos, 1974, Rumelhart et al., 1986] that implement gradient descent weight search. They have abilities to learn from incomplete and imprecise data. They have, however, some weaknesses that are difficult to avoid: 1) they require us to predefine the network architecture in advance, because it is not clear what size net can assimilate a given number of examples in order to achieve a valid generalization; and 2) the gradient descent search that they perform is susceptible to trapping at suboptimal local solutions as it goes to the minima in the nearest basin on the error surface without the potential to escape. Both of these disadvantages can be addressed using the GP paradigm to search for the optimal network topology and weights since they can avoid early convergence to inferior local optima.

Several backpropagation training techniques for polynomial networks are developed in Chapters 6 and 7 in the spirit of the feed-forward neural networks theory. Gradient descent training rules for higher-order networks with polynomial activation functions are derived. This makes it possible to elaborate first-order and second-order backpropagation training algorithms. In addition to this, advanced techniques proposed for neural networks, like second-order pruning, are applied to polynomial networks. After that, it is demonstrated how temporal backpropagation training of several kinds of networks with polynomial activation functions can be performed. All of these are reasons that allow us to call the multilayer polynomial networks equipped with gradient descent training rules Polynomial Neural Networks.

1.5 Bayesian Inference

The recent explorations into the theory of Bayesian inference enabled development of second-generation techniques for efficient neural computing [MacKay, 1992a, Buntine and Weigend, 1991b, Neal, 1996, Bishop, 1995, Doucet et al., 2001]. These novel techniques are extremely important for making practical applications where the data are usually uncertain to a great degree and contaminated by various kinds of noise. Such real data can be robustly processed by Bayesian methods which inherently deal with the data distributions, instead of simply with point data. The probabilistic methods are reliable because they provide formula that account for the uncertainty in the model parameters.

The main conceptual benefits of the probabilistic approach to polynomial neural network modelling are: 1) they provide a means for doing proper regularization, thus enhancing the generalization; 2) they provide strategies for automatic determination of the relevant model terms, thus contributing to doing model pruning and selection; 3) they provide formula for analytical computation of confidence intervals, thus giving evidence for the uncertainty of the inferred model.

The concepts of the Bayesian paradigm are elaborated here for polynomial networks. It is explained that according to the Bayesian theory, the network produces not a single point prediction but a probabilistic output that may be considered a combination of many outputs generated with each of the training inputs. The degree to which an output participates in the combination is determined by its posterior probability. The posterior probability is updated with the arrival of the data, and its evaluation reflects how certain the model becomes with the data. The network weight parameters are random variables that are updated with the information in the data; they are not simply point estimates. By changing the assumptions about the manipulated probability densities, we can obtain corresponding training algorithms for the cases of various kinds of noise distributions.

There are two main approaches to Bayesian learning with neural networks: the evidence framework [MacKay, 1992a] and the sampling network [Neal, 1996]. Algorithms for sparse Bayesian learning, recursive Bayesian learning, and probabilistic gradient-descent training based upon the evidence framework are developed here especially for PNN. These are algorithms for Bayesian inference with linear models that can be applied to both linear and nonlinear PNN, because even the nonlinear PNN are hierarchical compositions of linear submodels (activation polynomials) in the hidden network nodes. A Monte Carlo sampling algorithm for probabilistic PNN training is also presented.

1.6 Statistical Model Validation

The polynomial neural networks are statistical tools for data analysis. They are nonlinear regression and classification models which may be preferred over the traditional statistical and numerical optimization algorithms due to their ability for robust inductive learning. Another reason to use PNN for nonlinear regression and classification is that sometimes it is easier and faster to apply them to practical data without the need to analyze the data thoroughly before processing them.

The applicability of PNN, as well as artificial neural networks, is enhanced using statistical validation estimates. Such estimates are necessary to determine the degree of belief in the accuracy and predictability of the learned models. Without estimates of the standard error and the confidence intervals, it is impossible to judge whether a model is useful in the statistical sense. Estimates for statistical diagnostic of PNN models are discussed in Chapter 8. Derivations of confidence intervals for PNN are made regarding them as neural networks. These statistical estimates are computed using second-order error derivatives which are calculated by backpropagation techniques.

1.7 Organization of the Book

This book is organized as follows. Chapter 2 provides the mechanisms of inductive GP with PNN models. It elaborates the tree-like PNN representation, the linear implementation of PNN trees, the genetic learning crossover and mutation operators, as well as an algorithm for measuring tree-to-tree distance, and random tree generation algorithms. Chapter 3 offers the tree-like polynomial network representations. The following sections illustrate what kinds of static and dynamic polynomial models can be made upon tree-like structures. Fitness functions for search guidance using contemporary model selection criteria are designed in Chapter 4. Next, Chapter 5 designs the mechanisms for evolutionary search navigation based on the fitness landscape metaphor. Search performance measures are also defined.

The backpropagation techniques for high-order PNN models are derived in Chapter 6. We show analytical derivations of the gradient vector with the first-order error derivatives with respect to the weights, and the Hessian matrix with the second-order error derivatives. Sections 6.2 and 6.3 develop the first-order and second-order backpropagation training algorithms for PNN. The popular second-order Conjugate Gradients and Levenberg-Marquardt algorithms are also given. The first-order and second-order error derivatives are considered in Section 6.4 to implement algorithms for pruning PNN. Temporal backpropagation techniques, especially for training recurrent PNN, are proposed in Section 7. These include dynamic training which can be accomplished using the versions of the backpropagation through time and real-time recurrent learning algorithms made for polynomial networks in Section 7.2 and Section 7.3. Second-order temporal backpropagation is explained in Section 7.5. Strategies for improved dynamic training are given in Section 7.4. Optimization techniques for recurrent polynomial networks are briefly studied in the final section, 7.6.

The techniques for Bayesian polynomial neural network learning are developed in Chapter 8. The basics of the Bayesian inference are provided in Section 8.1 which introduces the notion of Bayesian error function. Equations for finding weight variance hyperparameters and output noise hyperparameters are derived in Section 8.2.1. The hyperparameters are used next in Section 8.2.2 to implement local and global regularization, and in Section 8.2.4 to compute the predictive data distribution. Alternative Bayesian network pruning is discussed in Section 8.3. Section 8.4 presents an Expectation-Maximization algorithm for training PNN models. Section 8.5 gives a recursive Bayesian algorithm for sequential training of polynomial networks. At the end of this chapter a sampling algorithm for Monte Carlo training of PNN is designed.

Tools for statistical diagnostics of PNN are investigated in Chapter 9. It explains how to measure the standard error by decomposing it into bias and variance components. Practical approaches to computing the bias and variance estimates of the standard error using residual bootstrap sampling are given in Section 9.2. Section 9.4 shows how to compute confidence intervals for PNN models. Two approaches are discussed: one using second-order error derivatives from the Hessian, and another using bootstrap sampling. The following section, 9.5, gives methods for calculating prediction intervals for PNN.

Empirical results from PNN applications to real-world data are presented in Chapter 10. Section 10.2 shows how to preprocess the data before undertaking learning. Tasks from various application areas, such as chaotic time-series modeling and financial forecasting, are taken to compare the performance of PNN with Linear ARMA models (Section 10.3), genetically programmed functions (Section 10.4), statistical learning networks (Section 10.5), multilayer perceptrons (Section 10.6), kernel models (Section 10.7) and recurrent networks (Section 10.8). The empirical investigations demonstrate that PNN models evolved by GP and improved by backpropagation are successful at solving real-world tasks.

Chapter 2

INDUCTIVE GENETIC PROGRAMMING

Inductive Genetic Programming (IGP) is a specialization of the Genetic Programming (GP) paradigm [Koza, 1992, Koza, 1994, Koza et al., 1999, Koza et al., 2003, Banzhaf et al., 1998, Langdon and Poli, 2002, Riolo and Worzel, 2003] for inductive learning. The reasons for using this specialized term are: 1) *inductive* learning is a search problem and GP is a versatile framework for exploration of large multidimensional search spaces; 2) GP provides *genetic* learning operators for hypothetical model sampling that can be tailored to the data; and 3) GP manipulates *program*-like representations which adaptively satisfy the constraints of the task. An advantage of inductive GP is that it discovers not only the parameters but also the structure and size of the models.

The basic computational mechanisms of a GP system are inspired by those from natural evolution. GP conducts a search with a population of models using mutation, crossover and reproduction operators. Like in nature, these operators have a probabilistic character. The mutation and crossover operators choose at random the model elements that will undergo changes, while the reproduction selects random good models among the population elite. Another characteristic of GP is its flexibility in the sense that it allows us to easily adjust its ingredients for the particular task. It enables us to change the representation, to tune the genetic operators, to synthesize proper fitness functions, and to apply different reproduction schemes.

This chapter demonstrates how to incorporate these mechanisms into a basic IGP framework so as to organize efficient stochastic search of vast hypothesis spaces. A subject of particular interest is the automatic synthesis of tree-structured polynomial networks by IGP. The computational mechanisms of IGP are general to a great degree and similar to those of traditional GP, so they may be used directly for processing binary tree-like models in other systems for inductive learning. If necessary, the components of the presented framework may be easily modified because of their simplicity. Special attention is given to making efficient mutation and crossover learning operators. Differences between encoded and decoded tree implementations of the PNN models are explained.

2.1 Polynomial Neural Networks (PNN)

Polynomial neural networks are a class of feed-forward neural networks. They are developed with the intention of overcoming the computational limitations of the traditional statistical and numerical optimization tools for polynomial identification, which can only practically identify the coefficients of relatively low-order terms. The adaptive PNN algorithms are able to learn the weights of highly nonlinear models.

A PNN consists of nodes, or neurons, linked by connections associated with numeric weights. Each node has a set of incoming connections from other nodes and one (or more) outgoing connections to other nodes. All nonterminal nodes, including the fringe nodes connected to the inputs, are called hidden nodes. The input vector is propagated forward through the network. During the forward pass it is weighted by the connection strengths and filtered by the activation functions in the nodes, producing an output signal at the root. Thus, the PNN generates a nonlinear real valued mapping $P : \mathcal{R}^d \rightarrow \mathcal{R}$, which taken from the network representation, is a *high-order polynomial model*:

$$P(\mathbf{x}) = a_0 + \sum_{i=1}^{L} a_i \prod_{j=1}^{d} x_j^{r_{ji}} \tag{2.1}$$

where a_i are the term coefficients, i ranges up to a preselected maximum number of terms L: $i \leq L$; x_j are the values of the independent variables arranged in an input vector $\mathbf{x}$, i.e. $j \leq d$ numbers; and $r_{ji} = 0, 1, ...$ are the powers with which the j-th element x_j participates in the i-th term. It is assumed that r_{ji} is bounded by a maximum polynomial order (degree) s: $\sum_{j=1}^{d} r_{ji} \leq s$ for every i. The polynomial (2.1) is linear in the coefficients a_i, $1 \leq i \leq L$, and nonlinear in the variables x_j, $1 \leq j \leq d$. It should be noted that equation (2.1) provides a finite format for representing the power series expansion (1.1).

Strictly speaking, a power series contains an infinite number of terms that can represent a function exactly. In practice a finite number of them is used for achieving the predefined sufficient accuracy. The polynomial size is manually fixed by a design decision.

2.1.1 PNN Approaches

There are various approaches to making PNN models: 1) neural network implementations of discrete Volterra models [Wray and Green, 1994]; 2) multilayer perceptron networks with a layer of polynomial activation functions [Marmarelis and Zhao, 1997]; 3) linear networks of polynomial terms [Holden and Rayner, 1992, Liu et al., 1998, Pao, 1989, Rayner and Lynch, 1989]; 4) polynomially modelled multilayer perceptrons [Chen and Manry, 1993]; 5) Pi-Sigma [Gosh and Shin, 1992, Shin and Ghosh, 1995] and Sigma-Pi neural networks [Heywood and Noakes, 1996]; 6) Sigma-Pi neural trees [Zhang and Mühlenbein, 1995, Zhang et al., 1997]; and 6) hierarchical networks of cascaded polynomials [Barron, 1988, Elder and Brown, 2000, Farlow, 1984, Green et al, 1988, Ivakhnenko, 1971, Madala and Ivakhnenko, 1994, Ng and Lippmann, 1991, Pham and Liu, 1995, Müller and Lemke, 2000]. These PNN approaches are attractive due to their universal approximation abilities according to the Stone-Weierstrass theorem [Cotter, 1990], and their generalization power measurable by the Vapnik-Chervonenkis (VC) dimension [Anthony and Holden, 1994].

The differences between the above PNN are in the representational and operational aspects of their search mechanisms for identification of the relevant terms from the power series expansion, including their weights and underlying structure. The main differences concern: 1) what is the polynomial network topology and especially what is its connectivity; 2) which activation polynomials are allocated in the network nodes for expressing the model; are they linear, quadratic, or highly nonlinear mappings in one or several variables; 3) what is the weight learning technique; 4) whether there are designed algorithms that search for the adequate polynomial network structure; and 5) what criteria for evaluation of the data fitting are taken for search control.

An interesting approach to building discrete Volterra models is to assume that the hidden node outputs of a neural network are polynomial expansions [Wray and Green, 1994]. In this case, the weights of these hidden node polynomials can be estimated with a formula derived using the Taylor series expansion of the original node output function. Then the network weights are obtained by backpropagation training. After convergence, the coefficients of the polynomial expansion and the kernels of the Volterra model are calculated.

The multilayer networks with one hidden layer of polynomial activation functions [Marmarelis and Zhao, 1997] are enhancements of the multilayer perceptrons that offer several advantages: they produce more compact models in which the number of hidden units increases more slowly with the increase of the inputs, and they yield more accurate models. Their common shortcoming is the need to fix in advance the network structure. The idea behind Separable Volterra Networks (SVN) [Marmarelis and Zhao, 1997] is to directly simulate the Kolmogorov-Lorentz theorem for building a continuous function by a two-layer architecture. SVN uses a linear function at the output node and univariate polynomials at the hidden layer nodes. The univariate polynomials in the hidden layer make the higher-order monomials of the model. SVN trains only the weights from the input to the hidden layer.

The linear networks of polynomial terms [Holden and Rayner, 1992, Liu et al., 1998, Pao, 1989, Rayner and Lynch, 1989] increase horizontally a single hidden layer with monomials. The Functional Link Net (FLNet) [Pao, 1989] expands a single hidden layer network with heuristically selected high-order functions. These functions are monomials, called functional links. Unfortunately this algorithm attempts to make power series expansions directly and suffers from a combinatorial explosion of nodes. The Volterra Connectionist Model (VCM) [Holden and Rayner, 1992, Rayner and Lynch, 1989] makes linear networks in a similar way by extending the input variables using non-linear polynomial basis functions. Another similar approach is the Volterra Polynomial Basis Function (VPBF) [Liu et al., 1998] network which adds nodes in a stepwise manner using an orthogonal least squares algorithm.

The output of a MLP network can be expressed as a polynomial function of the inputs [Chen and Manry, 1993]. Such a MLP is trained by backpropagation and a matrix model of the node activation functions is created, assuming that a node output is a finite degree polynomial basis function. The coefficients of these alternative polynomial basis functions, which simulate the hidden node outputs, are estimated by mean square error minimization. This approach yields transparent polynomials however it suffers from the same disadvantages as the MLP, so it may be regarded simply as a model extraction technique.

The Pi-Sigma Networks [Gosh and Shin, 1992] have a hidden layer of linear summing units and a product unit in the output layer. Such a network produces a high-order polynomial whose maximal degree depends on the size of the hidden layer. The efficacy of PSN is that it requires us to train only the weights to the hidden layer as there are no weights from the hidden nodes to the output node. PSN networks have a smaller number of weights compared to the multilayer perceptron networks. The problem is that a single PSN is not a universal approximator. Ridge Polynomial Networks (RPN) [Shin and Ghosh, 1995] offer a remedy to this problem, providing enhanced approximation abilities. The RPN is a linear combination of PSN using ridge polynomials which can represent any multivariate polynomial.

Sigma-Pi neural networks [Heywood and Noakes, 1996] are a kind of MLP networks with summation and multiplicative units that are trained with a backpropagation algorithm for higher-order networks. The Sigma-Pi networks have polynomials as net functions in the summation units which are passed through sigmoids to feed-forward the nodes in the next layer. These networks usually implement only a subset from the possible monomials so as to avoid the curse of dimensionality. Their distinguishing characteristics are the dynamic weight pruning of redundant units while the network undergoes training, and the use of different learning rates for each monomial in the update rule.

Sigma-Pi Neural Trees (SPNT) [Zhang and Mühlenbein, 1995, Zhang et al., 1997] are high-order polynomial networks of summation and multiplication units. The sigma units perform weighted summation of the signals from the lower feeding nodes, and the product units multiply the weighted incoming signals. The neural trees may have an arbitrary but predefined number of incoming connections, and also an arbitrary but predetermined tree depth. SPNT provides the idea to construct irregular polynomial network structures of sigma and product units, which can be reused and maintained in a memory efficient sparse architecture. A disadvantage of this approach is that it searches for the weights by a genetic algorithm which makes its operation slow and inaccurate.

The multilayer GMDH polynomial networks [Barron, 1988, Elder and Brown, 2000, Farlow, 1984, Green et al, 1988, Ivakhnenko, 1971, Madala and Ivakhnenko, 1994, Müller and Lemke, 2000, Ng and Lippmann, 1991, Pham and Liu, 1995] are more suitable than the other networks for intensive evolutionary search. First, taken separately a polynomial is simply a binary tree structure which is easy to manipulate by IGP. Second, GMDH offers the opportunity to learn the weights rapidly by least squares fitting at each node. However, such weights are locally optimal and admit further coordination by additional training with gradient-descent and probabilistic tuning with Bayesian techniques.

2.1.2 Tree-structured PNN

The models evolved by IGP are genetic programs. IGP breeds a population $\mathcal{P}$ of genetic programs $\mathcal{G} \in \mathcal{P}$. The notion of a *genetic program* means that this is a sequence of instructions for computing an input-output mapping. The main approaches to encoding genetic programs are: 1) tree structures [Koza, 1992]; 2) linear arrays [Banzhaf et al., 1998]; and 3) graphs [Teller and Veloso, 1996]. The tree-like genetic programs originate from the expressions in functional programming languages where an expression is arranged as a tree of elementary functions in its nodes and variables in its leaves. The linear genetic programs are linear arrays of instructions, which can be written in terms of a programming language or written in machine code. The graph-based programs are made as directed graphs with stacks for their processing and memory for the variables. The edges in the graph determine the sequence for execution of the programs. Each node contains the function to be performed and a pointer to the next instruction.

Tree-like genetic programs are suitable for IGP as they offer two advantages: 1) they have parsimonious topology with sparse connectivity between the nodes, and 2) they enable efficient processing with classical algorithms. Subjects of particular interest here are the linear genetic program trees that are genotypic encodings of PNN phenotypes which exhibit certain input-output behaviors.

The Tree-like Representation. A genetic program has a *tree* structure. In it a node is below another node if the other node lies on the path from the root to this node. The nodes below a particular node are a subtree. Every node has a parent above it and children nodes under it. Nodes without children are leaves or terminals. The nodes that have children are nonterminals or functional nodes.

PNN are represented with *binary trees* in which every internal functional node has a left child and a right child. A binary tree with Z functional nodes has $Z+1$ terminals. The nodes are arranged in multiple levels, also called *layers*. The level of a particular node is one plus the level of its parent, assuming that the root level is zero. The *depth*, or height of a tree, is the maximal level among the levels of its nodes. A tree may be limited by a maximum tree depth or by a maximum tree size, which is the number of all nodes and leaves.

Trees are described here formally to facilitate their understanding. Let $\mathcal{V}$ be a vertex set from *functional nodes* $\mathcal{F}$ and *terminal leaves* $\mathcal{T}$ ($\mathcal{V} = \mathcal{F} \cup \mathcal{T}$). A *genetic program* $\mathcal{G}$ is an ordered tree $s_0 \equiv \mathcal{G}$, in which the sons of each node $\mathcal{V}$ are ordered, with the following properties:

- it has a distinguishing parent $\rho(s_0) = \mathcal{V}_0$, called the *root* node;

- its nodes are labelled $\nu : \mathcal{V} \rightarrow \mathcal{N}$ from left to right and $\nu(\mathcal{V}_i) = i$;

- any functional node has a number of children, called arity $\kappa : \mathcal{V} \rightarrow \mathcal{N}$, and a terminal leaf $\rho(s_i) = \mathcal{T}_i$ has zero arity $\kappa(\mathcal{T}_i) = 0$;

- the children of a node $\mathcal{V}_i$, with arity $k = \kappa(\mathcal{V}_i)$, are roots of disjoint subtrees $s_{i1}, s_{i2}, ..., s_{ik}$. A subtree s_i has a root $\rho(s_i) = \mathcal{V}_i$, and subtrees $s_{i1},..., s_{ik}$ at its k children: $s_i = \{(\mathcal{V}_i, s_{i1}, s_{i2}, ..., s_{ik}) \mid k = \kappa(\mathcal{V}_i)\}$.

This vertex labeling suggests that the subtrees below a node $\mathcal{V}_i$ are ordered from left to right as the leftmost child s_{i1} has smallest label $\nu(s_{i1}) < \nu(s_{i2}) < ... < \nu(s_{ik})$. This ordering of the nodes is necessary for making efficient tree implementations, as well as for the design of proper genetic learning operators for manipulation of tree structures.

The construction of binary tree-like PNN requires us to instantiate its parameters. The terminal set includes the explanatory input variables $\mathcal{T} = \{x_1, x_2, ..., x_d\}$, where d is the input dimension. The function set contains the activation polynomials in the tree nodes $\mathcal{F} = \{p_1, p_2, ..., p_m\}$, where the number m of distinct functional nodes is given in advance. A reasonable choice are the incomplete bivariate polynomials up to second-order that can be derived from the complete one (1.2) assuming that some of its coefficients are zero. The total number of such incomplete polynomials is 25 from all $2^5 - 1$ possible combinations of monomials $w_i h_i(x_i, x_j)$, $1 \le i \le 5$, having always the leading constant w_0, and two different variables. A subset $p_i \in \mathcal{F}$, $1 \le i \le 16$ of them is taken after elimination of the symmetric polynomials (Table 2.1).

Table 2.1. Activation polynomials for genetic programming of PNN.

1.	$p_1(x_i, x_j) = w_0 + w_1 x_1 + w_2 x_2 + w_3 x_1 x_2$
2.	$p_2(x_i, x_j) = w_0 + w_1 x_1 + w_2 x_2$
3.	$p_3(x_i, x_j) = w_0 + w_1 x_1 + w_2 x_1 x_2$
4.	$p_4(x_i, x_j) = w_0 + w_1 x_1 + w_2 x_1 x_2 + w_3 x_1^2$
5.	$p_5(x_i, x_j) = w_0 + w_1 x_1 + w_2 x_2^2$
6.	$p_6(x_i, x_j) = w_0 + w_1 x_1 + w_2 x_2 + w_3 x_1^2$
7.	$p_7(x_i, x_j) = w_0 + w_1 x_1 + w_2 x_1^2 + w_3 x_2^2$
8.	$p_8(x_i, x_j) = w_0 + w_1 x_1^2 + w_2 x_2^2$
9.	$p_9(x_i, x_j) = w_0 + w_1 x_1 + w_2 x_2 + w_3 x_1 x_2 + w_4 x_1^2 + w_5 x_2^2$
10.	$p_{10}(x_i, x_j) = w_0 + w_1 x_1 + w_2 x_2 + w_3 x_1 x_2 + w_4 x_1^2$
11.	$p_{11}(x_i, x_j) = w_0 + w_1 x_1 + w_2 x_1 x_2 + w_3 x_1^2 + w_4 x_2^2$
12.	$p_{12}(x_i, x_j) = w_0 + w_1 x_1 x_2 + w_2 x_1^2 + w_3 x_2^2$
13.	$p_{13}(x_i, x_j) = w_0 + w_1 x_1 + w_2 x_1 x_2 + w_3 x_2^2$
14.	$p_{14}(x_i, x_j) = w_0 + w_1 x_1 + w_2 x_2 + w_3 x_1^2 + w_4 x_2^2$
15.	$p_{15}(x_i, x_j) = w_0 + w_1 x_1 x_2$
16.	$p_{16}(x_i, x_j) = w_0 + w_1 x_1 x_2 + w_2 x_1^2$

The notion of *activation polynomials* is considered in the context of PNN instead of transfer polynomials to emphasize that they are used to derive backpropagation network training algorithms (Chapter 6).

The motivations for using all distinctive *complete* and *incomplete* (first-order and second-order) bivariate activation polynomials in the network nodes are: 1) having a set of polynomials enables better identification of the interactions between the input variables; 2) when composed, higher-order polynomials rapidly increase the order of the overall model, which causes overfitting even with small trees; 3) first-order and second-order polynomials are fast to process; and 4) they define a search space of reasonable dimensionality for the GP to explore. The problem of using only the complete second-order bivariate polynomial (1.2) is that the weights of the superfluous terms do not become zero after least squares fitting, which is an obstacle for achieving good generalization.

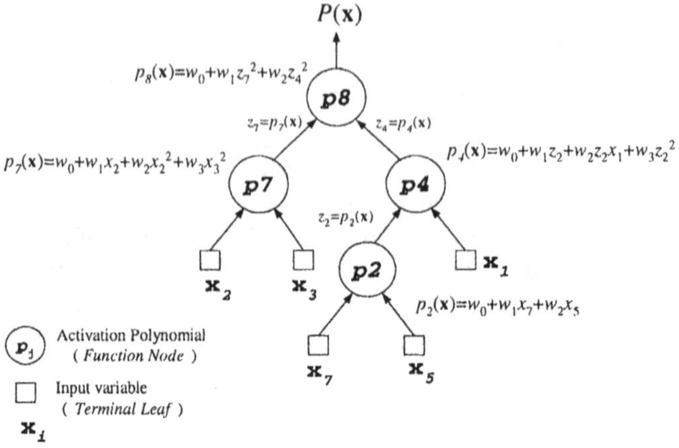

Figure 2.1. Tree-structured representation of a PNN.

Figure 2.2. illustrates a hierarchically composed polynomial extracted from the PNN in Figure 2.1 to demonstrate the transparency and easy interpretability of the obtained model.

Hierarchically Composed Polynomial

```
(( w0 + w1 * z7^2 + w2 * z4^2 )
        z7=( w0 + w1 * x2 + w2 * x2^2 + w3 * x3^2 )
             x2
             x3 )
        z4=( w0 + w1 * z2 + w2 * z2 * x1 + w3 * z2^2 )
             z2=( w0 + w1 * x7 + w2 * x5 )
                  x7
                  x5 )
             x1 ))
```

Figure 2.2. Polynomial extracted from the tree-structured PNN in Figure 2.1.

The accommodation of a set of complete and incomplete activation polynomials in the network nodes makes the models versatile for adaptive search, while keeping the neural network architecture relatively compact. Using a set of activation polynomials does not increase the computational demands for performing genetic programming. The benefit of having a set of activation polynomials is of enhancing the expressive power of this kind of PNN representation.

An example of a tree-structured polynomial using some of these activation polynomials is illustrated in Figure 2.1. The computed polynomial $P(\mathbf{x})$ at the output tree root is the multivariate composition: $P(x_1, x_2, x_3, x_5, x_7) = p_8(p_7(x_2, x_3), p_4(p_2(x_7, x_5), x_1))$.

The Search Space of Binary Trees. The number of terminals, instantiated by the input variables, and the number of functional nodes, instantiated by the activation polynomials, is important for the evolutionary learning of PNN because they determine the search space size and, thus, influence the probability for finding good solutions. When conducting evolutionary search by IGP, the size of the search space of tree-structures may be controlled by varying the number of activation polynomials or by the number of input variables.

Let the tree nodes be labelled by $\mathcal{F}$, which is the number of the hidden and fringe nodes. Let the tree leaves be labelled by $\mathcal{T}$, which is the number of the input variables that are passed through the leaves. Then, the number of different binary trees up to a predefined depth S is obtained by the following recursive formula [Ebner, 1999]:

$$\begin{aligned} Trees(0) &= \mathcal{T} \\ Trees(S) &= \mathcal{F}.Trees^2(S-1) + \mathcal{T} \end{aligned} \tag{2.2}$$

where $Trees(S)$ is the number of binary trees of depth up to S.

The tree depth impacts the search space size, but it should be noted that it also affects the convergence properties of polynomials. The maximal tree depth may be defined as a logarithmic function of the maximal order so as to restrict the network size: $S - 1 = log_2(MaxOrder)$. The most probable maximal polynomial order $MaxOrder$ may be determined in advance and considered as a tree depth limit to constrain the IGP search space. The $MaxOrder$ can be found by increasing the order of a randomly generated PNN, and measuring its error on the concrete sample: $\sigma^2 = \sum_{n=1}^{N}(y_n - P(\mathbf{x}_n))^2/(N - W - 1)$, where W is the number of the model weights. The denominator makes the error increase if the model becomes larger than the most probable degree.

Linear Implementation of PNN Trees. The design of tree- structured polynomial networks involves three issues: 1) how to represent the tree nodes; 2) how to represent the topological connections between the nodes; and 3) how to perform tree traversal. Taking these issues into consideration is crucial with respect to memory and time efficiency, as they impact the design of IGP systems.

From an implementation point of view the topology of a PNN tree can be stored as: a pointer-based tree, a linear tree in prefix notation, or a linear tree in postfix notation [Keith and Martin, 1994]. Pointer-based trees are such structures in which every node contains pointers to its children or inputs. Such pointer-based trees are easy to develop and manipulate; for example a binary tree can be traversed using double recursion. The problem of pointer-based trees is that the connections between the nodes are directly represented by pointers which incurs a lot of processing time. The reason is that most of the contemporary programming language implementations make these pointers to address dynamic memory locations, and their reference in run time is time consuming. The operating systems usually arrange the dynamic memory in different data segments which increases the time overhead for fetching data. That is why the speed of manipulating pointer-based tree structures may be several times slower than linearized trees.

Linear trees encapsulate nodes in arrays where the parent nodes precede the children nodes [Banzhaf et al., 1998]. Tree traversal of such linearized trees is made using stacks or recursion. The nodes in a linear tree can be allocated using prefix, infix or postfix notation. Most suitable for GP are the prefix and postfix notations. The prefix notation arranges the nodes as sequences that are traversed in the following order: parent, left subtree, and right subtree. *Linear trees* in prefix notation are preferred for GP because they enable us to make fast genetic learning operators that operate on array representations. Here, *prefix trees* for encoding PNN models are adopted in correspondence to the chosen labeling. The prefix trees are evaluated by recursive preorder tree traversal. The recursive preorder tree traversal visits a node, and then visits recursively its left and right subtrees.

Linearized Tree Genotypes. The tree implementation of PNN influences the development of IGP, and thus impacts the structural search process. This is because the implementation determines which neighboring trees can be sampled, that is it determines the search directions. The linearized tree-structures are genotypic representations of the PNN models, and they do not directly affect their phenotypic characteristics. One may envision that each variable length linear genotype has a corresponding PNN phenotype. The trees are means for representing the structures of PNN and they determine the sampling of polynomial models. However, they also indirectly influence their approximation qualities.

The linearized tree implementation can be described in biological terms in order to explain how the development of computational IGP mechanisms reflects knowledge about natural evolution. IGP relies on notions from biology, but they are only loose associations with the originals because its mechanisms only loosely simulate their biological counterparts in natural organisms.

The genotypic encoding of a genetic program is called a *genome*. The genome is a kind of a linear array of *genes* and has a variable length. In the case of IGP, the genome is a linearly implemented tree. The genes in the genome are labelled by *loci*. The position of each gene within the genome is its *locus*. A locus actually corresponds to the node label $\nu(\mathcal{V}_i)$, $\nu : \mathcal{V} \rightarrow \mathcal{N}$ of the particular tree node $\mathcal{V}_i$. The value of the node $\mathcal{V}_i$, which could be either an activation polynomial function $\mathcal{F}$ or a terminal $\mathcal{T}$, is called an *allele*. The alleles of the functions are in the range $[1, m]$ when $\mathcal{F} = \{p_1, p_2, ..., p_m\}$, while the alleles of terminals are in the range $[1, d]$ when $\mathcal{T} = \{x_1, x_2, ..., x_d\}$. In the case of a functional node, the gene carries the kind of the activation polynomial in its allele and its weights. In the case of a terminal node, the allele is the index for accessing the corresponding input variable from the example database. The tree traversal algorithm examines the tree by visiting its loci and fetches its alleles when necessary to evaluate the fitness.

2.2 IGP Search Mechanisms

IGP performs evolutionary search that explores global as well as local search regions. The power of IGP is due to several characteristics that distinguish it from the traditional search algorithms: 1) it manipulates the encoded implementation of the genetic program-like models rather than the individual models directly; that is the search is conducted in the genotype space; 2) it performs search simultaneously with a population of candidate solutions; and 3) the search is probabilistic and guided by the fitnesses of the individuals. The stochastic nature of IGP is a consequence of the nondeterministic changes of the population and the randomized selection of promising individuals.

IGP is intentionally developed to have characteristics that loosely mimic the principles of natural evolution. The key idea is to make computational mechanisms that operate like the corresponding biological mechanisms in nature. The ultimate goal behind the inspiration from nature is to pursue the powerful learning ability of the evolution process. Simulation of the natural evolutionary processes is organized at three levels: in the *genotype space* of linear tree representations, in the *phenotype space* of tree-structured PNN models, and in the *fitness space* which is the fitness landscape of PNN fitness values. The genetic learning operators act on the linear tree genotypes. Thus, genetic program-like PNN phenotypes are sampled. These PNN phenotypes are distinguished by their properties, e.g. the fitness. The computational IGP system examines the genotype search space with the intention of finding phenotypic solutions with desired fitnesses.

The evolutionary IGP search has two aspects: *navigation*, carried by the genetic sampling and selection operators, and *landscape*, determined by the fitness function and the variable length representation. There are two main genetic sampling operators: recombination, also called crossover, and mutation. They sample polynomials by probabilistically modifying their trees. The selection operator directs the search by randomly choosing and promoting elite individuals having high fitness. The search navigation moves the population on a landscape surface built of the genetic program fitnesses. The sampling and selection operators should push the population on the fitness landscape. The IGP mechanisms together should have the capacity to guide the population toward very deep landscape basins of good solutions.

2.2.1 Sampling and Control Issues

A critical problem in evolutionary IGP is the enormous dimensionality of the search space. In order to organize an efficient search process, the above two issues should be carefully analyzed.

The first issue is to make such mutation and crossover operators that can potentially visit every landscape region. These are also called learning operators because they sample individuals and thus contribute to finding the model structure. The learning operators for tree structures should be general and should not restrict the representation. These operators should avoid genetic program tree growth, known as bloating phenomenon, which worsens the IGP performance [Koza, 1992, Banzhaf et al., 1998, Langdon and Poli, 2002]. This is difficult to achieve because the tree growth usually implies improvement in fitness. Operators that allow tree bloat are unable to push the population progressively to promising landscape areas and cause search stagnation.

The second issue is that the population flow on the fitness landscape strongly depends on how the landscape has been created. The design of the fitness function can tune the landscape and mitigate the search difficulties. Fitness functions, fitness landscapes and their measures are investigated in separate chapters (Chapters 4 and 5).

A distinguishing feature of IGP is that its search mechanisms are mutually coordinated so as to avoid degenerated search. The size of the genetic programs serves as a common coordinating parameter. Size-dependant crossover, size-dependant mutation, and selection operators (that also depend on the tree size through their fitnesses) are designed. Making a common size biasing of the sampling operators and the fitness helps to achieve continuously improving behavior.

2.2.2 Biological Interpretation

The development of IGP systems follows the principles of natural evolution [Fogel, 1995, Paton, 1997]. Natural evolution acts on individuals having varying hereditary traits causing survival and reproduction of the fittest. Evolution is a term denoting changes of a population of individuals, called chromosomes, during successive generations. A chromosome plays the function of a genome and is a sequence of genes. The chromosomes have different lengths and shapes as they have different portions of traits. The hereditary traits are carried by the genes. The genes can be separated from the traits that they specify using the notion of a genotype. Genotype means the genes in an individual chromosome structure. The observable traits of an individual are referred to using the notion of a phenotype. Thus, the notions of a genotype and phenotype serve to make a distinction between genes and the traits that they carry. A gene can have different molecular forms that indicate different information about the traits called alleles.

Evolution keeps the most common alleles in the population and discards the less common alleles. The evolution involves updating the allele frequencies through the generations. The alleles in the population undergo modifications by several mechanisms: natural selection, crossover, and mutation. Natural selection reproduces individuals; it exchanges genetic material between the individuals in two populations during successive generations. Natural selection may have different effects on the population: 1) stabilization occurs when it maintains the existing range of alleles in the population, that is when it retains the individuals that contain the most common alleles; 2) shifting happens when it promotes individuals whose range of alleles changes in certain directions; and 3) disruption results when it deliberately favors concrete traits while destroying others. The crossover shuffles individuals, while the mutation changes the alleles.

Individuals in nature compete to survive during the generations. The successful individuals produce increasing numbers of offspring, while the unsuccessful ones produce less or no offspring. Natural selection picks more and more fit individuals, which when reproduced and mutated, lead to even better descendants. The adaptation of the individuals is not perfect. Their continuous evolution is driven probabilistically with respect to their fitness by selection. The population is in permanent movement along the generations.

Individuals are simulated in IGP by the genetic programs. In our case, these are the tree-structured PNNs. Each individual is associated with a fitness measure of its potential to survive in the population. The fitness of an individual accounts for its ability to reproduce, mutate, and so to direct the search. There is a fitness function that maps a genetic program into its fitness value. The most essential property of a genetic program is its *fitness*. The fitness helps to computationally simulate the biological principle of survival of the fittest. The biologically inspired idea is to promote, with higher probability, the fitter PNNs. In this way, the population moves toward promising areas in the search space seeking to locate the globally best solution.

2.3 Genetic Learning Operators

When a tree is modified, neighboring trees are sampled. The two main modification operators for genetic learning have different roles: the mutation performs local search in the vicinity of the parent tree, while the crossover conducts global search of distant search space areas. Both learning operators should be considered in IGP so as to achieve exploration and exploitation of the tree search space. Good solutions can be found only if the genetic learning operators are properly developed so as to sample every structurally possible tree, because every tree is hypothetically likely to be a solution of the task.

The operators for linear trees have to meet several criteria in order to keep the structural consistency of the genetic programs: 1) they should preserve the parent-child relationships among the vertices; and 2) they should not change the prefix ordering $\nu(s_i) < \nu(s_j)$ between the vertices after applying a series of operators $\nu(M(s_i)) < \nu(M(s_j))$.

The operator has to sample only the closest neighbors of the selected node in order to attain high correlation between the parent and the offspring. This requires keeping of the inclusion property between the corresponding subtrees from the parent s_i and the offspring s_j trees: $s_j \subset M(s_i)$ or $s_i \subset M(s_j)$. Tree transformations that satisfy these three topological properties of the trees may be expected to improve the search if properly coordinated with the other IGP mechanisms.

2.3.1 Context-preserving Mutation

Mutation is a genetic learning operator that modifies one parent tree into one offspring. The mutation operator is considered efficient when it causes slight changes of the fitness after transforming a tree. In order to facilitate the evolutionary search process there should be maintained high correlation between the fitness of the parent and that of the offspring. Such a relation is called strong causality [Rosca and Ballard, 1995a, Igel, 1998, Sendhoff et al., 1997]. Having strong causality ensures continuous progress in evolutionary search.

The *context-preserving mutation* (CPM) operator is a means for organizing local search. This mutation edits a tree structure subject to three restrictions: 1) maintaining the approximate topology of the genetic program tree by keeping the representation relationships among the tree vertices; 2) preserving the inclusion property between the subtrees; and 3) affecting only the nearest tree vertices to the chosen mutation point. The genetic program trees shrink and grow slightly, which contributes to the overall improvement of the evolutionary search.

A genetic program with a tree-like structure $\mathcal{G}$ of vertices $\mathcal{V}_i$, each of which has below a subtree $s_i = \{(\mathcal{V}_i, s_{i1}, s_{i2}, ..., s_{ik}) \mid k = \kappa(\mathcal{V}_i)\}$, can be transformed by the following three *elementary context-preserving mutations* $M : \mathcal{G} \times \mathcal{V} \times \mathcal{V} \to \mathcal{G}'$, $M(s, \mathcal{V}_i, \mathcal{V}_i') = s'$:

- *insert* M_I: adds a subtree $s_i' = \{(\mathcal{V}_i', s_{i1}', \mathcal{T}_{i2}', ..., \mathcal{T}_{il}') \mid l = \kappa(\mathcal{V}_i')\}$, so that the old subtree s_i becomes a leftmost child of the new subtree at the new node $\mathcal{V}_i'$, i.e. $s_{i1}' = s_i$;

- *delete* M_D: moves up the only subtree $s_i' = \{(\mathcal{F}_i', s_{i1}', ..., s_{il}') | 1 \le l \le \kappa(\mathcal{F}_i')\}$ of s_i iff $\exists \mathcal{F}_{ij} = \rho(s_{ij})$, for some $1 \le j \le \kappa(\mathcal{V}_i)$ to become root $\mathcal{F}_i' = \mathcal{F}_{ij}$, and all other leaf children $\forall k, ik \neq j, \rho(s_{ik}) = \mathcal{T}_{ik}$, of the old $\mathcal{V}_i$ are pruned. This deletion is applicable only when the node to be removed has one child subtree, which is promoted up;

- *substitute* M_S: replaces a leaf $\mathcal{T}_i = \rho(s_i)$, by another one $\mathcal{T}_i'$, or a functional $\mathcal{F}_i = \rho(s_i)$ by $\mathcal{F}_i'$. If the arity $\kappa(\mathcal{F}_i') = k$, then $s_i' = \{(\mathcal{F}_i', s_{i1}, ..., s_{ik}) \mid k = \kappa(\mathcal{F}_i')\}$. When $\kappa(\mathcal{F}_i') = l$ only $l = k \pm 1$ is considered. In case $l = k + 1$ it adds a leaf $s_i' = \{(\mathcal{F}_i', s_{i1}, ..., s_{ik}, \mathcal{T}_{il})\}$ else in case $l = k - 1$ it cuts $s_i' = \{(\mathcal{F}_i', s_{i1}, ..., s_{il})\}$.

There are various mutation operators, but many of them do not help to achieve progressive search. Many mutation operators augment the tree or trim it by whole subtrees, such as the hierarchical variable length mutation (HVLM) [O'Reilly, 1995]. HVLM inserts a randomly generated subtree before a randomly chosen vertex, deletes a randomly chosen node so that its largest subtree is promoted to replace it, and substitutes a randomly chosen node by another one with the same arity. HVLM generates quite different offspring models from their parents.

A useful idea is to develop a *uniform replacement mutation* (URM) *operator*. The URM operator successively traverses the tree nodes and changes every visited node or leaf with a probabilistically selected corresponding node or leaf. This operator allows us to make large steps in the search space because it makes larger tree changes than CPM. The difference between crossover and URM is that the latter is applied to a single tree and does not transfer material from another parent, rather it randomly updates the parent so as to produce an offspring.

Alternatively to the above transformation there could be made a *replacement mutation* (RM) which substitutes with a predefined probability each allele by a different, randomly chosen allele. While traversing the tree each functional node has the chance to be exchanged with another node, and each terminal leaf has the chance to be exchanged with another leaf. This RM operator may be applied after doing crossover so as to sustain the useful diversity of good alleles in the population.

Figure 2.3 displays an application of the context-preserving mutation operator to a concrete tree.

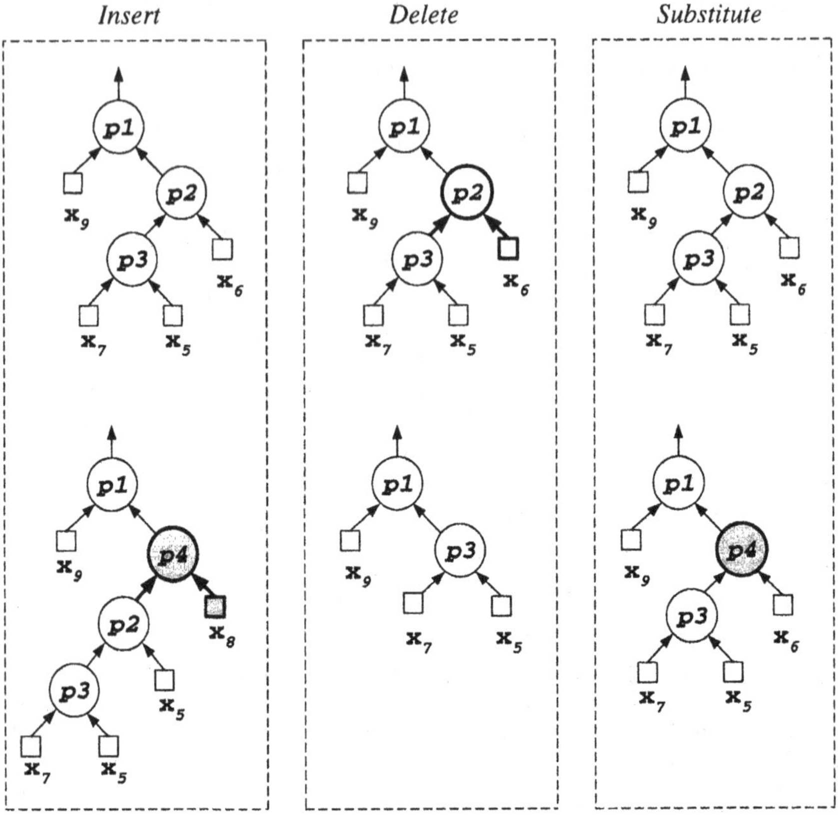

Figure 2.3. Context-preserving mutation (CPM) for tree-structured models.

2.3.2 Crossover Operator

The *crossover* operator should recombine node material by cutting or splicing two parent trees. Material exchange is made by selecting a cut point node in each tree, and swapping the subtrees rooted in the cut point nodes. The offspring trees may become larger than their parents. When a tree is of short size, it is not cut but added as a whole subtree at the crossover point in the other tree. If the two trees are short, they are spliced together. This crossover by cut and splice prevents the trees from rapid shrinking in the case of minimizing fitness functions. The recombination is restricted by a maximum tree size. This is a non-homologous crossover which does not preserve the topological positions of the swapped subtrees. Figure 2.4 illustrates an application of the crossover operator to two arbitrary trees.

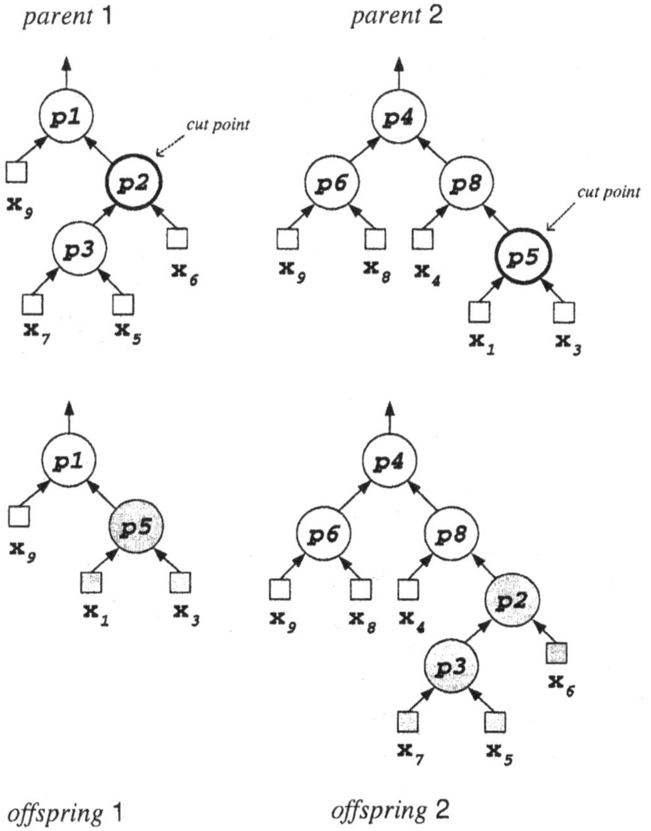

Figure 2.4. Crossover by cut and splice for tree-structured PNN models.

2.3.3 Size-biasing of the Genetic Operators

IGP conducts progressive search when the genetic learning operators climb easily on the fitness landscape. One aspect of the search control is to coordinate the fitness function and the genetic operators with a common bias parameter. The convergence theory of IGP (Section 2.6) suggests to use tree size biasing. The rationale is that small tree-like PNN usually do not fit the data well enough. Larger tree-like PNN exhibit better accuracy but do not necessarily generalize well on future data. While the fitness function only evaluates the genetic programs they need to be properly sampled. Early focusing to very small size or large size genetic programs can be avoided by size dependant navigation operators. The size-biased application of crossover and mutation helps to adequately counteract the drift to short or long programs.

The genetic learning operators should sample trees in such a way that the average tree size adapts without becoming very small or very large. Preferably small trees should be grown and large trees should be pruned. The operators have to prevent the tree bloat phenomenon which disturbs the evolutionary search [Banzhaf et al., 1998, Langdon and Poli, 2002]. Tree bloat occurs when the GP uses a fitness function that accounts only for the degree of fitting the data. When a tree expands, it pushes the search to a particular direction on the landscape which cannot be further avoided if there are no forces to shrink the tree for redirection. A similar disastrous search effect is the uncontrolled tree shrinking phenomenon. A population dominated by shrinking or growing genetic programs may drift to erroneous landscape areas where the evolutionary search stagnates.

The *size-biased mutation* operator for IGP performs context-preserving mutation with probability p_m defined as follows:

$$p_m = \mu \times |g|^2 \tag{2.3}$$

where μ is a free parameter [Goldberg et al., 1989], g is the linear implementation of the genetic program tree $\mathcal{G}$, and $|g|$ is its size. This operator usually modifies large trees.

The *size-biased crossover* operator for IGP splices or crosses two genetic program trees with probability p_c defined as follows:

$$p_c = \kappa / \sqrt{|g|} \tag{2.4}$$

where κ is a free parameter. More precisely, the probability whether to cut either of the trees is determined independently from the other. The cut points are randomly selected within the parents.

The free parameters serve as knobs with which one may carefully regulate the evolutionary search efficacy. The proper values for μ and κ may be identified with the autocorrelation function (Section 4.3.1).

2.3.4 Tree-to-Tree Distance

The development tools for IGP that manipulate trees should include an algorithm for estimating the distance between the trees. The topological similarity among trees is quantified by the *tree-to-tree distance* metric. Having an algorithm for computing the distance between the trees is useful because it can be applied for analysis and improvement of the GP mechanisms (Section 5.3).

The tree-to-tree distance is defined with respect to the basic concrete tree transformations which should be elaborated in advance. Distance $Dist(\mathcal{G}, \mathcal{G}')$ between two trees $\mathcal{G}$ and $\mathcal{G}'$ is the the minimum number $\sharp$ of elementary mutations $M \in [M_I, M_D, M_S]$ required to convert one of the trees $\mathcal{G}$ into the other $\mathcal{G}'$:

$$Dist(\mathcal{G}, \mathcal{G}') = \min\{\sharp\theta(M) | M \in [M_I, M_D, M_S], M(\mathcal{G}) = \mathcal{G}'\} \qquad (2.5)$$

where θ is a unit distance function associated with each of the elementary mutations. The unit distance from making a substitution is $\theta(M_S(\mathcal{V}, \mathcal{G}, \mathcal{V}'))$ which can be 1 if $\mathcal{V} \neq \mathcal{V}'$, and otherwise 0. The unit distance from using either of the insertion or deletion suboperators is $\theta(M_I(\mathcal{V}, \mathcal{G})) \equiv \theta(M_D(\mathcal{V}, \mathcal{G})) = 1$ because they always modify the trees on which they have been applied, that is they always change the trees.

This tree-to-tree distance (2.5) is a distance metric as it meets the following mathematical requirements: 1) it is symmetric $Dist(\mathcal{G}, \mathcal{G}') = Dist(\mathcal{G}', \mathcal{G})$; 2) it is nonnegative $Dist(\mathcal{G}, \mathcal{G}') = 0$ only if $\mathcal{G} = \mathcal{G}'$; and, 3) it obeys the triangle inequality.

The algorithm for computing the distance between trees should reflect their implementation and structural relationships between the parent and child nodes. The PNNs manipulated by IGP are implemented as labelled trees using preorder notation. The preorder labelling determines not only the arrangement of the nodes in the tree but it preserves also their structure. Let $\mathcal{V}_i$ be a node at position i in a tree. According to the preorder labeling, the following properties hold: 1) for each pair of labels $i_1 < i_2$, the node $\mathcal{V}_{i_1}$ is an ancestor of node $\mathcal{V}_{i_2}$; 2) for labels i which are related by the inequality $i_1 < i \leq i_2$, the nodes $\mathcal{V}_i$ are descendants of $\mathcal{V}_{i_1}$; and 3) the parent node $\mathcal{V}_{i_3}$ of node $\mathcal{V}_{i_2}$ is either $\mathcal{V}_{i_2-1}$ or an ancestor of $\mathcal{V}_{i_2-1}$, and $\mathcal{V}_{i_3}$ is on the path from node $\mathcal{V}_{i_1}$ to node $\mathcal{V}_{i_2-1}$.

A tree-to-tree distance algorithm for labelled trees in preorder notation using dynamic programming [Tai, 1979] is considered and modified to use the elementary context-preserving mutations $[M_I, M_D, M_S]$ from Section 2.3.1. Given two trees, the similarities between them are detected in three steps. The third step calculates the actual distance, while the first and second steps ensure that only distances achievable through legal context-preserving elementary mutations are counted.

The tree-to-tree distance algorithm using the elementary transformations from the CPM operator (Section 2.3.1) is given in four consecutive tables. Table 2.2b provides the function for computing the similarities between all subtrees from the first tree and all subtrees from the second. It uses the catalog updating function from the previous Table 2.2a. The function for counting the internode distances between arbitrary nodes in labelled preordered trees is shown in Table 2.2c. Finally, the three steps of the tree-to-tree distance algorithm are collected in Table 2.2d. The data arrays are common for all functions and are defined globally.

Table 2.2a. Function for filling the catalog of distances among all subtrees.

Catalog Filling

Algorithmic sequence

```
UpdateSD( r, u, i, q, z, j, x, y )
{
  if ((( r == u ) and ( u == i )) and (( q == z ) and ( z == j )))
     SD[ r ][ u ][ i ][ q ][ z ][ j ] = θ( i, j );
  else
     if ((( r == u ) and ( u == i )) or (( q < z ) and ( z == j ))) {
        p2=parent( j,G' )
        SD[ r ][ u ][ i ][ q ][ z ][ j ] = SD[ r ][ u ][ i ][ q ][ p2 ][ j − 1 ] + θ( 0, j );}
     else
        if ((( r < u ) and ( u == i )) or (( q == z ) and ( z == j ))){
           p1=parent( i,G )
           SD[ r ][ u ][ i ][ q ][ z ][ j ] = SD[ r ][ p1 ][ i − 1 ][ q ][ z ][ j ] + θ( i, 0 );}
        else
           SD[ r ][ u ][ i ][ q ][ z ][ j ] =
              Min( SD[ r ][ x ][ i ][ q ][ z ][ j ],
                   SD[ r ][ u ][ i ][ q ][ y ][ j ],
                   SD[ r ][ u ][ x − 1 ][ q ][ z ][ y − 1 ] + SD[ x ][ x ][ i ][ y ][ y ][ j ] );
}
```

Table 2.2b. Function for computing the structural similarity between each subtree from the first tree and each subtree from the second tree.

Distance Cataloging

Algorithmic sequence

```
CatalogDistances()
{
  for ( i = 1; i < treeSize1; i++ )
    for ( j = 1; j < treeSize2; j++ ) {
      u = i;
      while ( u > 0 ) {
        r = u;
        while ( r > 0 ) {
          z=j;
          while ( z > 0 ) {
            q=z;
            while ( q > 0 ) {
              UpdateSD( r, u, i, q, z, j, x, y );
              q = parent( q,G' ); }
            y=z;z = parent( z,G' ); }
          r = parent( r,G ); }
        x=u;u = parent( u,G ); }}
}
```

Table 2.2c. Function for counting the distances between arbitrary nodes in labelled preordered trees, necessary for measuring tree-to-tree distance.

Internode Distance Counting

Algorithmic sequence

```
CountDistances()
{
  ND[ 1 ][ 1 ] = 0;
  for ( i = 2; i < treeSize1; i++ )ND[ i ][ 1 ] = i;
  for ( j = 2; j < treeSize2; j++ )ND[ 1 ][ j ] = j;
  for ( i = 2; i < treeSize1; i++ )
    for ( j = 2; j < treeSize2; j++ ) {
      ND[ i ][ j ] = MAXINT;
      r = parent( i,G );
      while( r > 0 ) {
          q = parent( j ,G');
          while( q > 0 ) {
              p1=parent(i,G); p2= parent(j,G')
              ND[ i ][ j ] = Min( ND[ i ][ j ],
                  ND[ r ][ q ] + SD[ r ][ p1 ][ i − 1 ][ q ][p2 ][ j − 1 ] - θ( r, q ));
              q = parent( q,G' );}
          r = parent( r,G );}
      ND[ i ][ j ] = ND[ i ][ j ] + θ( i, j );}
}
```

Table 2.2d. Algorithm for measuring the distance between labelled preordered trees using the elementary transformations from the CPM operator.

Tree-to-Tree Distance Algorithm

	Algorithmic sequence
1.Initialization	MAXN maximal tree size, MAXD maximal tree depth *SD*[MAXN][MAXN][MAXD][MAXD][MAXD][MAXD]; *D*[MAXN][MAXN]; *ND*[MAXN][MAXN]; θ unit distance function, G genetic program tree
2. Perform Cataloging	*CatalogDistances*() [*Tables 2.2.a* and *2.2.b*]
3. Counting Distances	*CountDistances*() [*Table 2.2.c*]

4. Determine the minimal tree-to-tree distance	`D[ 1 ][ 1 ] = 0;`
	`for ( i = 2; i < treeSize1; i++ )`
	`  D[ i ][ 1 ] = D[ i − 1 ][ 1 ] + θ( i, 0 );`
	`for ( j = 2; j < treeSize2; j++ )`
	`  D[ 1 ][ j ] = D[ 1 ][ j − 1 ] + θ( 0, j );`
	`for ( i = 2; i < treeSize1; i++ )`
	`  for ( j = 2; j < treeSize2; j++ )`
	`  {`
	`    D[ i ][ j ] = Min( ND[ i ][ j ],D[ i − 1 ][ j ] + θ( i, 0 ),`
	`                  D[ i ][ j − 1 ] + θ( 0, j ));`
	`  }`

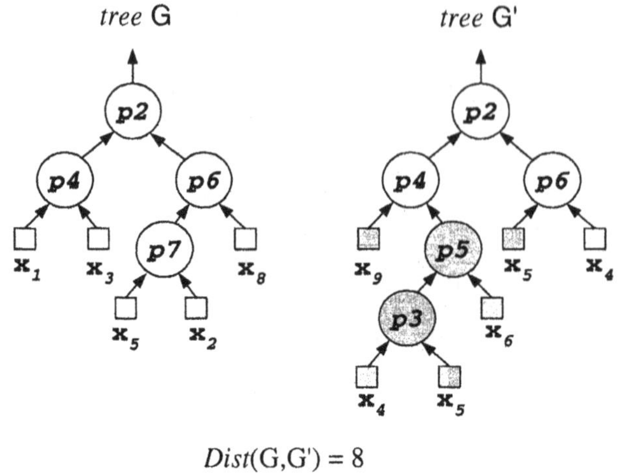

Figure 2.5. Tree-to-tree structural distance between two trees G and G' counted as the number of applications of the elementary operations $M \in [M_I, M_D, M_S]$.

This tree-to-tree distance algorithm is general and it serves for measuring the distance among trees with different branching factors. The algorithm implementation can be instantiated for binary trees in a straightforward manner. It should be noted that this tree-to-tree distance algorithm is computationally relatively expensive having complexity proportional to $\mathcal{O}(LL'S^2S'^2)$, where L and L' are the numbers of the nodes in the corresponding trees, and S and S' are their depths.

Figure 2.5 illustrates an example for the distance between two trees with respect to the mutations $M \in [M_I, M_D, M_S]$.

2.4 Random Tree Generation

The random tree generation algorithm impacts the evolutionary search performance. Its effect is through the ability to sample with equal probability each point from the search space. If the initial population has not been sampled well, the search may not converge to an optimal solution even if the IGP navigation is good. Since apriori information about the optima is usually not available, each search region should be sampled possibly with equal probability.

There are several methods available for random tree generation used in the GP community: naive methods [Koza, 1992], improved naive methods [Koza, 1992, Luke, 2000], and methods for construction of nearly uniformly distributed random trees such as uniform tree sampling [Salustowicz and Schmidhuber, 1997], stratified sampling [Iba, 1994] and compound derivations [Böhm and Geyer-Schulz, 1996].

The traditional method for random tree generation is the *Grow* algorithm [Koza, 1992]. It creates a tree-like genetic program by random generation of functionals and terminals until reaching the predefined depth. If a functional node is made, the algorithm continues recursively with attachment of random children nodes. The next node to install in the tree could be, with equal probability, a functional or a terminal from the node pool. This algorithm, however, does not allow to control the tree shape, therefore nonuniform, skewed distributions of trees result. One remedy to this unbalancing problem is to use the *Full* algorithm [Koza, 1992] which constructs complete trees up to a given depth.

Another improved method is the *ModifiedGrow* [Luke, 2000] which assigns user-defined probabilities to each functional node and terminal leaf so as to control their appearance in the trees. These probabilities are determined offline to speed up the tree construction. If the probability for choosing functionals over terminals is predetermined, random trees could be created around some desired average tree size. This algorithm, as well as the *Full* and *Grow*, does not necessarily produce truly random trees, rather it simply makes trees of different shape.

Better alternatives are provided by the methods that try to generate uniformly distributed random tree structures [Böhm and Geyer-Schulz, 1996, Iba, 1994, Salustowicz and Schmidhuber, 1997]. Such is the uniform sampling algorithm for initializing *probabilistic prototype trees* [Salustowicz and Schmidhuber, 1997]. A probabilistic prototype tree is a complete n-ary tree in which the nodes contain an initial probability threshold for selection of either a function or a terminal filling. A tree is generated by visiting every possible node from the complete tree. When the complete tree is traversed, a random number from the interval $[0; 1)$ is uniformly generated and compared with the threshold. If it exceeds the threshold, a terminal leaf is installed in the tree. Otherwise, a functional node with its children is inserted. The sum of probabilities for selecting the functions is equal to one.

An almost truly random tree generation algorithm can be implemented according to the bijection method [Iba, 1994]. This sophisticated algorithm produces random trees based on uniformly sampled words of symbols from a simple grammar of only two letters. This is a strategy for production of random words with n letters of the one kind and $n-1$ letters of the other kind. Next, the algorithm makes random permutations of the words, and builds corresponding trees of n nodes using a stack machine when reading the words. The generation of distinct tree structures is restricted by the desired node arities. The number of possible distinct trees and the construction of the solution are proportional to the Catalan number for trees with n nodes.

Exact uniform generation of complete trees can be accomplished using context-free grammars [Böhm and Geyer-Schulz, 1996]. This is a method for uniform sampling of populations of distinct words written in terms of a predefined context-free language. Distinct trees leading to different derivations of the same word are produced with each invocation of this algorithm. This algorithm recursively grows a complete derivation tree by randomly choosing the next context-free grammar rule for expanding the tree. The limit on the number of derivation steps constraints the tree depth. This tree generation algorithm can be applied to IGP after modifying the grammar rules to build functional models.

2.5 Basic IGP Framework

The IGP paradigm can be used for the automatic programming of polynomials. It provides a problem independent framework for discovering the polynomial structure in the sense of shape and size, as well as the weights. The IGP learning cycle involves five substeps: 1) ranking of the individuals according to their fitness; 2) selection of some elite individuals to mate and produce offspring; 3) processing of the chosen parent individuals by the crossover and mutation operators; 4) evaluation of the fitnesses of the offspring; and 5) replacement of predetermined individuals in the population by the newly born offspring. Table 2.3 presents the basic IGP algorithmic framework.

The formalization of the basic framework, which can be used for implementing an IGP system, requires some preliminary definitions. The IGP mechanisms operate at the genotype level; that is, they manipulate linearly implemented genetic program trees g. The basic control loop breeds a population $\mathcal{P}$ of genetic programs g during a number of cycles τ, called generations. Let n denote the size of the population vector; that is, the population includes $g_i, 1 \leq i \leq n$ individuals. Each individual g is restricted by a predefined tree depth S and size L in order to limit the search space to within reasonable bounds. The initial population $\mathcal{P}(0)$ is randomly created (Section 2.4).

The function *Evaluate* estimates the fitness of the genetic programs using the fitness function f to map genotypes $g \in \Gamma$ into real values f: $\Gamma \rightarrow R$. The fitness function f takes a genetic program tree g, decodes a phenotypic PNN model from it, and measures its accuracy with respect to the given data. All the fitnesses of the genetic programs from the population are kept in an array of fitnesses F of size n. The selection mechanism *Select*: $\Gamma^n \rightarrow \Gamma^{n/2}$ operates according to a predefined scheme for randomly picking $n/2$ elite individuals which are going to be transformed by crossover and/or mutation.

The recombination function *CrossTrees*: $\Gamma^{n/4} \times R \rightarrow \Gamma^{n/4}$ takes the half $n/4$ from the selected $n/2$ elite genetic programs, and produces the same number of offspring using size-biased crossover using parameter κ (Section 2.3). The mutation function *MutateTrees*: $\Gamma \times R \rightarrow \Gamma$ processes half $n/4$ from the selected $n/2$ elite genetic programs, using size-biased context-preserving mutation using parameter μ (Section 2.3).

The resulted offspring are evaluated, and replace inferior individuals in the population *Replace*: $\Gamma^{n/2} \times \Gamma^{n/2} \times N \rightarrow \Gamma^{n}$. The steady-state reproduction scheme is used to replace the genetic programs having the worst fitness with the offspring so as to maintain a proper balance of promising individuals (Section 5.1). Next, all the individuals in the updated population are ordered according to their fitnesses.

Table 2.3. Basic framework for IGP.

Inductive Genetic Programming

step	*Algorithmic sequence*
1. Initialization	Let the generation index be $\tau = 0$,and the pop size be n
	Let the initial population be: $\mathcal{P}(\tau) = [g_1(\tau), g_2(\tau), ..., g_n(\tau)]$ where g_i, $1 \leq i \leq n$, are genetic programs of depth up to S. Let μ be a mutation parameter, κ be a crossover parameter. Create a random initial population: $\mathcal{P}(\tau) = RandomTrees(n)$, such that $\forall g, Depth(g) < S$. Evaluate the fitnesses of the individuals: $F(\tau) = Evaluate(\mathcal{P}(\tau), \lambda)$ and order the population according to $F(\tau)$.
2. Evolutionary Learning	a) Randomly select $n/2$ elite parents from $\mathcal{P}(\tau)$ $\mathcal{P}'(\tau) = Select(\mathcal{P}(\tau), F(\tau), n/2)$.
	b) Perform recombination of $\mathcal{P}'(\tau)$ to produce $n/4$ offspring $\mathcal{P}''(\tau) = CrossTrees(\mathcal{P}'(\tau), \kappa)$.
	c) Perform mutation of $\mathcal{P}'(\tau)$ to produce $n/4$ offspring $\mathcal{P}''(\tau) = MutateTrees(\mathcal{P}'(\tau), \mu)$.
	d) Compute the offspring fitnesses $F''(\tau) = Evaluate(\mathcal{P}''(\tau), \lambda)$.
	e) Exchange the worst $n/2$ from $\mathcal{P}(\tau)$ with offspring $\mathcal{P}''(\tau)$ $\mathcal{P}(\tau + 1) = Replace(\mathcal{P}(\tau), \mathcal{P}''(\tau), n/2)$.
	f) Rank the population according to $F(\tau + 1)$ $g_0(\tau + 1) \leq g_1(\tau + 1) \leq ... \leq g_n(\tau + 1)$.
	g) Repeat the Evolutionary Learning (*step* 2) with another cycle $\tau = \tau + 1$ until the termination condition is satisfied.

2.6 IGP Convergence Characteristics

Theoretical studies of the convergence characteristics of GP have been performed in two main directions: to formulate a schema theorem for GP, and to develop a Markov model for GP. The research in these directions examines the evolutionary computation process from different points of view and reveals different factors that affect the search convergence. The theory given in this subsection can help to understand how the system propagates useful subsolutions of the task. A schema theorem valid for IGP is discussed next and an original Markov model for simplified IGP with fitness proportionate selection and context-preserving mutation is proposed for theoretical convergence analysis.

2.6.1 Schema Theorem of IGP

A formal explanation of the GP search performance can been made using the schema convergence theorem [Poli and Langdon, 1998, Rosca and Ballard, 1999, Langdon and Poli, 2002]. The schema theorem establishes a relationship between the individuals in the population and the mechanisms of the GP system. This theorem quantifies the expected behavior of similar individuals that are matched by a common pattern called schemata. The schema theorem describes the rates with which a schemata representing a region on the landscape grows and shrinks, thus allowing us to reason how the search progresses. During evolutionary search, schema of individuals with fitness greater than the average population fitness usually produce more offspring.

Individuals with close structural characteristics are summarized by a schemata. A schemata is a similarity pattern modelling a set of trees that are identical at certain positions; that is, they have coinciding functional and terminal nodes. Imposing a schemata on trees means that it can be taken to generate all similar trees with the property of having the common nodes. The common nodes are fixed positions, while the remaining positions can match any subtree, and are called wildcards.

Most convenient for describing the IGP performance is the rooted-tree schema theorem [Rosca and Ballard, 1999]. This theorem provides an expression for predicting the frequencies of individuals matched by rooted-tree schemata in the population depending on how their fitnesses relate to the average population fitness and depending on the effects of the selection, crossover, and mutation operators. A rooted-tree schemata is a tree fragment of certain order with a common root. The order of the schemata is the number of all its functional and terminal nodes without the wildcard symbols. Due to the fixed root, a schemata matches different trees having a similar shape. The different rooted-trees belong to disjoint subsets of the search landscape; therefore a rooted-tree schemata covers a concrete search region. When the search proceeds, the schema in the population shrink and grow, thus indicating how the evolutionary search effort is distributed on the search landscape.

Let the population contain schemata $\mathcal{H}$ and let there be $m(\mathcal{H}, \tau)$ instances of it at generation τ. Suppose that the average population fitness is $\bar{f}\ (\tau)$, and the average fitness of all schemata instances $\mathcal{H}$ at this moment is $\bar{f}_{\mathcal{H}}\ (\tau)$. The *rooted-tree schema convergence theorem* for traditional GP systems states that [Rosca and Ballard, 1999]:

$$m(\mathcal{H}, \tau+1) \geq m(\mathcal{H}, \tau)\frac{\bar{f}_{\mathcal{H}}\ (\tau)}{\bar{f}\ (\tau)}\left[1-(p_m+p_c)\frac{\sum_{i\in\mathcal{H}} f_i(\tau)/l_i}{\sum_{i\in\mathcal{H}} f_i(\tau)/O(\mathcal{H})}\right] \quad (2.6)$$

where i enumerates the instances of the schema $\mathcal{H}$, l_i is the size of instance i, $O(\mathcal{H})$ is the order of the schema, p_m is the mutation probability, and p_c is the crossover probability.

The above theorem shows that the survival of individuals depends not only on their fitness but also on their size. Search strategies can be developed using the tree size as a parameter in the following way: 1) size-biased mutation and crossover operators for tree size adaptation can be made (Section 2.3); and 2) size-biased fitness functions for search guidance and regulation of the tree complexities in the population through selection can be designed (Section 4.1.1). These two strategies have the potential to combat the tree growth problem and contribute to sustaining progressive search.

Although the formalism of the schema theorem gives some clues of how to improve the behavior of the evolutionary system, it has been widely criticized because it can hardly be used for online performance investigation [Vose, 1999]. The schema are difficult to detect and can hardly be identified while the GP system operates in real-time, and so in practice we cannot collect average statistics for the expected number of similar individuals in the population.

2.6.2 Markov Model of IGP

The Markov model of IGP provides a formalization of the probability distribution of chains from populations. The distribution of the populations evolved by the system during the generations allows us to analyze theoretically whether IGP can be expected to converge to a uniform distribution or not. If the population distribution reaches a uniform distribution within a finite number of steps, this means that the search will terminate. Having theoretical results from such analysis may be useful to realize how the genetic operators impact the evolutionary search.

IGP carries a stochastic process of continuous production of successive populations. It can be envisioned that each successive population in this evolutionary process depends only on the last population, and it does not depend on the process history. This is why the evolved populations may be considered a Markov chain. This reasoning allows us to develop a Markov model of the population-based IGP search. For simplicity, it is assumed here that the random effects are caused by selection and mutation operators which act on a population of a fixed size.

The IGP behavior can be studied following the related Markov theory of genetic algorithms [Davis and Principe, 1993], bearing in mind that the genetic programs have variable size. Assume that the IGP genotypes are represented using a language with alphabet $\mathcal{A}$. A genotype written in terms of this language of size no greater than L is a set of such symbols $\mathcal{G} = \{\mathcal{A}+\varepsilon\}^L$, where ε is the empty symbol. Markov chain analysis helps us to find the distribution of populations from such genotypes. Let the genotypes be specified by $g \in \mathcal{G}$ and $h \in \mathcal{G}$. Suppose that two successive populations are denoted by π and υ, and note that they have equal size $|\pi| = |\nu| = n$. The number of times that a particular genotype g appears in the population may be specified by $\pi(g)$. The population is then $\pi = [\pi(g_1), \pi(g_2), ...]$ as it contains genotypes $g_1, g_2, ...$ some of which are repeated and we have $\sum_{g\in\mathcal{G}} \pi(g) = n$. Clearly π is a distribution of n genotypes over $|\{\mathcal{A}\}^L|$ bins, where the symbol $|.|$ denotes the cardinality of a set. The genotype space that the IGP system can explore is a subset of the whole problem solution space $\{\pi\}$, which is the set of all possible populations. Since each population is a distribution of genotypes, it can be assumed that the genetic programming system produces a Markov chain of genotype distributions.

When the IGP manipulates the population using only the selection operator, the *probability for selection* $\Pr_l(g|\pi)$ of an individual g from population π is:

$$\Pr_l(g|\pi) = \frac{\pi(g)f(g)}{\sum_{h\in\mathcal{G}} \pi(h)f(h)} \tag{2.7}$$

where h enumerates all individuals in the population having their particular frequencies $\pi(h)$, $f(g)$ is the fitness value of individual g and f is usually a real number.

The *probability* $\Pr_l(\nu|\pi)$ *for producing a population* ν from population π after n independent samplings with returning of genotypes is:

$$\Pr_l(\nu|\pi) = \frac{n!}{\prod_{g\in\mathcal{G}} \nu(g)!} \prod_{g\in\mathcal{G}} \Pr_l(g|\pi)^{\nu(g)} \tag{2.8}$$

where n is the population size, and $\nu(g)$ is the number of occurrences of genotype g in population ν (note that $\sum_{g\in G} \nu(g) = N$).

These two probabilities allow us to obtain a boundary for the convergence of the population due to the forces exerted by the selection operator toward states of uniform populations. The expected number of transitions $E(\nu|\pi)$ from population to population until reaching a uniform population, is given by the inequality [Davis and Principe, 1993]:

$$E(\nu|\pi) \leq \left(\frac{nf_{\max}}{f_{\min}}\right)^{2n} < \infty \tag{2.9}$$

where $f_{\max}$ and $f_{\min}$ are the possible maximal and minimal fitness values.

Consider the case when IGP manipulates the population using two operators: selection and mutation. Since the stochastic effects from the selection operator have been investigated, it remains to study the effects from the context-preserving mutation. The *probability* $\Pr_m(g|h)$ *to obtain by mutation* individual g from individual h is:

$$\Pr_m(g|h) = \frac{1}{|\mathcal{A}|+1}\binom{L}{k} p_m^k (1-p_m)^{L-k} \tag{2.10}$$

where $|\mathcal{A}|+1$ is the alphabet size plus one empty symbol ε for deletion. The alphabet is $\mathcal{A} = F \cup T$, L is the size of genotype h, k is the number of modified alleles by the mutation, and p_m is the mutation probability.

The emergence of a genotype is a two-stage process: selection of a candidate from the population, and mutating it according to the mutation probability. Thus, the *probability* $\Pr_{lm}(g|\pi)$ *for obtaining by selection and mutation* a genotype g from population π is:

$$\Pr_{lm}(g|\pi) = \sum_{h\in\pi} \Pr_l(h|\pi) \Pr_m(g|h) \tag{2.11}$$

Then, the *probability* $\Pr_{lm}(\nu|\pi)$ *for producing a population* ν from population π by the combined use of selection and mutation is:

$$\Pr_{lm}(\nu|\pi) = \frac{n!}{\prod_{g\in\mathcal{G}} \nu(g)!} \prod_{g\in\mathcal{G}} \Pr_{lm}(g|\pi)^{\nu(g)} \tag{2.12}$$

where $\nu(g)$ is the frequency of genotype g in the next population.

It is proven that for such combined use of selection and mutation, the chain of population distributions cannot converge to a homogeneous state because the following relationship holds [Davis and Principe, 1993]:

$$\frac{n!}{\prod_{g\in\mathcal{G}} \nu(g)!} \left(\frac{p_m}{(1-p_m)^2}\right)^{nL} = \Pr_{lm}(\nu|\pi) \tag{2.13}$$

which is an indication for a stationary distribution.

The theoretical results from this Markov chain analysis of the population characteristics generated by an IGP system show that selection and mutation are not sufficient to organize successful evolutionary search; that is, there is a need for crossover as well. From another point of view, the Markov chain analysis demonstrated that the IGP performance depends on the mutation. Although some GP systems do not use it, one can realize that the mutation operator is not only useful but it is a necessary mean to sustain diversity in the population. The maintenance of enough diversity is a condition for achieving sustained exploration of the search space, and thus progressive search.

2.7 Chapter Summary

This chapter presented the basic structure of tree-like PNN models suitable for IGP. The PNN trees were related to other polynomial networks to emphasize the key differences between them, and to strengthen the confidence that tree-structured PNN are more flexible for doing evolutionary search by the mechanisms of IGP. The polynomial network models are allocated in binary tree structures for reducing the dimensionality of the search space and for making the network topology search process more efficient. The trees are implemented as linearized arrays to achieve fast computational speed.

Loosely simulating principles from natural evolution led to the development of the basic mechanism for genetic programming with PNN. A context-preserving mutation operator and a crossover operator were made. They can be applied to transform PNN structures with size-biasing in order to prevent degeneration of the search performance toward very small or very large trees. With the IGP, other mutation and crossover operators can be designed if it is necessary to improve the evolutionary search. The IGP framework provides a basic algorithm which can also be enhanced with novel features.

The presented brief theoretical analysis of the convergence behavior of IGP explained which factors affect the essential behavior of the system and provided clues as to what can be done in order to attain sustained evolution. It has been explained theoretically that: 1) it is beneficial to use size-biasing of the genetic learning operators and the fitness function because they influence the size of the offspring and avoid generating large complex trees which overfit the data and are harder to manage; and 2) it is beneficial to employ a mutation operator, in addition to the traditionally used crossover and selection in GP, because it helps to maintain high population diversity.

Chapter 3

TREE-LIKE PNN REPRESENTATIONS

Inductive machine learning requires determination of the mathematical format of the relationship between the given input and output data. The different kinds of mathematical models have different expressive power for describing data. Each practical data set has specific characteristics that should be approximated with a properly chosen model. The mathematical models can be distinguished according to the properties of the functional mappings that they offer. They can be divided into several groups: 1) linear or nonlinear models; 2) global or local, including piecewise, models; 3) discrete or continuous models; 4) models for periodic or aperiodic functions; etc..

The research experience indicates that functional identification from real-world data often uses nonlinear models. Linear models often fail to capture well the inherent properties and complex dynamics exhibited by natural data generating processes. Among the available various nonlinear function models we focus on high-order multivariate polynomials. The objective that motivates their study is twofold: 1) to incorporate the features of these various models, such as monomials, harmonics, kernels, recurrences, etc., into polynomials; and 2) to elaborate polynomials as connectionist models in order to enable using contemporary approaches, such as genetic programming for finding the model structure, neural network and Bayesian inference techniques for improving the weight parameters, for learning them efficiently.

This chapter investigates flexible nonlinear PNN specifications that are especially suitable for evolutionary computation by IGP mechanisms. The model specification involves two stages: 1) model representation, which requires us to determine the functional form of the polynomial mapping and how to accommodate it within the chosen structure; and

2) model identification, which requires us to decide how to extract parsimonious, less complex but faithful models from the chosen representation. The polynomial representations are allocated into tree-like neural network architectures.

The developed PNN can be divided in two groups: linear and nonlinear polynomial networks. A linear PNN has a structure that expands a power series by one term at each network node, so the overall model is a linear-in-the-weights polynomial of relatively low-order. A nonlinear PNN is essentially a multilayer neural network in which each node is fed by the activation polynomial outputs from its child nodes, and the overall function becomes a high-order polynomial. While a linear PNN gradually expands one power series, a nonlinear PNN builds a hierarchical composition of activation polynomials. The linear PNN can be used to make standard horizontal polynomials and kernel polynomials. The nonlinear PNN can be used to make block polynomials, orthogonal polynomials, rational polynomials, and dynamic polynomials. Two orthogonal models are demonstrated: Chebishev polynomials and polynomial trigonometric hybrids. Rational PNN using polynomial fractions are also proposed. The proposed dynamic models are recurrent PNN.

The common feature of all these polynomial representations is that they are allocated on tree-like neural network structures which are especially suitable for evolutionary search by IGP. The PNN models inherit the general format of discrete Volterra series and they possess universal approximation abilities. Their approximation properties can be explained using the generalized Stone-Weierstrass theorem and the Kolmogorov-Lorentz superposition theorem. Such evolved polynomials have been extensively tested on various inductive tasks (Chapter 10), and they have been found amenable to computational learning.

3.1 Discrete Volterra Series

The polynomials are nonlinear multivariate functions. Those considered here are Kolmogorov-Gabor polynomials (1.4,2.1). They are discrete analogs of the *Volterra models* [Volterra, 1959] whose popularity comes from their potential to describe any analytical nonlinearity by series expansions of the form [Schetzen, 1980]:

$$y(t) = w_0 + \sum_{i=1}^{\infty} V_i[x(t)] \tag{3.1}$$

built from convolution terms $V_i[x(t)]$, also called Volterra functionals.

The convolution terms are summations of products made as follows:

$$V_i[x(t)] = \sum_{\tau_1=1}^{\infty} \dots \sum_{\tau_i=1}^{\infty} \nu_i(\tau_1, \tau_2, \dots, \tau_i) \prod_{j=1}^{i} x(t - \tau_j) \tag{3.2}$$

where $\nu_i(\tau_1, \tau_2, \dots, \tau_i)$ are Volterra kernels, $x(t)$ are the discretely sampled inputs, and $y(t)$ are the targets. The Volterra kernels completely characterize the mapping and for finite series of reasonable length they can be found by geometric and algebraic computation approaches.

Different nonlinear models can be derived from the canonical discrete Volterra series by developing different terms. The common difficulties are how to determine the format of the terms, how many terms to use for achieving the desired accuracy, and how to find the kernels, also referred to as coefficients. The increase in the input dimension leads to a combinatorial explosion of terms which often causes numerical problems when trying to estimate the coefficients. In order to construct such polynomials, one has to be certain what their common features are, and what their expressive power is for describing functions.

In order to unify the discrete analogs of such Volterra series representations, this book adopts the following common format for *polynomials*:

$$P(\mathbf{x}) = a_0 + \sum_{i=1}^{S} a_i X_i + \sum_{i=1}^{S} \sum_{j=i}^{S} a_{ij} X_i X_j + \sum_{i=1}^{S} \sum_{j=i}^{S} \sum_{k=j}^{S} a_{ijk} X_i X_j X_k + \dots \tag{3.3}$$

where a_i are the polynomial coefficients that play the role of Volterra kernels $\nu_i(\tau_1, \tau_2, \dots, \tau_i)$, X_i are the input variables that capture the characteristics of the data $x(t - \tau_j)$, and $P(\mathbf{x})$ is the model output like $y(t)$.

When the provided input variables are passed through nonfunctional or functional transformations, the resulting models can have different descriptive characteristics such as kernel polynomials, high-order polynomials, orthogonal polynomials, trigonometric polynomials, rational polynomials, and dynamic polynomials. Such polynomials are developed in this chapter using binary tree-like structures.

3.2 Mapping Capabilities of PNN

The universal approximation property of PNN justifies the belief that these models are sufficient in most cases for addressing real-world applications. The PNNs presented have *universal approximation capabilities* as they can represent any arbitrary continuous function, defined over a finite interval, to any desired degree of accuracy if there are enough terms available. The existence of polynomial network models for such functions follows from the generalized *Stone-Weierstrass theorem* for multivariate functions [Davis, 1975]. This theorem states that for any continuous function on a compact interval there is a family of uniformly convergent polynomials. More formally, for any bounded monotonically increasing continuous function $f : R^d \to R$, $f(\mathbf{x}) = f(x_1, x_2, ..., x_d)$, and a closed definition region $\mathcal{D} = \{\mathbf{x} | -a \leq x_i \leq b, 1 \leq i \leq d\}$, there exists a PNN model $P(\mathbf{x})$ with polynomial nonlinearities which approximates $f(\mathbf{x})$ within some precision $\varepsilon > 0$ over $\mathcal{D}$: $\| f(\mathbf{x}) - P(\mathbf{x}) \| < \varepsilon$ for all $x \in \mathcal{D}$, where $\| \cdot \|$ denotes Euclidean distance.

The Stone-Weierstrass theorem was originally proven for functions in the closed interval $[0, 1]$, but it can be extended on an arbitrary interval $[a, b]$ in a straightforward manner using the linear transformation: $\widetilde{x} = a + (b - a)x$, so that $\| f - P \|_{[a,b]} = \max_{x \in [a,b]} |f(\mathbf{x}) - P(\mathbf{x})| < \varepsilon$.

Having the universal approximation property means that the PNN representations can potentially achieve satisfactory results provided that the network architecture contains enough nodes, since the number of nodes in the polynomial network structure determines the number of terms in the overall polynomial model. One should expect to attain a higher accuracy from a larger polynomial network architecture, as a larger network provides a larger polynomial expansion of higher degree. It should be noted however, that some real-world functions may require descriptions by indefinitely large numbers of network nodes which can not be implemented in practice.

The universal mapping abilities of PNN are their essential advantage over traditional MLP networks. It has been shown that certain MLP networks fail to satisfy the universal representation theorem [Hornik et al., 1989]. Although the theorem does not apply to some MLP, neural networks with two layers of neurons, with sigmoidal nonlinear activation functions, are universal approximators [Cybenko, 1989]. Alternative neural network architectures can be developed so as to satisfy the Stone-Weierstrass theorem but they require specialized network design decisions [Cotter, 1990]. Such difficulties can be avoided with the consideration of PNN. These polynomial networks are global models which can easily be analyzed with general purpose mathematical tools.

The generalized Stone-Weierstrass theorem for multivariate functions is considered a corollary to the Kolmogorov-Lorentz superposition theorem [Barron, 1988], and the universal mapping capabilities of PNN can also be explained with the latter. The superposition theorem of Kolmogorov [1957], elaborated further by Lorentz [1976], says that every continuous function on a bounded set can be represented exactly as a sum of compositions from continuous functions of one variable. Using properly selected continuous one-dimensional functions φ_i,$1 \leq i \leq 2d+1$, and fixed special continuous increasing functions ψ_{ij}, $1 \leq j \leq d$, defined on the unit cube $I = [0,1]^d$, we can write each continuous multivariate function $f(\mathbf{x})$ on I^d as follows:

$$f(\mathbf{x}) = f(x_1, x_2, ..., x_d) = \sum_{i=1}^{2d+1} \varphi_i \left(\sum_{j=1}^{d} \psi_{ij}(x_j) \right) \tag{3.4}$$

where $\mathbf{x} = [x_1, x_2, ..., x_d]$ is the input vector, and d is its dimension.

The Kolmogorov-Lorentz theorem suggests that it is possible to represent any continuous function on a bounded set arbitrarily well, but it does not specify exactly what could be the building functions φ_i and ψ_{ij}. Whilst one may hypothesize on the nature of the most appropriate functions to use, it is interesting to note that we may select these functions in such a way that the polynomial models can be derived from the above formula. Suppose that the one-dimensional functions ψ_{ij} are identity functions, that is $\psi_{ij}(x_j) = x_j$ for any i and j. Then, the inner summation gives: $z = \sum_{j=1}^{d} \psi_{ij}(x_j) = x_1 + x_2 + ... + x_d$ for all indices i. The functions φ_i can be chosen as follows:

$$\varphi_1(z) = a_1 z \tag{3.5}$$

$$\varphi_2(z) = a_2 zz = a_2 z^2 \tag{3.6}$$

$$\varphi_3(z) = a_3 zzz = a_3 z^3 \tag{3.7}$$

$$...$$

$$\varphi_n(z) = a_n z^n \tag{3.8}$$

Hence, the multivariate function model becomes:

$$f(\mathbf{x}) = \sum_{i=1}^{n} \varphi_i \left(\sum_{j=1}^{d} \psi_{ij}(x_j) \right) = a_1 z + a_2 z^2 + ... + a_n z^n \tag{3.9}$$

which is equivalent to the Kolmogorov-Gabor polynomial.

This result demonstrates that polynomials can be obtained from the Kolmogorov-Lorentz theorem as universal approximators. The polynomial degree n need not be restricted by $2d+1$. In general, $n > 2d+1$; for example, if $\psi = x^2$, $\psi = x^3$, etc..

3.3 Errors of Approximation

3.3.1 Approximation Error Bounds

An important question that arises when addressing inductive computation tasks is: what are the approximation error bounds of the adopted model, as in practice only limited amounts of training data are available, which are only samples from the complete data distribution? The learning process involves estimation of hypothetical solutions with finite data samples, which leads to uncertainties in the results. The preliminary belief in the results can be judged by formulae for the accuracy of approximation that can be attained in relation to the number of provided data. The fundamental question is: what is the approximation quality of a model as a function of the data and its representation properties such as the order and the input dimension?

The approximation theory provides ready theoretical results for the error bounds of least squares polynomials [Barron, 1988]. Assuming that the task is to fit normally distributed empirical data using the Euclidean distance measure, that is the L_2 norm, the minimax rate of *convergence of the total error (risk)* is:

$$\varepsilon_N = N^{-2q/(2q+d)} \tag{3.10}$$

where N is the number of the given data, q is the order of the bounded derivatives of the model, and d is the input dimension. The convergence rate indicates how the error decreases when adding terms to the partial sums that make the polynomial. This formula (3.10) shows that the number of data necessary for achieving good approximation grows enormously with the input dimension, and it is mitigated by the model smoothness as indicated by the order parameter.

The total error (1.1) (Section 1.1) is associated with the ability of the model to generalize; this is the difference between the polynomial output and the unknown true model. The above total error convergence formula (3.10) holds for polynomial networks and can be used to quantify the combined impact of the data, the order, and the dimension necessary to reach a satisfactory generalization. It shows how the polynomial complexity and the error are related. For example, using a polynomial of order $q = 10$ and input dimension $d = 10$ with $N = 1000$ training data, implies a convergence rate $\varepsilon_N = 0.01$. When growing very high-order polynomials using PNN faster convergence, lower errors can be obtained with the same data size in comparison to lower-order polynomials. This formula (3.10) also indicates that there is a risk of exponential impact of the dimensionality. Theoretically speaking, the curse of dimensionality is not avoided, rather it can be alleviated to a certain extent by growing compositions of simple activation polynomials according to the Multilayer GMDH approach [Ivakhnenko, 1971].

3.3.2 Empirical Risk

The problem of inductive learning is how to restore the dependencies in the empirical data. The notion of empirical data means that finding an optimal solution to the inductive task is difficult because there is no certainty in the properties of the training data necessary to produce theoretically precise results. The ultimate goal of finding a function that describes, with a minimal discrepancy, the desired output can be achieved by minimizing the *error (risk) functional* [Vapnik, 1992, Vapnik, 1995]:

$$E(\mathbf{w}) = \int L(\mathbf{y}, P(\mathbf{x}, \mathbf{w})) d\,\Pr(\mathbf{x}, \mathbf{y}) \tag{3.11}$$

where $L(\mathbf{y}, P(\mathbf{x}, \mathbf{w}))$ is the loss measured with a selected error function, $P(\mathbf{x}, \mathbf{w})$ is the output of polynomial P having weights $\mathbf{w}$ when estimated with input $\mathbf{x}$, and $\Pr(\mathbf{x}, \mathbf{y})$ is the joint probability distribution of the inputs $\mathbf{x}$ and the desired outputs $\mathbf{y}$. The obstacle to solving the integral in formula (3.11) is the unknown nature of the joint probability: $\Pr(\mathbf{x}, \mathbf{y}) = \Pr(\mathbf{y}|\mathbf{x}) \Pr(\mathbf{x})$. Assuming that the training examples are independent helps to develop the following tractable *empirical risk functional* [Vapnik, 1992, Vapnik, 1995]:

$$E_R(\mathbf{w}) = \frac{1}{N} \sum_{n=1}^{N} L(\mathbf{y}_n, P(\mathbf{x}_n, \mathbf{w})) \tag{3.12}$$

which does not involve the unknown joint probability distribution. Minimization of the empirical risk functional (3.12) gives bounds on the rate of convergence alternative to those from the approximation theory.

The empirical risk functional converges with a certain probability to the so-called *actual risk*. The rate of uniform convergence of the *average probability of the errors* to the actual risk is given by the inequality:

$$E'(\mathbf{w}) < E_R(\mathbf{w}) + 2\varepsilon_0^2(N, h, \alpha) \left(1 + \sqrt{1 + \frac{E_R(\mathbf{w})}{\varepsilon_0^2(N, h, \alpha)}} \right) \tag{3.13}$$

where $E'(\mathbf{w})$ is the average frequency toward which the error converges, $E_R(\mathbf{w})$ denotes the empirical risk functional associated with the training error, N is the number of the provided training data, and $\varepsilon_0(N, h, \alpha)$ is a confidence boundary given by:

$$\varepsilon_0(N, h, \alpha) = \sqrt{\frac{h}{N}\left[\ln\left(\frac{N}{h}\right) + 1\right] - \frac{\ln \alpha}{N}} \tag{3.14}$$

where α is a confidence level factor, and h is the VC-dimension of the model. The confidence level factor can be computed by the equation $\alpha = 1/\sqrt{N}$ which suggests that larger confidence intervals result from larger data samples. The inequality for rate of uniform convergence of the average probability (3.13) holds with probability $1 - \alpha$.

The Vapnik-Chervonenkis (VC) dimension [Vapnik and Chervonenkis, 1971] is a measure of the learning potential of the model. The VC-dimension of a polynomial of degree q is: $h = q + 1$ [Cherkassky et al., 1999]. In order to study the convergence properties of a PNN, the polynomial should be extracted from it into a power series format.

With the increase of the VC-dimension of the model the training error decreases but the generalization error becomes worse. That is how the empirical risk minimization principle leads to the idea of trading-off the model complexity with the model accuracy in order to attain good generalization performance. The means for improving the generalization are regularization, pruning and Bayesian techniques. The empirical risk can be estimated and used as evidence for the total risk.

3.4 Linear Polynomial Networks

A polynomial (3.3) is a linear superposition of terms. Such a linear model can be built starting with a single term and growing the structure term by term until the desired level of accuracy is reached. The problem is exactly which terms from the power series to include in the model so as to achieve a sufficient level of generalization. The inductive task is to search for the most plausible polynomial structure of terms which can be carried out efficiently using IGP. This section presents tree-structured representations made especially for IGP so that the tree traversal successively adds a new term at each hidden tree node. Two kinds of such networks are proposed: horizontal PNN and kernel PNN.

A distinguishing property of these polynomials is that they are linear-in-the-weights. This implies that it is easier to navigate the evolutionary search with them because each such model is overall linear and has a unique global minimum of the error function. Applying least squares weight estimation techniques leads directly to the global minimum on the error surface. The population-based evolutionary search for the best model is facilitated as the PNN are globally optimized, so there is no danger of attaining suboptimal solutions by the IGP system.

3.4.1 Horizontal PNN Models

Polynomials can be built using trees by gradual horizontal expansion of a partial model, adding one term at each intermediate node during tree traversal, the new term being indicated by the concrete activation polynomial at that node [Nikolaev and Iba, 2001b]. The weight of the new term is computed, while the old partial polynomial weights passed from the subtree below are only updated. Thus, the weights remain linear and are not raised to higher powers. Such a horizontal technique for polynomial construction from trees has been developed using the iterative least squares fitting method [Fadeev and Fadeeva, 1963].

The horizontal technique for polynomial construction from trees imposes special requirements on the selection of the set of activation polynomials in order to be suitable for an evolutionary IGP style search. The first requirement on the activation polynomials is that they enable successive growth of the partial polynomial by exactly one new term at each node. The second requirement is that the activation polynomials are short enough to be manipulated efficiently, even by OLS fitting, when they are at the lowest, fringe tree nodes having two leaf terminals. These two requirements can be met by designing a fixed set of six bivariate activation polynomials (Table 3.1). When an intermediate functional tree node is visited during the tree traversal process, the rightmost activation polynomial term specifies which new term to add.

Table 3.1. Activation polynomials for linear PNN learning.

1.	$p_1(\mathbf{x}) = w_0 + w_1 x_1 + w_2 x_2$
2.	$p_2(\mathbf{x}) = w_0 + w_1 x_1 + w_2 x_1^2 x_2$
3.	$p_3(\mathbf{x}) = w_0 + w_1 x_1 + w_2 x_1 x_2^2$
4.	$p_4(\mathbf{x}) = w_0 + w_1 x_1 + w_2 x_2^2$
5.	$p_5(\mathbf{x}) = w_0 + w_1 x_1 + w_2 x_1 x_2$
6.	$p_6(\mathbf{x}) = w_0 + w_1 x_1 + w_2 x_2^3$

Figure 3.1 gives an example for horizontal expansion of a partial polynomial. The partial polynomial passed from a subtree may be expanded, but also may feed an input variable at the parent node activation polynomial and thus, be suppressed from further expansion. There are two cases to consider, depending on the tree structure: 1) at a functional node with one leaf child, left or right, the partial polynomial is extended with the variable at the leaf (node p_2 in Figure 3.1); and 2) when a functional node has two children functional nodes, the partial sub-polynomial from the left child is extended (root node p_6 in Figure 3.1). The right partial sub-polynomial outcome is used to feed the second input variable, and it is not extended (node p_3 in Figure 3.1). The effect is extension of the partial polynomial by the right sub-polynomial whose weights are updated during a kind of restricted least squares regression.

The *iterative least squares* (ILS) method [Fadeev and Fadeeva, 1963] (pp.163-167) serves to implement iterative regression by adding successively new variables to the model. The horizontal technique employs ILS to learn the weights in all functional nodes except the fringe nodes. The ILS supplies formulae for direct computation of the new term weight, and for recurrent updating of the inverse covariance matrix $\mathbf{C}^{-1} = (\mathbf{\Phi}^T\mathbf{\Phi})^{-1}$. The benefit of this is in eliminating the need to conduct numerically unstable matrix inversions, which allows us to achieve reliable identification of the partial polynomials at the intermediate nodes.

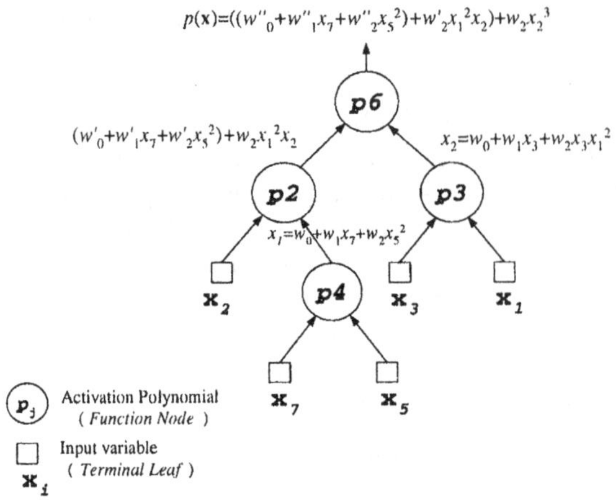

Figure 3.1. Horizontal polynomial construction using a tree-like PNN architecture.

Assume that a partial polynomial $p_i(\mathbf{x})$ with i terms $(1 \leq i \leq S)$ has been generated somewhere at an intermediate functional tree node. The normal matrix equation (1.7) can be simplified using the substitutions:

$$\left[\begin{array}{cc} \mathbf{C}_i & \mathbf{h}_i \end{array} \right] \equiv \left[\begin{array}{cc} \mathbf{\Phi}_i^T \mathbf{\Phi}_i & \mathbf{\Phi}_i^T \mathbf{y} \end{array} \right] \tag{3.15}$$

where $\mathbf{C}_i \equiv \mathbf{\Phi}_i^T \mathbf{\Phi}_i$ and $\mathbf{h}_i \equiv \mathbf{\Phi}_i^T \mathbf{y}$.

The least squares weight estimates are produced by the equation:

$$\mathbf{w}_i = \mathbf{C}_i^{-1} \mathbf{h}_i \tag{3.16}$$

where $\mathbf{C}_i^{-1}$ is the inverse of the covariance matrix $\mathbf{C}_i$.

After adding the $(i+1)$-th variable to the partial polynomial $p_i(\mathbf{x})$, the matrix $\mathbf{\Phi}_{i+1}$ becomes one column larger $\mathbf{\Phi}_{i+1} = [\ \mathbf{\Phi}_i \quad \phi_{i+1}\ ]$, where: $\phi_{i+1} = [\phi_{i+1}(\mathbf{x}_1), \phi_{i+1}(\mathbf{x}_2), ..., \phi_{i+1}(\mathbf{x}_n)]^T$. Then, the updated weights $\mathbf{w}_{i+1}$ are obtained with the equation:

$$\mathbf{w}_{i+1} = \left[\begin{array}{cc} \mathbf{C}_i & \mathbf{c}_{i+1} \\ \mathbf{c}_{i+1}^T & j_{i+1} \end{array} \right]^{-1} \left[\begin{array}{c} \mathbf{h}_i \\ k_{i+1} \end{array} \right] \tag{3.17}$$

where $\mathbf{c}_{i+1}$, j_{i+1}, and k_{i+1} are bordering elements of the old $\mathbf{C}_k$.

The bordering components substituted in (3.17) are as follows:

$$\mathbf{c}_{i+1} = \mathbf{\Phi}_i^T \phi_{i+1} \tag{3.18}$$

$$j_{i+1} = \phi_{i+1}^T \phi_{i+1} \tag{3.19}$$

$$k_{i+1} = \phi_{i+1}^T \mathbf{y} \tag{3.20}$$

where ϕ_{i+1} is a $N \times 1$ vector with the values of the new $(i+1)$-st variable.

The novel coefficient vector $\mathbf{w}_{i+1} = \mathbf{C}_{i+1}^{-1}\mathbf{h}_{i+1}$ may be obtained without inversion of the covariance matrix $\mathbf{C}_{i+1} = \mathbf{\Phi}_{i+1}^T\mathbf{\Phi}_{i+1}$, but rather incrementally using the known quantities $\mathbf{C}_i^{-1}$ and $\mathbf{h}_i$ available from the computation of the polynomial with i variables.

The elements of the vector $\mathbf{w}_{k+1}$ are derived by solving the equation $\mathbf{C}_{i+1}\mathbf{C}_{i+1}^{-1} = \mathbf{I}$, where $\mathbf{I}$ is a $(i+1)\times(i+1)$ identity matrix. The solution requires several steps. First, the components $\mathbf{c}_{i+1}$ (3.18), j_{i+1} (3.19), and k_{i+1} (3.20) are used to build the new matrix $\mathbf{C}_{i+1}^{-1}$. After transforming the resulting block matrix, one infers the element v_{i+1} for the lowest right corner of the matrix $\mathbf{C}_{i+1}^{-1}$. It is scalar computable as follows:

$$v_{i+1} = (j_{i+1} - \mathbf{c}_{i+1}^T\mathbf{C}_i^{-1}\mathbf{c}_{i+1})^{-1} \tag{3.21}$$

where $\mathbf{C}_i^{-1}$ and $\mathbf{c}_{i+1}$, as well as the scalar j_{i+1}, are known.

Second, this scalar v_{i+1} is used in (3.17) to express the remaining blocks of the matrix $\mathbf{C}_{i+1}^{-1}$. After that, multiplication of the matrix $\mathbf{C}_{i+1}^{-1}$ with the vector $\mathbf{h}_{i+1}$ is performed, resulting at $\mathbf{w}_{i+1}$. The resulting vector $\mathbf{w}_{i+1}$ is simplified by taking into account that $\mathbf{w}_i = \mathbf{C}_i^{-1}\mathbf{h}_i$ (3.16). This yields at the bottom of the column vector $\mathbf{w}_{i+1}$, a formula for direct estimation of the new weight w_{i+1}:

$$w_{i+1} = -v_{i+1}(\mathbf{c}_{i+1}^T\mathbf{w}_i - k_{i+1}) \tag{3.22}$$

Third, the new weight w_{i+1} is used in the upper block of $\mathbf{w}_{i+1}$:

$$\mathbf{w}_{i+1} = \begin{bmatrix} \mathbf{w}_i - w_{i+1}\mathbf{C}_i^{-1}\mathbf{c}_{i+1} \\ w_{i+1} \end{bmatrix} \tag{3.23}$$

to update the old weights $\mathbf{w}_i$ by the amount $w_{i+1}\mathbf{C}_i^{-1}\mathbf{c}_{i+1}$.

Finally, the new inverse matrix $\mathbf{C}_{i+1}^{-1}$ for successive computations is obtained:

$$\mathbf{C}_{i+1}^{-1} = \begin{bmatrix} \mathbf{C}_i^{-1} + v_{i+1}\mathbf{C}_i^{-1}\mathbf{c}_{i+1}\mathbf{c}_{i+1}^T\mathbf{C}_i^{-1} & -v_{i+1}\mathbf{C}_i^{-1}\mathbf{c}_{i+1} \\ -v_{i+1}\mathbf{c}_{i+1}^T\mathbf{C}_i^{-1} & v_{i+1} \end{bmatrix} \tag{3.24}$$

The matrix $\mathbf{C}_i^{-1}$ is symmetric, and therefore only half of the operations are sufficient to find the weights $\mathbf{w}_{i+1}$ and the new inverse $\mathbf{C}_{i+1}^{-1}$.

ILS require us to calculate the column vector $\mathbf{C}_i^{-1}\mathbf{c}_{i+1}$, used three times in (3.21, 3.23, 3.24), and after that its transposed version necessary for building the matrix (3.24) is easily derived. The scalar v_{i+1} also needs to be computed once. The weights vector $\mathbf{w}_{k+1}$ is next estimated with these known blocks. The block components, namely the column vector $\mathbf{C}_i^{-1}\mathbf{c}_{i+1}$, its transposed version $\mathbf{c}_{i+1}^T\mathbf{C}_i^{-1}$, and the scalar v_{i+1} are saved, ready to construct the new inverse matrix $\mathbf{C}_{i+1}^{-1}$ by formula (3.24) which is computationally stable and efficient.

3.4.2 Kernel PNN Models

Linear models using kernels have become increasingly popular for classification and regression [Vapnik, 1998, Cristiani and Shawe-Taylor, 2000, Schölkopf and Smola, 2002]. Kernel models consist of basis functions that translate the input space into a feature space of inter variable dependencies, which feature space is high dimensional. The kernels allow us to construct high-dimensional models by means of low-dimensional components. Making tree-like PNNs with kernels passed through the leaves enables us to build linear-in-the-weights high-dimensional functions without explicit computations in the feature space.

Kernels and Linear Models. A *Kernel* is a similarity function that maps the differences between two vectors, usually considered in the Euclidean space, into a scalar number. Kernels are most often associated with dot products (inner vector products) in the input space. The notation $\langle \mathbf{x}, \mathbf{x}' \rangle$ indicates a dot product of two vectors which is calculated as follows: $\langle \mathbf{x}, \mathbf{x}' \rangle = \sum_{i=1}^{d} x_i \cdot x_i'$. The general r-th order polynomial kernel is:

$$\langle \mathbf{x}, \mathbf{x}' \rangle^r = \left(\sum_{i=1}^{d} x_i \cdot x_i' \right)^r = \sum_{i_1=1}^{d} \sum_{i_2=1}^{d} \cdots \sum_{i_r=1}^{d} x_{i_1} \cdot x_{i_r} \cdot x_{i_1}' \cdots \cdot x_{i_r}' \tag{3.25}$$

which is a sum of monomials. Each monomial is a feature. For example, a second order polynomial kernel of two vectors $\mathbf{x} = (x_1, x_2)$ and $\mathbf{x}' = (x_1', x_2')$ is the product: $\langle \mathbf{x}, \mathbf{x}' \rangle = x_1^2 x_1'^2 + 2x_1 x_2 x_1' x_2' + x_2^2 x_2'^2$.

A composite function can be made by combining the similarities of a vector to all available previous vectors from the data set. A *linear kernel model* is defined in the feature space by the following superposition:

$$y(\mathbf{x}) = \sum_{n=1}^{N} w_n K(\mathbf{x}, \mathbf{x}_n) + w_0 \tag{3.26}$$

where $K(\mathbf{x}, \mathbf{x}_n)$ stands for a preselected kernel function $K(\mathbf{x}, \mathbf{x}_n) = f(\langle \mathbf{x}, \mathbf{x}_n \rangle)$ applied to each of the data vectors $\mathbf{x}_n$, $1 \leq n \leq N$.

The representative power of such linear kernel models is determined by the particular kind of kernel basis function. The most popular positive definite, real value transformations, which lead to power series models are the *polynomial kernel* [Schölkopf and Smola, 2002]:

$$K(\mathbf{x}, \mathbf{x}_n) = (\langle \mathbf{x}, \mathbf{x}_n \rangle + 1)^r \tag{3.27}$$

and the following *spline kernel*:

$$K(\mathbf{x}, \mathbf{x}_n) = 1 + \langle \mathbf{x}, \mathbf{x}_n \rangle + (1/2) \langle \mathbf{x}, \mathbf{x}_n \rangle \min(\mathbf{x}, \mathbf{x}_n) - (1/6) \min(\mathbf{x}, \mathbf{x}_n)^3 \tag{3.28}$$

which is actually a cubic polynomial.

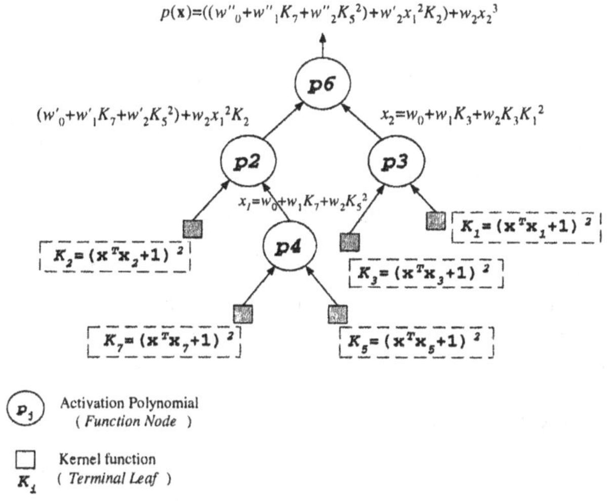

Figure 3.2. Tree-structured PNN modeling with kernel functions.

Learning Kernel Polynomials. Learning *kernel* PNN *models* involves the selection of a kernel, choosing basis activation polynomials, and regularizers. Here, linear-in-the-weights PNN are built using polynomial kernels. Localized polynomials of higher-order can be synthesized by relating the input vector $\mathbf{x}$ to another input vector $\mathbf{x}_i$:

$$K_i = (\mathbf{x}^T\mathbf{x}_i + 1)^2 \tag{3.29}$$

where $\mathbf{x}^T\mathbf{x}_i$ is computed as a dot product of two vectors. A linear tree-like PNN using polynomial kernels is illustrated in Figure 3.2.

Using the activation polynomials from Table 3.1 to construct network models causes some kernels to enter cross-product terms. This is not a problem because it is known that products of such kernels also produce valid kernels [Schölkopf and Smola, 2002], so the overall model retains the properties of linear models. The process of training such a polynomial network using kernels involves estimation of the weights by iterative least squares fitting using regularization. There are statistical and Bayesian techniques for finding proper regularization parameters (Chapter 8).

Polynomial kernel functions have been suggested as means for exact interpolation, but if a large number of them are taken, they tend to interpolate the data too closely. Since the inductive learning objective is to achieve good extrapolation, a fairly small number of kernels should be identified that compromises the goodness of fit with the generalization. The number of relevant kernel functions to enter the model may be determined by IGP style evolutionary search.

3.5 Nonlinear Polynomial Networks

Universally approximating Kolmogorov-Gabor polynomials can be composed hierarchically using multilayer PNN architectures. These nonlinear PNNs are essentially feed-forward neural networks in which each hidden network node output feeds the activation function in the higher layer node. Thus, the overall model is not only highly nonlinear, but also it is nonlinear in the weights which require specific training algorithms. Polynomial functions are extracted from such multilayer PNN according to the vertical technique suggested by the original Multilayer GMDH [Ivakhnenko, 1971]. Starting from the tree leaves, the overall polynomial model is composed by cascading the activation polynomials in the hidden network nodes during bottom-up tree traversal.

3.5.1 Block PNN Models

The PNN developed according to the multilayer GMDH impose a strong bias toward overparsimonious models. This happens because when polynomials are hierarchically cascaded, their order rapidly increases while only a small number of terms enter the model. A better representation for adaptive search can be made by injecting more terms in the tree-structured models, for example by passing summations. This can be performed using a *polynomial block reformulation* of the power series [Marmarelis and Zhao, 1997, Nikolaev and Iba, 2003]:

$$P(\mathbf{x}) = b_0 + \sum_{i=1}^{d} b_1(i) X_i + \sum_{i=1}^{d}\sum_{j=i}^{d} b_2(i,j) X_i X_j + \sum_{i=1}^{d}\sum_{j=i}^{d}\sum_{k=j}^{d} b_3(i,j,k) X_i X_j X_k + \ldots \tag{3.30}$$

where b_i are the weights, and X_i are summation blocks.

The blocks X_i suggest that summations or variables x_i enter the PNN as terminals:

$$X_i = \begin{cases} \sum_{m=1}^{d} x_m & \\ x_i & otherwise\ (1 \leq i \leq d) \end{cases} \tag{3.31}$$

This summation block (3.31) is a linear block $X_i = \sum_{m=1}^{d} \varphi(m) x_m$, where the functions $\varphi(m)$ are fixed to one. The weights b_1, b_2, b_3,... are indexed by the order of the monomial term in front of which they appear. These weights b_i are related to the coefficients a_i in the original power series (3.3) by the equations:

$$a_0 = b_0, a_i = \sum_{i=1}^{d} b_1(i), a_{ij} = \sum_{i=1}^{d}\sum_{j=i}^{d} b_2(i,j), a_{ijk} = \sum_{i=1}^{d}\sum_{j=i}^{d}\sum_{k=j}^{d} b_3(i,j,k) \ldots \tag{3.32}$$

where the indices $i, j, k, \ldots$ are limited by the input dimension d.

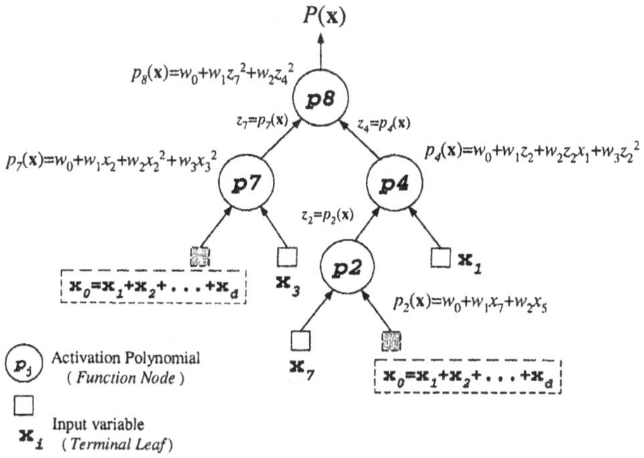

Figure 3.3. Tree-like PNN representation of a block structured polynomial.

According to formula (3.31), a terminal may be either a sum of all variables up to the given dimension or simply a single variable. In this way, the terminals inject more terms into the PNN model. At the same time, a polynomial generated with this formulation will include some, but not all, possible terms up to a given, predefined order. The weights of the activation polynomials are estimated by OLS fitting.

Figure 3.3 displays the allocation of a block reformulated high-order polynomial. The lowest terminal node here is a summation leaf, as well as the lowest right terminal leaf which is also a summation block.

3.5.2 Orthogonal PNN Models

When the data are prearranged into linear systems of normal equations they are usually overdetermined, and this causes numerical problems when attempting to solve them. Such learning problems are: 1) there may be linear dependencies in the data, because of which it may not be possible to infer a solution; the reason is that mean square error methods are not necessarily computationally stable in such cases; 2) when solving the normal equations by mean square error methods, the noise in the data and the rounding errors are multiplied in the inferred weights leading to numerical inaccuracies; and 3) even if the mean square error methods work, they may be very slow and may not be acceptable for the concrete application.

The learning of polynomials can be facilitated by inclusion of orthogonal terms. Having orthogonal terms can make the computation of the weights more stable, more accurate, and more rapid. Here stability is the robustness of the learning process with respect to different data sets.

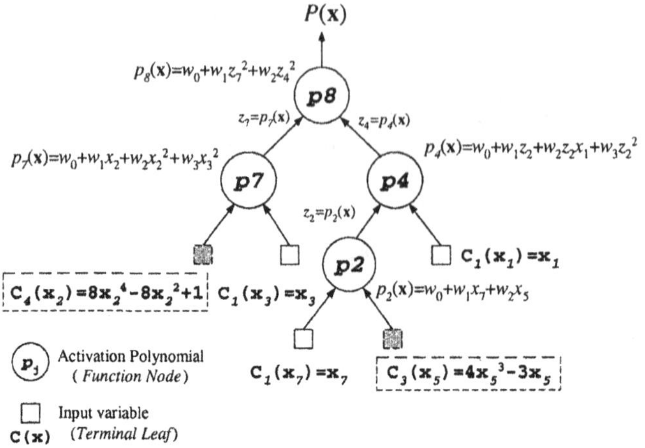

Figure 3.4. A tree-structured PNN that uses Chebishev terminals.

The tree-like PNN construction of multilayer GMDH adds high-order terms to the model which are not necessarily well structurally related to the data. One remedy for such problems is to use model components that capture common information in the data known as building blocks. The assumption is that the unknown function is resolvable in building block components, and they are learnable by IGP. A reasonable choice of such components are the Chebishev polynomials [Lanczos, 1957].

Chebishev polynomials can be incorporated as building blocks in tree-structured PNN [Nikolaev and Iba, 2001d] (Figure 3.4) in order to better capture the regularities in the data, as done by neural networks [Namatame and Ueda, 1992]. Thus, useful building blocks can be identified and propagated during the IGP search process. This idea is similar to the GP approaches that use automatically defined functions (ADF) [Koza, 1994], modules (MA) [Angeline, 1994], and adaptive representations (AR) [Rosca and Ballard, 1995b]. The Chebishev polynomials $C_i(x)$, passed as terminals X_i to enter the PNN models, are derived with the following recurrent formula [Lanczos, 1957]:

$$X_i \equiv C_i(x) = 2xC_{i-1}(x) - C_{i-2}(x) \tag{3.33}$$

where i is the polynomial order, and the starting model is $C_1(x) = x$.

The development of a PNN representation using Chebishev polynomials helps to achieve: 1) encapsulation of partial structural information in the polynomials so that they become sparser, and thus increasing of their generalization capacity; 2) better description of the oscillating properties in time series; 3) decreasing of the search space size due to the decrease of the tree size; and, 4) accelerating the search convergence.

3.5.3 Trigonometric PNN Models

Harmonic terms can be used as building blocks in IGP for enhancing the abilities of polynomials, especially in order to describe better oscillating time series data. Polynomial terms and harmonics can be used both to extend the expressive power of the network representation, and to develop tree-structured polynomial trigonometric networks [Nikolaev and Iba, 2001c]. The rationale for using polynomials and harmonics together is: 1) the polynomials are suitable as they approximate well the monotonic curvatures, as well as the discrepancies and gaps in the time series; 2) the harmonics are suitable as they approximate well oscillating components, spikes, and critical changes in the series curvature.

Rationale for Hybrid Modelling. Time series from observations of natural phenomena, in the fields of ecology, meteorology, financial forecasting etc., usually exhibit oscillating character. The oscillations are conveniently described by trigonometric functions which are sums of harmonics from the corresponding Fourier expansions. There are two possibilities to consider when one tries to find which harmonics should enter the time series model:

1) *periodically oscillating series* with repeating characteristics assume descriptions by sums of harmonics $T_i(t)$ with multiple frequencies $v_i = 2\pi i/N$, $1 \leq i \leq h$. The sum of harmonics $\sum_{i=1}^{h} T_i(t)$ in this case is a periodic function of t. The basis functions sin and cos are orthogonal, which guarantees decreasing of the mean squared error, and convergence in the limit, almost everywhere on the true function, when $h \to \infty$;

2) *aperiodically oscillating series* without repeating characteristics assume descriptions by sums of harmonics $T_i(t)$ with nonmultiple frequencies v_i. Having nonmultiple frequencies means that the sum of harmonics is not a periodic function of t. The basis functions sin and cos applied with nonmultiple frequencies are not orthogonal, and the attempts to model the data in this case can be done by searching for those harmonics that build the closest function to the true one.

The real-world data are often not exactly periodic, and can be modelled well by trigonometric functions that are sums of harmonics with unknown frequencies:

$$T(t) = \sum_{i=1}^{h} [A_i \sin(v_i t) + B_i \cos(v_i t)] \tag{3.34}$$

where A_i and B_i are the real-value harmonic amplitudes or coefficients, and the number of harmonics h is bounded by $max(h) \leq N/3$.

Distinct harmonics for making trigonometric PNN can be derived analytically using Prony's method [Hildebrand, 1987]: 1) calculate the non-multiple frequencies v_i, $1 \leq i \leq h$, of each harmonic component i; and 2) estimate the harmonic coefficients A_i and B_i, which enables us to determine the coefficients c_i, and the phases ϕ_i, for computing the separate harmonics using the concise equation $c_i \cos(v_i t - \phi_i)$.

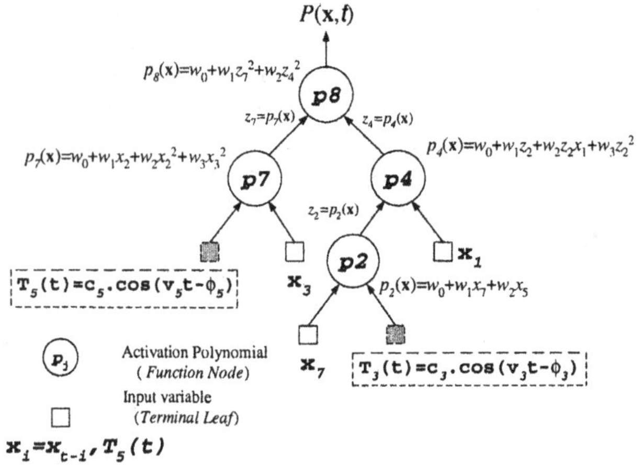

Figure 3.5. A tree-structured PNN that builds a polynomial trigonometric model.

Polynomial, Harmonic and Hybrid Terms. The functions $X_i(\mathbf{x}, t)$ that compose the polynomials can be hybrids of either polynomial or harmonic terms. For *polynomial terms*, we can take the input variables $p_i(\mathbf{x}, t) = x_{t-i}$, where x_{t-i} means i time units behind t, $i \leq d$. The *hybrid terms* can be formulated as follows:

$$X_i = \begin{cases} T_i(t) = c_i \cos(v_i t - \phi_i) \\ p_i(\mathbf{x}, t) = x_{t-i} \end{cases} \qquad (3.35)$$

where i is the harmonic number $1 \leq i \leq h$, c_i is the real-value harmonic amplitude, v_i is the harmonic frequency $0 < v_i < \pi$, such that $v_i \neq v_j$ for $i \neq j$, and ϕ_i is the phase angle. In the case of multiple frequencies, i.e. $v_i = 2\pi i/N$, the harmonics are $h = (N-1)/2$ when N is odd, and $h = N/2$ when N is even.

Figure 3.5 illustrates a polynomial trigonometric model represented as a tree-like PNN whose leaves feed harmonic components, with pre-computed frequencies and phases, and input variables directly.

Depending on the term variables, two cases arise: 1) *polynomial and harmonic cross-product*: in this case, the polynomial curvatures are transferred to the harmonic, and they amplify the spectrum of the harmonic in places determined by the polynomial; and 2) *harmonic and harmonic cross-product*: in this case, the product curvature will contain new frequency components from the spectra of the harmonics.

Identification of Harmonic Terminals. The nonmultiple frequencies v_i can be determined from an h-th degree algebraic equation which is derived from $T(t)$ (3.34). The derivation includes finding the coefficients $\alpha_q \in \mathcal{R}$ using lagged series values, substituting these coefficients α_q to instantiate the algebraic equation, and then solving it for v_i [Hildebrand, 1987, Madala and Ivakhnenko, 1994]. The weighting coefficients α_q, $0 \leq q \leq h-1$ are estimated by solving the following system of $N-2h$ equations by applying the least squares technique:

$$\sum_{q=0}^{h-1} \alpha_q (y_{t+q} + y_{t-q}) = y_{t+h} + y_{t-h} \tag{3.36}$$

where y_t denotes the t-th value from the given series, and the range is $t = h+1, ..., N-h$. These coefficients α_q are used to instantiate the equation for the frequencies v_i as follows:

$$\alpha_0 + \sum_{q=1}^{h-1} \alpha_q \cos(v_i q) = \cos(v_i h) \quad \text{for } v_i, 1 \leq i \leq h \tag{3.37}$$

After expressing all $\cos(iv)$ as polynomials of degree i in $\cos(v)$, equation (3.37) becomes an h-th degree algebraic equation in $\cos(v)$ for the nonmultiple frequencies [Hildebrand, 1987]:

$$\alpha'_0 + \alpha'_1 \cos(v) + \alpha'_2 \cos^2(v) ... + \alpha'_h \cos^h(v) = 0 \tag{3.38}$$

where the new coefficients α'_q result from (3.37).

Equation (3.38) is of the kind $g(v) = 0$ and can be solved by the Newton-Raphson method. Thus, h approximate roots are found which are the frequencies v_i, $1 \leq i \leq h$, of the h harmonics. Among these calculated h roots for $\cos(v)$, the admissible values are those that lie between -1 and 1, since $|\cos(v)| \leq 1$, from frequencies in the interval $0 < v < \pi$.

The *significant harmonics* can be identified by drawing periodograms with plots of the intensity function [Kendall and Ord, 1983]:

$$I(v_i) = \frac{N(A_i^2 + B_i^2)}{4\pi} \tag{3.39}$$

where A_i and B_i are the coefficients of the i-th harmonic.

In case of nonmultiple frequencies, the trigonometric models $T(t)$ (3.34) are linear models of the kind $\mathbf{Tc} = \mathbf{y}$. The amplitudes $\mathbf{c} = (b_0, A_1, B_1, A_2, B_2, ..., A_h, B_h)$ are found by solving the normal trigonometric equation.

After that, the amplitudes c_i and phases ϕ_i are computed from the formulae:

$$c_i = \sqrt{A_i^2 + B_i^2} \qquad \text{and} \qquad \phi_i = \arctan(B_i/A_i) \tag{3.40}$$

where i denotes the concrete harmonic number.

In order to find the harmonic amplitudes A_i and B_i, $1 \leq i \leq h$, forming a vector $\mathbf{c} = (b_0, A_1, B_1, A_2, B_2, ..., A_h, B_h)$, one has to solve the normal trigonometric equation:

$$\mathbf{c} = (\mathbf{T}^T\mathbf{T})^{-1}\mathbf{T}^T\mathbf{y} \tag{3.41}$$

using the harmonic design matrix:

$$\mathbf{T} = \begin{bmatrix} 1 & \sin(v_1 x_1) & \cos(v_1 x_1) & \ldots & \sin(v_h x_1) & \cos(v_h x_1) \\ 1 & \sin(v_1 x_2) & \cos(w_1 x_2) & \ldots & \sin(v_h x_2) & \cos(v_h x_2) \\ \vdots & \vdots & \vdots & & \vdots & \vdots \\ 1 & \sin(v_1 x_N) & \cos(w_1 x_N) & \ldots & \sin(v_h x_N) & \cos(v_h x_N) \end{bmatrix} \tag{3.42}$$

of size $N \times (2h+1)$ as there are $2h$ coefficients, A_i and B_i, $1 \leq i \leq k$.

The multiplication $\mathbf{T}^T\mathbf{T}$ leads to the following $(2h+1) \times (2h+1)$ covariance matrix:

$$\begin{bmatrix} N & \ldots & \sum_{t=1}^N \cos(v_h x_t) \\ \sum_{t=1}^N \sin(v_1 x_t) & \ldots & \sum_{t=1}^N \sin(v_1 x_t)\cos(v_h x_t) \\ \sum_{t=1}^N \cos(v_1 x_t) & \ldots & \sum_{t=1}^N \cos(v_1 x_t)\cos(v_h x_t) \\ \vdots & & \ldots \\ \sum_{t=1}^N \sin(v_h x_t) & \ldots & \sum_{t=1}^N \sin(v_h x_t)\cos(v_h x_t) \\ \sum_{t=1}^N \cos(v_h x_t) & \ldots & \sum_{t=1}^N \cos^2(v_h x_t) \end{bmatrix} \tag{3.43}$$

where the summations are over all N points. The vector $\mathbf{T}^T\mathbf{y}$ of size $(2h+1) \times 1$ is:

$$\mathbf{T}^T\mathbf{y} = \begin{bmatrix} \sum_{t=1}^N y_t \\ \sum_{t=1}^N y_t \sin(v_1 x_t) \\ \sum_{t=1}^N y_t \cos(v_1 x_t) \\ \vdots \\ \sum_{t=1}^N y_t \sin(v_h x_t) \\ \sum_{t=1}^N y_t \cos(v_h x_t) \end{bmatrix} \tag{3.44}$$

where the outcome vector $\mathbf{y}$ contains N values y_t, $1 \leq t \leq N$.

Advantages of Polynomial Trigonometric Models. The benefit of using harmonic components in the polynomials is induction of additional nonlinearities in the target model. The employment of analytically discovered nonmultiple frequencies extends the expressive power of the hybrid representations because when used in the cross-product terms, they modify the curvatures that they imply. When a simple activation polynomial is taken, the resulting product curvatures contain new frequency components that arise as sums and differences from the participating frequencies. In addition to this, when other bases are selected, there will appear additional spectra with multiple frequencies due to the squared *cos* functions.

3.5.4 Rational PNN Models

The approximation theory [Braess, 1986] provides mathematical treatment of rational polynomials and shows that they are generalizations of ordinary polynomials. On approximation tasks, the rational polynomials can be superior to ordinary polynomials especially when modelling highly nonlinear functions and some discontinuous functions. Hence, the rational polynomials should be preferred for modelling data with severe nonlinearities. Influenced by this theory and the research into rational function neural networks [Leung and Haykin, 1993, Rodriguez-Vazquez and Fleming, 2000, Zhu, 2003], tree-structured rational PNN representations with polynomial fractions are outlined below.

The most attractive advantage of polynomial fractions for inductive problem solving is that they can describe with a small number of terms severe nonlinearities for which an ordinary polynomial needs a large number of terms. A rational polynomial can be developed using a tree-structured PNN representation with ordinary activation polynomials in the hidden network nodes and a division operator applied at the root node. The overall rational function is obtained as a fraction of the numerator polynomial provided by the left root child node and a denominator polynomial provided by the right root child node. The overall PNN model becomes a *polynomial fraction* of the kind:

$$P(\mathbf{x}) = \frac{p_n(\mathbf{x})}{p_d(\mathbf{x})} \tag{3.45}$$

where the numerator $p_n(\mathbf{x})$ and the denominator $p_d(\mathbf{x})$ are power series expansions. These two polynomials, $p_n(\mathbf{x})$ and $p_d(\mathbf{x})$, are hierarchically composed by cascading the activation polynomials in the network nodes. The activation polynomials in the left subtree below the root lead to expansion of the numerator polynomial $p_n(\mathbf{x})$, and the activation polynomials in the left subtree below the root lead to expansion of the denominator polynomial $p_d(\mathbf{x})$. At the root, the weights of the two immediate root children polynomials are learned.

In order to learn a rational polynomial $P(\mathbf{x})$ allocated in a PNN network, the weights of the constituent ordinary activation polynomials in the hidden network nodes have to be estimated, and the weights of the polynomial fraction $p_n(\mathbf{x})/p_d(\mathbf{x})$ have to be determined by a relevant technique for system identification of rational models [Billings and Zhu, 1991]. According to this technique, since a ratio $p_n(\mathbf{x})/p_d(\mathbf{x})$ is a nonlinear model, it is expressed as a linear model, and then its weights are estimated by least squares fitting. The weights estimation formula is derived from the fraction of polynomials as follows:

$$y = \frac{p_n(\mathbf{x})}{p_d(\mathbf{x})} = \frac{p_n(x_i, x_j)}{p_d(x_k, x_l)} = \frac{\phi_n(x_i, x_j)\mathbf{w}_n}{1 + \phi_d(x_k, x_l)\mathbf{w}_d} \tag{3.46}$$

where y is the desired target output provided by the training sample, and x_i, x_j, x_k, x_l are the input variables that enter the bivariate activation polynomials $p_n(\mathbf{x})$ and $p_d(\mathbf{x})$ (defined in Table 2.1).

These polynomials are $p_n(x_i, x_j) = \phi_n(x_i, x_j)\mathbf{w}_n$ and $p_d(\mathbf{x}) = 1 + \phi_d(x_k, x_l)\mathbf{w}_d$ respectively. The weight vector is obtained after performing the transformation:

$$y = \phi_n(x_i, x_j)\mathbf{w}_n - y\phi_d(x_k, x_l)\mathbf{w}_d \tag{3.47}$$

which leads to the following matrix equation:

$$\begin{bmatrix} \mathbf{w}_n \\ \mathbf{w}_d \end{bmatrix} = (\mathbf{\Phi}^T\mathbf{\Phi})^{-1}\mathbf{\Phi}^T\mathbf{y} \tag{3.48}$$

where $\begin{bmatrix} \mathbf{w}_n & \mathbf{w}_d \end{bmatrix}^T = [w_{n0}, w_{n1}, ..., w_{nm}, w_{d1}, w_{d2}, ..., w_{ds}]^T$, assuming that the size of the polynomial $p_n(\mathbf{x})$ is $m + 1$ and the size of $p_d(\mathbf{x})$ is s. The design matrix $\mathbf{\Phi}$ consists of the following elements:

$$\mathbf{\Phi} = \begin{bmatrix} \phi_{n0}(\mathbf{x}_1) & \phi_{n1}(\mathbf{x}_1) & \dots & \phi_{nm}(\mathbf{x}_1) & -y\phi_{d1}(\mathbf{x}_1) & \dots & -y\phi_{ds}(\mathbf{x}_1) \\ \phi_{n0}(\mathbf{x}_2) & \phi_{n1}(\mathbf{x}_2) & \dots & \phi_{nm}(\mathbf{x}_2) & -y\phi_{d1}(\mathbf{x}_2) & \dots & -y\phi_{ds}(\mathbf{x}_2) \\ \vdots & \vdots & \vdots\ \vdots & & \vdots & \vdots\ \vdots & \\ \phi_{n0}(\mathbf{x}_N) & \phi_{n1}(\mathbf{x}_N) & \dots & \phi_{nm}(\mathbf{x}_N) & -y\phi_{d1}(\mathbf{x}_N) & \dots & -y\phi_{ds}(\mathbf{x}_N) \end{bmatrix} \tag{3.49}$$

which size is $N \times (m + s + 1)$.

There are several alternatives to the above least squares algorithm [Billings and Zhu, 1991] that can be explored to perform efficient weight training in rational polynomial networks: 1) a rational version of the backpropagation algorithm for gradient descent search of the most optimal rational function weights can be made [Zhu, 2003]; and 2) a recursive least squares fitting algorithm can be elaborated for finding the rational function weights [Leung and Haykin, 1993].

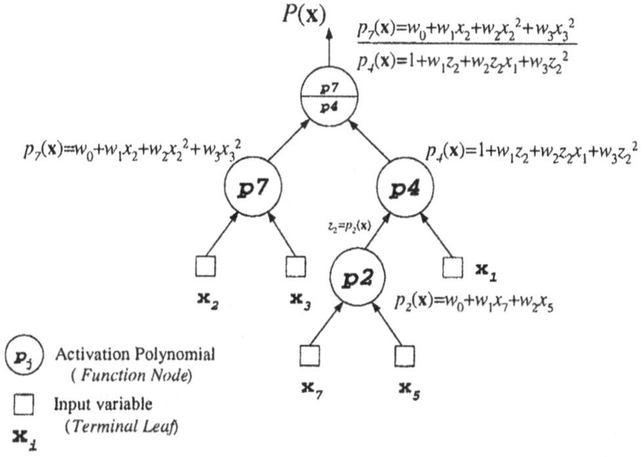

Figure 3.6. Tree-structured PNN representation of a polynomial fraction.

A polynomial fraction made as a tree-like PNN is shown in Figure 3.6.

A rational backpropagation algorithm for weight optimization in high-order rational PNN is developed in Section 6.4. It is useful for further improvement of the PNN weights, especially when the data are uncertain and contaminated by noise. The recursive least squares algorithm given in Section 7.6 may be chosen if faster training is desired. These two additional backpropagation techniques can be beneficial for training rational polynomial networks after the above least squares learning algorithm [Billings and Zhu, 1991] because it depends too much on the noise in the provided training targets.

The rational PNN, however, should be carefully considered for addressing practical tasks, because problems can arise due to the inherent limitations of the fractional models [Braess, 1986]: 1) the rational model behavior may seriously deviate in certain directions if the fraction becomes zero, and 2) the fraction derivatives can be unbounded, thus causing difficulties in the weight identification.

3.5.5 Dynamic PNN Models

Practical time series data requires models that capture time relationships between the data in addition to nonlinearities. There are two possibilities to build time in polynomial networks: 1) to incorporate the time in a static PNN, so that the static network structure models the nonlinear dependencies between the data while a kind of additional short-term memory is simulated to model time dependencies; and 2) to create dynamic PNN models with special network architectures of nodes having feedback connections for capturing the time information in the data. The central issue when intending to handle the time is how to make memory take account of the dynamic properties.

The dynamic properties of a function describing real-world phenomena can be expressed as being dependent on temporal variables. Temporal variables are taken at consecutive time steps. Such time variables provide sensitivity to temporal events. As this approach to dynamical modelling suggests dividing the time into regular, spacially distant intervals, it is referred to as spacial representation of time [Elman, 1990].

The dynamic polynomial formats using temporal variables provide rich, expressive power, especially for time series modelling, because they encapsulate better spatiotemporal patterns. There are high-order terms with temporal variables which offer powerful abilities for sequence learning. The usual problems that arise in learning dynamic polynomials are: what should the time windows be, how to find the model size and the model order. These problems concern finding the proper polynomial structure for the given task which can be addressed by evolutionary search [Gómez-Ramírez et al, 1999, Rodriguez-Vazquez, 1999].

Following this idea, we developed recurrent PNN. These recurrent PNN have universal approximation capabilities for modelling almost any dynamic characteristics, provided the temporal variable values are compact subsets of finite length [Sontag, 1992]. The generalization bounds of these dynamic PNN strongly depend on the maximal input length, and can be obtained only with some preliminary assumptions about the data distribution, or by restricting the topology [Hammer, 2001].

A common feature of dynamic PNNs is that they are state-space models of process behavior [Williams and Zipser, 1989, Narendra and Parthasarathy, 1990]. The states generalize information about the internal excitations to the applied inputs, so they supply additional information for better tracking of behavioral patterns. Recurrent PNNs belong to the class of recurrent neural networks [Jordan, 1986, Rumelhart et al., 1986, Elman, 1990, Tsoi and Back, 1994]. While traditional recurrent neural networks are black-box models from which it is difficult to extract the model, dynamic PNNs produce easily interpretable polynomials. Dynamic PNNs are attractive modeling tools as they are open-box state space models which may be evolved without using prior knowledge about the target function. Rather, the best recurrent polynomial structure can be found using the stochastic mechanisms of the genetic programming paradigm.

Recurrent PNN models can be developed by feeding back the errors from the activation polynomials as variables to enter any of the hidden network nodes [Iba et.al, 1995]. The intermediate errors from the activation polynomials serve as memory terminals [Iba et.al, 1995]. They keep information about the learning history and allow us to better capture the dynamic properties of time varying data. The memory terminals are evidence of the reaction of the parts of the model to a single temporal input pattern since there is a separate response from each hidden node to this pattern. In this way, the neural network learns to reflect the dynamics of the given inputs in the sense that it generalizes the temporal data characteristics. The hidden network nodes fed by memory terminals become context nodes, as they retain the temporal context.

The recurrent polynomials are represented as tree-structured neural networks with feedback connections. These are partially recurrent PNN because each memory terminal provides a feedback that enters some, but not all, functional nodes. In this way, global as well as local recurrences are implemented. The global recurrences are due to the use of the errors produced at the output root network node, which may enter any activation polynomial in the internal nodes. The local recurrences are due to the use of intermediate activation polynomial errors which may also be passed to any functional node as well as to itself. When the recurrences are passed through activation polynomials, the order of the time-dependencies increases, leading to improvement of the long-term mapping capabilities of the network model.

Recurrent PNNs are flexible representations whose learning by IGP leads to sparse models. Sparse recurrent networks with asymmetric irregular topologies may be found because the evolutionary search may discover the most relevant errors for the model; that is, not only necessarily predetermined error terms enter the activation polynomials. One problem of recurrent PNN is how to find the weights. They can be found in two steps: 1) estimate the weights of the cascaded activation polynomials using OLS fitting, and 2) reestimate the activation polynomials in the hidden nodes with the added error terms to produce the overall polynomial. This two-step process is a computational burden but it comes with the benefit of achieving more accurate models.

The original approach to learning weights in recurrent tree-like PNN suggests initialization of all weights with random values, and then application of an error-propagation training algorithm [Iba et.al, 1995]. Another problem is how to evaluate the fitness of the recurrent PNN after the application of the crossover and mutation operators. One possibility is to reestimate the whole PNN using the above two-step algorithm. Another possibility is to retrain only the subtrees below the modified nodes by an error correction algorithm [Iba et.al, 1995]. A recurrent PNN model made upon a tree-like network is illustrated in Figure 3.7.

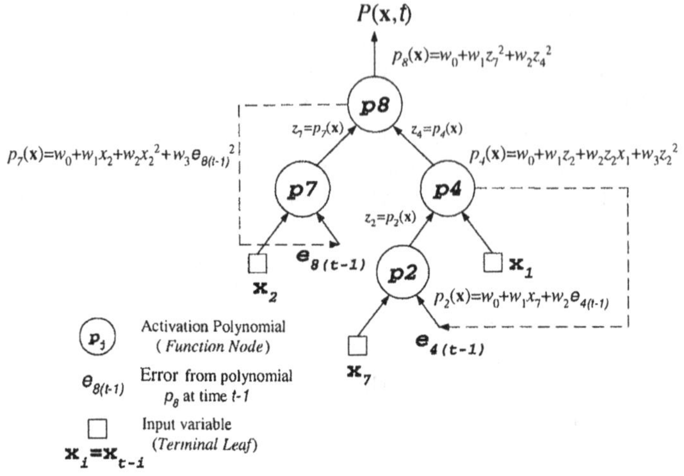

Figure 3.7. Recurrent polynomial constructed as a tree-like PNN with feedback connections from any hidden to any hidden network node.

3.6 Chapter Summary

This chapter studied various polynomial models suitable for regression and approximation tasks and showed how they can be implemented efficiently to facilitate their inductive learning from data. The theoretical approximation ability of polynomials was explained, and approximation error bounds that can be expected from such models were given. Their powerful expressive capacity serves as a motivation to develop various tree-like PNN representations of polynomials. The representations of polynomials as trees are especially suitable for organizing their structural learning by the mechanisms of the IGP paradigm. The fact that these trees serve to allocate PNN models on them enables further retraining by efficient connectionist approaches.

Whilst various kinds of tree-structured representations of polynomials were discussed, these are not exhaustive. The intention behind the models constructed in this chapter is to point out how basic polynomial mappings can be elaborated, and they may serve as patterns that provide hints of how to elaborate other versions. For example, making wavelet polynomials incorporating not only local but also frequency information in the selected wavelet basis functions, or making neuro-fuzzy models [Kasabov, 2002]. In this sense there is a lot of potential for research into enhancing the expressive power of polynomial functions designed in PNN format.

Chapter 4

FITNESS FUNCTIONS AND LANDSCAPES

IGP conducts search by modification of a population of genetic programs and by navigation of the population in the search space. The search space can be metaphorically considered a *fitness landscape* [Stadler, 1996, Wright, 1932]. The fitness landscape is an abstract discrete model that has three components [Jones, 1995]: a finite set of genetic programs, a fitness function that assigns a value to each genetic program, and a neighborhood relation specified by a genetic operator. Neighbors of a genetic program are all individuals reachable by one application of the operator. Each genetic operator creates its own landscape, according to the so-called one operator one landscape view [Jones, 1995]. There are considered to be mutation, crossover, and reproduction landscapes. The mutation landscape is different from the crossover and the selection landscapes. The landscape studies require explicit clarification as to which operator in combination with which fitness function is used.

At genotype level Γ the genetic programs are linearly implemented trees $g \in \Gamma$. The fitness function f maps a genetic program to a feature value $f : \Gamma \rightarrow R$. Since there is one-to-one correspondence between the linearly encoded trees and the genetic programs obtained from them, without loss of precision we may assume that the fitness function can be applied to a genome $f(g)$ as well as to its phenotype $f(\mathcal{G})$. When investigating the evolution of PNN one has to examine the dependencies between the linearly implemented networks and the corresponding polynomial fitting accuracy. Analogously, the neighborhood relation can be considered directly at phenotype level at which the phenotypic instance is the interpreted PNN model. Although the genotype and phenotype levels are separated, there exists a strong causal relation between them, and they can be used together to analyze the IGP performance.

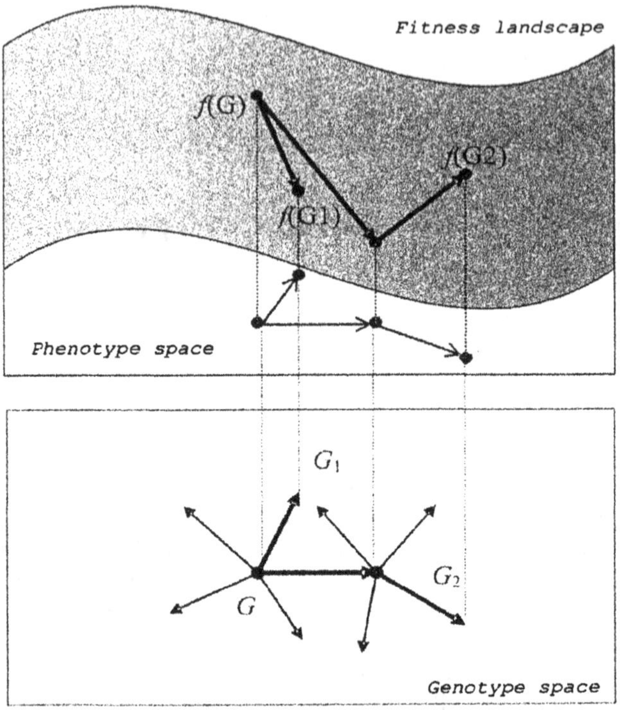

Figure 4.1. The fitness landscape illustrated: genotype-phenotype map (from the genotype space to the phenotype space) and phenotype-fitness map (from the phenotype space to the fitness space). The linear tree in the genotype space G, as its neighbors G_1 and G_2, are mapped (using dotted lines) into genetic program phenotypes, which are mapped (using dashed lines) into corresponding fitnesses.

Figure 4.1 provides an illustration of two mappings that build the fitness landscape: from the space of linear trees to the space of the genetic programs, this is the *genotype-phenotype map*, and from the genetic programs to their corresponding fitness values obtained by model evaluation, this is the *phenotype-fitness map*. The plot in Figure 4.1 shows that the genotype-phenotype map preserves the relationship between the linear trees and their genetic programs, and more precisely the direction and magnitude of their relationships. However the phenotype-fitness map does not preserve exactly all the properties of the relationships between the genetic programs and their fitnesses. It can be seen that the distance between the genotype $f(G_1)$ and its offspring $f(G_2)$ has a different direction and magnitude in the fitness space than the distances in the phenotype and genotype spaces.

The profile characteristics of the fitness landscape reflect the difficulty of the addressed task. The landscape examination is important for gaining insights into the evolutionary behavior of IGP [Kinnear, 1994]. Since the landscape depends on the fitness function, the design of proper fitness functions is crucial for achieving successful IGP performance. The following subsection studies the principles for elaboration of fitness functions for polynomial model selection. Computable measures for fitness landscape analysis are offered that allow us to study the suitability of the IGP components for adaptive search.

4.1 Fitness Functions

The fitness function is considered a driving force of the evolutionary search [Koza, 1992]. It has to reflect the characteristics that are desired from the solution of the inductive task. IGP, as with other inductive learning approaches, usually faces difficulty learning from a limited amount of provided training data. What remains in such situations is to decide how to efficiently use these data in order to acquire some information about the model structure. Having preliminary knowledge about the model features helps to focus the search toward not only highly fit, but also generalizing hypotheses. There are various criteria for estimating the generalization performance that usually include an error component and a complexity component.

Different techniques can be applied to design fitness functions with error and complexity components whilst trying to avoid overfitting with the data. Overfitting occurs when the model has a very small error on the training data, because it then tends to have a large error on unseen data from the same distribution. The overfitted models should be avoided from consideration during learning because they cannot extrapolate beyond the specificities of the current sample. This problem is addressed by making fitness functions that favor fit and sparse PNN.

IGP aims to learn well-performing polynomial models. Well-performing polynomials have the following three characteristics: they are *accurate*, *predictive*, and *parsimonious*. This requires us to design *fitness functions* with three ingredients: 1) an accuracy measurement that favors fit models; 2) a regularization factor that tolerates smoother mappings; and, 3) a complexity penalty that prefers short size models. Such functions augment the fitnesses of the good polynomials, make the good polynomials more clearly isolated on the fitness landscape, and thus help to direct the evolutionary search more precisely.

This section shows how to design *static* and *dynamic* fitness functions so that they become suitable for search control in IGP.

4.1.1 Static Fitness Functions

Static are those fitness functions whose mappings do not change; that is, they produce the same values when evaluated with the same genetic programs. The static fitness functions can be divided into four categories depending on the techniques with which they are obtained: *statistic*, *probabilistic*, *information-theoretic*, and *risk minimizing functions*.

The Inductive Learning Criterion. The objective of inductive learning is to learn a hypothesis that generalizes beyond the given data. The total approximation error is partly due to the insufficiency of the learning algorithm with the adopted representation, and partly due to the insufficient information in the available finite training sample. The learnability depends on the algorithm as well as on the data. In practice, the training data are provided by external sources and the most common assumption is that more data cannot be acquired. The issue that remains is how to manipulate the representation complexity so as to achieve sufficient power for data modelling. There is a strong interdependence between the representation complexity, sample size, and the generalization error. Complex models may exhibit low estimation errors on the given data, but they are inconsistent with unseen examples of the same input-output mapping. Simpler models may show higher estimation error but their prediction error is lower, so simpler models that exhibit satisfactory training errors should be preferred.

The supervised *inductive learning task* is: given a set of input vectors $\mathbf{x} = [x_1, x_2, ..., x_d]$, and corresponding targets y, find a function model P that describes the mapping $y = P(\mathbf{x}) + \varepsilon$, where ε is a zero mean, normally distributed noise. Viewing learning as search, the goal is to infer a map that minimizes the *risk (error) functional*:

$$E = \int L(y, P(\mathbf{x})) d \Pr(\mathbf{x}, y) \tag{4.1}$$

where $L(y, P(\mathbf{x}))$ is the loss, and $\Pr(\mathbf{x}, y)$ is the cumulative probability distribution. This functional is the ultimate learning criterion, however, it cannot be used directly as the probability $\Pr(\mathbf{x}, y)$ is not known.

The difficulty to obtain the unknown data distribution has lead to development of practically convenient learning criteria. Some of these criteria are derived using approaches that approximate the joint probability, while other criteria are reached by approaches that avoid the direct use of the joint probability. The most straightforward approach is to use the mean squared error as a loss function. The mean squared error may help to attain models with very low error on the training data (that is models with very low empirical risk) but it alone cannot guarantee achieving low prediction risk on future unseen data.

Average Error Functions. Several functions for estimating the empirical risk of the models without taking into account their structural characteristics are discussed. These functions are the mean squared error, the mean absolute deviation, and the relative averaged error.

Mean Squared Error. This is a basic measure of the deviation of the estimated output from the data when solving regression tasks. The best approximation $P(\mathbf{x})$ of the true unknown mapping $\tilde{P}(\mathbf{x})$ minimizes the distance: $\|\tilde{P}(\mathbf{x}) - P(\mathbf{x})\|^2$, where $\|.\|$ is the norm of the linear space L_2, defined: $\|P\| = \left(\int |P|^2 d\xi\right)^{1/2}$. The search for this best approximation can be performed using the *mean squared error* (MSE):

$$MSE = \frac{1}{N}\sum_{n=1}^{N}(y_n - P(\mathbf{x}_n))^2 = \frac{1}{N}\mathbf{e}^T\mathbf{e} \tag{4.2}$$

where y_n is the n-th outcome from in the provided training sample $\mathcal{D} = \{(\mathbf{x}_n, y_n)\}_{n=1}^{N}$, $P(\mathbf{x}_n)$ is the polynomial neural network outcome produced with the n-th input vector $\mathbf{x}_n = [x_{n1}, x_{n2}, ..., x_{nd}]$, and N is the data size. The vector $\mathbf{e} = [e_1, e_2, ..., e_n]$, of elements $e_n = y_n - P(\mathbf{x}_n)$, $1 \leq n \leq N$, is introduced to make the notation more concise.

The MSE is the most often used performance measure in practice as it is computationally feasible. However, it amplifies the discrepancies between the data too much and the estimated function mapping; that is, it exaggerates the large errors. The MSE measure cannot distinguish the small from the large errors, which may give an implausible picture of the approximation.

Mean Absolute Deviation. The median error is a robust measure of the mean model error as it does not allow us a small number of large errors to dominate over it. A version of this error is the *mean absolute deviation* (MAD) defined as follows:

$$MAD = \frac{1}{N}\sum_{n=1}^{N}|y_n - P(\mathbf{x}_n)| \tag{4.3}$$

where y_n is the target, and $P(\mathbf{x}_n)$ is the network output.

Relative Averaged Error. Evidence for the error of fit that do not depend on the magnitudes of the data can be obtained by scaling the sum of squared errors with the deviation of the given targets. This leads to the unitless estimate called *relative average error* (RAE):

$$RAE = \frac{\sum_{n=1}^{N}(y_n - P(\mathbf{x}_n))^2}{\sum_{n=1}^{N}(y_n - \overline{y})^2} \tag{4.4}$$

where $\overline{y}$ is the sample mean of the outputs $\overline{y} = (1/N)\sum_{n=1}^{N} y_n$.

Statistical Fitness Functions. Coherent measures that account for the fitting as well as for the parsimony of the models are provided by some specialized statistical functions. These are statistical criteria for minimization of the risk functional (4.1), assuming the loss function $L(y, P(\mathbf{x})) = (y_n - P(\mathbf{x}_n))^2$. Popular fitness functions for statistical model selection are the unbiased estimation of variance, the final prediction error, the predicted squared error, and the generalized cross validation.

Unbiased Estimation of Variance. Low generalization error can be attained if both the model interpolation quality and the number of its parameters are considered. In network learning, the *effective number of parameters* (weights)[Moody, 1992] is less than the number of the actual parameters. The good parameters can be included in the cost function according to the *Unbiased Estimation of Variance* (UEV) formula:

$$UEV = \frac{1}{N - \gamma}\mathbf{e}^T\mathbf{e} \tag{4.5}$$

where γ is the effective number of parameters computed as follows:

$$\gamma = W - \lambda trace(\mathbf{\Phi}^T\mathbf{\Phi})^{-1} \tag{4.6}$$

assuming that the model $P(\mathbf{x})$ is estimated using a regularization parameter λ, and $\mathbf{\Phi}^T\mathbf{\Phi}$ is the covariance matrix (Section 1.1.1).

The application of formula (4.5) to hierarchically cascaded polynomials requires some clarification. Since the developed PNN networks here use OLS fitting (1.7) to estimate the weights, partial effective parameters should be computed using (4.6) in every node. This is facilitated by the fact that the covariance matrix is available as a by-product from OLS fitting. The effective number of parameters in the whole network can be computed as a sum of all effective partial parameters.

Final Prediction Error. Another measure, derived using a second order Taylor series approximation of the generalization error, is the *Final Prediction Error* (FPE) [Akaike, 1970]:

$$FPE = \frac{N + \gamma}{N(N - \gamma)}\mathbf{e}^T\mathbf{e} \tag{4.7}$$

where γ are the effective parameters, and $\mathbf{e}$ is the vector of the errors.

This FPE measure accounts for both the degree of fitting and the model complexity. With the increase of the number of weights, the FPE reaches a minimum on the error surface. This error minimum is attained when the model has somewhere between zero weights and the number of weights equal to the data set size.

Predicted Squared Error. The intention to make an error measure that accounts for the model predictability without partitioning of the training set has lead to the development of a similar measure with a learning accuracy component proportional to the empirical error over the training data, and a structural complexity component proportional to the number of polynomial weights. This is the *Predicted Square Error* (PSE) [Barron, 1988, Barron and Xiao, 1991] defined as follows:

$$PSE = MSE + 2\frac{\gamma}{N}\sigma_y^2 \tag{4.8}$$

where MSE is the mean squared error (4.2), γ are the effective polynomial weights (4.6), and σ_y^2 is an estimate of the unknown error variance that can be obtained as follows:

$$\sigma_y^2 = \frac{1}{N}\sum_{n=1}^{N}(y_n - \overline{y})^2 \tag{4.9}$$

where $\overline{y}$ denotes the mean of the outputs. This empirical error variance σ_y^2 is practically useful since it does not depend on the model.

The PSE fitness function (4.8) also compromises between the error of fit and the model structure. What should be noted is that its second term, which penalizes overly complex models, is a linear function of the network weights. Because of this, when the number of weights increases, the slope of the PSE will begin to raise after reaching its minimum. The minimum is where the accuracy and complexity curves cross each other. This guarantees that the minimization of this error can lead to a well-performing polynomial due to its proper structure.

Generalized Cross Validation. A well-known approach in statistics for detecting the generalization capacity of a model is the leave-one-out cross validation. It requires us to perform successive error measurements of the studied model with each example as a separate testing set, after estimating the model with the remaining data. This idea can be applied analytically without reestimating the model. Although this analytical approach is strictly valid for linear models only, it can also be applied to polynomial networks using the following *Generalized Cross-Validation* (GCV) formula [Craven and Wahba, 1979, Wahba, 1990]:

$$GCV = \frac{N}{(N-\gamma)^2}\mathbf{e}^T\mathbf{e} \tag{4.10}$$

where $\mathbf{e}$ is the error vector, and γ are the effective model parameters. The justification of using this GCV formula is that it is applied after estimating the root activation polynomial which is linear in the weights.

Probabilistic Fitness Functions. Probabilistic fitness functions can be derived using the two main principal approaches: the Bayesian inference and the maximum likelihood [Bishop, 1995]. They also aim at minimization of the risk functional, but using other loss functions, which leads to estimates of the probability density of the given input-output pairs. The attempt to search for a functional description of the joint probability density of the data is known as the maximum a posteriori principle. It is assumed that the data are independent and identically distributed. Two distinguishing fitness functions from this category presented here are the Bayesian information criterion, and the maximum marginal likelihood.

Bayesian Information Criterion. The Bayesian approach allows us to obtain the mean of the joint posterior probability of the input-output data by decomposing it into a product of the dependence of the outputs on the model, and the prior belief in the model. This approach seeks to maximize the joint conditional density: $\Pr(\mathbf{x}, y) = \Pr(y|\mathbf{x}) \Pr(\mathbf{x})$, where $\mathbf{x}$ are the inputs, and y are the outputs. The objective of Bayesian model selection is maximization of this posterior probability, which for convenience, is transformed into a minimization problem by taking its negative logarithm. This reasoning motivated the development of the *Bayesian Information Criterion* (BIC) [Schwartz, 1978]:

$$BIC = \frac{N + (\ln(N) - 1)\gamma}{N(N - \gamma)} \mathbf{e}^T \mathbf{e} \tag{4.11}$$

where γ are the good parameters, and $\mathbf{e}$ is the error vector.

Maximum Marginal Likelihood. The maximum marginal likelihood approach helps to choose the most probable parameter values given the data. It differs from the Bayesian approach in that it involves the model with its weights. The goal of model selection is maximization of the unconditional posterior probability: $\Pr(y) = \int \Pr(y|\mathbf{x}) \Pr(\mathbf{x}) d\mathbf{x}$. Taking the logarithms, multiplying by minus two, and discarding the constants, leads to the following *Maximum Marginal Likelihood* (MML) [MacKay, 1992a] error estimate:

$$MML = \gamma \ln\left(\sigma_y^2\right) - \ln|\mathbf{R}| + \frac{1}{\sigma_y^2} \mathbf{e}^T \mathbf{e} \tag{4.12}$$

where σ_y^2 is an empirical estimate of the error variance (4.9), and $\mathbf{R}$ is the projection matrix. The construction of PNN makes the computation of the projection matrix for the whole polynomial model not so trivial because the covariance matrix of the overall model is not available. Fortunately, it is possible to approximate it using the covariance matrix produced for the estimation of the output node weights.

The projection matrix can be computed using the matrix equation:

$$\mathbf{R} = \mathbf{I} - \mathbf{\Phi}\mathbf{\Sigma}\mathbf{\Phi}^T \tag{4.13}$$

where $\mathbf{\Phi}$ is the design matrix formed to learn the output node weights, and $\mathbf{\Sigma}$ is the covariance matrix $\mathbf{\Sigma} = (\mathbf{\Phi}^T\mathbf{\Phi} + \lambda\mathbf{I})^{-1}$.

Information-theoretic Fitness Functions. There are several functions for evaluating both the degree of model accuracy and the degree of its complexity which have been derived using notions from the information theory. Such popular information-theoretic fitness functions are the Mallows' statistics, the Akaike's information criterion, and the minimum description length.

Mallows' Statistic. The total error of a regression model can be measured by the so-called *Mallows' Statistic* (C_p)[Mallows, 1973]:

$$C_p = \frac{1}{\sigma_y^2}\mathbf{e}^T\mathbf{e} + 2\gamma - N \tag{4.14}$$

where σ_y^2 is assumed as an estimate of the error variance (4.9), and γ is the number of effective parameters. The C_p function trades off the accuracy of fit with the model complexity.

Akaike's Information Criterion. The information content of a model increases with the decrease of the following *Akaike's Information Criterion* (AIC) function [Akaike, 1973]:

$$AIC = \frac{2}{N}\mathbf{e}^T\mathbf{e} + \frac{2}{N}\gamma \tag{4.15}$$

which penalizes models with larger number of effective parameters γ. In this way, the AIC function allows us to balance the relation between the model performance on the training data with the model complexity.

Minimum Description Length. Criteria that favor accurate and parsimonious models can be derived using the *Minimum Description Length* (MDL) [Rissanen, 1989] principle. This principle suggests to pursue not maximization of the posterior probability $\Pr(D|\mathcal{G}_i)\Pr(\mathcal{G}_i)$ of the genetic programs $\mathcal{G}_i$, $1 \leq i \leq \pi$, inferred from the data D, but rather minimization of its code length: $\min\{I(D|\mathcal{G}_i) + I(\mathcal{G}_i)|1 \leq i \leq \pi\}$, where $I(\mathcal{G}_i)$ denotes the coding length of the i-th genetic program alone $I(\mathcal{G}_i) = -\log_2 \Pr(\mathcal{G}_i)$, and $I(D|\mathcal{G}_i)$ is the coding length of this genetic program as a model of the data $I(D|\mathcal{G}_i) = -\log_2 \Pr(D|\mathcal{G}_i)$.

Adapted for polynomial network induction, the MDL principle can be stated as follows: given a set of data and an effective enumeration of their PNN models, prefer with greatest confidence the PNN which has both high learning accuracy (i.e. very closely approximates the data) and low syntactic complexity (i.e. has a small number of terms or weights). Such an MDL fitness function suitable for IGP is [Iba and de Garis, 1994]:

$$MDL = MSE + (n_{\mathcal{F}} + n_{\mathcal{T}}) + n_{\mathcal{F}} \log_2 \mathcal{F} + n_{\mathcal{T}} \log_2 \mathcal{T} \qquad (4.16)$$

where $n_{\mathcal{F}}$ is the number of functional nodes in the genetic program tree, $n_{\mathcal{T}}$ is the number of terminal leaves, $\mathcal{F}$ is the number of all possible functionals, and $\mathcal{T}$ is the number of all terminals.

A problem that arises in the application of this MDL formula (4.16) is how to trade off its two components, because they differ in magnitudes. One remedy to this problem is to balance the accuracy and the complexity by an adaptive parsimony factor. Denote the complexity cost by C, that is $C = (n_{\mathcal{F}} + n_{\mathcal{T}}) + n_{\mathcal{F}} log_2 \mathcal{F} + n_{\mathcal{T}} log_2 \mathcal{T}$. Then, the above MDL-based fitness function (4.16) can be balanced in the following way [Zhang and Mühlenbein, 1995]:

$$MDL2 = MSE + \rho(\tau)C \qquad (4.17)$$

where $\rho(\tau)$ is called adaptive Occam factor. Assuming that the error of the best genetic program at generation $\tau - 1$ is $MSE_{Best}^{\tau-1}$, and $C_{Best^{\tau}}$ is its expected complexity, the adaptive factor is computed with the formula [Zhang and Mühlenbein, 1995]:

$$\rho(\tau) = \begin{cases} N^{-2} MSE_{Best}^{\tau-1} / C_{Best^{\tau}}, & \text{if } MSE_{Best}^{\tau-1} \geq \epsilon \\ N^{-2} / \left(MSE_{Best}^{\tau-1} C_{Best^{\tau}} \right), & \text{otherwise} \end{cases} \qquad (4.18)$$

where ϵ is the suggested minimal error of the final solution. In the first case, the factor $\rho(\tau)$ decreases when $MSE_{Best}^{\tau-1} \geq \epsilon$ because the error is less than one. In the second case, when the error diminishes $MSE_{Best}^{\tau-1} < \epsilon$, the factor $\rho(\tau)$ increases, and thus, exaggerates the importance of the structure size during the later stages of the search process.

The MDL functions (4.16) and (4.17) add a complexity penalty to each error, and even if two genetic programs exhibit the same error, they will have different fitnesses if they have different structures. Thus, they make the local landscape slightly more rugged, but globally the landscape becomes smoother and easier for navigation.

Risk Minimizing Fitness Functions. Identification of well- generalizing models can be approached without measuring the joint distribution of the data [Vapnik, 1992]. According to the Vapnik-Chervonenkis theory [Vapnik and Chervonenkis, 1971, Vapnik, 1995], the risk functional can be reformulated to find the generalization error bounds in the following way: $(1/N) \sum_{n=1}^{N} L(y_n, P(\mathbf{x}_n))$. The function that describes the generalization error bounds may be taken as a model risk estimate.

The risk estimate can be used to direct the search because it is known that there exists a model with optimal complexity which for the given sample size has smallest prediction error. The *Structural Risk Minimization* (SRM) [Cherkassky et al., 1999] formula is:

$$SRM = \frac{1}{N}\left(1 - \sqrt{m - m\ln m + \frac{\ln N}{2N}}\right)^{-1} \mathbf{e}^T\mathbf{e} \tag{4.19}$$

where $\mathbf{e}$ is the error vector, and m is a factor computed using the VC-dimension $h = \gamma + 1$ as follows: $m = h/N$. The SRM estimate has confidence level: $1 - 1/\sqrt{N}$. It should be noted that this version of SRM is specialized for polynomial models.

The usefulness of the SRM is slightly limited due to its tendency to tolerate polynomials overfitting the data at the boundaries [Cherkassky et al., 1999]. That is why the boundary data can be removed from the training sample before using SRM.

4.1.2 Dynamic Fitness Functions

Dynamic fitness functions are those functions whose mappings change during the evolutionary process. This may happen when the examples from the training set are associated with a changing property. The fitness function can sustain improving search by driving the individuals in the population to compete, so as to fit data with more distinct properties. This competition between the individuals may help to accomplish reliable search in a similar way to the way in which the immune system learns [Farmer et al., 1986, Farmer, 1990, Bersini and Varela, 1991]. The motivation to mimic such biological learning abilities comes from the close similarity in the behavior of the immune system and the IGP system: 1) they both perform search for generalizations of fitted observations; and 2) they both use similar search mechanisms involving pattern matching, heuristic selection and gene modification.

Following an idiotypic network model of the immune system [DeBoer and Hogeweg, 1989], there a dynamic fitness function was developed which consists of two dynamic models that influence each other [Nikolaev et al., 1999]: 1) a model for propagating genetic programs that fit more important data, and stimulating them to match data from different subsets; and 2) a model for changing the importances of the data in dependence of the number of genetic programs that fit them. This dynamic function controls the search by encouraging complementary genetic programs to interact, and thus forms a kind of a network. The network connectivity is a source of diversity which is a spontaneous macroproperty that enables us to achieve continuous evolutionary search influenced by the importance of the data. Genetic program reinforcements with rewards for matched important examples occasionally provoke network perturbations which push the population on the landscape.

Genetic Program Dynamics. The *Dynamical Fitness Function* (DFF) is formed from a constant initial supply, plus a proportion from the previous fitness DFF_i^τ and proliferation due to arousal by fitted examples and evoked exciting interactions, without a death rate:

$$DFF_i^{\tau+1} = Z + DFF_i^\tau(\varsigma Prol(Ag_i^\tau, Id_i^\tau) - d) \tag{4.20}$$

where Z is influx constant, d is turnover constant, ς is proliferation constant, Ag_i^τ is the antigen score of the i-th genetic program at generation τ, Id_i^τ is the total anti-idiotype excitation of program i, and $Prol$ is the proliferation function. The fitness of a genetic program will increase when it fits more examples, and it also depends on their importances.

The *proliferation Prol* of a genetic program i in the next generation, according to this difference equation model, depends not only on the matched observations Ag_i^τ, but also on the extent of its interactions Id_i^τ with the other genetic programs:

$$Prol(Ag_i^\tau, Id_i^\tau) = \frac{Ag_i^\tau + Id_i^\tau}{\rho_1 + Ag_i^\tau + Id_i^\tau} \tag{4.21}$$

where ρ_1 is a free constant parameter.

The antigen score of a genetic program should account for the number of the examples that it fits and it should also depend on the importance of these eliciting examples. It is assumed that an example depends on the number and on the specificity of the structurally related genetic programs that match it. The *antigen score* Ag_i^τ of genetic program i can be defined as linearly proportional to the importance I_j^τ of the examples n which it matches, $1 \leq j \leq n$, $n \leq N$:

$$Ag_i^\tau = \sum_{j=1, i\neq j}^{n} B_{ij} I_j^\tau \tag{4.22}$$

where the binding B_{ij} of a program i is 1 if the genetic program matches the j-th example and 0 otherwise. For regression with continuous outcomes, the binding B_{ij} of a program i is redefined as follows:

$$B_{ij} = \begin{cases} 1 - \mathbf{e}_i^2/\mathbf{e}_A^2 & \textit{if } \mathbf{e}_{ij}^2 < \mathbf{e}_A^2 \\ 0 & \textit{otherwise} \end{cases} \tag{4.23}$$

where $\mathbf{e}_{ij}^2 = (y_i - P_i(\mathbf{x}_j))^2$ is the error between the outcome $P_i(\mathbf{x}_j)$ of the i-th program evaluated with input $\mathbf{x}_j$, and y_i is the target. The value of $\mathbf{e}_A^2$ is the sum of squared errors from all programs in the population.

Data Importance Function. The genetic program fitness dynamics should interact with the dynamics of the data. If more genetic programs recognize a particular example, then it should become less attractive. When a small number of unmatched exceptional examples remain, they have to reinforce those genetic programs in the population which cover them, and so to provoke search perturbation. The *importance* I_n^τ of example n is defined as proportional to the number of genetic programs that fit it, plus a term for constant recruitment γ_n:

$$I_n^{\tau+1} = I_n^\tau \left(\alpha - \sum_{j=1} \pi B_{jn} \frac{DFF_j^\tau}{F_{\max}^\tau N} \right) + \gamma_n \tag{4.24}$$

where α is a free constant parameter, and π is the population size.

Specifying the genetic program interactions A_{ij} is essential to drive the individuals to compete. The interactions should be such characteristics that reflect complementarity in behavior. Stimulating complementary behavior can be made by defining the affinity of the genetic programs to account for the difference in their mutual learning potential. Two genetic programs are complementary when they fit examples from disjoint subsets. The *affinity* A_{ij} between two genetic programs i and j may be defined as the set difference between the subset of examples:

$$A_{ij} = |D_i^\tau - D_j^\tau| \tag{4.25}$$

where D_i^τ is the subset of examples matched by program i at generation τ from all provided training data D: $D_i^\tau \subseteq D$, $D_j^\tau \subseteq D$.

The virtual *immune network* comprises all genetic programs in the population. This network is symmetric $A_{ij} = A_{ji}$ for $1 \leq i, j \leq \pi$, and also, the genetic programs do not recognize self $A_{ii} = 0$. The affinity A_{ij} stimulates the genetic programs to: 1) fit more examples; and 2) fit less overlapping data subsets.

The idiotypic influence among the genetic programs should estimate their mutual behavioral complementarity through the affinity interactions. The dynamic fitness uses such a factor to self-regulate so that together the individuals have the power to fit all data. The *anti-idiotype excitation* Id_i^τ is defined to favor a genetic program i if its interaction A_{ij} with the other $1 \leq j \leq \pi$ population members is high:

$$Id_i^\tau = \frac{1}{N\pi} \sum_{j=1, i \neq j} \pi A_{ij} DFF_j^\tau \tag{4.26}$$

where N is the data size, and π is the population size .

The evolution of the virtual immune network topology determines the ability of the IGP to conduct efficient search. It is important to realize how the network connectivity will correspond to the phases of evolutionary search. IGP usually begins with a random initial population, and the global excitation is large. When IGP performs global search, the interactions should be high, indicating exploration of large landscape areas. During local search, the wiring should be low as IGP exploits landscape areas in the vicinities of the reached local optima.

Finding of proper parameters for this dynamic function is a tedious task and may require a large number of trials. The following reference values are recommended: $Z = 0.1$, $d = 0.5$, $\rho_1 = 0.25$, $\varsigma = 1.1$, $\gamma_e = 0.001$, and $\alpha = 1.025$. The initial fitness is calculated by solving the above difference equation for a steady state $DFF_i^0 = DFF_i^{n+1}$, which leads to the formula: $DFF_i^0 = Z(\rho_1 + 1)/(\rho_1 + 1 + d + d\rho_1 - \varsigma)$.

The immune IGP dynamics have three aspects [Farmer et al., 1986]. The first aspect is the net topology dynamics. Here it is assumed that the immune network is symmetric and completely connected, but these are simplifications. Theoretically, the immune network should comprise programs interacting with a small number of other programs in the population. The affinity formula should not stimulate, however, formation of very sparse networks, since they make it impossible for perturbations to occur and so hinder the search. The second aspect is the parameter dynamics. The large number of free parameters in the fitness formula creates difficulties for finding and tuning their values. The third aspect is the concentration model dynamics of the genetic programs. These dynamics are very difficult to analyze because of the bell-shaped character of the activating proliferation function.

4.1.3 Fitness Magnitude

The fitness function can be transformed in several ways, if necessary, to make it more suitable for the evolutionary IGP search mechanisms. The main three formats of the fitness are [Koza, 1992]: *raw fitness*, *standardized fitness*, *adjusted fitness*, and *normalized fitness*. Raw fitness is the absolute quality of the genetic program as mapped by the fitness function which reflects the desired properties from the solution of the task. Standardized fitness is the minimizing version of the raw fitness, which in the case of evolving PNN, is the same as the raw fitness. Adjusted fitness is made by scaling the raw fitness with a particular method in order to improve the selection (Subsection 5.1). When fitness proportionate selection is used it is recommended to divide the adjusted fitness of an individual by the sum of all adjusted fitnesses from the population, which results in a normalized fitness.

4.2 Fitness Landscape Structure

The capacity of the evolutionary algorithm to perform efficient search is determined by its ability to move continuously on the underlying fitness landscape, that is by its ability to continuously push the population on the landscape. This suggests potential to traverse landscape valleys, climb on landscape peaks, walk on landscape ridges, and various other landscape profiles. When organizing population-based search on a fitness landscape, one may envision that each program moves along some trajectory. A program change leads to a move on the landscape toward another fitness value. Thus, during evolution each program makes a trajectory on the fitness landscape. The direction of the program movement reflects the rate of change of its fitness computed after one application of the modification operator.

Having knowledge about the fitness landscape structure helps to understand and control the evolutionary search process. The landscape can be envisioned as a three dimensional surface of points whose third dimension on the z-axis are fitnesses, and whose projections on the x-y plane are their corresponding genetic programs. The differences between the points form the *landscape structure*, in other words, the heights (magnitudes) of the fitnesses make the landscape. The fitness landscape profile consists of peaks, plateaus, saddles, and basins. The configurations of these forms indicate the structural characteristics of the landscape.

When the landscape structure includes peaks or basins with considerably different fitnesses, then the landscape is called *rugged* [Jones, 1995, Hordijk, 1996]. When mainly plateaus and large basins with comparative fitnesses build the structure, the landscape is *smooth* [Jones, 1995, Hordijk, 1996]. The fitness landscape characteristics show the difficulties that a searcher encounters when trying to find an extremum. There is no strict, generally accepted theory that explains exactly how the landscape characteristics influence the search. One of the views is that a rugged landscape is *complex* and difficult for search. A relatively smooth landscape is a *simple landscape* which is easy to search.

The ultimate goal of the search process is to locate the global optimum on the landscape. When a minimizing fitness function is considered, global optimum is the deepest basin point on the landscape. A genetic program $\mathcal{G}$ is a *global minimum* if it has smallest fitness than all other genomes $\mathcal{G}'$ on the whole landscape:

$$\forall \mathcal{G}, \mathcal{G}', f(\mathcal{G}) < f(\mathcal{G}') \tag{4.27}$$

The search has to avoid entrapment at inferior local optima. When a minimizing fitness function is considered, the local optimum is the lowest basin point on the landscape with equal fitness than all of its neighbors, reachable with the learning operator. A genetic program $\mathcal{G}$ is a *local minimum* if it has smallest fitness among all other genomes $\mathcal{G}'$ within a region with a certain radius r on the landscape:

$$\forall \mathcal{G}, \mathcal{G}', Dist(\mathcal{G}, \mathcal{G}') < r \Rightarrow f(\mathcal{G}) < f(\mathcal{G}') \tag{4.28}$$

where the radius r is defined using tree-to-tree distance *Dist*.

The fitness landscape structure can be described by different characteristics: 1) distribution of local optima; 2) heights of local optima; 3) dimensions of the basins between optimal points; 4) information that a point carries about distant points; 5) information that a point carries about optima, etc.. Before trying to investigate these features, one should realize that the genotype space in IGP is an irregular graph in which each genetic program has a different number of neighbors than the other genetic programs. The formal analysis of landscapes over irregular graphs is extremely difficult and still under investigation [Bastert et al., 2001], while there is a complete theory for the analysis of landscapes over regular graphs [Stadler, 1996] applicable to genetic algorithms.

4.3 Fitness Landscape Measures

The fitness landscape is a useful metaphor for analysis and understanding of the evolutionary search process. This metaphor is general and can be instantiated with particular learning operators and concrete fitness functions. Several measures for fitness landscape analysis are presented here, including statistical, probabilistic, information, and quantitative measures. It is demonstrated how to apply them to study landscapes derived with the mutation operator. The crossover and reproduction operators may be studied in an analogous way.

4.3.1 Statistical Correlation Measures

The search difficulties are monitored by the fitness landscape, and they are mainly in two aspects: *local* and *global search characteristics*. The local search characteristics depend on the relation between the fitness and the operator. Examinations of the local landscape features can be performed using the autocorrelation function [Manderick et al., 1991, Weinberger, 1990]. The global search characteristics depend on the correspondence between the fitness and the distance to a known global optima. Examinations of the global landscape can be made using the fitness distance correlation [Jones and Forrest, 1995].

The correlation landscape characteristics are only a necessary condition for the usefulness of the genetic operators and the fitness function. However, they do not guarantee that good search performance will be achieved. From a local perspective, a landscape with a single hill could have a high autocorrelation, but the evolutionary algorithm may climb slowly, making a long path on its slopes before reaching the global optima. From a global perspective, a landscape may feature by a good fitness distance correlation but if the global optima is surrounded by a lot of local optima, it will be arduous for the algorithm to search on it.

Autocorrelation Function. The *autocorrelation function* (ACF) of a fitness landscape [Manderick et al., 1991, Weinberger, 1990], in context of IGP, measures the statistical correlation between the fitnesses of genetic programs trees separated by a series of applications of the operator from which the landscape arises. The empirical autocorrelation ACF_d can be determined by the *fitness correlation coefficient* (FCC) of the operator that makes the landscape. The fitness correlation coefficient accounts for the characteristics of landscapes on trees at certain distance apart. The FCC, $FCC : R^n \times R^n \rightarrow R$, of the mutation landscape ($d = 1$) can be calculated with the fitnesses of n pairs of parent $\mathcal{G}_p$ and child $\mathcal{G}_c$ trees, taken during a random walk starting from an arbitrary initial tree through a set of trees generated by successive applications of the mutation operator [Manderick et al., 1991]:

$$FCC(F_p, F_c) = \frac{Cov(F_p, F_c)}{\sigma(F_p)\sigma(F_c)} \tag{4.29}$$

where: $Cov(F_p, F_c)$ is the covariance between the computed sequences $F_p = \{f_{p1}, ..., f_{pn}\}$ of parent fitnesses $f_p = f(\mathcal{G}_p)$, and $F_c = \{f_{c1}, ..., f_{cn}\}$ of child fitnesses $f_c = f(\mathcal{G}_c)$, $\sigma(F_p)$, and $\sigma(F_c)$ are the standard deviations of F_p and F_c respectively.

The autocorrelation ACF_d of a landscape over trees at distance d is:

$$\begin{aligned} \forall \mathcal{G}_p, \mathcal{G}_c, Dist(\mathcal{G}_p, \mathcal{G}_c) &= d, f(\mathcal{G}_p) \in F_p, f(\mathcal{G}_c) \in F_c \\ ACF_d &= FCC(F_p, F_c) \end{aligned} \tag{4.30}$$

When ACF_d is close to 1, the fitness and the operator are highly correlated, which indicates a locally smooth fitness landscape that is easy to search with the operator in most cases.

Strictly speaking, the ACF_d may be used to study *statistically isotropic* landscapes. A landscape is isotropic when the statistics do not depend on its examination by random walks. That is why several ACF_d have to be computed by walking different landscape subspaces, starting from different random trees. This helps to obtain a representative estimate for the entire landscape. Small deviations between the computed ACF_d indicate that the landscape subspaces look similar. In this case, the landscape may be considered statistically isotropic, and the application of the ACF_d formula (4.30) is valid subject to the assumption that the analysis is restricted to the walked subspaces [Hordijk, 1996].

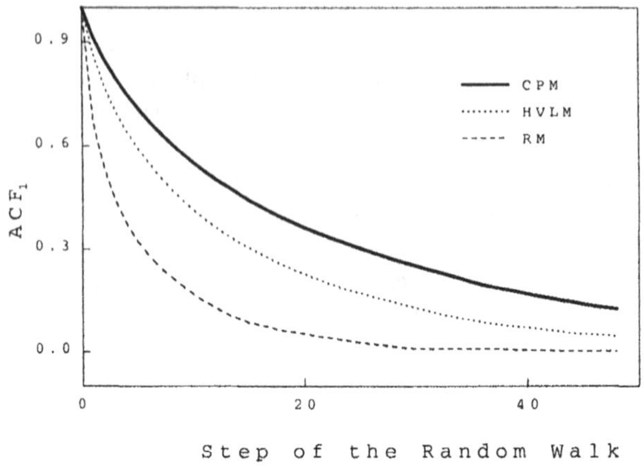

Figure 4.2. Autocorrelations of three different mutation landscapes produced with context-preserving mutation (CPM), hierarchical variable-length mutation ($HVLM$), and replacement mutation (RM). The MSE fitnesses are evaluated using the Mackey-Glass data, and averaged over 50 runs.

Figure 4.2 displays the ACF_1 of three mutation landscapes made using the operators CPM [Nikolaev and Iba, 2001a], $HVLM$ [O'Reilly, 1995], and RM (Subsection 2.2.2). One can see in Figure 4.2 that the landscape of the CPM operator [Nikolaev and Iba, 2001a] features highest autocorrelation, hence its landscape is smoother than the others.

The general algorithm for evaluating the ACF of a landscape of an irregular graph [Stadler, 1996] uses successive modifications of trees at different steps apart. The unified ACF from such different images, estimated with tree neighborhoods at increasing differences, is the average autocorrelation from them. This general algorithm that performs iteratively random sampling of trees and measures the unified ACF of averaged fitness landscape subspaces is given in Table 4.1.

Another look at the local fitness landscape characteristics can be made with the correlation length metric. The *correlation length* (CL) is a measure of the longest series of steps beyond which there could not be obtained meaningful information about the relationship among the fitnesses of two points on the landscape surface. The statistical estimate of the correlation length states that the largest lag for which there is still correlation between two points on the fitness landscape is the first step at which the ACF function becomes: $-2/\sqrt{n} \leq ACF \leq 2/\sqrt{n}$, where n is the number of sampled trees.

Table 4.1. General algorithm for measuring the autocorrelation function ACF of fitness landscapes that arise in IGP with tree-like genetic programs.

Measuring Autocorrelations in IGP

step	*Algorithmic sequence*
1. Initialization	Tree-to-tree distance $Dist : \mathcal{G} \times \mathcal{G} \rightarrow N$ and fitness $f : \mathcal{G} \rightarrow R$.
2. Perform	For several distances $d = 1$ to 10 do
a random	For a number of landscape subspaces $l = 1$ to 50 do
walk	a) Generate a parent tree $\mathcal{G}_p = RandomTree()$.
	b) For a large number of steps $n > 10^3$ do
	i) Sample an offspring $\mathcal{G}_c$ of $\mathcal{G}_p$ at $Dist(\mathcal{G}_p, \mathcal{G}_c) = d$.
	ii) Record the fitnesses: $f_p = f(\mathcal{G}_p)$ and $f_c = f(\mathcal{G}_c)$
	$F_p = \{f_{p1}, f_{p2}, ...\}$ and $F_c = \{f_{c1}, f_{c2}, ...\}$.
	iii) Replace the child to become parent: $\mathcal{G}_p = \mathcal{G}_c$.
	c) Compute the mean fitnesses
	$\overline{f}_p = \frac{1}{n}\sum_{i=1}^{n} f_{pi}, \overline{f_c} = \frac{1}{n}\sum_{i=1}^{n} f_{ci}$.
	d) Compute the covariance
	$Cov(F_p, F_c) = \sum_{i=1}^{n}(f_{pi} - \overline{f})(f_{ci} - \overline{f}_c)$.
	e) Compute the fitness deviations
	$\sigma(F_p) = \sqrt{\sum_{i=1}^{n}(f_{pi} - \overline{f}_p)^2}$
	$\sigma(F_c) = \sqrt{\sum_{i=1}^{n}(f_{ci} - \overline{f_c})^2}$.
	f) Calculate the AC for step d from subspace l
	$FCC_l(F_p, F_c) = Cov(F_p, F_c)/(\sigma(F_p)\sigma(F_c))$.
	Average the autocorrelations from the l subspaces
	$ACF_d = \frac{1}{50}\sum_{l=1}^{50} FCC_l$.
3. Calculate the	Compute the unified ACF from the available ACF_d
ACF	$ACF = \frac{1}{10}\sum_{d=1}^{10} ACF_d$.

Fitness Distance Correlation. The global search difficulties depend on the global landscape structure. On a relatively smooth fitness landscape, the distance to the global optimum decreases as the fitness improves. The relationship between the fitness and the distance to a known global optimum gives evidence of the global smoothness and ruggedness of the fitness landscape. This relation can be studied using the *fitness-distance correlation* (FDC) [Jones and Forrest, 1995] measure:

$$FDC(F, D) = \frac{Cov(F, D)}{\sigma(F)\sigma(D)} \tag{4.31}$$

where: $Cov(F, D)$ is the covariance between the fitnesses $F = \{f_1, ..., f_n\}$ of a set of n arbitrary trees and $D = \{d_1, ..., d_n\}$ are their distances to the chosen global optimum, $\sigma(F)$ and $\sigma(D)$ are their standard deviations.

When a fitness function with minimizing effect is employed, the value of FDC is 1 if there is a perfect correlation between the fitnesses of the trees and their distances to the optima. It is assumed that when the fitness-distance correlation is in the interval $0.15 \leq FDC < 1$, then the landscape is relatively mountable (that is such a landscape can be used for IGP). When the FDC is in the interval $-0.15 \leq FDC \leq 0.15$, the landscape is considered relatively difficult to search, and in case $FDC \leq -0.15$, the landscape is extremely hard to search. A hard landscape suggests that the fitness function or the representation should be improved so as to facilitate the search.

The fitness-distance correlation FDC can be estimated after making a large number of IGP runs and assigning the best tree as eventual global optimum. The rationale is that a large number of samplings are necessary to derive significant statistical evidence for the fitness landscape characteristics, since one does not know the global optima. After that, random trees should be generated, and their tree-to-tree distances to the selected global optimum should be computed.

As an example, investigations of a global mutation landscape were made using the Mackey-Glass series. Two fitness functions were taken: the generalized cross-validation (GCV) (4.10) and the mean squared error (MSE) (4.2). The calculated FDC values were as follows: 1) from the GCV fitness function in the interval $[0.17, 0.26]$; and 2) from the MSE fitness function in the interval $[0.05, 0.18]$. According to the above classification, the landscape of the GCV function seems relatively easier to search than that of the MSE.

Figure 4.3 shows a scatter plot of the fitness-distance correlation measured during the same runs with IGP using the Mackey-Glass data. One can see that average line through the scatter plot of the FDC obtained with the GCV is at a greater angle with the abscissa than this obtained with the MSE. This means that the GCV landscape features better correlation between the fitnesses and their distance to the optimal solution, therefore the GCV landscape is better for doing evolutionary search. From another point of view, the GCV landscape seem slightly more rugged from a local perspective, since individuals with equal error are estimated differently and have different fitnesses due to the complexity penalty. However, from a global perspective, the GCV landscape is smoother and the superior optima can be clearly distinguished on it; this is what makes the landscape mountable by the search algorithm. This is because the cross-validation factors in the GCV formula carry more information about the quality of the PNN models. Table 4.2 offers the algorithm for measuring FDC in IGP which has been used to make the scatter plots illustrated in Figure 4.3.

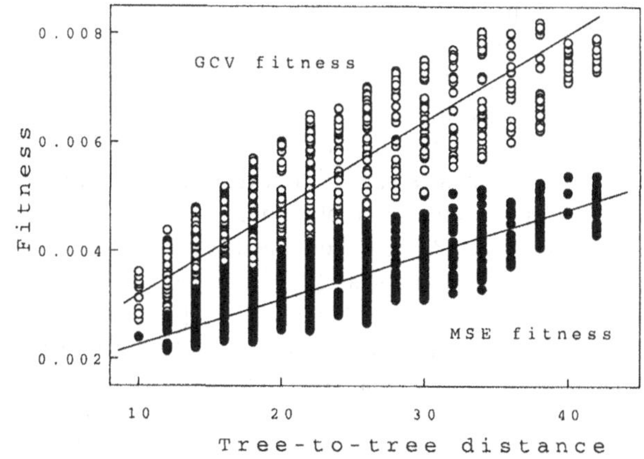

Figure 4.3. Scattered plots of the fitness-tree-to-tree-distance correlation calculated with 1000 randomly sampled tree-like PNN.

Table 4.2. Algorithm for measuring fitness-distance correlations *FDC* in IGP.

Measuring Fitness-Distance Correlations in IGP

step	*Algorithmic sequence*
1. Initialization	Let the distance function be $Dist : \mathcal{G} \times \mathcal{G} \rightarrow N$ and the fitness function be $f : \mathcal{G} \rightarrow R$ Find a virtual global optimum: $\mathcal{G}_g$.
2. Generate random trees	For a large number of steps $n > 10^3$ do a) Generate a tree: $\mathcal{G} = RandomTree()$. b) Evaluate its fitness: $f = f(\mathcal{G})$. c) Compute tree-to-tree distance to the global optima $Dist(\mathcal{G}, \mathcal{G}_g) = d$. d) Record the fitness f and the distance d $F = \{f_1, f_2, ...\}$ and $D = \{d_1, d_2, ...\}$.
3. Compute the variances and covariances	Compute the mean fitness and the mean distance $\overline{f} = \frac{1}{n}\sum_{i=1}^{n} f_i$, $\overline{d} = \frac{1}{n}\sum_{i=1}^{n} d_i$. Compute the covariance $Cov(F, D) = \sum_{i=1}^{n}(f_i - \overline{f})(d_i - \overline{d})$. Compute the deviations $\sigma(F) = \sqrt{\sum_{i=1}^{n}(f_i - \overline{f})^2}$,$\sigma(D) = \sqrt{\sum_{i=1}^{n}(d_i - \overline{d})^2}$.
4. Calculate the *FDC*	Compute the fitness/distance correlation $FDC(F, D) = Cov(F, D)/(\sigma(F)\sigma(D))$.

4.3.2 Probabilistic Measures

Practical development of IGP systems may be carried out using other fitness landscape measures that require less preliminary assumptions than the statistical correlation measures. Such is the *probabilistic causality measure* of the landscape ruggedness. Causality means that the distance between the genotypes in the phenotype space is kept proportional, as well in the fitness space. Small distances between a genotype and its neighbors imply small rate of change between the corresponding phenotypes and fitnesses. When the causality principle is satisfied, the landscape is smoother and the search is expected to be easier.

When the causality of the genotype-phenotype map is strong, a subject of particular interest in IGP is the phenotype-fitness map. This is because changes of the linear tree genotypes imply corresponding changes in the phenotypic genetic programs. The phenotype-fitness map establishes a relation between neighborhoods in the phenotype space and neighborhoods in the fitness space. The causality condition for the phenotype-fitness map in IGP with tree-like genotypes can be stated as follows [Igel, 1998, Rosca and Ballard, 1995a, Sendhoff et al., 1997]:

$$\begin{aligned} \forall \mathcal{G}_i, \mathcal{G}_j, \mathcal{G}_k, \text{ and } \mathcal{G}_j &\in M(\mathcal{G}_i), \mathcal{G}_k \in M(\mathcal{G}_i), \\ Dist(\mathcal{G}_i, \mathcal{G}_j) &< Dist(\mathcal{G}_i, \mathcal{G}_k) \Rightarrow \\ &\Rightarrow \|f(\mathcal{G}_i) - f(\mathcal{G}_j)\| < \|f(\mathcal{G}_i) - f(\mathcal{G}_k)\| \end{aligned} \tag{4.32}$$

where M are the immediate neighbors of a genetic program produced by mutation, f is the fitness function $f : \mathcal{G} \rightarrow R$, $Dist$ is the tree-to-tree distance $Dist : \mathcal{G} \times \mathcal{G} \rightarrow N$, and $\| \cdot \|$ is a distance operator.

The phenotype-fitness map can be analyzed by measuring the causal probability $\Pr(\Phi|\Pi)$ which is the probability of having the second condition from the above implication (4.32) in the fitness space $\Phi := \|f(\mathcal{G}_i) - f(\mathcal{G}_j)\| < \|f(\mathcal{G}_i) - f(\mathcal{G}_k)\|$ in case the first condition in the phenotype space $\Pi := Dist(\mathcal{G}_i, \mathcal{G}_j) < Dist(\mathcal{G}_i, \mathcal{G}_k)$ holds. The *causal probability* $\Pr(\Phi|\Pi)$ can be approximated by the number of causalities $C_{\Pi \Rightarrow \Phi}$ found in a number of experimental trials N_t [Sendhoff et al., 1997]:

$$\Pr(\Phi|\Pi) \approx C_{\Pi \Rightarrow \Phi} / N_t \tag{4.33}$$

where neighbors produced by the mutation operator are used to estimate the cases $C_{\Pi \Rightarrow \Phi}$. High causal probability indicates a smoother landscape which is usually easy to search. A higher causal probability $\Pr(\Phi|\Pi)$ means that IGP better fulfills the causality principle because each landscape point contains information about its neighbors. Genetic programs that carry such information about their neighbors preserve the graduality from the phenotype to the fitness space.

An algorithm for computing the probability $\Pr(\Phi|\Pi)$ is given in Table 4.3. It was applied to examine the causality in IGP and traditional GP using the same computational mechanisms and the Mackey-Glass series for fitness evaluations. It was found that the causal probability of IGP is $\Pr(\Phi|\Pi)_{IGP} = 0.64$, while that of traditional GP is lower $\Pr(\Phi|\Pi)_{GP} = 0.57$ which indicates that IGP searches on a smoother landscape and can be expected to perform better.

The causal probability $\Pr(\Phi|\Pi)$ measure offers several advantages over the statistical measures for analysis of fitness landscapes: 1) it does not depend on statistical assumptions about the properties of the fitness landscape in order to calculate the correlations; 2) it does not require knowledge about the extrema on the fitness landscape; and 3) it is invariant under reformulations of the fitness function. Similar advantages provide the information measures for landscape analysis.

Table 4.3. Algorithm for measuring the causal probability of the phenotype-fitness map in IGP with respect to tree-to-tree distance.

Measuring Causality in IGP

step	*Algorithmic sequence*
1. Initialization	Let the detected causalities be $C_{\Pi\Rightarrow\Phi} = 0$ $Dist : \mathcal{G} \times \mathcal{G} \rightarrow N, f : \mathcal{G} \rightarrow R$ $Neighbors(\mathcal{G}_i) = \{\mathcal{G}_j \| \mathcal{G}_j = M(\mathcal{G}_i)$, and $Dist(\mathcal{G}_i,\mathcal{G}_j) = 1\}$.
2. Perform trials	For a large number of trials $N^t > 10^3$ do a) Sample randomly a genotype $\mathcal{G}_i$ (from a uniform distribution). b) Generate two of its offspring by mutation $\mathcal{G}_j \in Neighbors(\mathcal{G}_i)$, $\mathcal{G}_k \in Neighbors(\mathcal{G}_i)$. c) Count the distances between the parent $\mathcal{G}_i$ and the offspring $\mathcal{G}_j$,$\mathcal{G}_k$ $Dist(\mathcal{G}_i, \mathcal{G}_j)$, $Dist(\mathcal{G}_i, \mathcal{G}_k)$. d) If $Dist(\mathcal{G}_i, \mathcal{G}_j) > Dist(\mathcal{G}_i, \mathcal{G}_k)$ exchange $\mathcal{G}_j$ with $\mathcal{G}_k$. e) If the causality condition $Dist(\mathcal{G}_i, \mathcal{G}_j) < Dist(\mathcal{G}_i, \mathcal{G}_k) \Rightarrow$ $\Rightarrow \|f(\mathcal{G}_i) - f(\mathcal{G}_j)\| < \|f(\mathcal{G}_i) - f(\mathcal{G}_k)\|$ is satisfied increment the cases $C_{\Pi\Rightarrow\Phi} = C_{\Pi\Rightarrow\Phi} + 1$.
3. Compute the probability	Evaluate the fraction $\Pr(\Phi\|\Pi) \approx C_{\Pi\Rightarrow\Phi}/N_t$.

4.3.3 Information Measures

The fitness landscape may be examined from the perspective of the information content of its structure [Vassilev et al., 2000]. Since the fitness landscape structure has a quite irregular profile, we are rather inclined to evaluate the informativeness of some elementary geometric objects that cover it, assuming that such landscape covering objects can be identified and estimated easily.

Information content of a fitness landscape is the entropy of the frequencies of the elementary objects that cover its structure. The elements of these covering objects should carry information about the instantaneous changes in the landscape profile, so they can simply be numbers from the triple: $\{-1, 0, 1\}$. This triple can be associated with the changes of the slopes of the landscape structure between two neighboring points as follows: when the slope goes down, then its covering element is -1; when the slope goes up, its covering element is 1; and when there is no change among two neighbors, the cover is 0. During a random walk on the landscape, the fitnesses $F = \{f_0, f_1, ..., f_n\}$ may be converted into a string cover $Q(\varepsilon) = \{q_0, q_1, ..., q_n\}$ of symbols from the alphabet $\{-1, 0, 1\}$. Each string $q_i \in \{-1, 0, 1\}$ may be envisioned as a landscape substructure component determined by means of a special function $q_i = \Psi(i, \varepsilon)$ defined as follows [Vassilev et al., 2000]:

$$\Psi(i, \varepsilon) = \begin{cases} -1, & \text{if } f_{i+1} - f_i < -\varepsilon \\ 0, & \text{if } \mid f_{i+1} - f_i \mid \leq \varepsilon \\ 1, & \text{if } f_{i+1} - f_i > \varepsilon \end{cases} \quad (4.34)$$

where ε is a real number $\varepsilon \in length[0, \max(f) - \min(f)]$. This parameter ε serves to control the precision of the cover. When $\varepsilon = 0$, the cover $Q(\varepsilon)$ will be very close to the landscape surface; that is, it will be sensitive to the landscape features. When ε increases, it will make the cover $Q(\varepsilon)$ insensitive to the underlying landscape characteristics.

The function $\Psi(i, \varepsilon)$ maps a step, which is a transition from a parent genetic program to an offspring on the landscape $\{f_i, f_{i+1}\}$ into an element from the string $q_i \in \{-1, 0, 1\}$. The frequencies of each two different steps, with elements $q \neq r$ on the landscape represented by a substring $[qr] \in Q(\varepsilon)$ of length two, can be estimated as follows:

$$\Pr_{[qr]} = \frac{n_{[qr]}}{n} \quad (4.35)$$

where $n_{[qr]}$ is the number of substrings $[qr]$ in the string $Q(\varepsilon)$ such that $q \neq r$, and n is the number of all substrings of length two within $Q(\varepsilon)$. Any substring $[qr]$, $q \neq r$, may be considered an informative object.

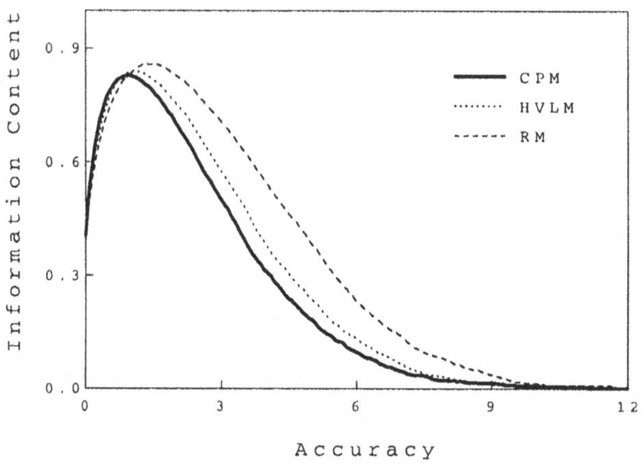

Figure 4.4. Curves of the information content of IGP mutation landscapes arising from the three operators: *CPM*, *HVLM*, and *RM*. Each curve is computed with 10000 points. The *MSE* fitnesses are evaluated using the Mackey-Glass series.

The *information content* (*INC*) of the fitness landscape is calculated as the entropy of the frequencies of the different slope changes in its cover [Vassilev et al., 2000]:

$$INC(\varepsilon) = -\sum_{q \neq r} \Pr_{[qr]} \log_6 \Pr_{[qr]} \tag{4.36}$$

where the base is 6 because this is the number of all substrings of length two that contain different elements from the alphabet $\{-1, 0, 1\}$.

The information content reveals whether the peaks remain visible when we observe the landscape from more and more distant points of view. If the peaks remain, this means that these are high peaks of a rugged landscape. The information content curves of three mutation landscapes arising in IGP are plotted in Figure 4.4.

Figure 4.4 shows that the context-preserving mutation (*CPM*) [Nikolaev and Iba, 2001a] has a smoother landscape than the hierarchical variable-length mutation (*HVLM*) [O'Reilly, 1995], and the replacement mutation (*RM*) operators (Subsection 2.2.2).

The smoother fitness landscape of the (*CPM*) operator can be explained with the changes of the information content curves of the studied landscapes as follows: 1) the curves start from a common point 0.41, which means that the three mutation operators have landscapes with approximately the same diversity of peaks; 2) the curve raisings in the interval $[0, 1.8]$ demonstrate that all the mutation operators climb or descend unevenly on their landscapes, which are rugged; 3) within the interval $[1.8, 9.5]$ the number and height of the insubstantial peaks on the landscape of the CPM operator is smaller than these on the landscapes of $HVLM$ and RM; that is, the CPM landscape is smoother; and, 4) the shared termination of the curves at 11.5 denotes that all landscapes have the same number of essential peaks. $\Pr_{[qr]} = n_{[qr]}/n$.

Table 4.4 presents the algorithm for measuring the information content of fitness landscapes. This algorithm involves initially performing a random walk to sample a large number of offspring and evaluating their fitnesses. After that, the recorded fitness arrays are used to: determine covers, estimate frequencies of substrings, calculate entropies, and increment the information content for a number of accuracies.

Table 4.4. Algorithm for measuring the information content of fitness landscapes that arise in IGP with tree-like genetic programs.

Measuring Information Content in IGP

step	*Algorithmic sequence*
1. Initialization	Let the fitness function be $f : \mathcal{G} \rightarrow R$. Generate a parent tree $\mathcal{G}_p = RandomTree()$.
2. Perform a random walk	For a large number of trials $n > 10^3$ do a) Sample an offspring $\mathcal{G}_c$ of $\mathcal{G}_p$. b) Record its fitness: $f_c = f(\mathcal{G}_c)$ in $F = \{f_1, f_2, ...\}$. c) Replace the child to become parent: $\mathcal{G}_p = \mathcal{G}_c$.
3. Compute the information content	For a number of accuracies $\varepsilon = 1$ to 20 do a) Consider the fitness array $F = \{f_1, f_2, ..., f_n\}$. b) Determine the cover $Q(\varepsilon)$ of elements $q_i = \Psi(i, \varepsilon)$ using the function $\Psi(i,\varepsilon) = \begin{cases} -1, & \text{if } f_{i+1} - f_i < -\varepsilon \\ 0, & \text{if } \mid f_{i+1} - f_i \mid \leq \varepsilon \\ 1, & \text{if } f_{i+1} - f_i > \varepsilon \end{cases}$. c) Estimate the frequencies of substrings $[qr]$, $q \neq r$, in $Q(\varepsilon)$ $\Pr_{[qr]} = n_{[qr]}/n$. d) Calculate the entropies $INC(\varepsilon) = -\sum_{q \neq r} \Pr_{[qr]} \log_6 \Pr_{[qr]}$. e) Increment the information content $INC = INC + INC(\varepsilon)$.

4.3.4 Quantitative Measures

Quantitative statistics for the fitness landscape structure can be obtained by counting such characteristics as the distribution of local optima, the depths of local optima, and the dimensions of the basins between them. These landscape characteristics can be measured by performing a large number of descents with the IGP algorithm to some near local optima. The downhill climbings on the landscape should be implemented as follows: start from a random genetic program whose fitness is a random point on the landscape, generate its neighbors, determine their fitnesses, select the fittest among the neighbors which is fitter than the current genetic program, and continue to move down until reaching a genetic program fitter than all of its neighbors.

Looking at a fitness landscape surface we are interested in finding out what the depths of the optima are, and how they are distributed. A large number of runs with IGP and GP were conducted to collect the depths and frequencies of the local minima on their mutation landscapes. One can see in Figure 4.5 that the mutation landscape in traditional GP features by more local optima. These local minima in GP occur more frequently, which means that its landscape is more rugged. The IGP landscape seems to be smoother with flatter hills.

A useful property of the fitness landscape, that can be detected using the same downhill climbing procedure, is the average basin radius. *Basin radius* is the number of steps performed by the algorithm until a particular local optimum is reached. The basin radius on the landscape can be computed as the average distance, in the sense of the number of steps from a parent to a child genetic program, traversed by the IGP system, after which it converges to a local optimum. Having information about the dimensions of the basins between the local optima on the landscape can be used to improve the IGP search navigation.

During the same runs with IGP and traditional Koza-style GP, there were recorded the number of downhill steps to reach the closest minima on their mutation landscapes. A scatter plot of the measured radiuses of the basins between the local optima is presented in Figure 4.6. This figure shows that the IGP system evolves on a landscape with larger basins as it makes longer walks. Respectively, the GP system quickly descends to the local minima as it seems that there are a lot of them.

The quantitative measurements of the landscape characteristics, illustrated in Figures 4.5 and 4.6, show that the local optima on the IGP landscape are less, and they feature by larger differences than from the other points. The mutation landscape in IGP is smoother, and the correct directions toward the optima on it could be identified faster. In this sense, one may think that the IGP landscape facilitates the search.

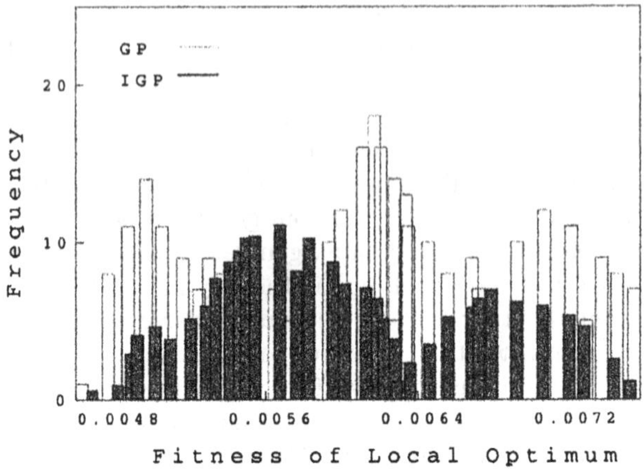

Figure 4.5. Distribution of local optima on a mutation landscape collected during 1000 downhill climbings to random optima.

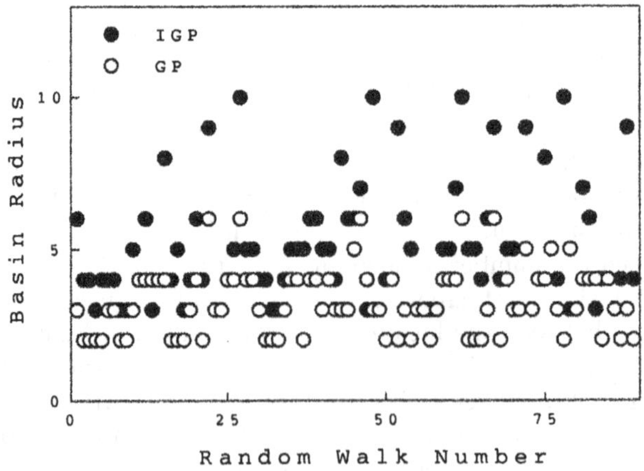

Figure 4.6. Average distance to local optima on a mutation landscape collected during 1000 downhill climbings to random optima.

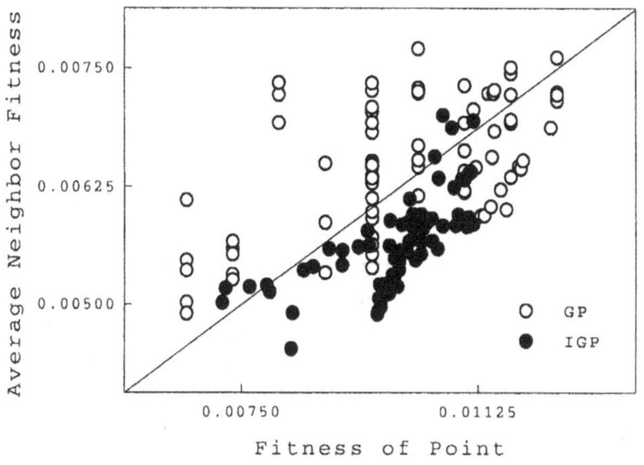

Figure 4.7. Steepness of the local optima on a mutation landscape collected during 1000 downhill climbings to random optima.

The next question that can be raised after knowing which landscape is smoother, is how smooth it is; that is, how steep are the optima on the fitness landscape. The *steepness of the local optima*, computed in the experiments with IGP and traditional Koza-style GP, are illustrated in Figure 4.7. It shows that the mutation landscape of traditional GP has local peaks with very steep slopes, which strengthens the confidence that its landscape is rugged, while the slopes of the mutation landscape of IGP are not so steep.

4.4 Chapter Summary

This section studied how to design fitness functions for evolutionary search control in IGP with polynomial networks. Empirical analysis of their usefulness was made with special measures, defined using the notion of fitness landscape. Assuming that the fitnesses of the individuals in the population bred by IGP form a fitness landscape, allows us to evaluate how the population moves during evolutionary search. The possibility to examine the population flow on the fitness landscape allows us to investigate the goodness of the IGP search mechanisms and provides hints as to which of them should improved.

The presented fitness functions are usually applied separately with respect to the inductive task and the desired characteristics from the solution. Another useful strategy followed often in practical applications is to design multiobjective fitness functions by collecting several criteria into one common fitness function. For example, statistical and probabilistic criteria could be incorporated into a shared fitness function. In such cases the fitness landscapes become slightly more complex, but they still remain amenable to analysis by the presented measures.

The recommendation for developing IGP systems is to study the suitability of all its micromechanisms by generating their landscapes using the selected fitness function for the given problem. The proposed fitness landscape measures are useful tools for examination of the evolutionary search control in IGP. They provide empirical evidence for the operation of the control machinery and reveal how it navigates the inductive learning process. The fitness landscape measures make IGP advantageous over the other machine learning and neural network paradigms because they can help to find which learning mechanisms need repair and show how the learning proceeds.

Chapter 5

SEARCH NAVIGATION

IGP is a general-purpose tripartite search system whose control mechanism works with three evolutionary operators: reproduction, crossover, and mutation. While the genetic crossover and mutation operators sample hypothetical solutions by changing the genetic programs, the reproduction operator implements the search heuristic. The reproduction has the role to stochastically direct the algorithm toward promising search areas, aiming to locate the best solution.

IGP systems are developed with the intention of performing efficient evolutionary search. Such a system may search efficiently if it is able to adapt to the characteristics of the fitness landscape, in the sense that it can escape entrapment in suboptimal local minima. It should have the potential for sustained exploitation as well as exploration of the landscape. The control mechanism should achieve broad examination of yet unvisited distant areas and narrow examination of close areas of the search space. The IGP adaptation on the fitness landscape is extremely difficult because its dimensionality is not known. The reason for having an enormous landscape is the irregularity of the neighboring relationships between the variable size genetic programs.

The stochastic IGP search strongly depends on capacity of the control mechanism to navigate the population successfully on the fitness landscape. An indication for successful navigation is continuous improvement of the fitnesses in the population. This can be done by maintaining high population diversity and using as much information as possible from the good, fit individuals. The good individuals carry and transmit information about the history of the evolution, thus they point out promising directions. There are, however, inferior locally optimal individuals that can cause search stagnation, as they can mislead the search.

This section studies how to implement control mechanisms for IGP search navigation, including several reproduction operators and advanced search control techniques. The reproduction operators determine the policy for breeding the successive populations. The mechanisms for advanced control contribute to moving the population continuously on the landscape, and to attaining progressive search.

An efficient IGP search navigation is one that has the capacity to adapt on the fitness landscape. This is the property of being able to generate better offspring, also known as evolvability [Altenberg, 1994a, Altenberg, 1994b]. The operators should act on the population in such a way so as to produce individuals with improving fitnesses. Assuming a concrete representation, the genetic learning and reproduction operators should proliferate partial solutions in the form of building blocks which with high probability improve the genetic programs. The learning operators should preserve and replicate the good building blocks within the genetic programs. The reproduction operator should keep and transmit individuals containing good building blocks.

The common aspect of the desired evolvability phenomena is how much the offspring differ from the parents. This aspect can be examined in IGP from different points of view through different observations of the search performance. Several easily computable performance measures are offered to facilitate practical studies into the evolutionary search behavior of IGP. Four groups of estimates are presented: measures of the evolvability of the fitnesses, convergence measures of the evolvability of the errors, diversity measures of the evolvability of the syntactic representations, and physical measures of the population dynamics. These measures can be used to tune the genetic learning and reproduction operators in order to improve the IGP system.

5.1 The Reproduction Operator

Reproduction is the operator for organizing survival of the fittest genetic programs; it decides which individuals should be propagated during the generations. Its role is twofold: to stimulate selection of highly fit individuals, and to maintain diversity in the population so as to sustain the evolution. In the beginning of the evolution it should impose a low pressure to the better individuals, otherwise they will take over the population too early and the search will stagnate prematurely. In the later stages it should exaggerate the differences between the individuals in order to identify the fitter individuals, because the fitnesses become very similar. Premature convergence occurs when the best individuals converge to a suboptimal basin on the landscape and remain there before reaching a sufficiently optimal minimum.

The reproduction has two ingredient phases implemented by corresponding strategies: selection and replacement. The selection strategy chooses the parents to produce offspring in the next generation. The replacement strategy decides which individuals to remove from the current population and exchange with offspring.

5.1.1 Selection Strategies

The selection operator should guide the search by imposing enough pressure on the good individuals in the population. The selection pressure can be measured by estimating the reproduction rate of the best individual during successive generations. Reproduction rate is the ratio between the copies of a particular individual before performing the selection step and after this step. If the reproduction rate of the best individual increases rapidly, this indicates that the selection pressure is high and the algorithm will eventually converge too early. At the other extreme, if the pressure is very low the algorithm may become too weak, disoriented and it may wander on the fitness landscape without being able to locate areas with promising individuals. This pressure depends on the chosen selection scheme and on their characteristics which are needed to develop working IGP systems.

The most popular selection strategies that can be used in IGP are fitness proportionate selection, ranking selection, truncation selection, and tournament selection. These selections were originally designed for genetic algorithms [Bäck and Hoffmeister, 1991, Bäck, 1996, Baker, 1987, Blickle and Thiele, 1997, Goldberg, 1989, Grefenstette and Baker, 1989], but they can be used in GP as well [Koza, 1992]. The problem is that there is no guarantee that their proven properties will be transferred directly because they have been derived for genetic algorithms that typically work with fixed length representations. Despite this rigorous analysis of selection properties such as takeover time, convergence time, selection variance, and selection intensity in the context of GP is still lacking. These selection schemes have to be studied in order to control the pressure that they impose during the evolution.

Fitness Proportionate Selection. The *fitness proportional selection* [Holland, 1975] gives each individual a probability $\Pr(\mathcal{G}_i^\tau)$ to reproduce proportional to its fitness and inversely proportional to the sum of all population fitnesses:

$$\Pr(\mathcal{G}_i^\tau) = \frac{f(\mathcal{G}_i^\tau)}{\sum_{j=1}^{\pi} f(\mathcal{G}_i^\tau)} \tag{5.1}$$

where $\mathcal{G}_i^\tau$ is the i-th individual (tree-like genetic program) at generation τ, and π is the population size.

Table 5.1. Algorithm for implementing roulette-wheel selection that can be used in IGP with tree-like genetic programs.

Fitness Proportionate Selection

step	*Algorithmic sequence*
1. Initialization	Population of genetic programs $\mathcal{G}_i, 1 \leq i \leq \pi$ Wheel with sections, starting with $s = 0$.
2. Develop the roulette wheel	For the whole population $i = 1$ to π Compute the sections $s_i = s_{i-1} + f(\mathcal{G}_i)/\sum_{j=1}^{\pi} f(\mathcal{G}_j)$.
3. Select promising individuals	For the whole population $i = 1$ to π a) Spin the wheel by drawing a random number $r = Rand(0,1)$; b) Pick a genetic program $\mathcal{G}_i$, such that $s_{i-1} \leq r < s_i$.

As the sum of the selection probabilities of all individuals in the population is one, we can imagine that the individuals are allocated in the slots of a roulette wheel, and each individual is granted a number of slots proportional to its selection percentage. The selection operator picks individuals using a pointer. The fitness proportional selection mechanism suggests to spin the wheel, and to take the current individual chosen by the pointer after each spin. When a parent is needed, the wheel is spun again and another individual is chosen. Thus, the fitness proportional selection transfers more copies of the fitter individuals to the next generation since they occupy larger slices from the wheel. Examination of the wheel allows us to determine how the search proceeds.

The fitness proportionate selection algorithm for reproduction of the whole population from one generation to the next is given in Table 5.1.

The fitness proportional selection is sensitive to the magnitude of the fitnesses. One remedy to this problem is to change the fitness scaling. The scaled raw fitnesses are called adjusted fitnesses [Koza, 1992]. The values of the objective function can be transformed into adjusted fitnesses so as to diminish the differences between them and to improve the competition. There are various scaling techniques such as linear scaling [Goldberg, 1989], truncation scaling [Goldberg, 1989], exponential scaling [Grefenstette and Baker, 1989], and logarithmic scaling [Grefenstette and Baker, 1989], that may also be used in IGP.

A drawback of fitness proportionate selection is that it does not allow control of the number of accepted offspring. It may happen that a small number of individuals contribute a large number of children to the next generation. The symptom of such degenerated performance is a rapid loss of diversity. One possibility to combat the loss of diversity is to assign different selection probabilities to each individual. This can be done by ranking the individuals so as to predetermine their involvement in the reproduction process.

Ranking Selection. The *ranking selection* [Grefenstette and Baker, 1989, Whitley, 1989] takes the individuals according to their arrangement in the population in increasing or decreasing order of fitness. The best individual is assigned rank one and the worst is given rank equal to the population size. The *linear ranking scheme* determines the selection probability of an individual with the following function [Baker, 1987, Grefenstette and Baker, 1989]:

$$\Pr(\mathcal{G}_i^\tau) = \frac{1}{\pi}\left(\alpha + (\beta - \alpha)\frac{rank(\mathcal{G}_i^\tau) - 1}{\pi - 1}\right) \tag{5.2}$$

where $\mathcal{G}_i^\tau$ is the i-th genetic program at generation τ, $rank(\mathcal{G}_i^\tau)$ is its rank in the population, π is the population size, α is the proportion for selecting the worst individual, and β is the proportional for selecting the best individual. When the conditions $\alpha + \beta = 2$ and $1 \leq \alpha \leq 2$ are satisfied, the best individual will produce no more than twice the offspring than the population average.

There are several modifications: linear ranking, nonlinear ranking, and exponential ranking [Blickle and Thiele, 1997, Michalewics, 1992]. They can be implemented using the same algorithmic framework given in Table 5.1 by exchanging formula (5.2) with formula (5.1). The linear ranking selection has been applied to GP [Koza, 1992] using a factor r_m for the parameters α and β that simulates the function gradient as follows: $\alpha = 2/(r_m + 1)$, $\beta = 2r_m/(r_m + 1)$.

Truncation Selection. A similar selection scheme is the uniform ranking [Bäck and Hoffmeister, 1991], also known as truncation selection [Mühlenbein and Schlierkamp-Voosen, 1995]. This scheme chooses for reproduction only top individuals having high rank in the current population, and these top individuals have the same chance to be taken. The fraction of the top individuals is defined by a rank threshold μ. The selection probability of the *truncation selection scheme* is:

$$\Pr(\mathcal{G}_i^\tau) = \begin{cases} 1/\mu, & 1 \leq rank(\mathcal{G}_i^\tau) \leq \mu \\ 0, & \text{otherwise} \end{cases} \tag{5.3}$$

where $rank(\mathcal{G}_i^\tau)$ is the rank of the i-th individual $\mathcal{G}_i^\tau$ in the population at generation τ. The fitnesses are used only for ordering of the population $f(\mathcal{G}_1^\tau) \leq f(\mathcal{G}_2^\tau) \leq ... \leq f(\mathcal{G}_\pi^\tau)$, and they do not participate in the selection. The advantage of truncation selection is that it is not affected directly by the fitnesses or by the scaled adjusted values.

Tournament Selection. Tournament selection is the most widely used scheme in GP [Koza, 1992]. The tournament selection randomly picks individuals from the population and promotes the best of them to survive. A tournament requires to draw random tuples $\{\mathcal{G}_{i_1}^{\tau}, \mathcal{G}_{i_2}^{\tau}, .., \mathcal{G}_{i_t}^{\tau}\}$, $1 \leq i \leq \pi$, of t individuals and next to choose the best one among them: $f(\mathcal{G}_i^{\tau}) \leq f(\mathcal{G}_{i_t}^{\tau})$, for each $\mathcal{G}_{i_t}^{\tau}$ from $\{\mathcal{G}_{i_1}^{\tau}, \mathcal{G}_{i_2}^{\tau}, .., \mathcal{G}_{i_t}^{\tau}\}$. Such t-tuples have to be drawn a number of times equal to the size of the population π for producing a whole new population. Assuming that the individuals are ordered so that the best individual has lowest index, the selection probability of *tournament selection* for picking the i-th individual can be determined as follows [Bäck, 1996, Blickle and Thiele, 1997]:

$$\Pr(\mathcal{G}_i^{\tau}) = \frac{1}{\pi^t}((\pi - i + 1)^t - (\pi - i)^t) \tag{5.4}$$

where π is the population size, and t is the tournament size. The selection pressure can be controlled by the tournament size. The tournament selection pressure toward the best individual becomes higher with the increase of the tournament size t.

The competition between the individuals in the tuples is also sensitive to the fitness values. This problem could be alleviated by organizing *Boltzmann tournaments* [Michalewics, 1992]. Boltzmann competitions are performed with pairs of individuals. The superiority of one of them is decided with the formula:

$$\Pr(\mathcal{G}_i^{\tau}) = \frac{1}{1 + \exp((f(\mathcal{G}_{i_1}^{\tau}) - f(\mathcal{G}_{i_2}^{\tau}))/T)} \tag{5.5}$$

where $f(\mathcal{G}_{i_1}^{\tau})$ and $f(\mathcal{G}_{i_2}^{\tau})$ are the fitnesses of the individuals from the tournament pair, and T is a regulating temperature parameter. Initially, T is set large so that the choice of a winner is random. By gradual decreasing of the temperature T, the strategy more clearly distinguishes the individuals with better fitnesses and they are given greater chances to win the tournament in the later generations.

Universal Selection. The above popular selection schemes can be generalized in a common *universal selection* mechanism [Blickle and Thiele, 1997]. The universal selection is developed with intention to reduce the large variation of the fitnesses after reproduction. It uses *stochastic universal sampling* (SUS) [Baker, 1987] for diminishing the variance of the number of offspring from each individual. The SUS algorithm spins the roulette wheel only once with fitness proportionate sections for each individual, rather than spinning it a number of times equal to the necessary offspring. The pointer is randomly generated, and after that equally spaced spikes pointing out which individuals to take for reproduction are installed.

Table 5.2. Algorithm for selection using stochastic universal sampling for IGP.

Universal Selection using SUS

step	*Algorithmic sequence*
1. Initialization	Population of genetic programs $\mathcal{G}_i, 1 \leq i \leq \pi$. Precomputed selection rates $S_i = \Pr(\mathcal{G}_i), 1 \leq i \leq \pi$. Wheel with sections, staring with $s = 0$.
2. Spin the wheel once	Spin the wheel by drawing a random number $r = Rand(0,1)$.
3. Select individuals using spikes	For the whole population $i = 1$ to π a) Let the offspring of i are $c = 1$. b) Compute the wheel slice $s = s + S_i$. c) While $(s > r)$ pick i using spikes r i) $c = c + 1$. ii) $r = r + 1$.

SUS can be made into a universal selection algorithm by using the selection probabilities $\Pr(\mathcal{G}_i^\tau)$, computed in advance to determine the slices in the roulette wheel. The SUS algorithm will produce the expected number of children only when the selection probabilities account precisely for the number of offspring. Then SUS is guaranteed to choose an individual $\mathcal{G}_i^\tau, 1 \leq i \leq \pi$, a number of times proportional to its selection rate $S_i = \Pr(\mathcal{G}_i^\tau)$. This universal selection algorithm for processing the whole population is presented in Table 5.2.

5.1.2 Replacement Strategies

After selecting promising individuals for the next generation, they have to be accommodated in the population. The accommodation involves removing inferior individuals from the population so that the promoted ones take their places. The decision of which individuals to remove can be made using the following *replacement strategies* [Chakraborty et al., 1996, De Jong and Sarma, 1992, Smith and Vavak, 1998, Syswerda, 1991]: random deletion, deletion of the worst individual by ranking, deletion of the worst individual by tournament, and deletion of the oldest in the sense generational persistence in the population.

The *random deletion* scheme suggests to remove randomly picked individuals from the population. This scheme is straightforward to implement, but it may destroy and lose many good individuals. The strategy *deletion of the worst by ranking* is to a great degree reasonable for large populations, however for smaller populations the worst individuals to die should be determined using tournaments. *Deletion of the worst by "kill tournament*" better preserves the nondeterministic character of the evolutionary search than deletion of the worst by ranking. The scheme *deletion of the oldest* may outperform the other replacement strategies, but the problem is how to determine for how many generations to keep the worst individuals. Conservative replacement is a policy that combines deletion of the oldest and kill tournament. The *conservative replacement* strategy performs inverse tournaments with pairs of individuals and removes the older of them.

5.1.3 Implementing Reproduction

The population can be updated with different implementations of the reproduction operator made according to several criteria [Bäck and Hoffmeister, 1991]: *dynamics*, *retention*, *elitism*, and *steadiness*.

The selection probability of the individuals depends on whether the promising parents are chosen with respect to their fitness or with respect to their ranks in the population. Since the fitnesses of the individuals change during the generations, a selection scheme is *dynamic* when it depends on the fitnesses of the individuals $\Pr(\mathcal{G}_i^\tau) \neq c_i$, $1 \leq i \leq \pi$, $\tau > 0$, where c_i are constants. Respectively, a selection scheme is called *static* when it depends on the ranks of the individuals which are fixed in the population $\Pr(\mathcal{G}_i^\tau) = c_i$, $1 \leq i \leq \pi$, $\tau > 0$, where c_i are constants.

There are selection schemes that allow any individual to generate offspring with non-zero probability, and there are schemes that completely discard some individuals from consideration. A selection scheme that gives greater than zero selection probability to each individual in the population $\Pr(\mathcal{G}_i^\tau) > 0$, $1 \leq i \leq \pi$, $\tau > 0$, is *preservative*. A selection scheme that deliberately discards some individuals by assigning zero selection probability to them $\Pr(\mathcal{G}_i^\tau) = 0$, $1 \leq i \leq \pi$, $\tau > 0$, is *extinctive*. The extinctive selection scheme enhances the diversity by choosing individuals at large distance apart.

The reproduction operator may give indefinite lifetime to the fitter individuals from the population. When the reproduction preserves and promotes a small number of best individuals to give birth of offspring until their fitness dominates the fitnesses of the remaining individuals in the population, it is called *elitist*. The extension of the lifetime of the better fitness individuals helps to reduce the fitness variance between the generations and to achieve more stable performance. The number of the best retained individuals is regulated by a coefficient of elitism k: $1 \leq k$, and $k \ll \pi$. Assuming a minimizing fitness function, a reproduction operator is k-elitist if $f(\mathcal{G}_i^\tau) \leq f(\mathcal{G}_i^{\tau-1})$ for each $i \in \{1, 2, ..., k\}$. If the reproduction operator does not keep any individuals, it is *pure*.

A reproduction operator that replaces the entire previous population with the offspring is called *generational*. The generational reproduction usually leads to a large fitness variance which, however, makes the search difficult to control. The recommended strategy (especially for IGP) is steady-state reproduction. The *steady-state reproduction* operator selects several individuals to mate, and replaces them with their offspring [De Jong and Sarma, 1992, Syswerda, 1991, Whitley, 1989]. The degree of overlapping between the populations can be monitored by a parameter for regulating the increase or decrease of the number of parents, called generation gap [De Jong and Sarma, 1992]. The generation gap is defined by the fraction i/π, where i denotes the desired portion of the population for replacement. If only one individual from the current population is exchanged, then the generation gap is $1/\pi$.

5.2 Advanced Search Control

The development of IGP systems needs not only different alternatives for making the evolutionary micromechanisms, like model representations, fitness functions and reproduction strategies, but it also needs different techniques for imposing adaptive search control. The notion of adaptive control means that the objective is to improve the navigation in such a way that the IGP search climbs and descends easier on the fitness landscape; that is, the population self-orients well on the concrete landscape. Otherwise, if the IGP guidance is not properly made the search may degenerate into random. Several advanced control techniques for macroevolutionary search, search by genetic annealing, demetic search, and coevolutionary search, are presented below.

5.2.1 Macroevolutionary Search

High diversity in the population can be achieved through examination of the relationships between the genetic programs. The interactions between the individuals can be used to improve the reproduction and to organize macroevolutionary search [Marin and Sole, 1999]. The macroevolutionary search exploits the connectivity among the individuals at a higher level of selection control, which is different from the clonal selection in the immune algorithm where the connectivity between the individuals is made at lower level within the fitness function.

The model of macroevolution decides which individuals will survive in dependence of their mutual interactions. In context of IGP, interactions can be the relationships between the fitnesses of the individuals because the fitnesses are the property that determines their survival probability. The selection may be elaborated to choose individuals with respect to their fitness difference from the other members of the population. Higher difference between the fitness of an individual and the remaining ones means that this genetic program carries specific information and has to be promoted further. The relationships among the individuals are such that the specific genetic programs are stimulated, while the similar genetic programs are suppressed. Similar genetic programs exploit the same area on the fitness landscape.

The strength of a link among two individuals $\mathcal{G}_i^\tau$ and $\mathcal{G}_j^\tau$, $1 \leq i, j \leq \pi$, can be defined as follows:

$$L_{ij}{}^\tau = \frac{f(\mathcal{G}_i^\tau) - f(\mathcal{G}_j^\tau)}{f_{\max}(\mathcal{G}^\tau)} \tag{5.6}$$

where $f(\mathcal{G}_i^\tau)$ and $f(\mathcal{G}_j^\tau)$ are the corresponding fitnesses, and $f_{\max}(\mathcal{G}^\tau)$ is the maximal fitness at this generation τ.

The reproduction operator has to be changed slightly for accommodating the connectivity relationships. The selection has to be modified to consider the macrofitnesses of the individuals. The *macrofitness* of a particular f' genetic program is the sum of its fitness distances from the remaining genetic programs:

$$f'(\mathcal{G}_i^\tau) = \sum_{j=1, j \neq i}^{\pi} L_{ij}^\tau \tag{5.7}$$

where L_{ij}^τ are the strengths of the interactions between the i-th individual and all other individuals available in the population at the current generation τ. Individuals with macrofitness less than a certain threshold, predefined in advance, become extinct. The extinct individuals may be replaced by copies of the surviving individuals, by their offspring, or by freshly generated random individuals.

5.2.2 Memetic Search

Memetic search [Moscato and Norman, 1992, Merz and Freisleben, 2000] is a hybrid technique that integrates local search in GP for better adaptation to the fitness landscape of the concrete task. The memetic algorithm performs population-based search with local improvement of the newly generated offspring. Following a hypothesis from the biological genetics, the idea is to conduct local search starting from each offspring. The local optima reached from the offspring is taken for continuation of the search instead of simply the offspring. Therefore, the memetic algorithm searches using locally optimal individuals rather than using arbitrary individuals. Although in the beginning the evolutionary search starts with random individuals, during the generations the locally optimized individuals tend to occupy the population.

Table 5.3. Algorithm for memetic search that can be used in IGP.

Memetic Search

step	*Algorithmic sequence*
1. Initialization	Population of genetic programs $\mathcal{G}_i, 1 \leq i \leq \pi$.
2. Memetic learning	For a number of generations τ
	For the whole population $i = 1$ to π
	a) Select, cross or mutate, to produce an offspring $\mathcal{G}_i$.
	b) Improve this offspring $\mathcal{G}_i$ by downhill climbing $\mathcal{G}'_i = LocalSearch(\mathcal{G}_i)$.
	c) Evaluate its fitness $f(\mathcal{G}'_i) = Eval(\mathcal{G}'_i)$.
	d) Replace the worst with this offspring.
	e) Rank the population according to fitness.
	If the termination condition is satisfied stop.

The effect of the genetic crossover and mutation operators in memetic search is performing large jumps on the landscape, while short downhill steps are performed by the local improvement operator. In case of a minimizing fitness function. the goal is descending to the deepest basin on the landscape. The crossover and mutation operators organize both exploration of the search space, while the local downhill climbings exploit the close neighborhoods of the search space. Local search algorithms operate until reaching the nearest local minima. In this sense, the memetic search is a hybrid technique because the role of the local search operator is different from the role of the genetic search operators.

There are two main approaches to implementing local search for the memetic algorithm: deterministic and stochastic. The deterministic local search samples all neighbors of the given individual, selects the best of these descendants, and so directs the process, pushing it downhill until reaching the closest minimum. The stochastic local search randomly generates only one neighbor of the given individual and takes it with probability proportional to its fitness. This stochastic version avoids the complete enumeration of all neighbors of the current search point. It is more efficient for IGP because the sizes of neighborhoods of tree-like individuals are usually large. Due to the nondeterministic selection of the next downhill move, it has abilities to avoid rapid convergence and entrapment into the closest optima, hence it can reach distant optima on the fitness landscape surface.

A memetic algorithm implemented for IGP style population-based search is illustrated in Table 5.3.

5.2.3 Search by Genetic Annealing

The reproduction can be improved using *simulated annealing* [Kirkpatrick et al., 1983]. Simulated annealing gives the conditions for choosing which among the parent and the offspring should be retained in the population. This algorithm more precisely guides the evolutionary search so that in the early stages, even not necessarily good individuals may be tolerated to stay in the population, while at the later stages focusing to better genetic programs is stimulated.

Simulated Annealing. Simulated annealing is conceived as an optimization algorithm [Kirkpatrick et al., 1983] that simulates evolution from an initial state to a random state in the search space, in the same way in which a physical system evolves from an initial configuration of its macroscopic variables to an equilibrium configuration that satisfies some constraints. The intention for using this algorithm is to perform guided transitions from one state in the space of hypotheses to another state, driven by the same dynamics as this that drives the behavior of the physical system. The motivation is that the dynamics of the physical system provides abilities to escape from early entrapment in suboptimal solutions. The two driving mechanisms that can be adopted for search control are relaxation and annealing.

The *relaxation mechanism* probabilistically samples hypotheses in the search space in such a way that it guarantees movement toward better solutions. It chooses hypotheses depending on their energy difference. Transition from a parent to an offspring hypothesis occurs with a probability defined using the Boltzmann distribution:

$$\Pr(\mathcal{G}_i) = \begin{cases} 1 & \text{if } \Delta En = En(\mathcal{G}_{i+1}) - En(\mathcal{G}_i) < 0 \\ \exp\quad(-\Delta En/kT) & \text{otherwise} \end{cases} \tag{5.8}$$

where $En(\mathcal{G}_{i+1})$ and $En(\mathcal{G}_i)$ are the energy characteristics of two successive hypotheses, k is a Boltzmann's constant, and T denotes the current step, usually called temperature. The notion of temperature means that the mechanism relaxes toward better hypotheses at each next step with the decrease of the temperature. A hypotheses with higher energy $\Delta En = En(\mathcal{G}_{i+1}) - En(\mathcal{G}_i) \geq 0$ may occasionally have a chance to be accepted, mostly in the early generations when the temperature is high.

The *annealing mechanism* serves to control the convergence so that it proceeds according to a predefined cooling schedule. The schedule specifies with what rate to lower the temperature so as to favor the appropriate hypotheses at the current step. If the schedule decreases the temperature too rapidly, some good hypotheses may be rejected, or if it decreases the temperature too slowly the hypotheses may become indistinguishable. This is why a sufficiently slow modification of T is recommended: $T^{\tau+1} = T^{\tau}/ln\tau$, where τ is the number of the iterative step. The temperature parameter is initialized according to the equation: $T^0 = -\triangle En^0/ln0.99$, where $\triangle En^0$ is the expected largest difference between the energies. The typical values for the Boltzmann's constant lie in the interval $k \in [0.5, 0.9]$.

Table 5.4. Algorithm for evolutionary population-based search by genetic annealing that can be used in IGP with tree-like genetic programs.

Genetic Annealing

step	*Algorithmic sequence*
1. Initialization	Population of genetic programs $\mathcal{G}_i, 1 \le i \le \pi$. Energies $En_i = f(\mathcal{G}_i)$, Boltzmann's constant $k \in [0.5, 0.9]$. Temperature $T = -\triangle En^0/ln0.99$.
2. Genetic annealing	For a number of generations τ For the whole population $i = 1$ to π a) Select, cross, or mutate, evaluate the offspring $\mathcal{G}_i$. b) Perform relaxation with the following loop i) Compute the energy $En(\mathcal{G}_{i+1}) = f(\mathcal{G}_{i+1})$. ii) if $En(\mathcal{G}_{i+1}) - En(\mathcal{G}_i) < 0$ Accept, and put $\mathcal{G}_{i+1}$ in the population else Accept with probability $\Pr(\mathcal{G}_i) = exp(-(En(\mathcal{G}_{i+1}) - En(\mathcal{G}_i))/kT)$. Update the cooling schedule $T^{\tau+1} = T^{\tau}/ln\tau$. Continue genetic annealing: go to step 2 until the termination condition is satisfied.

Relaxation and Annealing. The search process can be focused using genetic annealing with two phases: genetic relaxation with probabilistic acceptance of the offspring, and annealing by cooling with the temperature parameter. This algorithm can be applied to IGP using the fitnesses as energy characteristics. The survival of an individual is determined relatively to the energy of its parent. If an offspring has a lower energy then its parent, then it is promoted to the next population. Otherwise, if an offspring is worse than its parents, the survival of the offspring is decided probabilistically according to the Boltzmann's distribution. The genetic annealing algorithm is given in Table 5.4.

The annealing process is controlled by a cooling schedule which helps to sustain the search progress. The operation of the cooling schedule depends on a special temperature parameter. If the cooling temperature parameter is not adjusted properly the population may wander on the landscape without locating a good solution, or it may converge prematurely to an inferior solution. Most convenient is to perform uniform cooling with a common temperature parameter for all individuals in the population. There are various formula for updating the cooling schedule, some of which depend on the energies of the individuals. However, it is much more reliable to perform temperature cooling that does not depend on the individuals in the population.

5.2.4 Stochastic Genetic Hillclimbing

Stochastic genetic hillclimbing search [Ackley, 1987] is a complicated version of the genetic annealing algorithm. Stochastic genetic hillclimbing is a general algorithm for sustained adaptation on the search landscape that does not depend on the particular kind of the fitness function. It regulates the population through elaborated selection and replacement mechanisms. Individuals are picked with probability proportional to their displacement relative to the average population fitness, rather than proportional to the improvement from the parent. The probabilistic strategy is such that initially it tolerates arbitrary individuals, while later in the search it encourages individuals with above-average fitness. The average population fitness is enforced to decrease so as the population descends downhill on the landscape.

The selection mechanism in stochastic genetic hillclimbing determines the survival probability of an individual with respect to the average population fitness and the recent generational history of fitness values. An individual which is an improvement to the average population fitness and the fitness history is promoted further to the next generation, in other words, it is pushed to move on the landscape. The mean for stochastic control of the survival probabilities of the individuals is the recent fitness history. The recent history of fitness values θ is updated after evaluating each next offspring according to the equation:

$$\theta = \rho f_{av} + (1 - \rho)(f - \delta) \tag{5.9}$$

where f is the actual fitness of the offspring, f_{av} is the average population fitness, ρ is retention rate $0 < \rho < 1$, and δ is disturbance parameter.

The possibility to adjust the retention rate ρ in formula (5.9) allows us to balance the influence of the average population performance on the search process. The purpose of the disturbance parameter δ is to stimulate modification of even very good individuals. Otherwise, if there is no reinforcement of the good individuals, the search in their neighborhood stagnates and cannot progress in the vicinity of the landscape outside these locally optimal basins. The stochastic genetic hillclimbing algorithm is given in Table 5.5.

Table 5.5. Algorithm for doing stochastic genetic hillclimbing with IGP.

Stochastic Genetic Hillclimbing

step	*Algorithmic sequence*
1. Initialization	Population of genetic programs $\mathcal{G}_i, 1 \leq i \leq \pi$. Average population fitness f_{av}, Fitness history $\theta = f_{av}$, Retention rate $\rho = 0.5$, Disturbance $0 < \delta < 1$ Constant $k \in [0.5, 0.9]$, Temperature $T = -f_{av}/ln 0.99$.
2. Genetic hillclimbing	For a number of generations τ For the whole population $i = 1$ to π a) Select, cross, or mutate, evaluate the offspring $\mathcal{G}_i$. b) Perform relaxation with the following loop i) Compute the offspring fitness $f(\mathcal{G}_{i+1})$. ii) if $f(\mathcal{G}_{i+1}) - \theta < 0$ Accept, and replace the parent $\mathcal{G}_i$ with $\mathcal{G}_{i+1}$ else Accept with probability $\Pr(\mathcal{G}_i) = exp(-(f(\mathcal{G}_{i+1}) - \theta)/kT)$. c) Calculate the average population fitness f_{av}. d) Recompute the recent fitness history $\theta = \rho f_{av} + (1 - \rho)(f - \delta)$. Update the cooling schedule $T^{\tau+1} = T^{\tau}/ln\tau$. go to 2 until the termination condition is satisfied.

5.2.5 Coevolutionary Search

A promising IGP control strategy for hard inductive learning tasks is to distribute the evolutionary search effort among coevolving subpopulations. The idea is to create subpopulations that correspond to the substructures of the fitness landscape [Slavov and Nikolaev, 1997]. The search is facilitated by making subpopulations flowing on the substructures of the complex landscape. The distribution of the evolutionary search on the sublandscapes of the complex landscape means that the IGP attempts to solve the given task by solving its simple subtasks. In order to improve the search, there has to be made a proper cooperation between subpopulations flowing on the simple landscapes and the population flowing on the complex landscape.

The stages of this approach to coevolutionary search are: 1) determine the simple landscape substructures of the complex landscape; 2) for each simple landscape construct an appropriate evolutionary algorithm with a subpopulation easily flowing on it; that is, make special searchers for the particular landscape substructures; and 3) establish a mechanism for cooperation among the subpopulations.

Landscape Substructures. The profile of a fitness landscape is often a complex curve which may be replaced by elementary curves [Bastert et al., 2001]. Since the landscape arises from the fitness function, this idea requires one to identify the smoother component curves of a given function curve. The fitness function may be represented as a superposition of basis functions according to some analytical expansion. A rugged function curve $f(\mathcal{G})$ can be closely approximated by a sum of smoother function curves $f_i(\mathcal{G})$ from a predefined basis:

$$f(\mathcal{G}) = \sum_{i=1}^{\infty} a_i f_i(\mathcal{G}) \tag{5.10}$$

where a_i are the corresponding amplitudes.

This functional equation points out that one may think of a *complex fitness landscape structure* as a superposition of *simple (smoother) landscape substructures*. The superpositioned structure inherits the essential characteristics from the substructures, and that is why it may be expected that the search on some of the simple substructures will be easier. The inheritance of the essential landscape characteristics means that the search on the substructures will provide relevant building blocks for the search on the superpositioned landscape structure.

The interesting question in the design of such a mechanism is how to isolate some of the simple component functions from the expansion of the original fitness function. If some simple components of a complex fitness landscape can be identified, then efficient coevolutionary search on these simple substructures can be organized. The searches on the substructures may transfer by migration useful information for directing the search on the complex landscape, which will help to speed up the convergence of the primary population. The efficacy of the coevolution is sensitive to the mechanism for integrating the searches.

Two Subpopulations on Two Sublandscapes. The IGP control may be enhanced by maintaining two subpopulations: primary and secondary. The *primary subpopulation* should be made to search on the primary complex superpositioned landscape, while the *secondary subpopulation* should be made to search on one of its simple substructures. The secondary subpopulation has to contribute to the primary search by repeated migration of elite individuals to the primary subpopulation.

This approach to coevolutionary search with two subpopulations flowing on two landscapes can be implemented in IGP using different fitness functions. The genetic programs in the primary subpopulation may use an arbitrary fitness function f for the given task. The genetic programs $\mathcal{G}_2$ in the secondary subpopulation should use another fitness function f_2 which may be the average from the fitnesses of the neighbors evaluated using the primary fitness f [Slavov and Nikolaev, 1997]:

$$f_2(\mathcal{G}_2) = \frac{\sum_{\mathcal{G}'_2 \in M(\mathcal{G}_2)} f(\mathcal{G}'_2)}{\mid M(\mathcal{G}_2) \mid} \tag{5.11}$$

where $\mid M(\mathcal{G}_2) \mid$ is the number of neighbors of the genetic program $\mathcal{G}_2$. Neighbors are the genetic programs reachable from the current $\mathcal{G}_2$ by one application of the mutation operator M (Section 2.3.1).

The coevolutionary process has to be coordinated by migrating individuals from the secondary to the primary subpopulation. The migration helps to balance between good individuals in the two subpopulations in the following way. Consider binary tournament for selection of a promising individual $\mathcal{G}_2$ from the elite of the secondary subpopulation. Next, take the best neighbor $\mathcal{G}_2$ of this genetic program. In case of using a minimizing function, this is the individual with lowest fitness value:

$$\min\{f_2(\mathcal{G}'_2) | \mathcal{G}'_2 \in M(\mathcal{G}_2)\} \tag{5.12}$$

where f_2 is the fitness function used in the secondary population. As the number of neighbors of a genetic program may be very large, only a small fraction of them could be taken.

Two subpopulations developed in this way cooperate in the sense that they mutually focus the search. A requirement for cooperation is that the subpopulations use related fitness functions. Only then, the migration from the secondary to the primary subpopulation will exert pressure to highly fit individuals, and the migration will promote diversity.

The empirical studies into coevolutionary IGP search show that the secondary subpopulation flows on a smoother landscape than the primary subpopulation. It has been found that [Slavov and Nikolaev, 1997]: 1) the secondary subpopulation features a smaller number of local optima than those on the primary one; 2) the secondary landscape has flatter hills and basins; it has larger basins as it makes longer walks between the optimal points on its fitness landscape. These are indications which allow us to think that the individuals in the secondary population have potential to see ahead in the search space; they are able faster to identify the concrete uphill or downhill search direction.

This approach to searching on structured complex landscapes has several aspects. First, the approach is problem independent. This means that it could be used in IGP systems that utilize different genetic program representations. Second, the presented implementation migrates the best from the promising neighbors of the elite in the secondary subpopulation, chosen by binary tournament selection. Its advantage is that it preserves the probabilistic nature of the evolutionary search process.

5.2.6 Distributed Search

Efficient search can be organized by distributing the individuals only within local groups in the population. Such local subpopulations are often called *demes* in GP [Tackett and Carmi, 1994], and this notion comes from the theoretical biology [Wright, 1932]. The population is divided into demes with limited communication between them. The sub-populations are autonomous; they evolve in different search directions and exchange a small number of individuals at a predefined rate. Changing the migration rate allows control of the mixing between the demes so as to achieve better exploration of the search space, while exploitation of the search space is performed by the local demes.

The distributed search begins by partitioning the population into demes, each of which can be of different size. Within each deme, a basic IGP search is executed. The selection mechanism uses tournaments with small numbers of competitors. The competing individuals are probabilistically chosen from the local deme, but occasionally they may be picked from neighboring demes. The local search within the demes continues for a certain period so that the individuals between the demes mature enough in order to transmit useful genetic material when passed to other demes. The subpopulations evolve autonomously, and after that, individuals are migrated. The migration features by size and magnitude, which determine the search dynamics. There are exchanged better individuals, usually from the population elite.

This demetic search is suitable for maintaining high diversity in the population, but it has been criticized for the large number of parameters.

5.3 Performance Examination

The simulation of the biological mechanisms mutation, crossover and reproduction is not guaranteed to provide universal learning capabilities. These natural operators are necessary but not sufficient means for adaptation on complex search landscapes. Moreover, these mechanisms should be properly designed and tailored to the task so that the variability that they cause leads to improvement. When the IGP shows continuous improvement during search, it is said to possess the property evolvability [Altenberg, 1994b]. Such a property is required from every component of IGP that impacts the production of offspring.

The development of IGP systems should involve empirical investigations into how each of its components impacts the performance improvement. Each genetic operator should contribute to achieving evolvability. Using various performance measures, this section explains how the evolutionary IGP search process can be observed.

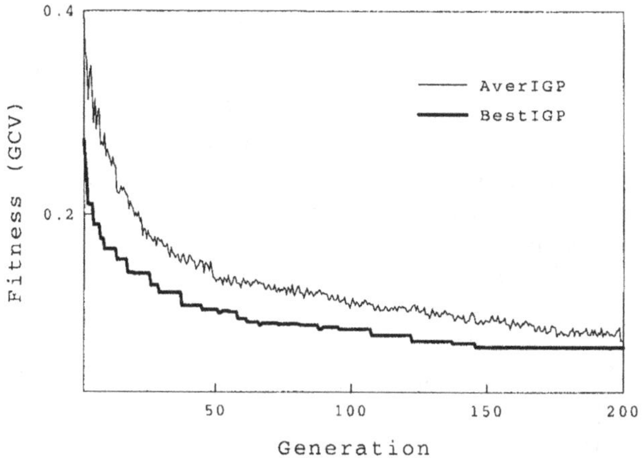

Figure 5.1. Evolvability of the best and average population fitness recorded during a representative run of the IGP system using the Mackey-Glass series.

5.3.1 Fitness Evolvability

Evidence about the progress of the evolutionary search can be acquired through measures of the fitness of the best individual and the average population fitness taken from a number of generations [Goldberg, 1989]. In the typical case, when a minimizing fitness function is used, the function that returns the *fitness of the best population member* $Best(\mathcal{P}^\tau)$ can be defined as follows:

$$Best(\mathcal{P}^\tau) = \min\{f(\mathcal{G}_i^\tau) | 1 \leq i \leq \pi, \forall \mathcal{G}_i^\tau \in \mathcal{P}^\tau\} \tag{5.13}$$

where the index i enumerates the genetic programs $\mathcal{G}_i^\tau$ in the population $\mathcal{P}^\tau$ at generation τ.

The *average population fitness* $Average(\mathcal{P}^\tau)$ shows whether the population as a whole moves on the search landscape:

$$Average(\mathcal{P}^\tau) = \frac{1}{\pi} \sum_{i=1}^{\pi} f(\mathcal{G}_i^\tau), \forall \mathcal{G}_i^\tau \in \mathcal{P}^\tau \tag{5.14}$$

where $\mathcal{P}^\tau$ is the population of programs $\mathcal{G}_i^\tau$ at generation τ. The population should converge slowly to the best individual without reaching it rapidly, such that the fraction $\lim_{\tau \to \infty}(Best(\mathcal{P}^\tau)/Average(\mathcal{P}^\tau)) \neq 1$. Otherwise, when the population average reaches the best one, the search will practically terminate. Figure 5.1 displays the best and average fitness curves recorded during runs of the IGP system.

5.3.2 Convergence Measures

During evolutionary search the IGP population leaves a trajectory, which is a path of its moves on the fitness landscape. This path can be identified by recording the errors of the elite individuals in the population. Then Principal Component Analysis (PCA) [Jolliffe, 1986] may be applied to reduce all errors into three dimensions in order to visualize them [Nikolaev and Iba, 2001d]. The PCA error trajectory computed in this way may be considered a *convergence measure* that illustrates the search problems encountered during evolutionary learning.

The PCA application for convergence examination may be explained as follows. The mean squared errors $m^\tau = (1/N)\sum_{n=1}^{N}(y_n - P(\mathbf{x}_n))^2$, of the elite PNN models are recorded at each generation τ, and error vectors are formed: $\mathbf{m}^\tau = [m_1^\tau, m_2^\tau, ..., m_k^\tau]$, where m_k^τ is the error of the k-th genetic program from the elite, $1 \leq k < \pi_{el}$.

Let each error vector $\mathbf{m}$ be a point in the k-dimensional error space. Such a vector may be represented as a linear combination of basis vectors: $\mathbf{m} = \sum_{i=1}^{k} m_i \mathbf{u}_i$, where $\mathbf{u}_i$ are unit orthonormal vectors such that $\mathbf{u}_i^T \mathbf{u}_j = \delta_{ij}$, and δ_{ij} is the Kroneker delta. The individual errors are $m_i = \mathbf{u}_i^T \mathbf{m}$. The PCA helps to change the coordinate system and to project the errors on the dimensions in which they exhibit largest variance. The basis vectors $\mathbf{u}_i$ are changed with new basis vectors $\mathbf{v}_i$ in the new coordinate system: $\mathbf{m} = \sum_{i=1}^{n} z_i \mathbf{v}_i$. This can be made by extracting $\mathbf{v}_i$ as eigenvectors of the covariance matrix $\mathbf{\Sigma}$ of the error trajectory recorded during a number of generations Υ:

$$\mathbf{\Sigma}\mathbf{v}_i = \lambda_i \mathbf{v}_i \tag{5.15}$$

where λ_i is the i-th eigenvalue of the covariance matrix $\mathbf{\Sigma}$:

$$\mathbf{\Sigma} = \sum_{\tau=1}^{\Upsilon} (\mathbf{m}^\tau - \bar{\mathbf{m}})^T (\mathbf{m}^\tau - \bar{\mathbf{m}}) \tag{5.16}$$

and the mean vector is $\bar{\mathbf{m}} = (1/\Upsilon)\sum_{\tau=1}^{\Upsilon} \mathbf{m}^\tau$.

The extent to which the i-th principal component captures the error variance can be measured as follows: $E_{pc} = \lambda_i^2 / \sum_i \lambda_i^2$. The theoretical studies suggest that the first two principal components (PCs) capture the most essential variations in the errors. The first and the second principal components of the errors are calculated as follows:

$$\mathbf{pc} = \sum_{i=1}^{2} z_i \mathbf{v}_i \tag{5.17}$$

where $\mathbf{pc} = (pc_1, pc_2)$, and z_i are the rotated coordinate coefficients.

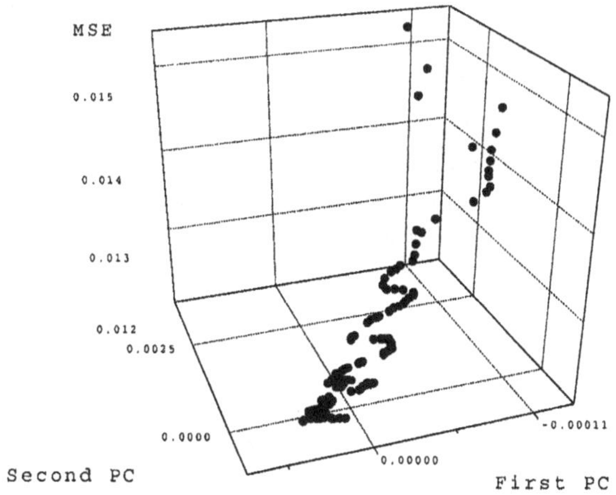

Figure 5.2. Error trajectory of the 30 elite polynomials (from a population of size 100) evolved with IGP applied to the Mackey-Glass data series.

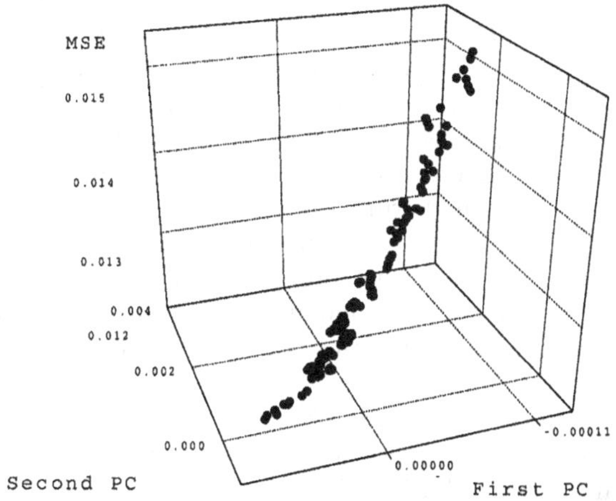

Figure 5.3. Error trajectory of the 30 elite polynomials (from a population of size 100) evolved with traditional GP applied to the Mackey-Glass data series.

Table 5.6. Algorithm for computing the error trajectory of IGP using PCA.

PCA Error Trajectory

step	*Algorithmic sequence*
1. Initialization	Population of genetic programs $\mathcal{G}_i$, $1 \le i \le \pi$, π_{el}=30%. Data set $D = \{(\mathbf{x}_j, y_j)\}_{j=1}^{N}$.
2. Perform an IGP run	For a number of generations τ do Record the errors m^τ of the elite k, $1 \le k < \pi_{el}$, individuals $\mathbf{m}^\tau = (m_1^\tau, m_2^\tau, ..., m_k^\tau)$.
3. Compute the error trajectory	a) Make the covariance matrix $\mathbf{\Sigma}$ $\mathbf{\Sigma} = \sum_{\tau=1}^{\Upsilon} (\mathbf{m}^\tau - \bar{\mathbf{m}})^T (\mathbf{m}^\tau - \bar{\mathbf{m}})$, where: $\bar{\mathbf{m}} = (1/\Upsilon) \sum_{\tau=1}^{\Upsilon} \mathbf{m}^\tau$. b) Compute the eigenvectors $\mathbf{v}_i$ and eigenvalues λ_i of $\mathbf{\Sigma}$ $\mathbf{\Sigma}\mathbf{v}_i = \lambda_i \mathbf{v}_i$. c) Select the largest eigenvectors: $\mathbf{v}_1$ and $\mathbf{v}_1$. d) Determine the coefficients z_i $z_i = \mathbf{v}_i^T \mathbf{m}$. e) Calculate the first and second principal components $\mathbf{pc} = \sum_{i=1}^{2} z_i \mathbf{v}_i$, where: $\mathbf{pc} = (pc_1, pc_2)$.

Plots of the error trajectory can be made by drawing the average mean square error (MSE) of the population elite against the first two principal components pc_1 and pc_2. Figures 5.2 and 5.3 depict the error trajectories obtained from separate experiments conducted with two genetic programming systems: the IGP. and a traditional Koza-style GP using the Mackey-Glass data. Each trajectory is computed from the errors recorded during a single run. Figure 5.2 shows that the variation of the elite error in Koza-style GP slopes down with a zig-zag movement during the evolutionary learning process (which can be seen from the changing error directions). Its population moves in curved directions on the search landscape, since it seems rugged and difficult to search with the particular genetic mechanisms.

The error trajectory in Figure 5.3 shows that the IGP search moves straight forward from the beginning until the end, and it progresses directly toward the final basin following almost a straight line direction of error decrease. In this sense, its population orients well on the search landscape. The plots in Figures 5.2 and 5.3 are meaningful because these PCs capture respectively pc_1=85.25% and pc_2=12.47% of the variance of all elite errors, which make us certain about the search behavior. The algorithmic framework with which these curves in Figures 5.2 and 5.3 have been produced is given in Table 5.6.

5.3.3 Diversity Measures

The evolvability of the genetic programs within the population can be investigated using diversity measures. The diversity measures give information about the alterations of the genetic program structures. That is why they account for the structural evolvability of the individuals in the population. The ability of IGP to maintain high diversity in the population can be examined using two easily computable measures: the syntactic population diameter and the structural population entropy. Investigations with these diversity measures can help to understand how the IGP population evolves during the generations.

Syntactic Population Diameter. Having enough diversity of genetic programs means that the IGP system has sufficient power to conduct efficient search. Otherwise, if it looses diversity, it usually rapidly converges to suboptimal solutions. The diversity can be examined with the population diameter. High population diameter indicates that the IGP system is able to maintain high diversity of dissimilar genetic programs in the population. The *syntactic population diameter* (SPD) can be estimated as the mean tree-to-tree distance among the elite individuals that have better fitness values:

$$SPD = \frac{1}{\pi_{el}} \sum_{i=1,j=1,i\neq j}^{\pi_{el}} Dist(\mathcal{G}_i, \mathcal{G}_j) \qquad (5.18)$$

where the population elite is usually $\pi_{el} = 40\%$.

Figure 5.4 shows the impact of three different mutation operators on the population diversity estimated using the syntactic population diameter metric. The SPD curves are calculated during experiments with the same IGP system implemented with fitness proportionate selection and steady-state reproduction. Three versions of this IGP were made with three different mutation operators: context-preserving mutation (CPM), hierarchical variable-length mutation ($HVLM$), and replacement mutation (RM) (Section 2.3.1). A close look at the plots in Figure 5.4 allow us to reason that when IGP searches with the context-preserving mutation operator, it supports highest variety of tree structures in the population. The replacement mutation RM operator seems worse because it is unable to sustain the diversity in the population, and therefore it could be expected to be inefficient for similar tasks. The $HVLM$ mutation is also inferior to CPM as it features by a lower syntactic population diameter.

Such empirical studies using SPD can be performed to analyze the effects of the other genetic learning operators and IGP mechanisms on the search process with intention to improve them.

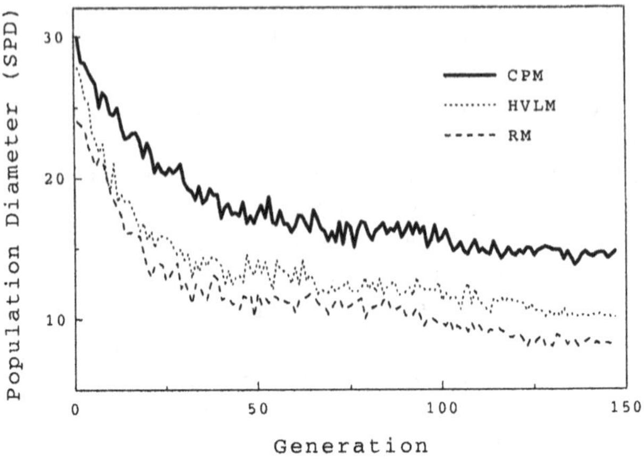

Figure 5.4. Population diameter computed during IGP runs with 50 genetic programs using different mutation operators: context-preserving mutation (CPM), hierarchical variable-length mutation ($HVLM$), and replacement mutation (RM).

Population Clustering. Evidence about the structural diversity in the population can be acquired by unsupervised clustering of the genetic programs [Nikolaev et al., 1999]. The evolutionary search should maintain a large number of clusters in order to achieve successful performance. Higher numbers of clusters indicates that there is a high diversity of genetic program structures. The number of population clusters should be recorded after each generation during a run of the IGP system.

The implementation of a clustering program for genetic programming systems with tree-like genetic programs requires the tree-to-tree distance algorithm. The tree-to-tree distance algorithm, given in Section 2.3.4, has to be developed in advance as a separate function and is invoked at the end of each reproductive cycle.

The population can be analyzed using an incremental clustering algorithm. The set of genetic programs are partitioned into a number of clusters with similar elements. The intercluster similarity is measured using the tree-to-tree distance to the mean of the particular cluster. The clustering algorithm starts with the two most distant genetic programs in the population as initial cluster centers. The remaining genetic programs are processed incrementally and classified relatively to the average tree-to-tree distance between the existing centers.

The average tree-to-tree distance between the centers is defined in the following way:

$$d = \frac{2}{K(K-1)} \sum_{k=1}^{K-1} \sum_{i=k+1}^{K} Dist(\mathcal{G}_k, \mathcal{G}_i) \tag{5.19}$$

where K is the number of all clusters of programs in the population.

When a genetic program $\mathcal{G}$ comes, its tree-to-tree distances to the centers of available population clusters is computed. If the maximal from the distances between the genetic program to the cluster centers is greater than the average distance between the centers, this genetic program becomes a new cluster; that is, it is promoted as center of a completely new cluster. Otherwise, it is added to the cluster whose elements seem most similar to it in tree-to-tree distance sense:

$$Dist(\mathcal{G}, \mathcal{G}_i) \leq Dist(\mathcal{G}, \mathcal{G}_j), 1 \leq i, j \leq K, j \neq i \tag{5.20}$$

where $\mathcal{G}_i$ and $\mathcal{G}_j$ denote cluster centers.

After adding the next genetic program to a particular cluster, its cluster center is recomputed and the average distance between the centers is updated. The genetic program which is at smallest tree-to-tree distance to the remaining genetic programs in the cluster becomes its center:

$$\mathcal{G}_k = \min \left\{ \sum_{i=1}^{n_k} Dist(\mathcal{G}_k, \mathcal{G}_i) | \mathcal{G}_k \in Z_k \right\} \tag{5.21}$$

where Z_k denotes the k-th cluster in the current population, $\mathcal{G}_k$ is the center genetic program of this k-th cluster, and n_k is the number of the members in cluster Z_k.

Figure 5.5 illustrates the clusters computed during representative runs of the IGP and traditional Koza-style GP systems using the Mackey-Glass data series. The traditional GP was implemented with the MSE fitness function, while IGP used the GCV fitness function. The difference is that IGP was made using the context-preserving mutation operator, while the Koza-style GP used mutation at random points. Figure 5.5 shows that the population of the IGP system during evolutionary search contains more clusters; that is, it maintains higher diversity of genetic programs. The higher number of clusters are indication that the IGP system is capable of continuous adaptation on the search landscape. It is interesting to note that traditional GP also has a relatively large number of syntactically different programs in its population. The computational algorithm for incremental population clustering, used to prepare this figure, is shown in the next Table 5.7.

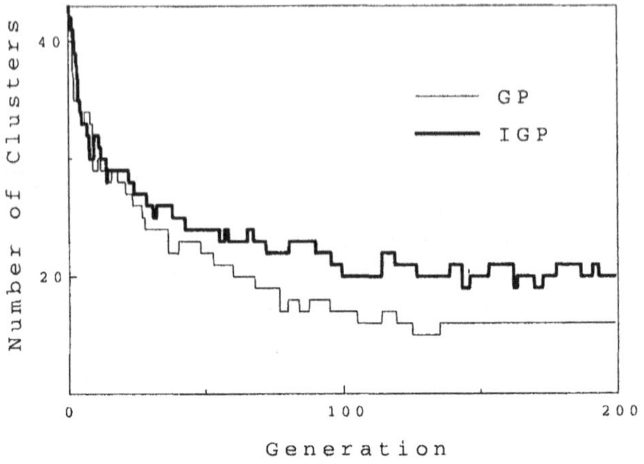

Figure 5.5. Population clustering of IGP and traditional Koza-style GP using populations of size 100 genetic programs and the Mackey-Glass data series.

Table 5.7. Algorithm for unsupervised incremental clustering that may be applied after each generation in a particular run of the IGP system.

Unsupervised Population Clustering for IGP

step	*Algorithmic sequence*
1. Initialization	Current population of genetic programs $\mathcal{G}_i$, $1 \leq i \leq \pi$. Take the two most distant individuals as centers: $Z_1 = \{\mathcal{G}_1\}$ and $Z_2 = \{\mathcal{G}_2\}$, so the current clusters are $K = 2$. Let d be the average distance between cluster centers.

2. Process consecutively all genetic programs	For each next genetic program $\mathcal{G}$ do
	a) Calculate its tree-to-tree distance to each center
	$Dist(\mathcal{G}, \mathcal{G}_i)$, $1 \leq i \leq K$.
	b) if $d < Dist(\mathcal{G}, \mathcal{G}_i)$
	Make this genetic program
	a new cluster center $Z = \{\mathcal{G}\}$
	else
	Allocate it in the cluster with closest center $\mathcal{G}_i$
	$Dist(\mathcal{G}, \mathcal{G}_i) \leq Dist(\mathcal{G}, \mathcal{G}_j)$, $1 \leq i, j \leq K$, $j \neq i$.
	c) Recompute the center of this cluster
	$\mathcal{G}_k = \min\left\{\sum_{i=1}^{n_k} Dist(\mathcal{G}_k, \mathcal{G}_i) \mid \mathcal{G}_k \in Z_k\right\}$.
	d) Update the average cluster distance
	$d = (2/K(K-1)) \sum_{k=1}^{K-1} \sum_{i=k+1}^{K} Dist(\mathcal{G}_k, \mathcal{G}_i)$.

Structural Population Entropy. The diversity of genotype structures bred by IGP can be measured by the population entropy. It is defined in such a way that a low entropy indicates that the IGP system evolves from a random population to an internally structured one. The tendency in the search process should be toward evolving generations with decreased structural randomness compared to the structural content of the initial population. This may happen if the population is capable of keeping information about the individuals, like homogenous compositions, and transmitting it further so that there is no loss of useful genetic program structures.

Structural population entropy is the average entropy of the sequences of genes that make the genetic programs. It estimates the structural similarity between the genotypes available in the population. A sequence of genes may be collected by traversal of the corresponding linear genetic program tree. After that, the linear trees have to be arranged consecutively one by one in a population table. The population table should include a number of rows equal to the population elite. The columns should contain the alleles from the genotype loci. The loci from the genotype correspond to the vertices in the linear tree representation, which may be functional nodes and terminal leaves.

The probability Pr of an allele a in a particular locus column is computed by its relative frequency $freq$ in this column contributed by the elite genetic programs:

$$\Pr(a) = \frac{freq(a)}{\pi_{el}} \tag{5.22}$$

where π_{el} denotes the size of the population elite.

The entropy h of a locus l is therefore the sum of the entropies of its alleles a_i from its locus column $i, 1 \leq i \leq \pi$ in the population table:

$$h_l = -\sum_{i=1}^{\pi_{el}} \Pr(a_i) \times \log_2 \Pr(a_i) \tag{5.23}$$

The structural population entropy H is the sum of the entropies of all vertices v_i occupying the successive loci: $1 \leq l \leq |\mathcal{G}|$, divided by the size of the longest, in sense of number of nodes and leaves, genetic program $|\mathcal{G}|$ in the population under study:

$$H^\tau = \frac{1}{|\mathcal{G}|} \sum_{l=1}^{|\mathcal{G}|} h_l \tag{5.24}$$

where H^τ is the entropy at generation τ. In order to obtain correct and meaningful results, this procedure should be applied with at least 100 different populations recorded during consecutive generations.

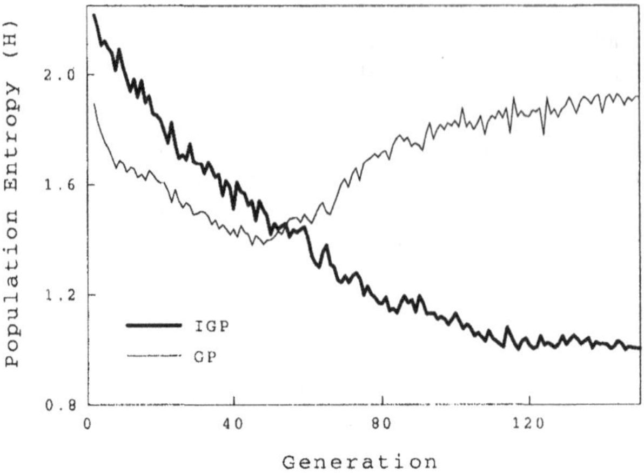

Figure 5.6. Population entropy averaged from 10 runs of IGP and traditional GP with populations of 100 genetic programs, $\pi_{el} = 40\%$, using mutation parameter $\mu = 0.085$, and crossover parameter $\kappa = 5$.

Figure 5.6 displays the changes of the population entropy calculated with separate runs of IGP and traditional Koza-style GP. The IGP system is implemented with the *GCV* fitness function, and the context-preserving mutation operator. The traditional GP uses the *MSE* function and mutation at random points. The remaining mechanisms in both systems are the same: they use fitness proportional selection, steady-state reproduction, and were trained on the Mackey-Glass data series.

Figure 5.6 displays that the ensemble of genetic programs maintained by the IGP system continuously becomes more and more homogenous. Evidence for this homogeneity is the overall sloping down IGP entropy curve. On the contrary, the population entropy in traditional GP changes variably. The observation that the traditional GP entropy tends to increase after a certain generation suggests that the individuals lose useful structural content during the transformations by the genetic learning operator, and they are unable to search efficiently on the fitness landscape. A reason for the better behavior of IGP is that its sampling context-preserving mutation operator and the fitness function are coordinated through the common genetic program size parameter. One is inclined to think that this size-base coordination helps to install useful structural information in the population.

The computational algorithm for measuring the entropy picture of the population during runs with IGP is given in Table 5.8.

Table 5.8. A computational algorithm for making a picture of the structural population entropy in IGP.

Measuring Structural Population Entropy in IGP

step	*Algorithmic sequence*
1. Initialization	Population of genetic programs $\mathcal{G}_i, 1 \leq i \leq \pi$. the best 40% of which are population elite π_{el}.
2. Conduct an IGP run and make entropy picture	For a number of generations τ do a) Isolate the genotypes of the population elite π_{el} and arrange them in a population table *PopTable*. b) For each loci $l = 1$ to $\|\mathcal{G}_l\|$, where $\|\mathcal{G}_l\|$ is the longest genome. i) Compute the frequences of alleles in this locus column $\Pr(a) = (freq(a))/\pi_{el}$. ii) Calculate the entropy of this locus $h_l = -\sum_{i=1}^{\pi_{el}} \Pr(a_i) \times \log_2 \Pr(a_i)$. c) Estimate the population entropy $H^\tau = (1/\|\mathcal{G}\|) \sum_{l=1}^{\|\mathcal{G}\|} h_l$.

5.3.4 Measures of Self-Organization

The evolutionary algorithms exhibit complex dynamical behavior that can be investigated using measures from the physics of complex systems. The behavior of the IGP population may be envisioned as analogical to this of a cloud of physical particles thrown on a hilly landscape surface. The population moves on the fitness landscape like an ensemble of particles which are pulled by the gravity force, decreases their speed due to friction, and finally stops at some landscape basin or trough with a particle in the lowest point. While the population flows on the landscape, as a result of the internal changes in the population, its potential energy is expected to be transformed with losses into kinetic energy. A slowly decreasing total population energy is a dynamic characteristic which implies feasibility of the evolutionary algorithm to search.

The dynamics of IGP can be studied with the following physical measures [Nikolaev and Slavov, 1998]: potential population energy, kinetic population energy, and total population energy. These are physical estimates which provide evidence for such dynamical characteristics of the algorithm performance like the transmission of useful information, the self-organization, the movement, and the stabilization of the population.

Potential Population Energy. IGP should maintain individuals that contain different partial solutions. A larger repertoire of dissimilar fit genetic programs means that there is a greater chance for their arrangement into better ones. Therefore, the IGP should distribute the search effort on clusters of fit genetic programs. The theory of thermodynamics provides the potential energy as a characteristic of the ability of a system to self-organize toward configurations that increasingly satisfy given macroscopic constraints. Starting with individuals randomly scattered on the fitness landscape, the behavior of an evolutionary searcher will converge when the fit genetic programs in the population resemble each other, or the distances between them slowly decrease.

In order to observe the diversity from a macroscopic point of view, the *potential population energy* E_P of an IGP dynamic system can be defined as follows:

$$E_P = \frac{1}{\pi_{el}^2} \sum_{i=1}^{\pi_{el}} \sum_{j=1}^{\pi_{el}} Dist(\mathcal{G}_i, \mathcal{G}_j) f_i f_j \tag{5.25}$$

where $f_i = f(\mathcal{G}_i)$ and $f_j = f(\mathcal{G}_j)$ are the fitnesses of the possible pairs of genetic programs $\mathcal{G}_i$ and $\mathcal{G}_j$ from the population elite of size π_{el}, and $Dist(\mathcal{G}_i, \mathcal{G}_j)$ is the tree-to-tree distance between them.

The potential population energy will decrease with the decrease of the distances between the genetic programs. This will be an indication that the evolutionary algorithm improves and the population self-organizes. The potential population energy is considered here to compare the performance of IGP with a traditional Koza-style GP. IGP features by the GCV fitness function and the context-preserving mutation operator. The traditional GP uses the MSE fitness function and mutation at random points. The remaining micromechanisms are the same: crossover at random points, fitness proportional selection, and steady-state reproduction. Both GP were evaluated with the Mackey-Glass series.

The potential energy curves plotted in Figure 5.7 demonstrate that the IGP system achieves higher population variety compared to the traditional GP. During the experiments, IGP show abilities to produce continuously modified configurations with varying but overall fitter genetic programs, and to relax to an energetic equilibrium. The IGP system seems capable of balancing well between the sizes of the programs and their fitnesses, which enables the population to reach together an equilibrium configuration with very good solutions. The potential energy of traditional GP decreases quickly as it gets trapped rapidly into imperfect configurations of relatively fit but suboptimal programs with close tree shapes that quickly dominate the population.

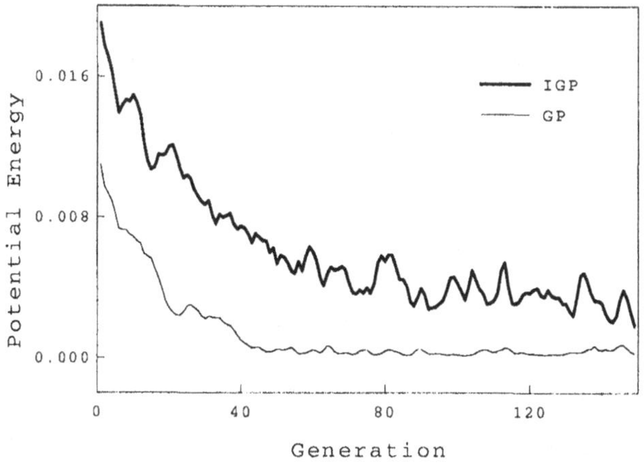

Figure 5.7. Potential population energy E_P averaged over 10 runs with IGP using small populations of 100 genetic programs, elite $\pi_{el} = 40\%$, genetic operator parameters $\mu = 0.05$, $\kappa = 3$, and fitnesses evaluated using the Mackey-Glass data.

Kinetic Population Energy. The kinetic energy can be used for estimating the IGP search effort made to push the population on the fitness landscape. An increasing kinetic energy will be an indication that the algorithm performance improves, in the sense that it has abilities to alter the search toward unexplored landscape regions. The search performance depends on the provided examples, and they are an important factor for redirecting the search. The genetic programs should compete within the population to capture more unique examples from the data.

The *kinetic population energy* could be estimated by summing the speeds s_i of the genetic programs $\mathcal{G}_i$ $(1 \leq i \leq \pi_{el})$ multiplied by their fitnesses f_i, averaged with respect to the population elite number π_{el}:

$$E_K = \frac{1}{\pi_{el}} \sum_{i=1}^{\pi_{el}} s_i f_i \tag{5.26}$$

The speed is a global characteristic of the motion of a genetic program, which is representative for the global performance of the IGP system. The speed expresses the instantaneous tendency of a genetic program to modify its capacity to interpolate the given data precisely. In context of IGP, the speed of a genetic program quantifies the rate of variation of the interpolated exceptional examples. An example vector becomes exceptional and hence, important when less genetic programs from the population match it with error lower than a preselected threshold.

The *speed* s_i of a genetic program $\mathcal{G}_i$ should be defined in two different ways for the two typical kinds of application problems: classification and regression. When performing classification by IGP the speed could be the sum of the importances $I \in R$ of the examples that the genetic program matches $M(\mathcal{G}_i, (\mathbf{x}_j, y_j), \varepsilon) = true$ or $false$, $M : \mathcal{G} \times D \times R \rightarrow B$. When performing regression by IGP, the speed could be the number of data points that the genetic program approximates with error lower than a predefined threshold $\varepsilon \in R$:

$$s_i = \sum_{M(\mathcal{G}_i, (\mathbf{x}_j, y_j), \varepsilon)} I_j \tag{5.27}$$

where $(\mathbf{x}_j, y_j)$ is an example from the given data. The speed s_i will be largest when the genetic program $\mathcal{G}_i$ correctly recognizes all examples.

The extent to which an example is matched by all genetic programs in the population is called importance. It should be evaluated with its relative displacement from the remaining examples in the sample using a dynamic characteristic like the fitness. The importance I_j of the j-th example $(\mathbf{x}_j, y_j)$ is the normalized difference between the fitnesses of all genetic programs from the population elite π_{el} and the fitnesses f_i of these individuals $\mathcal{G}_i$ that match it $M(\mathcal{G}_i, (\mathbf{x}_j, y_j), \varepsilon)$ with low error less than the predefined threshold ε:

$$I_j = \frac{\sum_{k=1}^{\pi_{el}} f_k - \sum_{M(\mathcal{G}_i, (\mathbf{x}_j, y_j), \varepsilon)} f_i}{\sum_{k=1}^{\pi_{el}} f_k} \tag{5.28}$$

The values produced by this normalized formula grow when the portion of genetic programs $\mathcal{G}_i$ classifying correctly the j-th example $(\mathbf{x}_j, y_j)$ decreases: $\lim_{i \rightarrow 0} I_j = 1$.

The justification for this definition is that when the number of genetic programs that match an example increase, more individuals carry information about its features and the example becomes less influential for the search. The importance of an example is a sign for its identity compared to the remaining examples. Capture of such a distinct example may cause a search perturbation, and may be expected to contribute to improvement of the search process. Recognition of a yet unmatched example by an individual says that this genetic program is in a promising search direction. In order to search well, the algorithm should tolerate speedy genetic programs which at each next generation match more important examples.

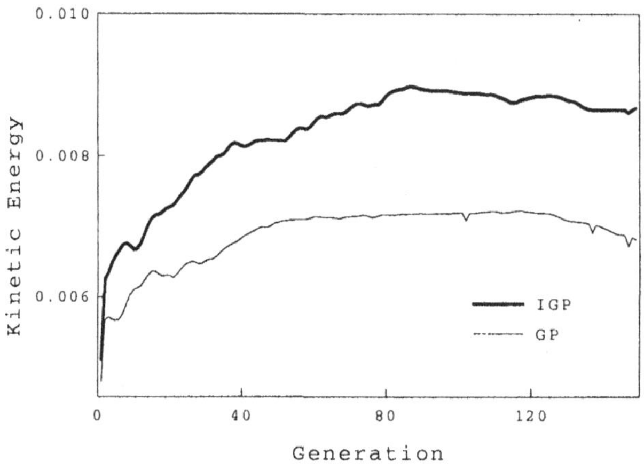

Figure 5.8. Kinetic population energy E_K averaged over 10 runs with IGP using small populations of 100 genetic programs, elite N_{el} = 40%, genetic operator parameters $\mu = 0.05$, = 3, and fitnesses evaluated using the Mackey-Glass data.

Figure 5.8 shows the kinetic population energies of IGP and traditional Koza-style GP measured while learning the Mackey-Glass series. These GP differ in that IGP uses size-biased context-preserving mutation and *GCV* fitness function, while traditional GP uses ordinary mutation at random points and *MSE* fitness function. When looking at the kinetic energy curves, one notes that the kinetic energy of IGP gradually rises. Because of this we are inclined to think that using the size-biased genetic learning operators and fitness function helps to match increasingly more exceptional examples. The speedy genetic programs in IGP prevail in the population, which from a global perspective leads interpolation of more examples.

The curves in Figure 5.8 demonstrate that the genetic programs pursue adaptation with mutual competition to match exceptional data. This competition is regulated by the size-integrated navigation and fitness biases, which provide the capacity to make considerable population changes. This ensures motion of the population on the fitness landscape and continuous performance improvement. The traditional GP tends to converge relatively fast to a population of individuals having close shapes and size, and there are no forces that can push the population so as to reorient the search. This reasoning follows from the almost unchanging kinetic population energy of traditional GP, although in the beginning of the search process it slightly increases.

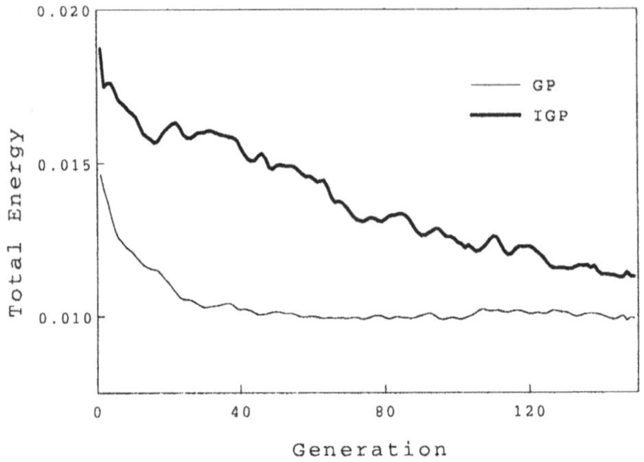

Figure 5.9. Total population energy E_T averaged over 10 runs with IGP using small populations of 100 genetic programs, elite N_{el} = 40%, genetic operator parameters $\mu = 0.05$, = 3, and fitnesses evaluated using the Mackey-Glass data.

Total Population Energy. IGP may be considered a dissipative computational system [Yang et al., 1996] that relies on the principles of information absorbation, change, and transmission. There is energy consumption for accumulating information in the population, modifying this information, as well as distributing the information among the individuals. The total energy is a representative measure for the collective behavior of the genetic programs in the population.

The total population energy $E_T = E_P + E_K$, describes the degree of IGP stabilization. During evolutionary search, the potential population energy is expected to be transformed with losses into kinetic energy. The energy losses are due to dissipation plus energy consumption for aggregation of useful partial solutions in the form of building blocks. The hypothesis is that an evolutionary search algorithm is a kind of an open system, which dissipates energy from its useless genetic programs discarded to the environment and conserves the energy of its elite genetic programs [Yang et al., 1996]. The elite genetic programs should carry the essential information and compete to take over the population, and thus diminish the population randomness.

The total population energy is used here to relate the performance of IGP to this of a traditional Koza-style GP. IGP features by the *GCV* fitness function and the context-preserving mutation operator. The traditional GP uses the *MSE* fitness function and mutation at random points. The plots in Figure 5.9 display that the traditional GP search rapidly saturates compared to IGP. The decreasing character of the total population energy can be interpreted as a process of consuming energy from the environment to foster the fit genetic programs, which is accompanied with freeing the energy of inferior individuals. The rapid energy flux to the environment in traditional GP says that it accumulates incorrect information, possibly because it converges to genetic programs of similar size and shape. The slow energy decline of IGP shows that it continually absorbs energy in the form of useful genetic material.

Physical Population Picture. The population energy estimates can be taken to make physical pictures of the dynamics of evolutionary algorithms (Table 5.9). They reveal general behavioral patterns and allow one to derive explanations about the search quality of the GP system.

Table 5.9. Algorithm for taking a physical picture of the IGP dynamics.

Making a Physical Population Picture in IGP

step	*Algorithmic sequence*
1. Initialization	Initial population, the best 25% are population elite π_{el} Data $D = \{(\mathbf{x}_j, y_j)\}_{j=1}^{N}$, and error threshold ε.

2. Conduct runs	For a number of runs do
	For a number of generations do
	a) Perform recombination, mutation, and selection: select elite π_{el}.
	b) With all elite $\mathcal{G}_i$ and $\mathcal{G}_j$ compute potential energy $E_P = (1/\pi_{el}^2) \sum_{i=1}^{\pi_{el}} \sum_{j=1}^{\pi_{el}} Dist(\mathcal{G}_i, \mathcal{G}_j) f_i f_j$.
	c) In order to measure the kinetic energy do
	i) Determine the importances I_j of the examples $I_j = (\sum_{k=1}^{\pi_{el}} f_k - \sum_{M(\mathcal{G}_i,(\mathbf{x}_j,y_j),\varepsilon)} f_i) / \sum_{k=1}^{\pi_{el}} f_k$.
	ii) Measure the speed s_i of each elite program $\mathcal{G}_i$ $s_i = \sum_{R(\mathcal{G}_i,(\mathbf{x}_j,y_j),\varepsilon)} I_j$.
	iii) Compute the kinetic population energy $E_K = (1/\pi_{el}) \sum_{i=1}^{\pi_{el}} s_i f_i$.
	d) Compute the total population energy $E_T = E_P + E_K$.
	Collect the energies during into corresponding arrays.

3. Terminate	Perform averaging of each energy array E_T, E_P, E_K.

The above energy estimates demonstrated how one can analyze the characteristics of IGP in the three stages: start, global, and local search. The IGP starts with a random population which has a low kinetic energy and a high potential energy. After that, the IGP system enters the stage of global search during which it rapidly accelerates and traverses large landscape areas. This behavior is indicated by the slightly sloping-down potential energy and the increasing kinetic population energy. When IGP focuses at a region with a good solution, it shows behavior on the edge between global and local search. Then it moves with a slow velocity, since changes of the investigated search directions still happen. During this transitional search stage the potential energy oscillates with large magnitudes, and the kinetic energy varies slightly.

5.4 Chapter Summary

This section presented control micromechanisms for IGP. It was shown how to implement reproduction and replacement strategies. There were given algorithms for fitness proportionate, ranking, truncation, and tournament selection of promising individuals from the population. There were given several replacement mechanisms, including: random deletion, deletion of the worst individual by ranking, deletion of the worst by tournament, and deletion of the oldest individual from the population.

The main contributions of this chapter to the research in genetic programming are the offered measures for examination of the evolutionary search performance. There were proposed four groups of measures: fitness evolvability measures, convergence measures, diversity measures, and measures of the self-organizing behavior. These are general measures whose implementation does not depend on the concrete implementation of the GP system and its micromechanisms, so these measures can be applied to investigate the performance of any GP system. These measures are useful because they provide valuable information about different aspects of the search algorithm. Having this information, one can tune and improve the GP system components so as to achieve faster and reliable convergence to good solutions.

The possibility to take a picture of the physical characteristics, like the potential and kinetic energies, makes the IGP a promising application tool, as with these measures a researcher can be convincing about the self-organizing potential of the system. Taking a picture of the self-organizing behavior of the IGP provides evidence about the adaptive capacity of the evolutionary search, and it may be considered to examine it as a dynamical system for real-world problem solving.

Chapter 6

BACKPROPAGATION TECHNIQUES

The presented methodology for inductive learning of polynomial networks includes three groups of techniques for: 1) finding the network architecture, i.e. polynomial terms; 2) improving the network weights, i.e. polynomial term coefficients; and 3) adapting the network weights with respect to their variances and the noise variance of the adopted probability distribution. After evolving an adequate PNN topology by genetic programming, the weights can be improved further by BackPropagation (BP) techniques. This is crucial to successful learning because the weights of the polynomial are essential in describing the data, and so they impact PNN training as well as generalization performance. Estimating the PNN weights by OLS fitting often does not lead to sufficiently good solutions. That is why additional retraining could be made by backpropagation [Rumelhart et al., 1986], elaborated for higher-order networks of polynomial activation functions.

The constructive polynomial network algorithms from the GMDH family do not guarantee achieving coherence between the higher and the lower layer weights. These algorithms build the network without achieving enough mutual cooperation between the weights so that together they fit the data. This happens because while growing the network, the weights are estimated vertically in a bottom-up manner from the lowest layers near the inputs toward the higher layers near the output. When estimated in this way, the weights in the lower layers are frozen and do not depend on the weights in the higher layers. The weights in the lower layers are not coordinated with the weights in the higher layers, while the weights in the higher layers are coordinated with the weights in the lower layers. This is the rationale for recommending further mutual synchronization of all the weights in such constructive networks.

The representation of polynomials as multilayer feed-forward PNN enables us to develop efficient BP techniques for their tuning. The basic BackPropagation Algorithm (BPA) [Rumelhart et al., 1986, Werbos, 1974] conducts gradient descent search in the direction of the most rapid error decrease by changing the weights. This could be envisioned as changing the weights so as to move downhill on the error surface, aiming at reaching the deepest basin. BPA performs two passes through the multilayer structure of the network: a forward pass and a backward pass. During the forward pass it computes the outputs from the hidden nodes and the overall output. During the backward pass it updates the weights using an error correction rule. BPA is an error-correction procedure that presents the training data many times and modifies the weights until the network produces outputs satisfactory close to the provided desired outputs. In the case of PNN, typically the Euclidean distance (L_2- norm) is preferred as a closeness criterion.

Backpropagation techniques are specialized here for nonlinear PNN to make them reliable supervised learning systems [Nikolaev and Iba, 2003]. Several BPA based on first-order (Section 6.2) and second-order optimization methods (Section 6.3) are developed for nonlinear PNN weight learning. The second-order BP algorithms are those based on the Newton's method, the pseudo-Newton training method, the conjugate gradients method, and the Levenberg-Marquardt method. The issue of weight regularization is considered in the context of the first-order properties and revisited using the second-order properties of these networks. After that, design of first-order and second-order pruning methods is detailed. Approaches to learning step control are briefly discussed.

6.1 Multilayer Feed-forward PNN

PNN are connectionist computational devices for mathematical modelling. They consist of processing units, called neurons or hidden network nodes, linked in irregular network topologies to model functions. Each neuron has several incoming connections, an outgoing connection, and a basis activation function. In the case of tree-structured PNN, each neuron has exactly two incoming links. The node inputs are passed through an activation function that generates the nonlinear output signal. The PNN use low-order activations, more precisely, bivariate linear and quadratic activation polynomials (Table 2.1). Since the coefficients of an activation polynomial weight the effects of the input signals, they are simply called weights. The input signals are sent through the incoming connections; that is, the connections carry the signals. The signals can be outputs from other neurons or input variables.

The neurons in PNN are organized hierarchically in multiple layers, also called levels: an input layer of fringe nodes that receive the input variables, hidden layers of functional nodes fed with outputs from other nodes and/or input variables, and an output layer having a root node that produces the overall model output. Such PNN are essentially feed-forward networks because the computed output from a node does not influence its inputs either directly or indirectly. When cascaded hierarchically, the node activation polynomials in such a multilayer structure compose a high-order function of the inputs.

Polynomials are suitable as activation functions since they are both: 1) nonlinear, thus when cascaded they imply abilities for representing highly nonlinear functions; and, 2) continuous, thus differentiable and so enable gradient descent learning. Employing activation polynomials in the nodes of neural networks is sufficient for learning higher-order multivariate functions and eliminates the need to consider other kinds of functions such as the usual sigmoid and hyperbolic tangent.

6.2 First-Order Backpropagation

BPA [Rumelhart et al., 1986, Werbos, 1974] performs gradient descent weight search in training steps called cycles or epochs. Each cycle is an iteration over the data and it involves: 1) a forward pass with one input vector through the network which generates outputs from each node, and finally a network output; 2) a backward pass of error signals; and, 3) changes of the weights proportional to the errors. The forward pass propagates the effects of the lower layer weights toward the higher layer weights encoded as input signals. The backward pass propagates down through the network, from the root to the fringe nodes, the effects of the higher layer weights on the lower layer weights encoded as error signals. The error signals carry information not only for the difference between the estimated outputs and the targets, but also about the magnitudes of the weights on the distinct paths from the root to the concrete node. In this way BPA, achieves precise tuning of the weights that reflects their mutual dependencies.

Backpropagating of the errors enables us to adjust each weight in proportion to its influence on the output. A large modification of a weight is done if it causes a large reduction of the error. In order to perform optimal weight update, BPA exploits several influences of the network model components on the computation of the gradient in the weight space: how the changes of a weight influence the output of the concrete node, how the nodes in the next layer influence a particular weight change in the previous layer, and how the network root node output influences a particular weight change.

Viewing learning as a weight optimization problem, the task is to find such weights that minimize the squared error:

$$E(\mathbf{w}) = \frac{1}{2}\sum_{n=1}^{N} e_n^2 \tag{6.1}$$

$$e_n = y_n - P(\mathbf{x}_n, \mathbf{w}) \tag{6.2}$$

where $\mathbf{w}$ is the weight vector of the network which applied to given input $\mathbf{x}_n$ produces output $P(\mathbf{x}_n, \mathbf{w})$, and e_n is the error from the n-th training example. The derivative of this error with respect to the weights gives the amount for updating the weight vector.

6.2.1 Gradient Descent Search

The *gradient descent search algorithm* prescribes to make specific weight updates so that the network output error, as a function of all these weights, achieves steepest decrease. The direction of steepest error decrease is opposite to the gradient vector of the error function. In this sense, weight learning is a search process of moving downhill on the error landscape. In nonlinear PNN, the surface of the error function (6.1) has multiple optima and minima. The ultimate goal of the search process organized with the concrete network is to find a weight vector that possibly corresponds to the lowest minima on the error surface, in the deepest basin on the error landscape. Pushing the weight vector, which is an argument of the error function, causes moves of the error point, determined by the network output, on the error surface.

The gradient descent weight search can be terminated when the gradient becomes sufficiently small, below a predefined threshold, that is even before or near the global minimum on the error surface where the gradient is zero. Because of the somewhat unknown nature of the error in practice it may be difficult to decide which is a sufficiently good solution. That is why the search is stopped after performing a fixed number of iterations or until there is no longer error minimization.

A necessary means for developing weight learning rules that optimally decrease the error are the first-order and second-order derivatives of the error function with respect to the weights. They serve to elaborate the mechanisms of the BPA. The first-order error derivatives form the so-called *gradient vector* $\mathbf{g} \equiv \nabla E$ (6.36,6.37) on the error surface obtained with weight vector $\mathbf{w}$. The first-order error derivatives are of the kind $\partial E(\mathbf{w})/\partial w_i$, $1 \leq i \leq W$, where $E(\mathbf{w})$ is the error obtained from PNN with weights $\mathbf{w} = [w_0, w_1, ..., w_W]^T$ when evaluated with the n-th example, and W is the number of weights.

The activation polynomials used in the nodes of the polynomial networks are continuous functions which assume gradient descent learning [Nikolaev and Iba, 2003]. Having different network topologies and activation functions requires different analytical expressions for the gradient vector. The derivation of the expressions for the gradient vector in polynomial networks relies on the following assumptions: 1) every functional network node, hidden and output, uses inputs that are signals coming from its two children nodes; and, 2) in every hidden node, linear or quadratic activation polynomials are allocated. These polynomials play the roles of both net functions that collect the input signals, and activation functions that provide the nonlinearities.

Although the presented derivations do not involve bounding the activation polynomial outputs by passing them through appropriate additional filters, such as the sigmoidal or tangential functions, they can be incorporated in the following algorithms in a straightforward manner as suggested in the classical literature. It should be noted that bounding the activation polynomial outputs through additional nonlinearities may be necessary to stabilize the generalization on future data as suggested in the introduction, especially for PNN.

6.2.2 First-Order Error Derivatives

Weight training algorithms can be implemented using the exact gradient vector or using an approximation to the gradient vector. The second approach is preferred for explaining the derivation of the canonical BPA.

Let the instantaneous error between the desired output y_n and the estimated PNN output produced with the input vector $\mathbf{x}_n$ from the same example pair $(\mathbf{x}_n, y_n)$ be:

$$E_n = \frac{1}{2} e_n^2 \tag{6.3}$$

where e_n is the error (6.1) obtained from the n-th training example.

The BPA training rule is derived for an arbitrary node with weight w on one of its incoming connections, and after that it is specialized for the output node and for the hidden nodes. The first-order derivatives of the instantaneous error after this node with respect to the weight is:

$$\frac{\partial E_n}{\partial w} = \frac{\partial E_n}{\partial p} \frac{\partial p}{\partial w} \tag{6.4}$$

where p is the activation polynomial at the node whose output influences the error, and w is a weight parameter. Such error derivatives $\partial E_n / \partial w$ are calculated not only for each weight from this polynomial but also for each weight in the whole network.

The first component $\partial E_n/\partial p$ in the error derivative reflects the node error change as a function of the change in the input feeding that node. In case of tree-structured PNN, the node inputs can be weighted by any of the activation polynomials $p_1, p_2, ..., p_{16}$ defined in Table 2.1. The second component $\partial p/\partial w$ reflects the error change as a function of the specific weight w in the node polynomial. When the complete bivariate quadratic polynomial is used, there are five partial derivatives:

$$x' = \frac{\partial p}{\partial w}; \frac{\partial p}{\partial w} = x_1, \frac{\partial p}{\partial w} = x_1^2, \frac{\partial p}{\partial w} = x_2, \frac{\partial p}{\partial w} = x_2^2, \frac{\partial p}{\partial w} = x_1 x_2 \quad (6.5)$$

Two kinds of error derivatives $\partial E_n/\partial w$ are obtained: one for the output node, and one for the hidden network nodes.

Let's assume that the output node is indexed by k and the hidden nodes with outgoing connections feeding it are indexed by j. The error derivative for the output node with respect to its weights is:

$$\frac{\partial E_n}{\partial w_{kj}} = \frac{\partial E_n}{\partial p_k} \frac{\partial p_k}{\partial w_{kj}} \quad (6.6)$$

where p_k is the activation polynomial at the output root node, and w_{kj} is the weight from a child node at the j-th level to the root k.

Since the activation polynomial determines the output $P(\mathbf{x}) = p_k$, the derivative with respect to this polynomial is:

$$\frac{\partial E_n}{\partial p_k} = -(y_n - P(\mathbf{x}_n)) \quad (6.7)$$

where y_n is the desired output, and $P(\mathbf{x}_n)$ is the estimated PNN output with the n-th example. The output $P(\mathbf{x}_n)$ is used instead of p_k to emphasize that if additional bounding is applied at the output node, for example using the sigmoidal squashing function, then this equation (6.7) should be multiplied by its derivative.

The error derivative with respect to a weight reflects the fact that the error depends on the weight through the activation polynomial that is fed by a signal multiplied by this weight. The error is actually a result of the hierarchical cascade of activation polynomials. The error derivative with respect to a weight on a connection feeding hidden node at level j by a node output from the immediate lower i-th level, can be obtained using the chain rule as follows:

$$\frac{\partial E_n}{\partial w_{ji}} = \frac{\partial E_n}{\partial p_j} \frac{\partial p_j}{\partial w_{ji}} \quad (6.8)$$

where w_{ji} is the weight on the link from node i up to higher parent node j in the tree. The difficulty to obtain this derivative comes from the problem to determine the first multiplier $\partial E_n/\partial p_j$.

The multiplier $\partial E_n / \partial p_j$ accounts for the sensitivity of the error to the output of the node. Finding these error derivatives, with respect to the activation polynomials in the hidden nodes, is involved as it is influenced by the complex interrelationships between the polynomials. The complex dependencies arise due to their composition within the tree structures. The partial derivatives $\partial E_n / \partial p_j$ for hidden nodes in layer j depend on the errors committed by nodes k in the higher layer:

$$\frac{\partial E_n}{\partial p_j} = \frac{\partial E_n}{\partial p_k} \frac{\partial p_k}{\partial p_j} \tag{6.9}$$

where p_k is the activation polynomial in the parent node at depth k, and p_j is the activation polynomial in the child node at the lower depth j. Thus, the error sensitivities are computed backwards from the root output node to the fringe nodes, and historically it is referred to as backpropagated error and the algorithm backpropagation.

The derivative $\partial p_k / \partial p_j$ also remains a polynomial. There are two alternatives for this derivative $p'_{kj} = \partial p_k / \partial p_j$, depending on whether the j-th node is fed with argument x_1 or with argument x_2. For example, the derivatives of the polynomial $p_4(\mathbf{x}) = w_0 + w_1 x_1 + w_2 x_1 x_2 + w_3 x_1^2$ are: $p'_{41} = w_1 + w_2 x_2 + 2 w_3 x_1$ with respect to the feeding signal x_1, and $p'_{42} = w_2 x_1$ with respect to the signal x_2. Since the variable x_1 always comes from the left child, the first derivative is called the left derivative. Analogously, since the second variable x_2 comes from the right child node, the second derivative is called the right derivative.

An activation polynomial in binary tree-structured PNN could be fed in three ways: 1) directly with input variables passed from the leaves x_i, $0 \leq i \leq d$; 2) with polynomial outcomes from lower layer nodes $x_i = p_i(\mathbf{x})$, $1 \leq i \leq 16$, or 3) with an input and an activation polynomial output from a lower layer node.

Delta Training Rules. The BPA for PNN training traverses the network three times. It carries out [Nikolaev and Iba, 2003]: 1) a forward pass by bottom-up tree traversal for computing the output; 2) a backward pass by top-down tree traversal for collecting the error derivatives; and, 3) bottom-up tree traversal, again for adjustment of the weights. The network weights are modified in the direction of the optimal error decrease which is opposite to the gradient on the error surface. The amount of steepest error decrease shows what individual weight changes should be made so that the outputs, as a function of these weights, approaches the true mapping. The weight learning formula that uses derivative information from the gradient is called the generalized delta rule.

The *generalized delta rule* for adjustment of the network weights after each n-th training example $(\mathbf{x}_n, y_n)$ is defined as follows:

$$w = w + \Delta w \tag{6.10}$$

where Δw is the weight update. It is computed in the optimal direction opposite to the error gradient with the formula:

$$\Delta w = -\eta \frac{\partial E_n}{\partial w} \tag{6.11}$$

where η is the learning rate, and E_n is the instantaneous error (6.3) measured between the target y_n and the network output $P(\mathbf{x}_n)$.

The calculation of the two kinds of error derivatives $\partial E_n / \partial p$, for the output node and for the hidden network nodes, leads to different learning rules for the output and hidden nodes. While the root node directly influences the output error, the hidden node errors are filtered through the hierarchical network architecture. These two main kinds of error derivatives can be applied to the three combinations of signals that enter a node through its incoming connections: 1) feeding two inputs; 2) feeding two lower layer node outputs; and 3) feeding an input and a lower layer node output. This is why several training rules are developed below, and have to be instantiated for each of these cases.

Delta Rule for Output Node Weights. Assume that the output node is indexed by k and the hidden nodes with outgoing connections feeding them are indexed by j. Then, the partial derivative for the output node is $\partial E_n / \partial p_k = -(y_n - P(\mathbf{x}_n))$ (6.7). This amount is traditionally substituted in the expression for the error derivative with respect to the weight $\partial E_n / \partial w_{kj} = (\partial E_n / \partial p_k)(\partial p_k / \partial w_{kj})$ as a separate variable called *backprop error*, which is also referred to as local gradient:

$$\delta_k = \frac{\partial E_n}{\partial p_k} \tag{6.12}$$

After introducing this substitution for the root polynomial network node $\delta_k = y_n - P(\mathbf{x}_n)$, assuming that $P(\mathbf{x}_n) = p_k$, the *delta rule for the output node* becomes:

$$\Delta w_{kj} = -\eta \frac{\partial E_n}{\partial w_{kj}} = \eta \delta_k x'_{kj} \tag{6.13}$$

where x'_{kj} is the derivative of the k-th node activation polynomial with respect to the weight $x'_{kj} = \partial p_k / \partial w_{kj}$. Such delta rules should be specialized for all of the available weights: w_0, w_1,..., $w_{d'}$, $1 \leq d' \leq 5$.

Delta Rule for Hidden Node Weights. Suppose that the hidden nodes are indexed by j as above and the hidden nodes in the previous, lower network layer whose outgoing connections feed them are indexed by i. Since in tree-like PNN each node output feeds exactly one parent higher in the network, the backprop error $\partial E_n/\partial p_j = (\partial E_n/\partial p_k)(\partial p_k/\partial p_j)$ obtained using the chain rule is:

$$\delta_j = \frac{\partial E_n}{\partial p_j} = (-\delta_k)p'_{kj} \tag{6.14}$$

where $\delta_k = \partial E_n/\partial p_k$ is the local gradient from the parent node, and p'_{kj} denotes the backward propagated derivative from the k-th node down to the j-th node $p'_{kj} = \partial p_k/\partial p_j$.

Using the error δ_j in the derivative $\partial E_n/\partial w_{ji} = (\partial E_n/\partial p_j)(\partial p_j/\partial w_{ji})$, leads to the following the *delta rule for the hidden nodes*:

$$\Delta w_{ji} = -\eta \frac{\partial E_n}{\partial w_{ji}} = \eta \delta_j x'_{ji} \tag{6.15}$$

where $x'_{ji} = \partial p_j/\partial w_{ji}$. Again, the weight update Δw_{ji} should be instantiated for all of the available weights: w_0, w_1,..., $w_{d'}$, $1 \leq d' \leq 5$.

As an illustrative example let consider the PNN given in Figure 6.1. The activation polynomials allocated in the network nodes are:

$$p_3 = w_{30} + w_{31}p_5 + w_{32}p_5x_4 \tag{6.16}$$

$$p_5 = w_{50} + w_{51}x_3 + w_{52}p_4^2 \tag{6.17}$$

$$p_4 = w_{40} + w_{41}x_1 + w_{42}x_1x_2 + w_{43}x_1^2 \tag{6.18}$$

The output node derivatives with respect to weights w_{31} and w_{32} are easy to determine as they are directly proportional to the output error $(y_n - P(\mathbf{x}_n))$ and the particular signal feeding the corresponding polynomial term:

$$\frac{\partial E_n}{\partial w_{31}} = -(y_n - P(\mathbf{x}_n))p_5 \tag{6.19}$$

$$\frac{\partial E_n}{\partial w_{32}} = -(y_n - P(\mathbf{x}_n))p_5x_4 \tag{6.20}$$

where $P(\mathbf{x}_n) = p_3$, p_5 is the output from the left root child produced with input vector $\mathbf{x}_n$, and x_4 is the fourth element of the same input vector $\mathbf{x}_n$. Note that here the feeding signal is not directly the polynomial output from the child node because it is transformed into a monomial term. For example, when dealing with weight w_{32}, the parent node with activation polynomial p_3 is not fed exactly by the output of the child polynomial p_5, but with the product p_5x_4. This is because the signals coming from the lower layers are expanded to enter the corresponding terms of the bivariate activation polynomials.

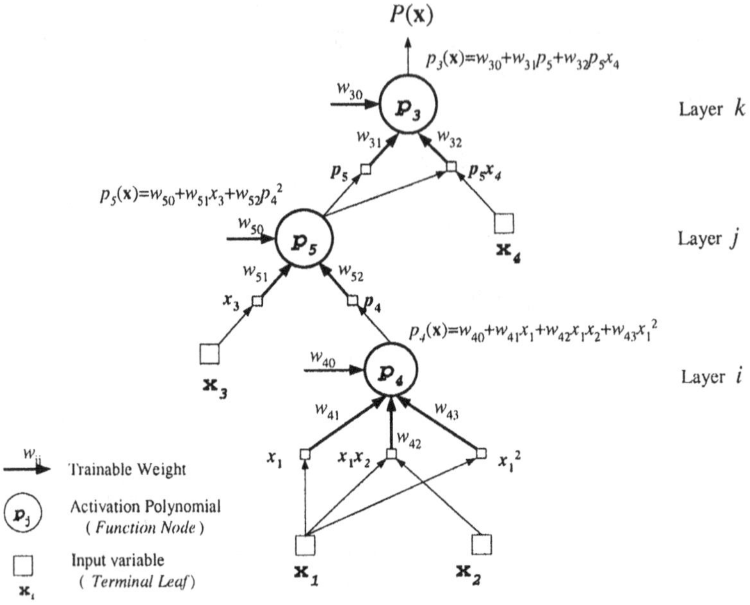

Figure 6.1. A detailed view of a tree-structured Polynomial Neural Network with explicitly shown expanded connections and their weights.

The derivatives for the hidden left child node (node 5 at layer j in Figure 6.1) with respect to its weights are:

$$\frac{\partial E_n}{\partial w_{51}} = -(y_n - P(\mathbf{x}_n))\frac{\partial p_3}{\partial p_5}\frac{\partial p_5}{\partial w_{51}} = -e_n(w_{31} + w_{32}x_4)x_3 \quad (6.21)$$

$$\frac{\partial E_n}{\partial w_{52}} = -(y_n - P(\mathbf{x}_n))\frac{\partial p_3}{\partial p_5}\frac{\partial p_5}{\partial w_{52}} = -e_n(w_{31} + w_{32}x_4)p_4^2 \quad (6.22)$$

where p_4 is the output from the right child, and x_3 and x_4 are the third and fourth elements of the input vector $\mathbf{x}_n$.

The derivatives for the hidden right child node 4 at layer i of node 5 with respect to its weights are computed using the chain rule:

$$\frac{\partial E_n}{\partial w_{41}} = \frac{\partial E_n}{\partial p_5}\frac{\partial p_5}{\partial p_4}\frac{\partial p_4}{\partial w_{41}} = \frac{\partial E_n}{\partial p_5}(2w_{52}p_4)x_1 \quad (6.23)$$

$$\frac{\partial E_n}{\partial w_{42}} = \frac{\partial E_n}{\partial p_5}\frac{\partial p_5}{\partial p_4}\frac{\partial p_4}{\partial w_{42}} = \frac{\partial E_n}{\partial p_5}(2w_{52}p_4)x_1x_2 \quad (6.24)$$

$$\frac{\partial E_n}{\partial w_{43}} = \frac{\partial E_n}{\partial p_5}\frac{\partial p_5}{\partial p_4}\frac{\partial p_4}{\partial w_{43}} = \frac{\partial E_n}{\partial p_5}(2w_{52}p_4)x_1^2 \quad (6.25)$$

where the chain derivative of the output error with respect to the parent node 5 is $\partial E_n/\partial p_5 = -(y_n - P(\mathbf{x}_n))(w_{31} + w_{32}x_4)$.

6.2.3 Batch Backpropagation

BPA can be implemented for training PNN in batch mode or in incremental mode. The *batch version* of BPA suggests that we update the weights after presenting all examples to the network; that is, after computing the exact gradient of the error function. It aims at minimizing the total error over all training examples. The weights in the exact gradient are produced by summation of the derivatives of the instantaneous errors with respect to the particular weight:

$$\Delta w = \Delta w + \Delta w_n \tag{6.26}$$

where Δw_n is the computed update from the n-th example.

Table 6.1. Batch BPA for training nonlinear tree-like PNN.

Backpropagation Algorithm for PNN (batch version)

step	*Algorithmic sequence*
1. Initialization	Data $\mathcal{D} = \{(\mathbf{x}_n, y_n)\}_{n=1}^{N}$ and learning rate $\eta = 0.1$. Initial deltas: $\Delta w_{kj} = \Delta w_{ji} = 0$.
2. Network Weight Training	Repeat for each epoch a) For each training example $(\mathbf{x}_n, y_n)$, $1 \leq n \leq N$, do i) Perform a forward pass with input $\mathbf{x}_n$ - calculate the output $P(\mathbf{x}_n)$. ii) Perform a backward pass - compute the output node error and delta $\delta_k = y_n - P(\mathbf{x}_n)$ $\Delta w_{n,kj} = \eta \delta_k x'_{kj}$ where $x'_{kj} = \partial p_k / \partial w_{kj}$. - compute the hidden node errors and deltas $\delta_j = (-\delta_k) p'_{kj}$ where $p'_{kj} = \partial p_k / \partial p_j$ $\Delta w_{n,ji} = \eta \delta_j x'_{ji}$ where $x'_{ji} = \partial p_j / \partial w_{ji}$. iii) Accumulate the weight changes $\Delta w_{kj} = \Delta w_{kj} + \Delta w_{n,kj}$ $\Delta w_{ji} = \Delta w_{ji} + \Delta w_{n,ji}$ b) Update the weights $w = w + \Delta\, w$. Until termination condition is satisfied.

The batch BPA works in the following way: the examples are passed through the network, the output error is calculated, this error is backpropagated, the weight changes are accumulated, and after exhausting the whole batch of given examples the weights are modified. The weights are adjusted only at the end of the training epoch with all examples. This batch training procedure is repeated until reaching satisfactory low error. A summary of this batch BPA is given in Table 6.1.

6.2.4 Incremental Backpropagation

The *incremental version* of the BPA updates the weights iteratively after each example. After presentation of a training vector and computing the weight changes, they are introduced immediately to adapt the weights, without accumulating all changes until the end of the epoch. This style of training is sometimes called stochastic training.

The stochastic training is expected to provide the ability to escape from entrapment at poor local minima on the error surface. This can happen as the shape of the error landscape changes with each example; actually, it is an instance of the complete error landscape which arises from the concrete training example. Because of this, the instantaneous error may become of such magnitude that it allows the algorithm to jump out of the current landscape basin. Theoretically however, it is impossible to precisely investigate this behavior. This is why the performance of the incremental BPA is arduous to analyze. A summary of the incremental BPA is given in Table 6.2.

Table 6.2. Incremental BPA for training nonlinear tree-like PNN.

Backpropagation Algorithm for PNN (incremental version)

step	*Algorithmic sequence*
1. Initialization	Data $\mathcal{D} = \{(\mathbf{x}_n, y_n)\}_{n=1}^{N}$ and learning rate $\eta = 0.1$.
	Initial deltas: $\Delta w_{kj} = \Delta w_{ji} = 0$.
2. Network	Repeat for each epoch
Weight Training	a) For each training example $(\mathbf{x}_n, y_n)$, $1 \leq n \leq N$, do
	i) Perform a forward pass with input $\mathbf{x}_n$
	- calculate the output $P(\mathbf{x}_n)$.
	ii) Perform a backward pass
	- compute the output node error and delta
	$\delta_k = y_n - P(\mathbf{x}_n)$
	$\Delta w_{kj} = \eta\delta_k x'_{kj}$ where $x'_{kj} = \partial p_k / \partial w_{kj}$.
	- compute the hidden node errors and deltas
	$\delta_j = (-\delta_k) p'_{kj}$ where $p'_{kj} = \partial p_k / \partial p_j$
	$\Delta w_{ji} = \eta\delta_j x'_{ji}$ where $x'_{ji} = \partial p_j / w_{ji}$.
	iii) Update the network weights
	$w_{kj} = w_{kj} + \Delta w_{kj}$
	$w_{ji} = w_{ji} + \Delta w_{ji}$.
	Until termination condition is satisfied.

Incremental vs. Batch Learning. The batch BPA is approximated by the incremental version. The latter computes an approximation of the gradient on the error surface, while the former computes the true complete gradient. This means that the batch algorithm more accurately follows the optimal direction of error decrease, and it could be expected to attain better results. An advantage of the batch BPA is that it is less sensitive to noise and outliers in the data. The disadvantage of the batch BPA is that it seems to oversmooth the weight correlations when accumulating the weight changes, which often drives the algorithm to the closest minima only. Although one cannot decide whether the closest minima will be the best, it often occurs that the batch BPA becomes prematurely trapped at suboptimal results.

In practice, the incremental version of the BPA frequently performs much better than the batch version in the sense of learning better weight values. This is mainly attributed to its stochastic character because when it tunes the weights after each example, the algorithm can avoid premature convergence and can achieve more sustained weight search. From a theoretical point of view, however, there is no guarantee that the incremental BPA will reach more accurate solutions than the batch BPA. From a computational point of view, the incremental version takes more time while the batch version consumes more memory. Both versions of the BPA for training high-order PNN exhibit time complexity $\mathcal{O}(\mathcal{F}^2)$ where $\mathcal{F}$ is the number of the hidden network nodes.

6.2.5 Control of the Learning Step

The convergence of the backpropagation algorithms can be improved by proper control of the learning steps that they take; that is, by tuning the delta rule for careful weight adjustment. When the BPA is applied to PNN, the learning step control needs special attention because the activation polynomials are fed by inputs with considerably different magnitudes which makes the operation of the training algorithm difficult to navigate. Another important factor that affects the BPA when applied to PNN is that the activation polynomials are often unbounded; their outputs are not filtered through the sigmoid function, rather they are used as they are. This may cause large output errors that are problematic to handle. The activation polynomials can be deliberately bounded but this could be detrimental to the overall accuracy.

There are two groups of approaches to controlling the weight learning step: 1) approaches that use additional factors in the delta rule for enforcing progressive search, such as adding a momentum term [Rumelhart et al., 1986]; and 2) approaches for tuning of the learning rate in the delta rule. The most typical approaches from the second group are the bold driver method [Battiti, 1989], search then converge [Darken and Moody, 1990], and the delta-bar-delta method [Jacobs, 1988].

Learning with Momentum. Research into neural network training has found that a momentum term is necessary for maintaining the operational stability of the BPA. The problem is that during gradient descent search the weight vector often oscillates. For example, when proceeding on a slow, narrow valley on the error surface, the BPA oscillates and does not make fast, downhill steps. The convergence of the BPA can be accelerated by adding a momentum term to the weight update rule. This strategy allows us to move the weight vector across even flat regions on the error landscape, and so helps to avoid unnecessary oscillations. The delta training rule using *momentum* proportional to the previous learning step is:

$$w_{n+1} = w_n + \Delta w_n + \alpha \Delta w_{n-1} \tag{6.27}$$

where w_n is the weight, Δw_n is the weight update computed according to the delta rule, Δw_{n-1} is the previous weight update, and α is the momentum rate. The momentum α is usually a small constant $0 < \alpha \leq 1$, and it can be used in both incremental and batch versions.

Learning Rate Tuning. Distinct methods for learning rate tuning have been proposed for the BPA. Common to these methods is the idea of changing the learning rate parameter at each step; in the incremental BPA we modify the learning rate after each training example, and in the batch BPA we modify the learning rate at the end of each training epoch. Tuning of the learning rate is reasonable as the error landscape has specific characteristics in the various regions, hence adapting the learning rate even by a constant factor, but depending on the underlying error surface, can be beneficial for stabilizing the performance. After developing such learning rate adaptation schemes, they can be applied in different ways: 1) traditionally using a global learning rate for all weights in the network; 2) using different learning rates for each hidden network node; 3) using a different local learning rate for each particular weight; and 4) using a different learning rate for each layer.

Learning Rate Calibration. The convergence properties of the learning algorithm have been studied from different perspectives. It is well-known that in order to guarantee convergence of the weight update rule in the mean, the learning rate η_n should be bounded by the following inequality [Ham and Kostanic, 2000]:

$$0 < \eta_n < \frac{2}{trace(\mathbf{H})} \tag{6.28}$$

where $\mathbf{H}$ is the Hessian matrix (6.39,6.40). Learning rates selected from this interval help to attain stable learning performance.

Bold Driver Method. This method prescribes to modify the learning rate by a constant factor in order to sustain the search if it progresses or to hinder it if it does not. The bold driver accelerates the weight convergence in the same direction if the last weight adjustment has reduced the error, and decelerates the search if the recent weight adjustment has failed to decrease the error. The *bold driver method* [Battiti, 1989] offers the following formula for updating the learning rate:

$$\eta_{n+1} = \begin{cases} \gamma^{+}\eta_n & \text{if } E_n < E_{n-1} \\ \gamma^{-}\eta_n & \text{otherwise} \end{cases} \tag{6.29}$$

where γ^{+} is an accelerating constant, γ^{-} is a decelerating constant, and η_{n+1} is the learning parameter to be used in the next iteration of the training algorithm. The accelerating constant γ^{+} is typically selected greater than one $\gamma^{+} > 1$. A formula that can help to determine its value is: $\gamma^{+} = (1 + (1 - \gamma^{-})c)$, where c is a constant $c = 10$. The decelerating constant is taken less than one $0 < \gamma^{-} < 1$.

Search Then Converge. This method suggests to tune the learning rate by a factor that varies during the search process: $\eta_{n+1} = c/\vartheta$, where c is a constant, and the parameter ϑ is defined separately for each iteration. The basic idea is to implement such a learning schedule that allows initially large jumps in the weight space, and after some training period, enforces more precise, slower focusing toward near minima. Thus, when the backprop training proceeds the search matures and replaces the phase of exploring the error landscape with a phase of exploiting the neighborhood areas. The formula for such a *search then converge* [Darken and Moody, 1990] schedule is:

$$\eta_{n+1} = \frac{\eta_0}{1 + n/\tau} \tag{6.30}$$

where η_0 is a preselected constant, n is the iteration number, and τ is the intended maximal number of training epochs.

A sophisticated version for implementing a *search then converge* [Darken and Moody, 1990] schedule is given by the rational function:

$$\eta_{n+1} = \eta_0 \frac{1 + (c/\eta_0)(n/\tau)}{1 + (c/\eta_0)(n/\tau) + \tau(n^2/\tau^2)} \tag{6.31}$$

where η_0 and c are constants, n is the iteration number, and τ is the epoch number. All parameters have to be selected heuristically.

Delta-Bar-Delta Method. This method relies on the idea that if the error derivative keeps unchanged during several consecutive iterations there is a steady error decrease and, hence, the learning step may be increased. Otherwise, if the sign of the error derivative changes, this indicates that the learning process oscillates and the learning step has to be decreased. The *delta-bar-delta method* [Jacobs, 1988] sets individual learning parameters for each weight according to the formula:

$$\Delta\eta_{i,n+1} = \begin{cases} \gamma^{+}\eta_{i,n} & \text{if } g_{i,n}g_{i,n-1} > 0 \\ \gamma^{-}\eta_{i,n} & \text{otherwise} \end{cases} \tag{6.32}$$

where $\eta_{i,n+1}$ denotes the learning rate for the i-th weight at the n-th iteration, $g_{i,n} = \partial E_n/\partial w_i$ is an averaged estimate of the error derivative with respect to the particular i-th weight, and γ^+ and γ^- are growth and shrinking parameters taken from the intervals $0 < \gamma^- < 1 < \gamma^+$. The averaged error derivative is computed using the equation:

$$g_{i,n} = (1-\kappa)\partial E_n/\partial w_i + \kappa\partial E_{n-1}/\partial w_i \tag{6.33}$$

where κ is a small positive constant $0 < \kappa < 1$, E_n is the instantaneous error, and w_i is the weight.

6.2.6 Regularized Delta Rule

The weight training performed using BPA can be controlled by regularization for producing smoother function mappings. When regularization is applied in backpropagation training, it also helps to stabilize the behavior of the learning algorithm. This improvement of the reliability in the training procedure is an effect of the incorporation of a penalty term in the cost function that accounts for the model complexity represented by the magnitudes of the network weights.

Viewed in context of the bias/variance dilemma, the idea behind regularization is to diminish the bias contribution to the error due to the average level of fitting by means of adding another complexity term. This correcting complexity penalty controls the smoothing during training because the training algorithm is derived by differentiation of the augmented cost function. This additional term added to the error is usually a function of the weight magnitudes, and it is also known in the connectionist research as weight decay. After augmenting the cost function to $E = 0.5\left(\sum_{n=1}^{N}(y_n - P(\mathbf{x}_n, \mathbf{w}))^2 + \lambda\sum_{i=1}^{m} w_i^2\right)$, the following regularized delta rule for weight training is obtained:

$$w = (1-\eta\lambda)w + \Delta w \tag{6.34}$$

where λ is the regularization parameter, and η is the learning rate.

Neural network research has proposed many regularization functions [Haykin, 1999], each having own their advantages and disadvantages. The *weight decay* formula $\sum_j w_j^2$ [Hertz et al., 1991] may disproportionately favor many small weights because the curvature of this formula rapidly increases and does not enable us to make a precise difference between weights in the interval $-1.0 \leq w \leq 1.0$. The *weight elimination* formula $\sum_j (w_j^2/(1+w_j^2))$ [Weigend et al., 1992] discourages too many small weights and overcomes, to a certain extent, this problem. However, it is still steep in the interval $-1.0 \leq w \leq 1.0$. In addition to this, it arbitrarily favors significant weights $w \leq -2.0$ and $w \geq 2.0$.

6.3 Second-Order Backpropagation

The first-order BP techniques for neural network training explore the error surface inefficiently, since they change the weights in a modest way. A common drawback of the first-order BP techniques is their slow convergence. The weight vector often tends to oscillate in the basin of attraction on the error surface going downward on its slopes, or jumps from one slope to another until reaching the minimum. Gradient descent search strongly depends on the characteristics of the error landscape, which is extremely large and cannot be entirely traversed.

The problem is that it is impossible to determine the best configuration of network weights in an admissible time. It has been studied theoretically that the problem of learning the weights of a fixed neural network that performs exactly to the desired mapping is an NP-complete problem [Judd, 1990]. One possibility of avoiding such difficulties to a great degree is to start training not with arbitrary initial weights, but the weights estimated by least-squares fitting as suggested in the first IGP phase of learning PNN. Another possibility is to consider the discussed strategies for learning rate control, but they require us to heuristically introduce a lot of parameters. The tuning of the learning step may help to avoid entrapment into local minima on the slopes down to the minimum of the valley, but this is not guaranteed.

Ideas for implementing more powerful PNN training methods are provided by optimization theory. The optimization methods suggest that weight updates for faster convergence can be made using information about the second-order properties of the error surface. The optimal search direction can be determined using the second-order derivatives of the error function with respect to the weights vector.

The BP framework can also be extended to obtain the second-order derivatives, that is the Hessian matrix. The possibility of calculating the Hessian [Bishop, 1995, Buntine and Weigend, 1991a, Pearlmutter, 1994] in PNN enhances their potential because: 1) it helps to develop contemporary second-order BP techniques for efficient PNN training [Bishop, 1995, Shepherd, 1997]; 2) it allows us to implement second-order network pruning strategies [LeCun et al., 1990, Hassibi and Stork, 1993]; 3) it enables us to precisely compute the network complexity necessary for design of fitness functions; and 4) it provides a tool for adjusting various algorithm parameters. Several second-order techniques for BP are presented below. The corresponding delta rules of the kind: $\mathbf{w} = \mathbf{w} + \eta \Delta \mathbf{w}$ tell us how to make adjustments of the weights vector $\mathbf{w}$.

6.3.1 Second-Order Error Derivatives

The Hessian Matrix. The idea for using the Hessian matrix of second derivatives of the error with respect to the weights, comes from the Taylor series expansion of the error function in the vicinity of the current weight vector. The local neighborhood of the weight vector consists of all vectors within some predefined distance. If we assume that the current weight vector is $\mathbf{w}_0$, then the weight vector at the next step is: $\mathbf{w} = \mathbf{w}_0 + \Delta\mathbf{w}$, which is the weight vector modified by the learning operator. The Taylor series approximation of the error in the local neighborhood of this weight vector is:

$$E(\mathbf{w}_0 + \Delta\mathbf{w}) = E(\mathbf{w}_0) + \Delta\mathbf{w}^T\mathbf{g} + \frac{1}{2}\Delta\mathbf{w}^T\mathbf{H}\Delta\mathbf{w} + \mathcal{O}\left(||\Delta\mathbf{w}||^3\right) \quad (6.35)$$

where $\nabla E(\mathbf{w}_0)$ denotes the gradient at point $\mathbf{w}_0$ defined as follows:

$$\mathbf{g} \equiv \nabla E = \left.\frac{\partial E(\mathbf{w})}{\partial \mathbf{w}}\right|_{\mathbf{w}=\mathbf{w}_0} \quad (6.36)$$

$$\mathbf{g} \equiv \nabla E = \left[\frac{\partial E(\mathbf{w})}{\partial w_0}, \frac{\partial E(\mathbf{w})}{\partial w_1}, \ldots, \frac{\partial E(\mathbf{w})}{\partial w_W}\right]^T \quad (6.37)$$

where W is the number of the network weights in the model.

Let us assume the cost function: $E = 0.5\sum_{n=1}^{N}(y_n - P(\mathbf{x}_n, \mathbf{w}))^2$. Then the gradient vector entries can be computed as follows:

$$\frac{\partial E(\mathbf{w})}{\partial w} = -\sum_{n=1}^{N}(y_n - P(\mathbf{x}_n, \mathbf{w}))\frac{\partial P(\mathbf{x}_n, \mathbf{w})}{\partial w} \quad (6.38)$$

where $P(\mathbf{x}_n, \mathbf{w})$ is the PNN output computed with weights vector $\mathbf{w}$ when applied to input vector $\mathbf{x}_n$.

The Hessian matrix with the second-order error derivatives with respect to the weights is:

$$\mathbf{H} \equiv \nabla^2 E = \left.\frac{\partial^2 E(\mathbf{w})}{\partial \mathbf{w}^2}\right|_{\mathbf{w}=\mathbf{w}_0} \quad \text{with entries } H_{ij} \equiv [\mathbf{H}]_{ij} = \frac{\partial^2 E(\mathbf{w})}{\partial w_i \partial w_j} \quad (6.39)$$

where H_{ij}, specifies its element at row i and column j.

The *full Hessian matrix* is defined explicitly as follows:

$$\mathbf{H} = \begin{bmatrix} \frac{\partial^2 E(\mathbf{w})}{\partial w_1^2} & \frac{\partial^2 E(\mathbf{w})}{\partial w_1 \partial w_2} & \cdots & \frac{\partial^2 E(\mathbf{w})}{\partial w_1 \partial w_W} \\ \frac{\partial^2 E(\mathbf{w})}{\partial w_2 \partial w_1} & \frac{\partial^2 E(\mathbf{w})}{\partial w_2 \partial w_2} & \cdots & \frac{\partial^2 E(\mathbf{w})}{\partial w_2 \partial w_W} \\ \vdots & \vdots & & \vdots \\ \frac{\partial^2 E(\mathbf{w})}{\partial w_W \partial w_1} & \frac{\partial^2 E(\mathbf{w})}{\partial w_W \partial w_1} & \cdots & \frac{\partial^2 E(\mathbf{w})}{\partial w_W \partial w_W} \end{bmatrix} \tag{6.40}$$

where its size $W \times W$ is determined by the number of the weights W.

Assuming an error: $E = 0.5 \sum_{n=1}^{N} (y_n - P(\mathbf{x}_n, \mathbf{w}))^2 = 0.5 \sum_{n=1}^{N} {e_n}^2$, the Hessian entries are:

$$[\mathbf{H}]_{ij} = \sum_{n=1}^{N} \left\{ \left(\frac{\partial P(\mathbf{x}_n, \mathbf{w})}{\partial w_i} \right) \left(\frac{\partial P(\mathbf{x}_n, \mathbf{w})}{\partial w_j} \right)^T - e_n \left(\frac{\partial^2 P(\mathbf{x}_n, \mathbf{w})}{\partial w_i \partial w_j} \right) \right\} \tag{6.41}$$

where $P(\mathbf{x}_n, \mathbf{w})$ is the polynomial network output.

The gradient vector and the Hessian matrix can be expressed by means of common subelements for developing concise formulae for second-order training algorithms. The common subelements are the network output derivatives with respect to the weights:

$$J_i = \frac{\partial P(\mathbf{x}_n, \mathbf{w})}{\partial w_i} \tag{6.42}$$

where $P(\mathbf{x}_n, \mathbf{w})$ is the network output from input $\mathbf{x}_n$. These subelements J_i are to be arranged in the so-called *Jacobian matrix* defined as follows:

$$\mathbf{J} = \begin{bmatrix} \frac{\partial^2 P(\mathbf{x}_1, \mathbf{w})}{\partial w_1} & \frac{\partial^2 P(\mathbf{x}_1, \mathbf{w})}{\partial w_2} & \cdots & \frac{\partial^2 P(\mathbf{x}_1, \mathbf{w})}{\partial w_W} \\ \frac{\partial^2 P(\mathbf{x}_2, \mathbf{w})}{\partial w_1} & \frac{\partial^2 P(\mathbf{x}_2, \mathbf{w})}{\partial w_2} & \cdots & \frac{\partial^2 P(\mathbf{x}_2, \mathbf{w})}{\partial w_W} \\ \vdots & \vdots & & \vdots \\ \frac{\partial^2 P(\mathbf{x}_N, \mathbf{w})}{\partial w_1} & \frac{\partial^2 P(\mathbf{x}_N, \mathbf{w})}{\partial w_2} & \cdots & \frac{\partial^2 P(\mathbf{x}_N, \mathbf{w})}{\partial w_W} \end{bmatrix} \tag{6.43}$$

where N is the number of the data, and W is the number of the weights.

The gradient can be expressed with the Jacobian in the following way:

$$\mathbf{g} = -\mathbf{J}^T \mathbf{e} \tag{6.44}$$

where $\mathbf{e} = [e_0, e_1, ..., e_N]$ (6.2) is the error vector.

The Hessian matrix can be formulated using the Jacobian as follows:

$$\mathbf{H} = \frac{1}{N} (\mathbf{J}^T \mathbf{J} - \mathbf{R}) \tag{6.45}$$

where the matrix $\mathbf{R}$ is made of elements $R = e_n (\partial^2 P(\mathbf{x}_n, \mathbf{w}) / \partial w_i \partial w_j)$.

$\mathcal{R}$-propagation Algorithm for PNN. The entries of the Hessian for feed-forward networks have been precisely specified [Bishop, 1995]. This specification, however, is difficult to implement with a computational algorithm despite the attempts of several authors who explained it in detail [Buntine and Weigend, 1991a]. A more efficient algorithm for evaluation of the complete Hessian is available that prescribes calculation of the second order error derivatives by making forward passes from the inputs to the tree root, and backward passes from the root node down to the fringe nodes. It is called $\mathcal{R}$-propagation [Pearlmutter, 1994], as its steps can be performed using the framework of the classical BPA. The advantage of $\mathcal{R}$-propagation is that it allows us to evaluate the second-order error derivatives along with the first-order error derivatives in linear time with respect to the number of network weights.

The *$\mathcal{R}$-propagation algorithm* [Pearlmutter, 1994] is specialized here for PNN. This algorithm reveals that the full Hessian matrix can be obtained by multiplying it with a binary vector of size equal to the number of weights. When successively setting the vector components to one, this algorithm generates the Hessian matrix column by column. The accumulation of all examples requires us to perform N forward and N backward passes, where N is the number of training examples. The $\mathcal{R}$-propagation algorithm adapted for PNN below makes successive forward and backward tree network traversals for computing the error derivatives, updates the Hessian matrix after each next example, and repeats such cycles W times, once for each column of the Hessian.

The basic idea is to produce the exact Hessian matrix as a result of the multiplication:

$$\mathbf{v}^T\mathbf{H} = \mathbf{v}^T\nabla^2 E = \mathbf{v}^T\nabla(\nabla E) \tag{6.46}$$

where $\mathbf{v}$ is a binary vector, and ∇ is the gradient operator. The $\mathcal{R}\{\cdot\}$ operator is defined as follows:

$$\mathcal{R} = \mathbf{v}^T\nabla \tag{6.47}$$

which is estimated by doing $\mathcal{R}$-propagation.

Let us assume again that the root node indexed by k produces output p_k using linear and nonlinear terms $p_k = \sum_j w_{kj}p_j$, where w_{kj} is a weight on connection from node with activation polynomial p_j toward node with p_k. Its terms are fed by its left and right child polynomial outputs $p_j = \sum_i w_{ji}p_i$ when the activation polynomial is fed by outputs from nodes below, or $p_j = \sum_i w_{ji}x_i$ when only input variables x_i enter the activation polynomial through leaves. These quantities are computed during the $\mathcal{R}$-forward propagation, along with the estimation of the $\mathcal{R}$-

operator in the following sequence:

$$\mathcal{R}\{p_j\} = \sum_i v_{ji} x_i \tag{6.48}$$

$$\mathcal{R}\{p_j\} = \sum_i w_{ji} \mathcal{R}\{p_i\} + \sum_i v_{ji} p_i \tag{6.49}$$

$$\mathcal{R}\{p_k\} = \sum_j w_{kj} \mathcal{R}\{p_j\} + \sum_j v_{kj} p_j \tag{6.50}$$

where $\mathcal{R}\{p_k\}$ is the operator applied at the root, and $\mathcal{R}\{p_j\}$ is the operator applied at hidden nodes separately for cases with terms entered directly by node outputs or by inputs.

The error derivatives are computed with the BPA. The output root network node and the hidden nodes are manipulated separately. At the root output node the deltas are computed: $\delta_k = y_n - P(\mathbf{x}_n)$. At the hidden functional nodes deltas are also computed but in a different way: $\delta_j = (-\delta_k) p'_{kj}$ where $p'_{kj} = \partial p_k / \partial p_j$. These deltas are used by the $\mathcal{R}$-backward propagation pass to estimate the $\mathcal{R}$-operator as follows:

$$\mathcal{R}\{\delta_k\} = \mathcal{R}\{p_k\} \tag{6.51}$$

$$\mathcal{R}\{\delta_j\} = \mathcal{R}\{-\delta_k\} p'_{kj} + (-\delta_k) \mathcal{R}\{p'_{kj}\} \tag{6.52}$$

where $\mathcal{R}\{\delta_k\}$ and $\mathcal{R}\{\delta_j\}$ are the applications of the operator at the root node and at hidden nodes of the network respectively.

The error derivatives with respect to the weights also have to be computed: $\partial E_n / \partial w_{kj} = -\delta_k x'_{kj}$, where $x'_{kj} = \partial p_k / \partial w_{kj}$, and $\partial E_n / \partial w_{ji} = -\delta_j x'_{ji}$, where $x'_{ji} = \partial p_j / \partial w_{ji}$. The $\mathcal{R}$-operator is instantiated as follows:

$$\mathcal{R}\left\{\frac{\partial E_n}{\partial w_{kj}}\right\} = -\mathcal{R}\{\delta_k\} x'_{kj} - \delta_k \mathcal{R}\{x'_{kj}\} \tag{6.53}$$

$$\mathcal{R}\left\{\frac{\partial E_n}{\partial w_{ji}}\right\} = -\mathcal{R}\{\delta_j\} x'_{ji} - \delta_j \mathcal{R}\{x'_{ji}\} \tag{6.54}$$

where the operators $\mathcal{R}\{x'_{kj}\}$ and $\mathcal{R}\{x'_{ji}\}$ are computed analogously, bearing in mind that their arguments x'_{kj} and x'_{ji} are monomial terms.

Several theoretical and practical clarifications concerning the computation of the full Hessian matrix (6.39,6.40) should be made: 1) the exact evaluation of the Hessian matrix according to the sophisticated algorithm of Bishop [Bishop, 1995] has space complexity $\mathcal{O}(W^2)$ and time complexity $\mathcal{O}(W^2)$; 2) the $\mathcal{R}$-propagation algorithm of Pearlmutter [Pearlmutter, 1994] is much faster and it is often preferred in practical implementation because it has only linear cost $\mathcal{O}(W)$; 3) when the

Hessian is inverted its cost increases to $\mathcal{O}(W^3)$; 4) diagonal approximations of the Hessian can be made with low, linear cost $\mathcal{O}$ (W) in several ways: using gradients $\partial^2 E(\mathbf{w})/(\partial w_i \partial w_j) = (\partial E(\mathbf{w})/\partial w_i)(\partial E(\mathbf{w})/\partial w_j)$; using finite differences according to Shepherd [Shepherd, 1997]; and using central differences after Nabney [Nabney, 2002].

Practical tasks however often lead to Hessian matrices which are not simply diagonal so the usefulness of the diagonal approximations may be limited [Bishop, 1995].

The algorithm for performing $\mathcal{R}$-propagation on polynomial network models is given in Table 6.3. Note that this implementation incorporates the steps of the backpropagation algorithm that evaluate the error gradients with respect to the weights, so there is no need for invocation of its components in several stages.

Table 6.3. Summary of the $\mathcal{R}$-propagation algorithm for tree-like PNN.

$\mathcal{R}$-propagation Algorithm for PNN

step	*Algorithmic sequence*
1. Initialization	Data $\mathcal{D} = \{(\mathbf{x}_n, y_n)\}_{n=1}^N$, and $\mathbf{v} = (0, 0, ..., 0)$ of size $1 \times W$.
2. Network Weight Training	For each weight c, $1 \le c \le W$ a) Set the vector entry $\mathbf{v}_c = 1.0$ b) Compute the product $\mathbf{v}^T\mathbf{H}$ in one epoch: For each example $(\mathbf{x}_n, y_n)$, $1 \le n \le N$, do i) Perform a forward pass and estimate $p_j = \sum_i w_{ji}x_i$, or $p_j = \sum_i w_{ji}p_i$ $\mathcal{R}\{p_j\} = \sum_i w_{ji}\mathcal{R}\{p_i\} + \sum_i v_{ji}p_i$ $p_k = \sum_j w_{kj}p_j$ $\mathcal{R}\{p_k\} = \sum_i w_{kj}\mathcal{R}\{p_j\} + \sum_i v_{kj}p_j$. ii) Perform a backward pass - calculate the output delta and derivatives $\delta_k = y_n - P(\mathbf{x}_n)$ $p'_{kj} = \partial p_k/\partial p_j$, and $x'_{kj} = \partial p_k/\partial w_{kj}$. - apply the R-operator $\mathcal{R}\{\delta_k\} = \mathcal{R}\{p_k\}$ $\mathcal{R}\{\partial E_n/\partial w_{kj}\} = \mathcal{R}\{-\delta_k\}x'_{kj} + (-\delta_k)\mathcal{R}\{x'_{kj}\}$. - calculate the hidden deltas and derivatives $\delta_j = (-\delta_k)p'_{kj}$, and $x'_{ji} = \partial p_j/\partial w_{ji}$. - apply the R-operator $\mathcal{R}\{\delta_j\} = \sum_k \mathcal{R}\{-\delta_k\}p'_{kj} + \sum_k(-\delta_k)\mathcal{R}\{p'_{kj}\}$ $\mathcal{R}\{\partial E_n/\partial w_{ji}\} = \mathcal{R}\{-\delta_j\}x'_{ji} + (-\delta_j)\mathcal{R}\{x'_{ji}\}$.
3. Evaluate the Hessian	Extract the Hessian from the dot product $\mathbf{v}^T\mathbf{H}$.

6.3.2 Newton's Method

The second-order Newton's method [Bishop, 1995, Haykin, 1999, Shepherd, 1997] may be followed to develop an accelerated PNN weight training algorithm. It suggests to use second-order error derivatives when computing the weight change direction for making the next learning step, and reaches a solution relatively quickly if the starting point is well located. The weight learning algorithm for implementing the Netwon's method can be derived starting from the Taylor's approximation of the error function. The quadratic approximation of the error using Taylor's expansion (6.35) is:

$$\nabla E(\mathbf{w}_0 + \Delta \mathbf{w}) = \nabla E(\mathbf{w}_0) + \mathbf{H}\Delta \mathbf{w} \tag{6.55}$$

where $\mathbf{w}_0 + \Delta \mathbf{w}$ is the weight vector after making a learning step $\Delta \mathbf{w}$, and $\mathbf{H}$ is the Hessian matrix (6.40). The optimal learning step $\Delta \mathbf{w}$ can be determined by seeking the minimum of this function. The minimum $\nabla E(\mathbf{w}_0 + \Delta \mathbf{w}) = 0$ can be found by differentiation with respect to $\Delta \mathbf{w}$. This gives the following update direction or *Newton's rule*:

$$\Delta \mathbf{w} = \mathbf{H}^{-1}\mathbf{g} \tag{6.56}$$

which can be taken to update the weights vector $\mathbf{w} = \mathbf{w} + \Delta \mathbf{w}$. Newton's rule includes, as a special case, the traditional first-order linear weight update rule: $\Delta \mathbf{w} = -\eta \nabla E(\mathbf{w}_0) = -\eta \mathbf{g}$.

Theoretically Newton's method should converge to the optimal weight vector. Practically, however, the convergence is not guaranteed because of the need to perform inversion of the Hessian matrix, which unfortunately is often ill-conditioned and may not be computationally invertible. Only when the Hessian is positive definite (that is, all its eigenvalues are positive), it is invertible and will lead to the minimum point. The most serious practical concern is that at each algorithmic step the exact Hessian has to be stored and computed.

What makes the Netwon's training rule attractive is the suggestion to use individual learning rates for each network weight. The individual learning rates can be obtained using second-order error derivatives. Netwon's rule actually makes the learning rate for each weight w_{ij} proportional to the corresponding diagonal element $[\mathbf{H}]_{ij}$ from the Hessian matrix. The use of individual learning rates helps to focus the weight search algorithm in the right direction at each algorithmic learning step. This is not guaranteed when only first-order gradients are used because they may not point in the right search direction, and as a consequence the learning algorithm may be unstable.

6.3.3 Pseudo-Newton Training

Due to the difficulties associated with the straightforward application of the Newton rule for training neural networks, including the PNN developed here, it has been found that a rough approximation of that rule is also useful in practice [Becker and LeCun, 1989]. The network weights can be trained using the following *pseudo-Newton rule*:

$$\Delta \mathbf{w} = -\mathbf{g}\frac{1}{\partial^2 E(\mathbf{w})/\partial \mathbf{w}^2} \tag{6.57}$$

which avoids the problematic inversion of the Hessian matrix (6.39).

In order to facilitate the learning process and to perturb the weights even when the weight vector appears to be a point on a flat region of the error surface, regularization should always be performed:

$$\Delta w_{ij} = -\frac{\partial E}{\partial w_{ij}} \bigg/ \left(\left| \frac{\partial^2 E}{\partial w_{ij}^2} \right| + \lambda \right) \tag{6.58}$$

where λ is the appropriately chosen regularization parameter, and $|\cdot|$ denotes the absolute value of its argument. The absolute value is necessary in order to properly handle negative curvatures of the error surface. Since classical statistical techniques are not directly applicable in the case of a highly nonlinear polynomial network model, the recommendation is to select the values for the regularization parameter heuristically, with respect to the inductive task addressed.

The practical pseudo-Newton rule above (6.58) can be considered for training polynomial networks by incorporating it in the algorithmic framework of the backpropagation algorithm.

6.3.4 Conjugate Gradients

The *conjugate-gradients* is a quasi second-order method that can be used for achieving faster convergence in network training [Bishop, 1995, Shepherd, 1997]. Its efficacy is in that it reaches the convergence speed of second-order methods without explicitly using second-order error derivative information; that is, without explicit reference to the Hessian matrix. The idea behind this algorithm is to compute the weight updates in direction conjugate to the previous updates, which has a stabilizing effect on the search performance and accelerates the downhill moves on the error landscape. The conjugate direction is perpendicular to the gradient of the quadratic function. The Hessian is used only for the theoretical derivation of the optimization algorithm, while its direct use is avoided assuming that it is almost constant in the neighborhood on the error surface especially when it is close to some minimum.

The weight modifications following the gradient can be written as a linear function of the previous modifications in the following way:

$$\Delta \mathbf{w}_{n+1} = -\mathbf{g}_{n+1} + \varsigma_n \Delta \mathbf{w}_n \tag{6.59}$$

where $\mathbf{g}_{n+1}$ is the gradient vector obtained at the current n-th iterative step, and ς_n is a parameter. Assuming that initially $\Delta \mathbf{w}_0 = -\mathbf{g}_0$, several rules for computing the parameter ς_n after each next training example can be applied. The two most popular rules that are often adopted in practice to identify the values of the parameter ς_n are:

- the Fletcher and Reeves rule [Fletcher, 1987]:

$$\varsigma_n = \frac{\mathbf{g}_{n+1}^T \mathbf{g}_{n+1}}{\mathbf{g}_n^T \mathbf{g}_n} \tag{6.60}$$

where $\mathbf{g}_{n+1}$ is the current gradient vector, and $\mathbf{g}_n$ is the previous gradient vector computed at the previous iteration of the training algorithm.

- the Polak-Ribiere rule [Polak, 1971]:

$$\varsigma_n = \frac{\mathbf{g}_{n+1}^T (\mathbf{g}_{n+1} - \mathbf{g}_n)}{\mathbf{g}_n^T \mathbf{g}_n} \tag{6.61}$$

where again $\mathbf{g}_{n+1}$ is the current gradient, and $\mathbf{g}_n$ is the previous gradient. The Polak-Ribiere formula (6.61) is found to be more efficient.

6.3.5 Levenberg-Marquardt Method

Newton's method (6.56) offers ideas for development of general second-order training algorithms for neural networks, and the gradient descent algorithm (6.11) may be considered its specialization. This line of reasoning has lead to the derivation of an optimization method that tunes the learning direction in the weight update rule by a single parameter. The Levenberg-Marquardt method [Levenberg, 1944, Marquardt, 1963] provides a stepwise weight modification formula that can be incorporated into a network training algorithm. The basic idea is to reduce the gradient to zero which can be envisioned as making jumps directly toward the closest minimum on the error surface.

The *Levenberg-Marquardt algorithm* may be applied for training PNN using the following weight modification formula:

$$\Delta \mathbf{w} = -(\mathbf{H}_d + \lambda \mathbf{I})^{-1} \mathbf{g} \tag{6.62}$$

where $\mathbf{H}_d$ is the diagonal approximation of the Hessian matrix with second-order error derivatives, $\mathbf{g}$ is the gradient vector (6.36,6.37), and λ is the regularization parameter.

The diagonal elements of the Hessian can also be written in terms of the Jacobian matrix entries of the derivatives of the polynomial outputs with respect to the weights:

$$[\mathbf{H}_d]_{ij} = \sum_{n=1}^{N} [\mathbf{J}]_{i,n} [\mathbf{J}]_{j,n} \tag{6.63}$$

where $[\mathbf{J}]_{i,n} = \partial P(\mathbf{x}_n)/\partial w_i$. Having this correspondence is useful for rewriting of the training algorithm in a more useful format.

The Levenberg-Marquardt training rule expressed using the elements of the Jacobian is given alternatively by the matrix equation:

$$\Delta \mathbf{w} = -(\mathbf{J}^T \mathbf{J} + \lambda \mathbf{I})^{-1} \mathbf{g} \tag{6.64}$$

where $\mathbf{g}$ and $\mathbf{J}$ can be obtained by backpropagation.

There are two important details to note in this formula (6.64): 1) in order to gain efficiency the diagonal approximation of the Hessian is adopted, which can be easily computed when backpropagating the error; and 2) in order to avoid numerical computation instabilities it includes a regularization factor. When the regularization tends to zero, $\lambda \to 0$, the Levenberg-Marquardt rule (6.64) approaches the Newton's rule (6.56). Respectively, when the regularization parameter goes to infinity, $\lambda \to \infty$, this rule (6.64) approaches the generalized delta rule (6.11) for gradient descent learning. The Levenberg-Marquardt method has an advantage over these methods as it is less sensitive to the ill-posedness of the Hessian matrix due to the use of regularization.

Use of the Levenberg-Marquardt algorithm is recommended for training neural networks and PNN in batch mode. Alternatively, it can be used in incremental mode with the formula [Bishop, 1995]:

$$\Delta \mathbf{w}_n = -\left(\frac{1}{[\mathbf{J}]_{i,n} [\mathbf{J}]_{j,n} + \lambda \mathbf{i}} \right) \mathbf{g}_n \tag{6.65}$$

where i and j are the weight vector indices.

6.4 Rational Backpropagation

Following the basic ideas of the backpropagation algorithm (Section 6.2), one can elaborate delta rules for gradient descent weight training of various polynomial network architectures. What is necessary is to reformulate the expressions for the error derivatives with respect to the concrete monomial terms in the activation function, and the derivatives of the parent node activation polynomials with respect to the incoming activation polynomial outputs from the preceding layer. This can be demonstrated by specializing the BPA for rational PNN.

The rational PNN (Section 3.5.4) computes a rational function as a fraction between the activation polynomial outputs provided by the left and right children of the root node. All other hidden network nodes below these root children in the tree-like network topology compute linear and quadratic bivariate functions (Table 2.1). The rational BPA for weight learning in such polynomial networks requires us to pay special attention to the two root children nodes while the update of the weights on connections to the remaining hidden nodes can be processed according to the generalized delta rules for standard PNN (Section 6.2).

In order to demonstrate the derivation of the rational BPA, let us assume that the output node calculates the following polynomial ratio:

$$p_k = \frac{p_n}{p_d} = \frac{w_{n0} + w_{n1}p_{i1} + w_{n2}p_{i2} + w_{n3}p_{i1}p_{i2} + w_{n4}p_{i1}^2 + w_{n5}p_{i2}^2}{1 + w_{d1}p_{i3} + w_{d2}p_{i4} + w_{d3}p_{i3}p_{i4} + w_{d4}p_{i3}^2 + +w_{d5}p_{i4}^2} \tag{6.66}$$

where p_n is the numerator and p_d is the denominator polynomial.

Since the numerator is passed by the left child node at the lower j-th layer, it is fed by node outputs and/or inputs from the previous i-th layer: $p_n = w_{n0} + w_{n1}p_{i1} + w_{n2}p_{i2} + w_{n3}p_{i1}p_{i2} + w_{n4}p_{i1}^2 + w_{n5}p_{i2}^2$. The denominator is also fed by signals coming from the previous i-th layer, but they are different, so the variables in its terms have different indices: $p_d = 1 + w_{d1}p_{i3} + w_{d2}p_{i4} + w_{d3}p_{i3}p_{i4} + w_{d4}p_{i3}^2 + w_{d5}p_{i4}^2$. The denominator in rational models always has a constant term equal to one.

This rational PNN should be equipped with two distinct training rules for the weights in the root child polynomials, while the weights from the root to its children remain fixed to one [Zhu, 2003]. The error derivative of the output with respect to the weights in the root children polynomials can be found using the chain rule. The key point in the derivation is to note that these weights participate in a fraction which has to be treated as a rational function. The weights w_n influence the output through the numerator polynomial p_n, while the weights w_d influence the output through the denominator polynomial p_d; however, they build the output together as a homogeneous function. The error derivative at the numerator polynomial in the output node is:

$$\frac{\partial E_n}{\partial w_{nj}} = \frac{\partial E_n}{\partial p_k}\frac{\partial p_k}{\partial p_n}\frac{\partial p_n}{\partial w_{nj}} = -\delta_k \frac{1}{p_d} x'_{nj} \tag{6.67}$$

where the numerator weights are indexed by nj because they participate in the j-th activation polynomial at the lower layer. This component x'_{nj} is essentially the same as the derivatives in standard PNN.

The weight modifications in the denominator polynomial are affected by the numerator polynomial. The error derivative with respect to the weights of the denominator polynomial in the output node is:

$$\frac{\partial E_n}{\partial w_{dj}} = \frac{\partial E_n}{\partial p_k} \frac{\partial p_k}{\partial p_d} \frac{\partial p_d}{\partial w_{dj}} = -\delta_k \frac{p_n}{p_d^2} x'_{dj} \tag{6.68}$$

where w_{dj} are the denominator weights in the activation polynomial allocated in the right child node at the preceding j-th layer.

The propagation of the output error down through the network depends on the rational polynomial in the root. The error backpropagation process starts by sending the effects of the output error toward the hidden node polynomials through the root fraction. A complication arises because the derivatives of a function have to be computed. In the tree-like rational PNN the backpropagation proceeds from the root children down toward the other hidden nodes; that is, the computation continues down from the i-th layer. The backpropagated error carries the following root node polynomial derivative $\partial p_k / \partial p_i$ with respect to an activation polynomial at the i-th layer:

$$p'_{ki} = \frac{\partial p_k}{\partial p_i} = \frac{1}{p_d^2} \left(\frac{\partial p_n}{\partial p_i} p_d - p_n \frac{\partial p_d}{\partial p_i} \right) \tag{6.69}$$

where p_j is an activation polynomial output from a child node.

The *rational backpropagation algorithm* for weight training and minimization of the instantaneous output error $E_n = 0.5e_n^2$ (6.3) in rational PNN includes: 1) two delta rules for the weights in the root: one rule for the numerator polynomial and one rule for the denominator polynomial, and 2) one delta rule for the hidden network nodes.

Rational Delta Rules for the Root Children Nodes. Consider the substitution $\delta_k = \partial E_n / \partial p_k$ for the error derivative at the k-th root node polynomial in the network. The two *rational delta rules for the root children node weights*, one for the numerator weights and one for the denominator weights, are:

$$\Delta w_{nj} = -\eta \frac{\partial E_n}{\partial w_{nj}} = \eta \delta_k \frac{1}{p_d} x'_{nj} \tag{6.70}$$

$$\Delta w_{dj} = -\eta \frac{\partial E_n}{\partial w_{dj}} = \eta \delta_k \frac{p_n}{p_d^2} x'_{dj} \tag{6.71}$$

where x'_{nj} denotes the activation polynomial derivative $x'_{nj} = \partial p_n / \partial w_{nj}$, and x'_{dj} is the derivative $x'_{dj} = \partial p_d / \partial w_{dj}$.

Rational Delta Rule for the Hidden Nodes. The rational BPA proceeds down the tree-like structure and computes the local gradients that are necessary to change the weights in the remaining hidden nodes. First the algorithm passes the previous backprop error $(-\delta_k)$ to produce the next one, $\delta_i = (-\delta_k)p'_{ki}$ (6.14). The estimation of the polynomial derivative $p'_{ki} = \partial p_k / \partial p_i$ (6.69) is specific due to the fractional character of the root polynomial. Using the substitution for the derivative $x'_{ji} = \partial p_j / \partial w_{ji}$ (6.15), the *rational delta rule for the hidden node weights* becomes:

$$\Delta w_{ji} = -\eta \frac{\partial E_n}{\partial w_{ji}} = \eta \delta_i x'_{ji} \tag{6.72}$$

where w_{ji} is the weight on the connection from a node in the i-th neural network layer toward a node in the j-th layer.

The convergence of this rational backpropagation is expected to be relatively fast if performed after structural model identification, during which the weights are usually learned approximately and so they are expected to be close to their optimal values. Table 6.4 presents the framework of the backpropagation algorithm for rational PNN.

Table 6.4. Incremental BPA for training high-order rational PNN.

Backpropagation for Rational PNN (incremental version)

step	*Algorithmic sequence*
1. Initialization	Data $\mathcal{D} = \{(\mathbf{x}_n, y_n)\}_{n=1}^{N}$ and learning rate $\eta = 0.1$. Initial deltas: $\Delta w_{kj} = \Delta w_{ji} = 0$.
2. Network Weight Training	Repeat for each epoch a) For each training example $(\mathbf{x}_n, y_n)$, $1 \le n \le N$, do i) Perform a forward pass using input $\mathbf{x}_n$, to produce output $P(\mathbf{x}_n)$. ii) Backward pass - compute the output node error and delta $\delta_k = y_n - P(\mathbf{x}_n)$. - compute backwards at the root children nodes left child node (numerator) $\Delta w_{nj} = \eta \delta_k (1/p_d) x'_{nj}$ where $x'_{nj} = \partial p_n / \partial w_{nj}$ right child node (denominator) $\Delta w_{dj} = \eta \delta_k (p_n / p_d^2) x'_{dj}$ where $x'_{dj} = \partial p_d / \partial w_{dj}$. - continue down toward the fringe nodes and compute $\delta_i = (-\delta_k) p'_{ki}$ where $p'_{ki} = \partial p_k / \partial p_i$ $\Delta w_{ji} = \eta \delta_i x'_{ji}$ where $x'_{ji} = \partial p_j / w_{ji}$. iii) Update the network weights $w_{kj} = w_{kj} + \Delta w_{kj}$ $w_{ji} = w_{ji} + \Delta w_{ji}$. Until termination condition is satisfied.

6.5 Network Pruning

The intention behind polynomial network pruning is to discard from the model redundant, less important terms which do not contribute significantly to optimal data fitting. It is known that too many terms cause overfitting and such models do not generalize well beyond the given data. The objective is to reduce the network complexity so that it still approximates the data well and improves the generalization. Implementing algorithms for trimming networks requires us to define criteria for termination of the weight removal. Guidelines for weight removal provides the bias-variance dilemma [Geman et al., 1992] (Chapter 9), according to which weights should be deleted until the sum of the statistical bias and variance reaches its minimum. The following pruning procedures can be repeated several times, and the resulting networks are retrained until settling at an acceptable solution.

Another way of deciding when to stop removing weights is to use statistical criteria such as UEV (4.5), FPE (4.7), PSE (4.8), and GCV (4.10). They require us to apply the $\mathcal{R}$-propagation algorithm (Section 6.3.1) for computing the *effective number of network parameters* γ:

$$\gamma_{NL} = W - \sum_{i=1}^{W} \frac{\lambda}{\alpha_i + \lambda} = W - \lambda trace(\mathbf{H}^{-1}) \tag{6.73}$$

where W is the number of weights, α_i are the eigenvalues of the Hessian, λ is the regularization parameter, and $\mathbf{H}^{-1}$ is the inverse Hessian.

The above two formulae for finding the efficient parameters γ_{NL} (6.73) may yield different values. This could happen due to computational inaccuracies during the computation of the eigenvalues, and during the inversion of the Hessian. In order to be convincing in the accuracy of the estimated number γ_{NL}, this number may be checked by relating it to the equivalent number γ that could be obtained using formula (4.6) applied as part of the OLS fitting procedure.

6.5.1 First-Order Network Pruning

The basic idea behind first-order network pruning is to exploit the information contained in the error gradient for better adapting the network structure to the data and for improving its generalization.

Stochastic Pruning. Weights that have less impact on the error gradient are less significant. Having computed the first-order error derivatives in the PNN by means of BP allows us to estimate the standard deviation of the gradient. Weights whose magnitudes, divided by the standard deviation of the gradient vector, produce a very small value may be trimmed from the network. The significance s_{ij} of a weight w_{ij}

can be measured by the following t-test formula, which may be applied for *stochastic network pruning* [Finnoff et al., 1992]:

$$s_{ij} = \frac{|w_{ij} + g|}{\sqrt{(1/N)\sum_{n=1}^{N}(g_n - \bar{g})^2}} \tag{6.74}$$

where the mean gradient entry $\bar{g}$ is : $\bar{g} = (1/N)\sum_{n=1}^{N} g_n$ made of elements $g_n = \partial E_n / \partial w_{ij}$ (6.36). This stochastic pruning is a kind of magnitude-based method with the advantage that it accounts for the error sensitivity to the particular network weights through first-order derivative information.

Pruning by Inverse Kurtosis. PNN can be pruned using only first-order information in the errors to judge the significance of the weights without taking into account their magnitudes. This can be done by comparing of the distributions of the gradients. When the distribution of a gradient with respect to a weight is broader, this means that its optimization depends on more data. Rrespectively, if the gradient distribution is peaked, this means that only a small number of data affect this weight. Therefore, a weight with a peaked gradient distribution is not likely to have a large impact on the network. Weights can be pruned after their ranking based on the differences between their gradient distributions in the following way [Neuneier and Zimmermann, 1998]:

$$s_{ij} = \frac{1}{\varepsilon + |diff_{w_{ij}}|} \tag{6.75}$$

where $\varepsilon = 0.001$, and $diff_{w_{ij}}$ is a kurtosis measure of the deviation from the normal distribution [Neuneier and Zimmermann, 1998]:

$$diff_{w_{ij}} = \left(\frac{(1/N)\sum_{n=1}^{N}(g_n - \bar{g})^4}{\left((1/N)\sum_{n=1}^{N}(g_n - \bar{g})^2\right)^2} - 3 \right)^2 \tag{6.76}$$

where a small value indicates to prune this weight.

6.5.2 Second-Order Network Pruning

Second-order information in the errors can also be exploited to prune networks with the aim of improving their extrapolation. Taylor's approximation of the error can be simplified further in addition to the elimination of its third-order and higher-order terms. When this approximation is taken to analyze a network that has already been trained, it can be expected that the weight vector has already approached some minima on the error surface. This idea can be applied to prune evolved

PNN whose weights have been estimated by OLS fitting. Since at the minimal error point the gradient is zero (that is, $\nabla E(\mathbf{w}_0) = 0$), the second term in Taylor's expansion (6.35) vanishes so that there remains only $E(\mathbf{w}_0 + \Delta\mathbf{w}) \cong E(\mathbf{w}_0) + 0.5\Delta\mathbf{w}^T\mathbf{H}\Delta\mathbf{w}$. This equation shows that a possible error change that can occur when a learning step from $\mathbf{w}_0$ to $\mathbf{w}_0 + \Delta\mathbf{w}$ is made, can be described with the *quadratic form*:

$$E(\mathbf{w}_0 + \Delta\mathbf{w}) - E(\mathbf{w}_0) \cong \frac{1}{2}\Delta\mathbf{w}^T\mathbf{H}\Delta\mathbf{w} \qquad (6.77)$$

where $\mathbf{w}_0$ is the weight vector and $\mathbf{H}$ is the Hessian matrix.

Equation (6.77) shows that the error change depends on the magnitudes of the weights as well as on their interrelationships described by the second-order derivatives from the Hessian. Weights with very small magnitudes and small Hessian entries only slightly affect the error. The greater the weights and their contribution to the Hessian, the larger their influence on the error. Therefore, the quadratic form $0.5\Delta\mathbf{w}^T\mathbf{H}\Delta\mathbf{w}$ provides the basis for deriving formulae for the significance of the weights that can be used for network pruning.

Optimal Brain Damage. The minimization of the quadratic form $\Delta\mathbf{w}^T\mathbf{H}\Delta\mathbf{w}$ can be approached from two perspectives: 1) using the diagonal approximation of the Hessian; and 2) using the full Hessian. The former approach to network pruning using the diagonal approximation of the Hessian is called *optimal brain damage* (OBD) [LeCun et al., 1990]. OBD removes weights having small saliency computed using second-order error derivatives according to the following formula:

$$s_{ij} = \frac{1}{2}\frac{\partial^2 E}{\partial w_{ij}^2} w_{ij}^2 = \frac{1}{2}[\mathbf{H}_d]_{ij} w_{ij}^2 \qquad (6.78)$$

where $[\mathbf{H}_d]_{ij}$ is the Hessian entry on the diagonal where $i = j$. The diagonal approximation of the Hessian is:

$$[\mathbf{H}_d]_{ij} = \sum_{n=1}^{N} \left\{ \left(\frac{\partial P(\mathbf{x}_n, \mathbf{w})}{\partial w_i} \right) \left(\frac{\partial P(\mathbf{x}_n, \mathbf{w})}{\partial w_j} \right)^T \right\} \qquad (6.79)$$

which can be estimated using the gradients obtained by backpropagation. The simplified format of this saliency is:

$$s_{ij} = \frac{1}{2} \left(\frac{\partial E}{\partial w_i} \frac{\partial E}{\partial w_j} \right) w_{ij}^2 \qquad (6.80)$$

where $\partial E/\partial w_i$ and $\partial E/\partial w_j$ are the error derivatives.

The OBD pruning approach is very efficient as its computational cost is linear in the number of weights in the network. OBD has the advantage that it accounts for the interdependencies between the network weights, while first-order pruning techniques (Section 6.5.1) and weight subset selection take into account only the weight magnitudes when calculating the saliences. OBD goes beyond weight size-based importance and enables us to judge more precisely how all the weights in the whole network cooperate for data modelling.

Optimal Brain Surgeon. *Optimal brain surgeon* (OBS) [Hassibi and Stork, 1993] is another approach to ranking the weights that uses the complete Hessian. OBS more precisely estimates the relationships between the weights using the complete Hessian (6.39,6.40). The weight saliencies according to OBS are determined with the following fraction:

$$s_{ij} = \frac{1}{2}\frac{w_{ij}^2}{[\mathbf{H}^{-1}]_{ij}} \tag{6.81}$$

where $[\mathbf{H}^{-1}]_{ij}$ is the inverse full Hessian entry in row i and column j.

The OBS approach is more time-consuming than OBD due to the necessity to evaluate the full Hessian, and then to invert it. In practice, the complete Hessian may be extremely large and/or ill-conditioned which means that it may be difficult or even impossible to invert. Therefore the OBS strategy may not always be applicable due to numerical inaccuracies. From another point of view, OBS has been found superior to OBD on many research problems, and it could be expected to perform favorably to OBD, first-order pruning techniques (Section 6.5.1), and weight subset selection. OBS has the same advantage as OBD in that it is a second-order method that can better capture the weight dependencies in polynomial networks.

6.6 Chapter Summary

This section strengthens the importance of the backpropagation algorithm as a computational mechanism for learning the weights of nonlinear network models. It demonstrated that the BP is efficient for retraining of nonlinear PNN after discovery of their relevant topology by IGP. IGP should be considered as a first step for polynomial identification from data because it helps to automatically resolve many problems that hinder the success of BP applied to conventional neural networks, such as: what should the initial weight values be, how many hidden layers should be used, how many should the hidden nodes be, and what should be the network connectivity. What remains is to improve the weights as IGP discovers the proper network structure by manipulating flexible, plastic tree-like network architectures.

The idea of using the backpropagation weight learning algorithm for further improvement of evolved PNN is general and it is applicable to other higher-order networks. The experiments with BP on nonlinear PNN demonstrate that polynomial networks, once constructed in a bottom-up manner, are suboptimal solutions which assume considerable error corrections because the BP training begins with weights determined by least squares fitting during IGP. The weights of the evolved polynomials position them on slopes of the error surfaces toward some optima, however close to some optima that has not been reached. In order to continue the descent on the slopes down toward the basin minima, very small learning rates have to be used to avoid overshooting the minima. Since the weights have been learned to some extent, the algorithm convergence is rapid in the sense that it takes fewer epochs.

Approaches were presented for learning step control and pruning that are especially suitable for PNN. There is a large amount of research material on developing learning rate control algorithms and neural network pruning strategies that can also be applied to PNN after proper modifications to reflect the specificities of the BP techniques studied here for high-order polynomial networks.

Concerning the ease of implementation, it is obvious that first-order BP techniques are straightforward to implement, but they are not so efficient as the second-order training methods. Amongst the second-order methods, the conjugate gradients method seems very attractive because it is fast and can be developed without difficulties. After that, the Levenberg-Marquardt method can be applied using the computed entries of the Jacobian matrix.

Chapter 7

TEMPORAL BACKPROPAGATION

There are many practical inductive tasks with data whose properties change over time. In order to track the inherent characteristics of such dynamically changing data, there are necessary representations that describe spatiotemporal information. These should be special dynamic representations which react to the provided inputs after a certain delay time; that is, they may not respond immediately to the inputs like traditional static models. The dynamic models include the time as a parameter that influences the mapping to reflect the time ordering, and in this way the dynamic models capture time dependencies.

Research into dynamic network models involves development of specialized temporal training algorithms that utilize sequentially arriving data. Such temporal training algorithms take into account the time relationships among the data. When performing parameter adjustment with dependence on the time ordering, the dynamic models may exhibit noninstantaneous response to the present inputs, which leads to non-zero transient response. Therefore, one serious problem that arises in temporal training is to stabilize the training procedure in order to achieve sufficiently accurate results. Other difficulties in temporal learning arise due to the increased complexity of the dynamic model structure because not only external inputs, but also feedback delays from the output and the hidden nodes, may have to be handled.

Two main kinds of polynomial networks for temporal data processing can be distinguished: time-delay (or time window) PNN (Section 3.4.1-3.5.4) using lagged variables, and recurrent PNN (Section 3.5.5) using links passing back node outputs as variables. Time-delay PNN enable the application of static BP techniques for weight learning, assuming both temporal and spacial dimensions. Such approaches, however, have several drawbacks: 1) they impose a strong limit on the duration of the temporal events as they process data through fixed time windows, moreover, in order to fix the window size they require predetermination of the embedding dimension; and 2) they face difficulties recognizing which are the absolute and which are the relative positions in the sequences, which makes it difficult to capture long-term time-varying relationships in the data. The first drawback can be avoided by the employment of powerful search techniques like IGP that may automatically discover the relevant time lags for the adopted model. The second drawback can be avoided by development of recurrent PNN.

The recurrent PNN with feedback connections (Section 3.8.3) are alternatives to the time-delay networks for temporal sequence learning. Recurrent PNN are made as discrete time models trainable by specialized backpropagation algorithms for weight adaptation derived from their specification as state-space models. Assuming that IGP has evolved the optimal recurrent PNN topology for the task, its weights can be improved using the exact gradient computation algorithms Back-Propagation Through Time (BPTT) [Rumelhart et al., 1986, Werbos, 1974] and Real-Time Recurrent Learning (RTRL) [Williams and Zipser, 1989, Williams and Zipser, 1995]. They conduct gradient descent search in the weight space, subject to the assumption that all connections are treated with the same delay of one time step $\Delta t = 1$. BPTT performs gradient calculations backward in time, while RTRL computes the gradient forward in time. Especially for discrete higher-order networks with polynomial activation functions, there are implemented the incremental RTRL, and two versions: real-time BPTT and epochwise BPTT. After that, a Recursive BackPropagation (RBP) [Shah et al., 1992, Puskorius and Felkamp, 1994] algorithm, based on minimum mean square weight estimation, is elaborated for faster training of recurrent PNN.

7.1 Recurrent PNN as State-Space Models

The recurrent PNN may be envisioned as state-space models of process behavior [Williams and Zipser, 1989, Chen et al., 1990, Narendra and Parthasarathy, 1990]. They formalize the input-output mapping, suggested by the given training data, by taking into consideration their dynamical properties. This is because not only external input variables, but also temporal variables representing internal states, enter the network. The states capture past node information and send it through the loops, thus providing memory that relieves the necessity to select time lags. The states generalize the information about the internal excitations to the inputs and supply additional activity information for better tracking of behavioral patterns.

The operation of a PNN node from a dynamic perspective can be described with the following coupled difference equations:

$$s(t+1) = p[x(t), s(t)] \tag{7.1}$$

$$z(t) = f[s(t)] \tag{7.2}$$

where $x(t)$ is the external input, $s(t)$ is the internal state, and $z(t)$ is the node output at time t. The first process equation (7.1) specifies that the next state $s(t+1)$ is a function of the input $x(t)$ and the present state $s(t)$. The second measurement equation (7.2) specifies that the output is produced as a function of the state.

The recurrent PNN use activation polynomial functions in the hidden and output network nodes. They can be expressed as dependent, on a discrete time parameter influencing the variables, according to the process equation (7.1) as follows:

$$s(t+1) \equiv p(t) = \sum_{m=0}^{5} w_m u_m(t) \tag{7.3}$$

where $p(t)$ is a partial activation polynomial (Table 2.1) derived from the complete one: $p(t) = w_0 + w_1 u_1(t) + w_2 u_2(t) + w_3 u_1(t) u_2(t) + w_3 u_1^2(t) + w_4 u_2^2(t)$. The temporal variables $u(t)$ are introduced for notational convenience to describe one of the following alternatives:

$$u(t) = \begin{cases} x(t) \\ p_a(t) \\ s(t) \equiv p(t-1) \end{cases} \tag{7.4}$$

that is, they could be either external inputs $x(t)$ or activation polynomial outputs $p_a(t)$ passed from a child node from the preceding network layer, or hidden node states $s(t)$ at time tick t which are recorded previous outputs of the corresponding node.

The problem of learning recurrent polynomial networks from data can be stated as follows: given a trajectory of inputs $x(1), x(2), ..., x(t)$ sampled at discrete times, their corresponding targets $y(1) = x(m+1), y(2) = x(m+2), ..., y(t-m) = x(t)$, and an initial state vector $s(1) = 0, s(2) = 0, ..., s(t-m) = 0$, find the structure and parameters of the PNN that best models the underlying mapping. Here, m denotes the input history; that is, the network output depends on m earlier inputs from the given trajectory. The weight tuning algorithm includes three steps repeated a large number of times: 1) make the next system states $s(t+1)$ from the previous inputs $x(t)$ and states $s(t)$ with the activation polynomials in the hidden nodes; 2) compute the network output; and 3) update the network weights.

The trajectory learning algorithms like BPTT and RTRL adapt the network output gradually to follow the provided data sequence. They implement different weight training rules obtained by differentiating the process and management dynamic equations (7.1,7.2) in two opposite directions, backward and forward in time.

There are several features of these algorithms for the case of PNN that deserve clarification: 1) it is assumed that the activation polynomials serve both as net-input functions and as transfer functions f; that is, the measurement equation (7.2) uses the identity function; 2) the activation polynomials p in the process equation (7.1) are higher-order functions of their variables; and, 3) the polynomial networks have a binary tree-like structure, which implies that every hidden node feeds exactly one parent, and every node has exactly two incoming connections.

7.2 Backpropagation Through Time

BPTT [Rumelhart et al., 1986, Werbos, 1974] as a notion, summarizes two (real-time and epochwise) training strategies for dynamic neural networks that collect the instantaneous error gradients from all temporal patterns backward in time. The BPTT strategies can be understood in context of the BP framework assuming that the network is unfolded, unrolled in the time. Unfolding is a process of transforming the temporal dependencies into spatial relationships. Copies of the temporally dependent nodes leading to a larger network are created, which may be considered static and thus trainable by static backpropagation. The states and the recurrent links through which they flow are duplicated at each time instant from the end, down to the beginning of the time interval. The weights on replicated connections between successive layers in the unraveled network are the same (Figure 7.1).

BPTT are trajectory learning algorithms that modify the weights in the opposite direction to the error gradient. Both BPTT algorithms create virtual networks by unfolding the original topologies on which backpropagation training is applied. The objective is to improve the weights so as to minimize the total error over the whole time interval. These algorithms collect the instantaneous errors on all data and update the weights after a complete presentation of the given sequence.

The instantaneous gradients are produced in a different manner: 1) the real-time BPTT estimates the current error, and uses it to obtain and accumulate the earlier derivatives from the current down to the initial moment; and 2) the epochwise BPTT adds the previous derivatives, as well as the network errors, taken in reverse order within the epoch boundaries and restarts the next epoch from another moment.

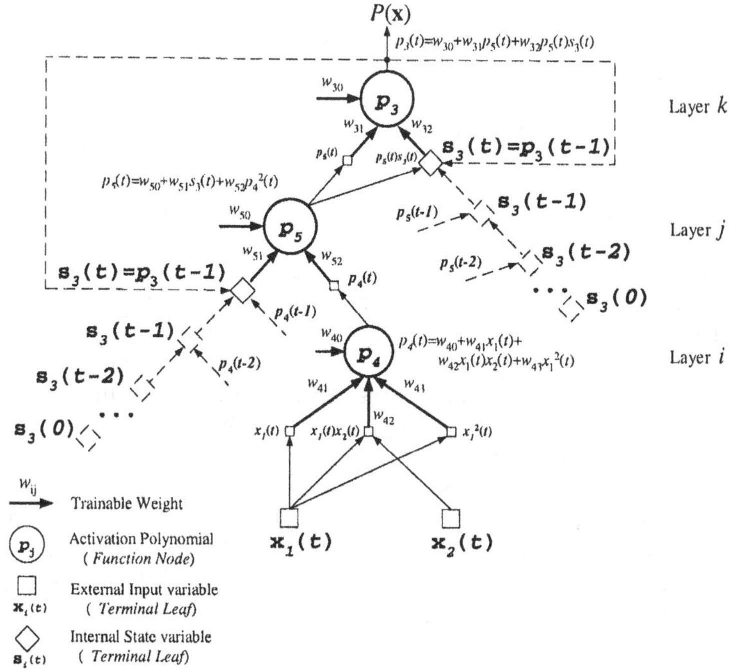

Figure 7.1. Unrolling in time of a tree-like recurrent PNN with two time layers.

7.2.1 Derivation of BPTT Algorithms

Let the given trajectory of observations encompass the period from t_0 to t_1 inclusive, that is the interval $(t_0, t_1]$. When the PNN is unrolled in time, the total error can be collected by summation of the instantaneous errors $E \equiv E(\tau)$ on the subtrajectory from the initial $t_0 + 1$ up to the final moment t_1, using the equation:

$$E(t_0, t_1) = \sum_{\tau=t_0+1}^{t_1} E(\tau) = \sum_{\tau=t_0+1}^{t_1} \frac{1}{2}(y(\tau) - P(\tau))^2 \qquad (7.5)$$

where τ indicates the time ticks from the given interval.

Both versions of BPTT share a common temporal delta training rule for weight updating that requires computation of the total error derivative over the whole temporal interval from t_0 to t_1 inclusive:

$$\Delta w = \frac{\partial E}{\partial w} = -\eta \sum_{\tau=t_0+1}^{t_1} \frac{\partial E}{\partial w(\tau)} \qquad (7.6)$$

where η is the learning rate parameter.

The following analysis shows how to make the derivatives $\partial E/\partial w(\tau)$, which are then specialized for making real-time or epochwise BPTT.

According to the process equation (7.1), explaining the operation of a node in recurrent networks, the error derivative $\partial E/\partial w(\tau)$ is sensitive to the weight through the internal state of the node:

$$\frac{\partial E}{\partial w(\tau)} = \frac{\partial E}{\partial s(\tau+1)}\frac{\partial s(\tau+1)}{\partial w(\tau)} = \frac{\partial E}{\partial s(\tau+1)}x'(\tau) \tag{7.7}$$

where the $x'(\tau)$ is the influence of the weight changes on the future state $x'(\tau) = \partial s(\tau+1)/\partial w(\tau)$, which can be obtained using the node output at the previous time instant $x'(\tau) = \partial p(\tau)/\partial w(\tau)$.

The first multiplier $\partial E/\partial s(\tau+1)$ accounts for the error sensitivity to the state variations over time. This sensitivity can be computed by ordering the partial derivatives in time [Werbos, 1974]: $E(1), E(2), ..., E(t)$. This ordering helps to infer the formula for the effect of the state on the error. The formula includes the explicit state influence at moment τ as well as the implicit state influences on the error arising in the future moments $\tau+1$. Let the instantaneous error derivative with respect to the current state at moment τ be substituted by the backprop error: $\delta(\tau) = \partial E/\partial s(\tau)$. Assuming that the unfolded network produces temporally arranged errors leads to the following backprop error:

$$\delta(\tau) = \frac{\partial E}{\partial s(\tau)} = \frac{\partial E}{\partial s^*(\tau)} + \sum_r \frac{\partial E}{\partial s_r(\tau+1)}\frac{\partial s_r(\tau+1)}{\partial s(\tau)} \tag{7.8}$$

where $\partial E/\partial s^*(\tau)$ is the explicit error sensitivity to the state at time tick τ, and $s_r(\tau+1)$ are the next implicit states sent via the recurrent links indexed by r. Equation (7.8) can be written more concisely as follows:

$$\delta(\tau) = -e(\tau) + \sum_r \delta(\tau+1)w_r \tag{7.9}$$

where $e(\tau)$ is the output error $e(\tau) = y(\tau) - P(\tau)$ at time τ, and w_r are the weights on the recurrent connections that enter the node.

The boundary condition for this formula (7.9) should be approached with care. At the end of the given time interval when $\tau = t_1$, the backprop error reduces to the impact of the network output error: $\delta(t_1) = -e(t_1)$, because there is no future evidence: $\delta(t_1+1) = 0$. At all earlier time instants for the period $\tau < t_1$, the backprop errors can be propagated and so they become available.

The time offset in formula (7.9) means that the error gradient is accumulated backward in time by traversing the trajectory from the final time step t_1 down to the beginning of the interval t_0+1. The earlier backprop errors are computed at each earlier time instant by successive application of the error formula (7.9). The instantaneous error derivatives are defined with respect to weights on connections to the output and respectively on links to the hidden nodes. They are elaborated here, especially for tree-like recurrent PNN leading to two temporal BPTT training rules. Since these rules can be applied to the time-unraveled network in the same way as the static BP, the algorithms are called backpropagation through time.

Temporal Delta Rule for Output Node Weights. The total error derivative with respect to a weight w_{kj} on connection from the hidden to the root network node suggests to update it with the following *temporal BPTT delta rule*:

$$\Delta w_{kj} = -\eta \frac{\partial E}{\partial w_{kj}} = \eta \sum_{\tau=t_0+1}^{t_1} \delta_k(\tau) x'_{kj}(\tau - 1) \tag{7.10}$$

where the backpropagated error at the particular time step is $\delta_k(\tau) = [-e_k(\tau) + \delta_k(\tau+1)w_r]$ according to formula (7.9), and the state derivative with respect to the weight is $x'_{kj}(\tau-1) = \partial p_k(\tau-1)/\partial w_{kj}(\tau-1)$. The above equation includes the particular error at time instant τ as $e_k(\tau) = y_k(\tau) - P(\tau)$, where the network output is actually the output produced by the activation polynomial at the root $P(\tau) = p_k(\tau)$.

Temporal Delta Rule for Hidden Node Weights. The *temporal BPTT training rule for the hidden node weights* is obtained in a similar way, leading to the following more complicated expression:

$$\Delta w_{ji} = -\eta \frac{\partial E}{\partial w_{ji}} = \eta \sum_{\tau=t_0+1}^{t_1} \delta_j(\tau) x'_{ji}(\tau - 1) \tag{7.11}$$

where $\delta_j(\tau)$ is the backprop error at node j, and $x'_{ji}(\tau-1) = \partial p_j(\tau - 1)/\partial w_{ji}(\tau-1)$. The backprop error $\delta_j(\tau)$ is more involved, it is not only the output error at the particular time step, because its explicit error sensitivity component reflects the position of the node in the network architecture. The expansion of the backprop error which accounts for the network architecture as well as for the time variations is:

$$\delta_j(\tau) = \left[-\delta_k(\tau)p'_{kj} + \delta_j(\tau+1)w_r\right] \tag{7.12}$$

where the first term $-\delta_k(\tau)p'_{kj}$ is the backpropagated error from higher layer nodes, and the second term is the time dependency on the state. The first term is the contribution of the derivatives: $\partial E/\partial s^*_j(\tau) = -\delta_k(\tau)p'_{kj}$, which is returned from the k-th output node to the concrete j-th node through the intermediate nodes as in static BP.

The BPTT algorithm applied to a tree-like recurrent PNN is illustrated using the network in Figure 7.1. This recurrent polynomial network is taken similar to the feed-forward PNN in Figure 6.1 in order to facilitate understanding the differences between the static BPA and the temporal dynamic versions of the BPA presented in this chapter. The hidden nodes in Figure 7.1 use the same activation polynomials:

$$p_3(t) = w_{30} + w_{31}p_5(t) + w_{32}p_5(t)s_3(t) \quad (7.13)$$

$$p_5(t) = w_{50} + w_{51}s_3(t) + w_{52}p_4^2(t) \quad (7.14)$$

$$p_4(t) = w_{40} + w_{41}x_1(t) + w_{42}x_1(t)x_2(t) + w_{43}x_1^2(t) \quad (7.15)$$

The instantaneous error derivatives at time τ with respect to the weights w_{31} and w_{32} on connections toward the output node are derived using the temporal delta rule (7.10) as follows:

$$\frac{\partial E}{\partial w_{31}(\tau)} = -e(\tau)p_5(\tau) \quad (7.16)$$

$$\frac{\partial E}{\partial w_{32}(\tau)} = [-e(\tau) + w_{32}\delta_3(\tau+1)]\, p_5(\tau)p_3(\tau-1) \quad (7.17)$$

where $e_3(\tau) = y(\tau) - P_3(\tau)$, and the backprop error is computed recursively $\delta_3(\tau) = [-e_3(\tau) + w_{32}\delta_3(\tau+1)]$ at all previous times $t_1 > \tau \geq t_0$.

The instantaneous derivatives for the left child node 5 at layer j of the root with respect to its weights w_{51} and w_{52} at time τ are:

$$\frac{\partial E}{\partial w_{51}(\tau)} = [-e_3(\tau)\,(w_{31} + w_{32}p_3(\tau-1)) + w_{51}\delta_5(\tau+1)]\, p_3(\tau-1) \quad (7.18)$$

$$\frac{\partial E}{\partial w_{52}(\tau)} = -e_3(\tau)\,(w_{31} + w_{32}p_3(\tau-1))\, p_4^2(\tau) \quad (7.19)$$

where $\delta_5(\tau) = [-e_3(\tau)\,(w_{31} + w_{32}p_3(\tau-1)) + w_{51}\delta_5(\tau+1)]$.

The instantaneous error derivatives for the right child node (node 4 at layer i in Figure 7.1) of node 5 with respect to its weights w_{41}, w_{42} and w_{43} at time τ are produced in a straightforward manner, as the output of node 5 depends only on the input variables x_1 and x_2:

$$\frac{\partial E}{\partial w_{41}(\tau)} = \frac{\partial E}{\partial p_5(\tau)}\,[2w_{52}(\tau)p_4(\tau)]\, x_1(\tau) \quad (7.20)$$

$$\frac{\partial E}{\partial w_{42}(\tau)} = \frac{\partial E}{\partial p_5(\tau)}\,[2w_{52}(\tau)p_4(\tau)]\, x_1(\tau)x_2(\tau) \quad (7.21)$$

$$\frac{\partial E}{\partial w_{43}(\tau)} = \frac{\partial E}{\partial p_5(\tau)}\,[2w_{52}(\tau)p_4(\tau)]\, x_1^2(\tau) \quad (7.22)$$

where $\partial E/\partial p_5(\tau) = -e(\tau)\,[w_{31}(\tau) + w_{32}(\tau)p_3(\tau-1)]$.

7.2.2 Real-Time BPTT Algorithm

The real-time BPTT algorithm involves a forward and a backward pass with each training temporal example. The forward pass sends the example through the network and calculates the node outputs, which become system states after shifting the state buffer one step back. The backward pass computes the output error at the current time tick. After that, it performs tree traversal from the root to the leaves and calculates: 1) the backprop errors in each hidden node according to the static delta rules for the current moment t; and 2) the backprop errors with respect to the states for all earlier time steps by unfolding the encountered hidden node if it has a recurrent link that feeds some state variable. The corresponding weight deltas are finally evaluated. The real-time BPTT algorithm is illustrated in Table 7.1.

Table 7.1. Real-time temporal backpropagation for tree-like recurrent PNN.

Real-Time BPTT Algorithm for PNN

step	*Algorithmic sequence*
1. Initialization	Input trajectory $x(1), x(2), ..., x(t_1)$, backprop errors $\delta_j(1) = \delta_j(2) = ... = \delta_j(t_1) = 0$ and states $p_j(1) = ... = p_j(t_1) = 0$ for each hidden node j.
2. Perform network training	For each consequtive step t, $t_1 \geq \tau \geq t_0 + 1$, do a) Forward pass: propagate the inputs $x(1), x(2), ..., x(m)$ and the states $p_j(t-1)$ to compute node outputs, save them to become next states. b) Backward pass: from the root down to the fringe nodes i) compute the backprop errors using the output $\delta_k(t) = -(y_k(t) - P_k(t))$ if this is the output node $\delta_j(t) = -\delta_k(t)p'_{kj}$ if this is a hidden node. ii) if this node has a recurrent connection then unfold it, compute and store the backprop errors for the earlier time steps by iterating backward in time with τ, $t - 1 \geq \tau \geq t_0 + 1$ $\delta_k(\tau) = \delta_k(\tau + 1)w_r$ at the output node $\delta_j(\tau) = \delta_j(\tau + 1)w_r$ at the hidden noded otherwise (when there is no recurrent link) $\delta_j(\tau) = -\delta_k(\tau)p'_{kj}$. c) Update the weights by accumulating the gradients $\Delta w_{kj} = \eta \sum_{\tau=t_0+1}^{t} \delta_k(\tau)x'_{kj}(\tau - 1)$, where $x'_{kj}(\tau - 1) = \partial p_k(\tau - 1)/\partial w_{kj}(\tau - 1)$ $\Delta w_{ji} = \eta \sum_{\tau=t_0+1}^{t} \delta_j(\tau)x'_{ji}(\tau - 1)$, where $x'_{ji}(\tau - 1) = \partial p_j(\tau - 1)/\partial w_{ji}(\tau - 1)$.

7.2.3 Epochwise BPTT Algorithm

The epochwise BPTT performs the same forward pass as the real-time version, but it makes different calculations during the backward pass. The reason is that the errors from the earlier moments are explicitly calculated and considered when computing the deltas so as to impact the weight changes. The main distinguishing characteristic of the epochwise BPTT is that the errors from the previous time steps are injected through $e_k(\tau)$, $t' \geq \tau \geq t_0 + 1$, in the derivatives $\delta_k(\tau) = [-e_k(\tau) + \delta_k(\tau+1)w_r]$ at the output root network node and through $e_j(\tau) = -\delta_k(\tau)p'_{kj}$ in $\delta_j(\tau) = \left[-\delta_k(\tau)p'_{kj} + \delta_j(\tau+1)w_r\right]$ at the hidden nodes. This means that the epochwise algorithm minimizes the total error from all previous instantaneous network errors (Table 7.2).

Table 7.2. Epochwise temporal backpropagation for tree-like recurrent PNN.

Epochwise BPTT Algorithm for PNN

step	*Algorithmic sequence*
1. Initialization	Input trajectory $x(1), x(2), ..., x(t_1)$, backprop errors $\delta_j(1) = \delta_j(2) = ... = \delta_j(t_1) = 0$ and states $p_j(1) = ... = p_j(t_1) = 0$ for each hidden node j.
2. Perform network training	Repeat for each epoch in the time period $(t_0, t']$, $t' \leq t_1$ a) For each time instant τ, $t' \geq \tau \geq t_0 + 1$, do i) Forward pass: propagate the inputs $x(1), ..., x(m)$ and the states $p_j(\tau - 1)$ to compute node outputs save them to become next states. ii) Backward pass: from the root down to the fringes - compute the output backprop error at the root $\delta_k(\tau) = -e_k(\tau) = -(y_k(\tau) - P_k(\tau))$, and $e_j(\tau) = -\delta_k(\tau)p'_{kj}$. - if this node has a recurrent connection then unfold it, compute and store the backprop errors for the earlier time steps by iterating backward in time from t' down to $t_0 + 1$ $\delta_k(\tau) = [-e_k(\tau) + \delta_k(\tau+1)w_r]$ at the output $\delta_j(\tau) = [-e_j(\tau) + \delta_j(\tau+1)w_r]$ at the hidden otherwise (when there is no recurrent link) $\delta_j(\tau) = e_j(\tau) = -\delta_k(\tau)p'_{kj}$. b) Update the weights by adding the epoch gradient $\Delta w_{kj} = \eta \sum_{\tau=t_0+1}^{t'} \delta_k(\tau)x'_{kj}(\tau-1)$, where $x'_{kj}(\tau-1) = \partial p_k(\tau-1)/\partial w_{kj}(\tau-1)$ $\Delta w_{ji} = \eta \sum_{\tau=t_0+1}^{t'} \delta_j(\tau)x'_{ji}(\tau-1)$, where $x'_{ji}(\tau-1) = \partial p_j(\tau-1)/\partial w_{ji}(\tau-1)$. c) Reinitialize the network.

7.3 Real-Time Recurrent Learning

Another temporal supervised learning algorithm for training dynamic neural networks that can be applied to PNN is *real-time recurrent learning* (RTRL) [Williams and Zipser, 1989, Williams and Zipser, 1995]. The name comes from its ability to perform weight tuning forward in time while the network is running. It computes weight changes at each time step along the given trajectory. The RTRL algorithm resembles BPTT in that it uses the same cost function and attempts to follow the true negative gradient of this error function. However, it relies on a different derivation of the temporal learning rules. While BPTT computes the gradient assuming decomposition of the weight in time, the RTRL computes the gradient assuming that the error function is decomposed in time. RTRL estimates the instantaneous error derivatives with respect to the weights at each time tick from the given interval while the network is continuously running forward on successive data.

The RTRL performance criterion is minimization of the total temporal error over the whole given interval, defined as follows:

$$E(t_0, t_1) = \sum_{t=t_0+1}^{t_1} E(t) = \sum_{t=t_0+1}^{t_1} \frac{1}{2}(y(t) - P(t))^2 \tag{7.23}$$

where $E(t) = 0.5(y(t) - P(t))$ is the instantaneous (local error).

The derivative of the total error with respect to any weight is determined assuming that the cost function is sensitive to the time, rather than assuming that the weight is sensitive to the time. Because of this, the initial states, the external inputs and the network weights, are kept fixed during the computations over the entire trajectory. The error derivative is found by a forward expansion of the instantaneous cost in time performed according to the chain rule:

$$\Delta w = \frac{\partial E}{\partial w} = \sum_{t=t_0+1}^{t_1} \frac{\partial E(t)}{\partial w} = \sum_{t=t_0+1}^{t_1} \frac{\partial E(t)}{\partial p(t)} \frac{\partial p(t)}{\partial w} = - \sum_{t=t_0+1}^{t_1} \delta(t) \frac{\partial p(t)}{\partial w} \tag{7.24}$$

which holds for any arbitrary weight on connection that enters the node. This equation suggests that the gradient of the total error can be computed by accumulating the derivatives of the instantaneous errors at each time tick t from the given interval.

The first multiplier in this equation for the error derivative (7.24) is the backprop error: $\delta(t) = \partial E(t)/\partial p(t)$. The second multiplier $\partial p(t)/\partial w$ is the so called *dynamic derivative* of the output with respect to the weight at time t. This dynamic derivative describes the impact of the weight change on the activation polynomial output and it can be expanded using partials with respect to the weight as follows:

$$\begin{aligned}\frac{\partial p(t)}{\partial w} &= \sum_{m=1}^{5} \frac{\partial}{\partial w}(w_m u_m(t)) \\ &= \sum_{m=1}^{5} \left[w_m \frac{\partial u_m(t)}{\partial w} + u(t) \right] \end{aligned} \tag{7.25}$$

where $u(t)$ is the temporal variable participating in the term $wu(t)$. Equation (7.25) can be simplified since the temporal derivatives of the external variables are zero, that $\partial u_m(t)/\partial w = 0$, so it vanishes when directly feeding external inputs $u_m(t) \equiv x_m(t)$.

There remains to find the partial temporal derivatives of recurrently passed output signals from other nodes. The differentiation of the polynomial output of the node with respect to a weight yields:

$$\frac{\partial p(t)}{\partial w} = \sum_{r} w_r \frac{\partial p_r(t-1)}{\partial w} + u(t) \tag{7.26}$$

only for recurrent connections w_r, $r < m = 5$ that feed past outputs p_r. This equation is produced by differentiation of the weighted incoming signals to this node $w_m u_m(t)$ with respect to the trained w. The summation over all recurrent links r accounts for the effect from other node outputs p_r sent via these recurrent connections weighted by w_r, and for the effect from the signal $u(t)$ on the trained link weighted by w. The signal $u(t)$ could be an external input, or a child node output, or a feedback signal from a higher layer node. The partial derivative of the instantaneous error $\partial E(t)$ at time t with respect to a weight w becomes:

$$\frac{\partial E(t)}{\partial w} = -\delta(t) \left[\sum_{r} w_r \frac{\partial p_r(t-1)}{\partial w} + u(t) \right] \tag{7.27}$$

where r enumerates the recurrent connections that enter the node.

Expression (7.27) shows that the error gradient can be handled forward in time along with the continuous evolution of the network dynamics according to the process (7.1) and measurement (7.2) equations.

Several cases arise from this formula in context of tree-structured recurrent PNN with irregular topologies. They can be divided in two main groups: error derivatives for the root node and error derivatives for the hidden network nodes. These two main groups can be further subdivided into subgroups due to the possibility for having combinations of forward and backward links toward a node. There are four possible combinations of network connections: 1) feeding two external inputs; 2) feeding two lower layer node outputs; 3) feeding an external input and a node output from a lower layer network node; and 4) feeding a recurrent signal coming from a higher layer node and a nonrecurrent signal, which can be either an input or a lower node output. For this reason, several RTRL training rules are developed below.

Temporal Delta Rules for Output Node Weights. Two cases arise at the root network node depending on its incoming connections. When the root network node is entered by signals along non-recurrent connections sending lower layer node outputs or external input variables directly, the temporal delta rule remains the same as the one used for static gradient descent training. Assuming that the root node is indexed by k and its links come from the j-th node or a variable below, the *temporal delta rule for the output node* is:

$$\Delta w_{kj}(t) = -\eta \frac{\partial E(t)}{\partial w_{kj}} = \eta \delta_k(t) x'_{kj}(t) \tag{7.28}$$

where η is the learning rate, $\delta_k(t)$ is the error $\delta_k(t) = y_k(t) - P(t)$, $P(t) = p_k(t)$, and $x'_{kj}(t)$ is the dynamic derivative of the node activation polynomial with respect to the weight $x'_{kj}(t) = \partial p_k(t)/\partial w_{kj}$.

Another different training rule is obtained when there is a connection feeding back the output of the root node to itself. This temporal training rule is common for the root node weights because the output error $\partial E(t)$ with respect to any weight w_{kj} from the j-th hidden node to the k-th root node in this moment, depends on the recurrent signal from the past step that enters the node. The recurrency requires elaboration of the derivative $\partial E(t)/\partial w_{kj}$ according to equation (7.27), which leads to the following *RTRL temporal delta rule for the output node*:

$$\Delta w_{kj}(t) = \eta \delta_k(t) \left[\sum_r w_{kr} \frac{\partial p_k(t-1)}{\partial w_{kj}} + u_j(t) \right] \tag{7.29}$$

where w_{kr} are the weights on the self-loops, p_k is the root polynomial, and u_j is the signal on the trainable link weighted by w_{kj}. There can be several recurrent links $r < m = 5$ since there may be up to four activation polynomial terms. This formula (7.29) is applied either with signal $u_j(t) = p_k(t-1)$ to train the self-recurrent connection weighted by w_{kr}, or with previous node output $u_j(t) = p_j(t-1)$, or with an external variable $u_j(t) = x(t)$ passed directly to the root node.

Temporal Delta Rules for Hidden Node Weights. There are three cases of feeding hidden nodes. The simplest case is when the node receives lower node outputs and/or external variables because it remains the same as in static gradient descent. Let the trained node be indexed by j and its incoming link come from the i-th polynomial or variable. Then the temporal delta rule for the hidden node weights is:

$$\Delta w_{ji}(t) = -\eta \frac{\partial E(t)}{\partial w_{ji}} = \eta \delta_j(t) x'_{ji}(t) \tag{7.30}$$

where $\delta_j(t) = -\delta_k(t) p'_{kj}(t)$ is the local backprop error, produced using the partial derivative of the output from the k-th node with respect to the output of the j-th node in some preceding level defined by $p'_{kj}(t) = \partial p_k(t)/\partial p_j(t)$, and the current dynamic polynomial derivative with respect to the trained weight is $x'_{ji}(t) = \partial p_j(t)/\partial w_{ji}$.

A hidden network node can receive an incoming signal through a recurrent connection from a higher layer node in the network or through a self-recurrent connection. These two cases are handled with a common weight training rule which involves different partial derivatives of the backward signal, depending on the link that provides it.

The common *RTRL temporal delta rule for training hidden node weights* w_{ji} in dynamic PNN is defined with the following equation:

$$\Delta w_{ji}(t) = \eta \delta_j(t) \left[\sum_r w_{jr} \frac{\partial p_l(t-1)}{\partial w_{ji}} + u_i(t) \right] \tag{7.31}$$

where w_{jr} is the weight on the looping connection, p_l is the activation polynomial output fed back from the network node, and u_i is the signal on the link weighted by w_{ji}.

This training rule (7.31) for any kind of weight w_{ji} on links to hidden network nodes is specialized into two ways corresponding to the two possible recurrent links associated with the weight w_{jr}. These specializations suggest producing two different dynamic derivatives from the recurrent signal $p_l(t-1)$ with respect to the trained weight w_{ji}: 1) by computing the dynamic derivative as $\partial p_j(t-1)/\partial w_{ji}$ when there is a self-recurrent link feeding back the output of the same node activation polynomial $p_l = p_j$; and 2) by computing the dynamic derivative as $\partial p_l(t-1)/\partial w_{ji}$ when there is a recurrent connection from some higher network node providing signal p_l through the loop.

The first case of a self-recurrency uses the previous node derivative which may be kept in a memory buffer associated with the node. The second case of a hidden node fed by a recurrent signal from a higher layer node leads to a more complicated dynamic derivative $\partial p_l(t-1)/\partial w_{ji}$. The reason is that there has to be taken into account the fact that the activation polynomial output passed from the higher node depends on the trained weight through all activation polynomial outcomes from the intermediate nodes between this higher node and the current node. The derivative in this situation is formed using the chain rule and requires to traverse the path from the higher layer node to the current one. During the topdown tree traversal all dynamic derivatives, at the particular time instant $t-1$, of the encountered node activation polynomials have to be collected in the following way:

$$\frac{\partial p_l(t-1)}{\partial w_{ji}} = \frac{\partial p_l(t-1)}{\partial p_j(t-1)} \frac{\partial p_j(t-1)}{\partial w_{ji}} \tag{7.32}$$

which holds when the l-th node is the immediate node above the current j-th node. The cases of higher nodes are obtained analogously.

Let's consider as an example the recurrent PNN given in Figure 7.2, which has the same architecture as the network in Figure 7.1. It is assumed that the hidden nodes in the PNN given in Figure 7.2 compute the same activation polynomials:

$$p_3(t) = w_{30} + w_{31}p_5(t) + w_{32}p_5(t)s_3(t) \tag{7.33}$$

$$p_5(t) = w_{50} + w_{51}s_3(t) + w_{52}p_4^2(t) \tag{7.34}$$

$$p_4(t) = w_{40} + w_{41}x_1(t) + w_{42}x_1(t)x_2(t) + w_{43}x_1^2(t) \tag{7.35}$$

The temporal error derivatives with respect to the output node weights w_{31} and w_{32} are computed according to equation (7.27) as follows:

$$\frac{\partial E(t)}{\partial w_{31}} = -(y(t) - P(t)) \left[w_{32} \frac{\partial p_3(t-1)}{\partial w_{31}} + p_5(t) \right] \tag{7.36}$$

$$\frac{\partial E(t)}{\partial w_{32}} = -(y(t) - P(t)) \left[w_{32} \frac{\partial p_3(t-1)}{\partial w_{32}} + p_5(t)p_3(t-1) \right] \tag{7.37}$$

where the output is $P(t) = p_3(t)$, the dynamic node derivatives with respect to the weights on the incoming connections are $\partial p_3(t-1)/\partial w_{31} = p_5(t-1)$, and respectively $\partial p_3(t-1)/\partial w_{32} = p_5(t-1)p_3(t-2)$.

The error derivatives with respect to the weights w_{51} and w_{52} entering the hidden left child node 5 at layer j, in Figure 7.2, at moment t are:

$$\frac{\partial E(t)}{\partial w_{51}} = e(t)\left[w_{31} + w_{32}p_3(t-1) \right] \left[w_{51} \frac{\partial p_3(t-1)}{\partial p_5(t-1)} \frac{\partial p_5(t-1)}{\partial w_{51}} + p_3(t-1) \right] \tag{7.38}$$

$$\frac{\partial E(t)}{\partial w_{52}} = e(t)\left[w_{31} + w_{32}p_3(t-1) \right] \left[w_{51} \frac{\partial p_3(t-1)}{\partial p_5(t-1)} \frac{\partial p_5(t-1)}{\partial w_{52}} + p_4^2(t) \right] \tag{7.39}$$

where $p_3(t-2) = \partial p_5(t-1)/\partial w_{51}$, and $p_4^2(t-1) = \partial p_5(t-1)/\partial w_{52}$.

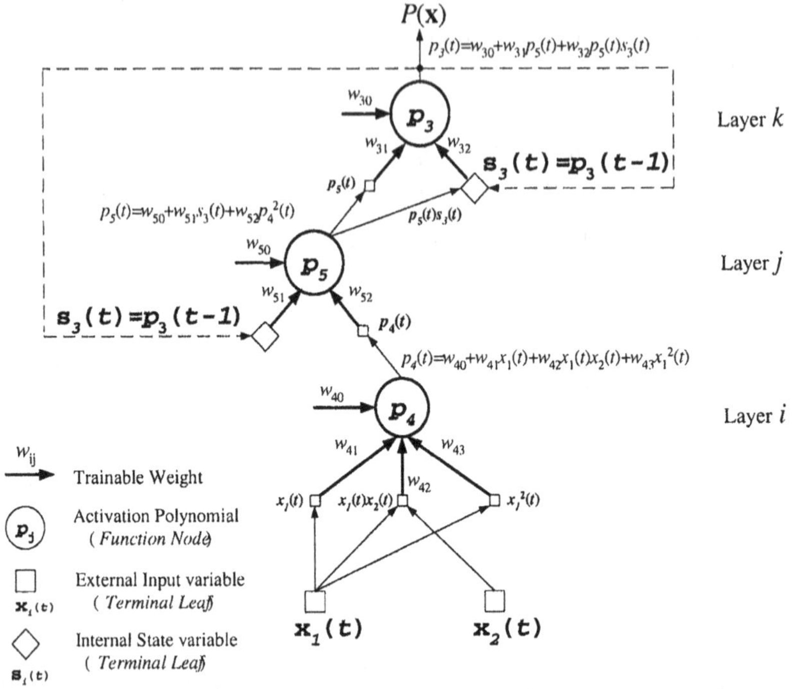

Figure 7.2. A detailed view of a tree-structured recurrent PNN with explicitly shown expanded connections and their weights.

The derivatives for the hidden right child node 4 at layer i of node 5, in Figure 7.2, at time tick t are easy to determine since there are no loops that send recurrent signals back to this node. The instantaneous error derivatives with respect to weights w_{41}, w_{42} and w_{43} are:

$$\frac{\partial E(t)}{\partial w_{41}} = \frac{\partial E(t)}{\partial p_5(t)}\frac{\partial p_5(t)}{\partial p_4(t)}\frac{\partial p_4(t)}{\partial w_{41}} = \frac{\partial E(t)}{\partial p_5(t)}\left[2w_{52}p_4(t)\right]x_1(t) \quad (7.40)$$

$$\frac{\partial E(t)}{\partial w_{42}} = \frac{\partial E(t)}{\partial p_5(t)}\frac{\partial p_5(t)}{\partial p_4(t)}\frac{\partial p_4(t)}{\partial w_{42}} = \frac{\partial E(t)}{\partial p_5(t)}\left[2w_{52}p_4(t)\right]x_1(t)x_2 \quad (7.41)$$

$$\frac{\partial E(t)}{\partial w_{43}} = \frac{\partial E(t)}{\partial p_5(t)}\frac{\partial p_5(t)}{\partial p_4(t)}\frac{\partial p_4(t)}{\partial w_{43}} = \frac{\partial E(t)}{\partial p_5(t)}\left[2w_{52}p_4(t)\right]x_1^2(t) \quad (7.42)$$

where $\partial E(t)/\partial p_5(t) = (y(t) - P(t))\left[w_{31} + w_{32}p_3(t-1)\right]$.

The RTRL algorithm is suitable for training recurrent PNN in incremental mode [Williams and Zipser, 1989, Williams and Zipser, 1995]. This incremental algorithm, shown in Table 7.3, modifies the weights at each step along the given data trajectory. The weight adjustments do not follow precisely the exact gradient on the error surface, but rather follow its estimate at the particular time tick. This means that RTRL updates the weights by approximating the exact gradient of the error function similar to standard incremental backpropagation. The approximation to the exact gradient is close when the learning rate is sufficiently small so that the magnitude of the weight changes are considerably smaller than the time magnitude of the network operation.

Table 7.3. Real-time recurrent learning algorithm for tree-like PNN.

RTRL Algorithm for PNN (incremental version)

step	*Algorithmic sequence*
1. Initialization	External data $x(t)$, states $s(t)$, and derivatives $\partial p(0)/\partial w = 0$.
2. Perform network weight training	Repeat many times a) For each time instant t, $t_0 \leq t \leq t_1 - 1$ do i) Forward pass: propagate inputs $x(t)$ and states $s(t)$ to compute the node outputs, i.e. the past states $s(t+1) \equiv p(t) = \sum_{m=1}^{5} w_m u_m(t)$, where $u(t) = \begin{cases} x(t) \\ s(t) \equiv p(t-1) \end{cases}$. ii) Backward pass: from the root down to the fringes - compute deltas for the output weights $\delta_k(t) = y(t) - P(t)$ if there is no recurrent connection $\Delta w_{kj}(t) = \eta \delta_k(t) x'_{kj}(t)$, where $x'_{kj}(t) = \partial p_k(t)/\partial w_{kj}$ else when there is a self-recurrent connection w_{kr} $\Delta w_{kj}(t) = \eta \delta_k(t) \left[w_{kr} \left(\partial p_k(t-1)/\partial w_{kj} \right) + u_j(t) \right]$. - compute deltas for hidden node weights $\delta_j(t) = -\delta_k(t) p'_{kj}(t)$, where $p'_{kj}(t) = \partial p_k(t)/\partial p_j(t)$ if there is no recurrent connection $\Delta w_{ji}(t) = \eta \delta_j(t) x'_{ji}(t)$, where $x'_{ji}(t) = \partial p_j(t)/\partial w_{ji}$ else when there is a self-recurrent connection from the l-th node above $\Delta w_{ji}(t) = \eta \delta_j(t) \left[w_{jr} \left(\partial p_l(t-1)/\partial w_{ji} \right) + u_i(t) \right]$ where if $j \neq l$ compute the chain derivative $\partial p_l(t-1)/\partial w_{ji} = \left[\partial p_l(t-1)/\partial p_j(t-1) \right] \left[\partial p_j(t-1)/\partial w_{ji} \right]$. iii) Update the network weights with the derivatives $w_{kj} = w_{kj} + \Delta w_{kj}(t)$ $w_{ji} = w_{ji} + \Delta w_{ji}(t)$. Until termination condition is satisfied.

7.4 Improved Dynamic Training

Recurrent PNN exhibit complex dynamics and their training is susceptible to entrapment in suboptimal weight configurations. Various strategies for improving the learning performance of recurrent networks as they run are available. They can help to decrease the computational complexity of the algorithms and to accelerate their convergence. Such specific techniques designed for extending the temporal backpropagation algorithms discussed here are teacher enforced training [Williams and Zipser, 1995], truncating in time [Williams and Zipser, 1995], and subgrouping [Williams and Zipser, 1995]. The truncating and subgrouping strategies compute the approximate error gradient.

7.4.1 Teacher Enforced Training

The speed of convergence of the dynamic PNN learning algorithms can be accelerated by teacher enforced training [Williams and Zipser, 1989, Williams and Zipser, 1995]. This is a technique that aims at better adjustment of the network dynamics to the data trajectory. The idea is to replace the looping node outputs, sent back recursively to feed lower layer nodes at certain time steps by the given target signals. Thus, the network weight search becomes more precisely guided by the teaching signal even if the network is unable to match the data. The desired signal may contribute to faster error reduction during learning as this teaching signal directly influences the weight adjustments.

Teacher forcing in recurrent PNN can be implemented by passing the desired signals to enter activation polynomial terms as follows:

$$u(t) = \begin{cases} d(t) & \text{for some } t \in D(t) \\ x(t) & t \notin D(t) \\ s(t) \equiv p(t-1) & t \notin D(t) \end{cases} \tag{7.43}$$

where $d(t)$ is the target from the selected set $D(t)$ at step t.

The teacher forcing causes only slight modifications of the temporal training rules for weight updating. Teacher guidance elaborated for the real-time BPTT algorithm means that when the future errors from the unfolded network in time are calculated they become zero at the selected desired values, and hence the backprop error is: $\delta_k(\tau) = 0$ and $\delta_j(\tau)$, for $t-1 \geq \tau \geq t_0+1$. Respectively, when the epochwise BPTT is enforced its backprop errors used for calculating the derivatives are simply reduced to the instantaneous errors at the current time step: $\delta_k(\tau) = -e_k(\tau)$ and $\delta_j(\tau) = -e_j(\tau)$, for $t-1 \geq \tau \geq t_0+1$.

Using teacher navigation in the RTRL training algorithm requires zeroing the activation polynomial derivatives $\partial p(t-1)/\partial w$ when computing the next derivative $\partial p(t)/\partial w$, since the derivative of the desired signal from the trajectory points with respect to any weight is zero.

7.4.2 Truncating in Time

Convergence of recurrent polynomial network training can be speeded up with the assumption that only a small subset of recent past data affects the network output. This truncation applied to BPTT [Williams and Zipser, 1995] requires unfolding the network only a small number of layers in time. Such time bounding relaxes the need to store the entire temporal history of the network, and so it enables a decrease in the complexity of the algorithm. However, the truncation may help to achieve a close approximation to the true gradient only if the outputs are not temporarily dependant on the external inputs from the distant past. It is recommended to apply the truncation mainly for repairing the real-time version of the BPTT algorithm.

Truncation in time can also be used to improve the RTRL algorithm [Catfolis, 1993] by computing the weight changes as dependent only on a small number of previous time ticks. The rationale for using short training trajectories is to make the temporal node output derivatives $\partial p(t)/\partial w$ sensitive to several recent steps only. This can be made by re-initializing the derivatives at a certain predefined number of steps. The size of the predefined time window is crucial for improving the learning performance; if it is closer to the optimal interval, then the convergence will be faster, otherwise the learning speed may be too slow and the algorithm may learn too little from the data.

7.4.3 Subgrouping

The subgrouping technique [Williams and Zipser, 1995] has been developed for reducing of the complexity of the RTRL algorithm for recurrent networks. The idea is to train separately smaller subnets of the network instead of training the whole network. When the network is partitioned into subnetworks, the learning is restricted to the individual subnetworks with considerably more sparse connectivity. The difficulty of how to identify the subnetworks of the studied recurrent network can be avoided by dividing it into subnetworks of approximately equal size in the sense of number of weights. The isolation of the subnetworks should be made in such a way that each of them has at least one node with the given desired values so as to enable separate training.

7.4.4 Common Temporal Training Problem

The most serious problem of temporal BP training of recurrent PNN arises from the so-called vanishing gradients [Bengio et al., 1994]. The magnitude of the temporal output derivatives tends to vanish to zero exponentially with the increase of the time steps. Because of this, the training process cannot converge to satisfactory solutions of the task, or converges extremely slowly. The recurrent network settles in configurations of weights that capture only short-term relationships in the data. One approach to avoiding this problem is to assume that the limited memory is an obstacle for storing information from arbitrary periods of time, and to try to extend it for handling longer periods. This idea suggests to consider larger PNN topologies with more hidden nodes, and respectively, more past hidden system states. Another approach is to perform second-order temporal training.

7.5 Second-Order Temporal BP

A general strategy for efficient learning is to use the second-order information from the error derivatives. The second-order gradient optimization methods (Section 6.3) can also be applied for improving the convergence of temporal BP training of recurrent PNN. The implementation of such methods requires calculation of the Hessian matrix (6.39). Knowing how to find the entries of the temporal Hessian enables us to develop versions of Newton's method, pseudo-Newton method, conjugate gradients, and Levenberg-Marquardt method for training recurrent PNN. Such temporal BP training methods can be designed in either of two ways: 1) by computing the full temporal Hessian, or 2) by computing a diagonal approximation to the temporal Hessian.

The diagonal approximation of the temporal Hessian can be made as in the static case by multiplying the first-order error derivatives of the network outputs with respect to the weights at the particular time instants: $(\partial P(t)/\partial w_i)\,(\partial P(t)/\partial w_j)^T$. The full temporal Hessian consists of second-order error derivatives of the PNN outputs with respect to the weights at the concrete time step:

$$[\mathbf{H}]_{ij}(t) = \sum_{t=t_0+1}^{t_1} \left\{ \left(\frac{\partial P(t)}{\partial w_i}\right) \left(\frac{\partial P(t)}{\partial w_j}\right)^T - e(t) \left(\frac{\partial^2 P(t)}{\partial w_i \partial w_j}\right)^2 \right\} \tag{7.44}$$

where $e(t) = y(t) - P(t)$ is the error at time t. These entries can be obtained by specializing the $\mathcal{R}$-propagation algorithm [Pearlmutter, 1994] for recurrent PNN.

$\mathcal{R}$-propagation for Recurrent PNN. The $\mathcal{R}$-propagation algorithm [Pearlmutter, 1994] performs forward and backward network traversals for estimating the derivatives, adapts the matrix after each next example, and repeats such cycles W times, once for each column of the Hessian. The temporal output derivatives in recurrent PNNs can be made in two ways: 1) using the BPTT algorithm (Section 7.2), or 2) using the RTRL algorithm (Section 7.3). The BPTT algorithm, however, may not produce the proper instantaneous derivative $\partial P/\partial w(\tau)$. That is, it may not be equal to the exact one $\partial P(t)/\partial w$, because it is usually computed with training history size much smaller than the size of the whole interval from the current moment down to the beginning of the training interval. Moreover, the gradient computed backwards becomes very small. This is known as the vanishing gradient problem [Bengio et al., 1994]. For this reason, the RTRL algorithm should be preferred for computing the temporal Hessian in recurrent PNN as it is more reliable for generating the instantaneous derivative $\partial P(t)/\partial w$.

According to the discrete-time equation (7.3), the network root node generates output $p_k(t) = \sum_j w_{kj}u_j(t)$, where w_{kj} is a weight on link from the j-th child node feeding an external variable $u_j(t) = x_i(t)$, an activation polynomial output $u_j(t) = \sum_i w_{ji}p_i(t)$, or a past state of some hidden node $u_j(t) = s(t)$ (7.4). The forward pass of the $\mathcal{R}$-operator applied to activation polynomials like $p_k(t)$ and $p_j(t)$ involves the computation of the following quantities:

$$\mathcal{R}\{p_j(t)\} = \sum_i v_{ji}x_i(t) \tag{7.45}$$

$$\mathcal{R}\{p_j(t)\} = \sum_i w_{ji}\mathcal{R}\{p_i(t)\} + \sum_i v_{ji}p_i(t) \tag{7.46}$$

$$\mathcal{R}\{p_k(t)\} = \sum_j w_{kj}\mathcal{R}\{p_j(t)\} + \sum_j v_{kj}p_j(t) \tag{7.47}$$

where $v_{ji} \in \mathbf{v}$ is an element from the binary unit vector $\mathbf{v}$ in $\mathcal{R} = \mathbf{v}^T\nabla$ (6.47). This is different from the static case because here there are discretely sampled external variables, and the polynomial outputs appear at discrete steps, which lead to different derivatives.

During the backpropagation pass, the $\mathcal{R}$-operator is applied to the backprop errors estimated at the root and at the hidden network nodes. The result at the root output node coincides with the operator application with the root polynomial. At the hidden nodes the backprop errors are: $\delta_j(t) = (-\delta_k(t))p'_{kj}(t)$ where the derivative is $p'_{kj}(t) = \partial p_k(t)/\partial p_j(t)$. Acting on these backprop errors with the $\mathcal{R}$-operator leads to the following two corresponding equations:

$$\mathcal{R}\{\delta_k(t)\} = \mathcal{R}\{p_k(t)\} \tag{7.48}$$

$$\mathcal{R}\{\delta_j(t)\} = \mathcal{R}\{-\delta_k(t)\}p'_{kj}(t) + (-\delta_k(t))\mathcal{R}\{p'_{kj}(t)\} \tag{7.49}$$

where $\mathcal{R}\{\delta_k(t)\}$ is the application of the operator at the root node, and $\mathcal{R}\{\delta_j(t)\}$ is the application of the operator at hidden nodes.

Traversing the tree-like PNN structure down from the root toward the leaves is accompanied by computing the error derivatives: $\partial E(t)/\partial w_{kj}$ (7.28, 7.29), and $\partial E(t)/\partial w_{ji}$ (7.30, 7.31). The application of the $\mathcal{R}$-operator to these error derivatives is as follows:

$$\mathcal{R}\left\{\frac{\partial E(t)}{\partial w_{kj}}\right\} = -\mathcal{R}\{\delta_k(t)\}u'_{kj}(t) - \delta_k(t)\mathcal{R}\{u'_{kj}(t)\} \quad (7.50)$$

$$\mathcal{R}\left\{\frac{\partial E(t)}{\partial w_{ji}}\right\} = -\mathcal{R}\{\delta_j(t)\}u'_{ji}(t) - \delta_j(t)\mathcal{R}\{u'_{ji}(t)\} \quad (7.51)$$

where for clarity, two additional variables u'_{kj} and u'_{ji} are used.

These variables u'_{kj} and u'_{ji} distinguish the effects of the recurrent connections in the network; they capture the impact of the backward links on the neural network output at the particular time step. The variables u'_{kj} and u'_{ji} are substitutions for the following equations:

$$u'_{kj}(t) = \sum_r w_{kr}\frac{\partial p_k(t-1)}{\partial w_{kj}} + u_j(t) \quad (7.52)$$

$$u'_{ji}(t) = \sum_r w_{jr}\frac{\partial p_l(t-1)}{\partial w_{ji}} + u_i(t) \quad (7.53)$$

where p_l is an arbitrary activation polynomial output sent via the corresponding recurrent connection. When the $\mathcal{R}$-operator is applied to these variables the summation goes in front and the operator acts on each incoming link that enters the node. Their corresponding applications $\mathcal{R}\{u'_{kj}(t)\}$ and $\mathcal{R}\{u'_{ji}(t)\}$ after some simplifications become:

$$\mathcal{R}\{u'_{kj}(t)\} = \sum_r \left(w_{kr}\mathcal{R}\left\{\frac{\partial p_k(t-1)}{\partial w_{kj}}\right\} + v_{kr}p_k{}' \right) + \mathcal{R}\{u_j(t)\} \quad (7.54)$$

$$\mathcal{R}\{u'_{ji}(t)\} = \sum_r \left(w_{jr}\mathcal{R}\left\{\frac{\partial p_l(t-1)}{\partial w_{ji}}\right\} + v_{jr}p_l{}' \right) + \mathcal{R}\{u_i(t)\} \quad (7.55)$$

where $p_k{}' = \partial p_k(t-1)/\partial w_{kj}$, $p_l{}' = \partial p_l(t-1)/\partial w_{ji}$, and the operators $\mathcal{R}\{\partial p_k(t-1)/\partial w_{kj}\}$ and $\mathcal{R}\{\partial p_l(t-1)/\partial w_{ji}\}$ denote applications to polynomials that can be made using the ready formulas (7.45, 7.46, 7.47).

Table 7.4. Summary of the $\mathcal{R}$-propagation algorithm for recurrent PNN.

$\mathcal{R}$-propagation for Recurrent PNN

step	*Algorithmic sequence*
1. Initialize	Data $\mathcal{D} = \{(\mathbf{x}_n, y_n)\}_{n=1}^{N}$, and a vector $\mathbf{v} = (0, 0, ..., 0)$
2. Train Network Weights	For each weight c, $1 \leq c \leq W$ a) Set the vector entry $\mathbf{v}_c = 1.0$. b) Compute the dot product $\mathbf{v}^T\mathbf{H}$ in one epoch as follows: For each training example $(\mathbf{x}_n, y_n)$, $1 \leq n \leq N$, do i) Perform a forward pass and estimate $u_j(t) = \sum_i w_{ji}p_i(t)_i$, or $u_j(t) = x_i(t)$ $\mathcal{R}\{p_j(t)\} = \sum_i w_{ji}\mathcal{R}\{p_i(t)\} + \sum_i v_{ji}p_i(t)$ $p_k(t) = \sum_j w_{kj}u_j(t)$ $\mathcal{R}\{p_k(t)\} = \sum_j w_{kj}\mathcal{R}\{p_j(t)\} + \sum_j v_{kj}p_j(t)$. ii) Perform a backward pass - calculate the output node delta and derivatives $\delta_k(t) = y(t) - P(t)$, $p'_{kj}(t) = \partial p_k(t)/\partial p_j(t)$, and $x'_{kj}(t) = \partial p_k(t)/\partial w_{kj}$. - apply the $\mathcal{R}$-operator $\mathcal{R}\{\delta_k(t)\} = \mathcal{R}\{p_k(t)\}$ $u'_{kj}(t) = \sum_r w_{kr}(\partial p_k(t-1)/\partial w_{kj}) + u_j(t)$ $\mathcal{R}\{u'_{kj}(t)\} = \sum_r R_r + \mathcal{R}\{u_j(t)\}$ $R_r = w_{kr}\mathcal{R}\{\partial p_k(t-1)/\partial w_{kj}\} + v_{kr}\partial p_k(t-1)/\partial w_{kj}$ $\mathcal{R}\{\partial E(t)/\partial w_{kj}\} = -\mathcal{R}\{\delta_k(t)\}u'_{kj}(t) - \delta_k(t)\mathcal{R}\{u'_{kj}(t)\}$. - calculate backwards hidden deltas and derivatives $\delta_j(t) = (-\delta_k(t))p'_{kj}(t)$, and $x'_{ji}(t) = \partial p_j(t)/\partial w_{ji}$. - apply the $\mathcal{R}$-operator $\mathcal{R}\{\delta_j(t)\} = \mathcal{R}\{-\delta_k(t)\}p'_{kj}(t) + (-\delta_k(t))\mathcal{R}\{p'_{kj}(t)\}$ $u'_{ji}(t) = \sum_r w_{jr}(\partial p_l(t-1)/\partial w_{ji})\partial p_l(t-1) + u_i(t)$ $\mathcal{R}\{u'_{ji}(t)\} = \sum_r R_r + \mathcal{R}\{u_i(t)\}$ $R_r = w_{jr}\mathcal{R}\{\partial p_l(t-1)/\partial w_{ji}\} + v_{jr}(\partial p_l(t-1)/\partial w_{ji})$ $\mathcal{R}\{\partial E(t)/\partial w_{ji}\} = -\mathcal{R}\{\delta_j(t)\}u'_{ji}(t) - \delta_j(t)\mathcal{R}\{u'_{ji}(t)\}$.
3. Evaluate	Extract the Hessian from $\mathbf{v}^T\mathbf{H}$.

Having algorithms for calculation of the temporal Hessian provides abilities not only to develop second-order temporal BP training algorithms for recurrent PNN, but also to implement second-order network pruning, as well as to realize approaches for estimation of confident, prediction intervals. Further discussions on recurrent network pruning and regularization are provided in subsections 7.7.1 and 7.7.2.

The algorithm for performing $\mathcal{R}$-propagation on recurrent PNN is given in the above Table 7.4.

7.6 Recursive Backpropagation

Recent research in temporal data processing points out that an efficient way to avoid many of the disadvantages of gradient descent search techniques for dynamic neural network training is to apply recursive least squares methods, which are closely related to Kalman filter methods [Haykin, 2001]. Instead of first-order or second-order gradient descent algorithms one can use recursive least squares for weight adaptation to achieve faster convergence. The recursive least squares methods are suitable for modeling dynamically changing data as they utilize the information in the data arriving as a sequence, and so enable us to capture time-varying effects. These methods are convenient for weight learning in PNN when processing temporal data where the traditionally used OLS suffers from numerical instabilities.

A *recursive backpropagation* (RBP) algorithm is developed here for minimum least-squares weight estimation in recurrent PNN. This is a kind of neuron-level Kalman filter training algorithm applied locally at each network node [Shah et al., 1992, Puskorius and Felkamp, 1994]. The recursive formula treats the activation polynomials in the polynomial network nodes as linear, since they are linearized by means of their output dynamic derivatives with respect to the weights. The RBP updates the weights using backward propagated dynamic derivatives. Since the dynamic derivatives are computed in the style of the backpropagation algorithm this gives the name RBP. RBP repeatedly performs a number of epochs, where each epoch involves an incremental presentation of all data from the beginning to the end of the given interval.

The learning objective of RBP training is minimization of the instantaneous cost function: $E(t) = (1/2)(y(t) - P(t))^2$. Assuming that the weights on links entering a particular network node at time t are arranged into a vector: $\mathbf{w}(t) = [w_1(t), w_2(t), ..., w_m(t)]$, and the approximate error-covariance matrix is $\mathbf{A}$ of size $m \times m$, the equations for calculating the weight updates are as follows:

$$\mathbf{r}(t) = \mathbf{A}^{-1}(t-1)\mathbf{j}(t) \quad (7.56)$$

$$\mathbf{k}(t) = \mathbf{r}(t)[\eta^{-1} + \mathbf{j}^T(t)\mathbf{r}(t)]^{-1} \quad (7.57)$$

$$\mathbf{w}(t) = \mathbf{w}(t-1) + \mathbf{k}(t)[y(t) - P(t)] \quad (7.58)$$

$$\mathbf{A}^{-1}(t) = \eta[\mathbf{A}^{-1}(t-1) - \mathbf{k}(t)\mathbf{j}^T(t)\mathbf{A}^{-1}(t-1)] \quad (7.59)$$

where $\mathbf{j}(t)$ is the vector with dynamic output derivatives with respect to the node weights from the previous time step: $\mathbf{j}(t) = \partial P(t)/\partial \mathbf{w}|_{\mathbf{w}=\mathbf{w}(t-1)}$, and η is a forgetting factor that plays a role similar to learning rate.

This set of recursive formula considers one weight vector and corrects it in pursuit of reaching a minimum mean squared error solution. Using the a priori vector $\mathbf{w}(t-1)$, a one step ahead prediction of the network output $P(t)$ is generated. The predicted output $P(t)$ is then related to the new presented measurement $y(t)$ to evaluate the discrepancy between them, which serves as innovation suggesting by what amount to adjust the weight. The a posteriori weight vector $\mathbf{w}(t)$ is computed by formula (7.58) in proportion to the innovation and another quantity called the Kalman gain (7.57). The computation of the Kalman gain requires one to recompute the covariance matrix $\mathbf{A}^{-1}(0)$ (7.59).

The dynamic derivatives at each time instant can be determined using the RTRL algorithm for recurrent PNN. These dynamic derivatives account for weights on connections feeding three kinds of inputs: external variables, activation polynomial outputs, and internal network states. The effect of the forgetting factor is to diminish the effect from distant data in the past. During incremental training the output $P(t)$ at time t captures information about the whole data history, and therefore the error $y(t) - P(t)$ also carries information about all observed data from time $t_0 + 1$ up to the present t. The forgetting parameter values are selected from the interval $\eta^{-1} \in [0 \div 1]$. The inverse of the approximate error-covariance matrix is initialized with large elements $[\mathbf{A}^{-1}(0)]_{ii} = c$, where c is a number in the range $c \in [10^3 \div 10^8]$.

Applying such recursive algorithms should be accompanied by adding artificial process noise $[\mathbf{Q}(0)]_{ii} \in [10^{-3} \div 10^{-6}]$ to the diagonal of the covariance matrix to speed up the training convergence [Haykin, 2001]. When training incrementally, the noise should be adapted over time so as to add a stochastic character to the learning process. A simple strategy to tune the noise is to modify it using simulated annealing so that it slowly diminishes with time.

When RBP is applied to tree-structured PNN where each hidden node feeds exactly one parent node, there is no need to perform matrix inversion because the quantity inside the brackets in equation (7.57) is a scalar. This avoidance of numerical computation difficulties makes RBP attractive for inductive problem solving. Another reason to use RBP is its relatively low computational complexity $\mathcal{O}(m^2\mathcal{F})$, where m is the number of weights per neuron, and $\mathcal{F}$ is the number of neurons in the network. This is only the complexity for evaluating the matrix equations (7.56, 7.57, 7.58, 7.59), however. Therefore, in order to obtain the full complexity of RBP, the overhead for computing the dynamic derivatives by the RTRL algorithm have to be added.

The recursive BPA training algorithm specialized for training recurrent PNN, using derivatives calculated according to the RTRL strategy, is illustrated in Table 7.5.

Table 7.5. BPA for training recurrent PNN using derivatives computed by RTRL.

Recursive Backpropagation for PNN (incremental version)

step	*Algorithmic sequence*
1. Initialization	External data $x(t)$, states $s(t)$, derivatives $\partial p(0)/\partial w = 0$, forgetting factor $\eta^{-1} = 0.9$, noise $[\mathbf{Q}(0)]_{ii} = 1.0e-3$ initial covariance matrix of elements $[\mathbf{A}^{-1}(0)]_{ii} = 1.0e3$.
2. Perform network weight training	Repeat a) For each time instant t, $t_0 \leq t \leq t_1 - 1$ do i) Forward propagate the inputs $x(t)$ and the states $s(t)$ to compute node outputs. ii) Backward pass: during top-down tree traversal do - if this is the root node compute the output error $\delta_k(t) = y(t) - P(t)$ and the dynamic derivatives $\mathbf{j}(t) = \partial P(t)/\partial \mathbf{w}_{kj}$. - else if this is a hidden node compute the derivatives $\mathbf{j}(t) = [\partial P(t)/\partial p_j(t)][\partial p_j(t)/\partial \mathbf{w}_{ji}]$. - calculate the Kalman gain $\mathbf{k}(t) = \mathbf{A}^{-1}(t-1)\mathbf{j}(t)[\eta^{-1} + \mathbf{j}^T(t)\mathbf{A}^{-1}(t-1)\mathbf{j}(t)]^{-1}$. - update the weights at this network node $\mathbf{w}(t) = \mathbf{w}(t-1) + \mathbf{k}(t)[y(t) - P(t)]$. - update the covariance matrix $\mathbf{V}(t) = \mathbf{k}(t)\mathbf{j}^T(t)\mathbf{A}^{-1}(t-1)$ $\mathbf{A}^{-1}(t) = \eta[\mathbf{A}^{-1}(t-1) - \mathbf{V}(t)] + \mathbf{Q}(t-1)$. - update the process noise $\mathbf{Q}(t) = F[\mathbf{Q}(t-1)]$. Until termination condition is satisfied.

7.7 Recurrent Network Optimization

The complexity of recurrent PNN should be optimized during and after their temporal backpropagation training. Their generalization performance could be improved because they may not be topologically relevant enough and tuned to the data, and also there may be redundant weights in the model. Even if the network has been learned by IGP, superfluous weights can still remain in it, or at least their effect on the output should be diminished in order to enhance the model predictability. When the network is complex, in the sense of having redundant weights or weights of excessive magnitudes, it tends to overfit the data and exhibits a large generalization error. In temporal BP training, the complexity of recurrent PNN can be controlled by applying regularization and optimized using pruning methods.

7.7.1 Regularization

Regularization can be implemented by adding a weight decay penalty to the total temporal training error function, thus making a regularized average error (RAE) similar to the one for static networks. The derived regularized temporal weight training rule, which is easy to instantiate for BPTT and RTRL in particular, remains essentially in the same format: $w = (1 - \eta\lambda)w + \Delta w$, where λ is the regularizer.

Recurrent PNN can also be regularized in a specific way so as to separately control the complexity of feed-forward and the complexity of backward connections. This idea for separate weight shrinking can be implemented by reformulating the regularized average error to account for the effects from the different groups of weights separately:

$$RAE = \frac{1}{t_1}\left(\sum_{t=t_0+1}^{t_1} (y(t) - P(t))^2 + \lambda_f \sum_f w_f^2 + \lambda_b \sum_b w_b^2\right) \qquad (7.60)$$

where f is the index of the forward links, and b is the index of the backward recurrent links. The different regularizers λ_f and λ_b can be found using the Bayesian regularization approach. When the Bayesian formula is applied to determine the proper values of one of the regularizers, the other should be kept fixed. The temporal weight training rules obtained as solutions to the above RAE equation set to zero at the minimum of the error surface are:

$$w_f = (1 - \eta\lambda_f)w_f + \Delta w_f \qquad (7.61)$$

$$w_b = (1 - \eta\lambda_b)w_b + \Delta w_b \qquad (7.62)$$

where η is the usual learning rate parameter.

7.7.2 Recurrent Network Pruning

A direct approach to optimizing the structural complexity of recurrent PNN is weight pruning. Network pruning methods are direct in the sense that they eliminate connections while regularization is an indirect method because it only diminishes the weight magnitudes without necessarily removing weights. Recurrent PNN can be pruned using the same methods developed for static PNN which are discussed in Section 6.5. There are first-order (Section 6.5.1) and second-order (Section 6.5.2) pruning methods. The difference is that they have to be implemented using the temporal gradient and the temporal Hessian which makes their design more involved [Pedersen and Hansen, 1995].

Training of recurrent PNN by recursive least squares also enables us to perform efficient pruning because the RBP algorithm computes the covariance matrix at every time step which contains important information about the network weights. A weight can be discarded from the recurrent network if its magnitude is small and its deviation during training is large. The saliency of a recurrent PNN weight is determined with the following formula:

$$s_{ij} = \frac{1-\eta^{-1}}{2}[\mathbf{A}^{-1}(t)]_{ij} w_{ij}^2 \tag{7.63}$$

where $[\mathbf{A}^{-1}(t)]_{ij}$ is the diagonal entry of the covariance matrix, and η is the forgetting parameter. The usefulness of this formula comes from the possibility of applying it with an arbitrary amount of data.

7.8 Chapter Summary

The backpropagation techniques BPTT and RTRL presented in this chapter are general approaches to gradient descent training of polynomial networks with arbitrary feedback connections. What makes RTRL different from BPTT is that the former attempts to determine the gradient vector directly by computing the errors at the available time steps, while the latter recovers past temporal information from which the gradient is obtained. BPTT is nonlocal in time but local in space, hence it is less complex to develop. RTRL is local in time and nonlocal in space, therefore much more complex to develop.

Each of these algorithms has its advantages and disadvantages that can be distinguished on the basis of their computational requirements. The main disadvantage of the real-time BPTT algorithm is that it needs unlimited memory resources when running indefinitely through time, while the epochwise BPTT seems more attractive with respect to memory resources as it considers limited time intervals between predefined boundaries. The major criticisms of the RTRL algorithm are that it is computationally intensive, and it communicates nonlocal information between the nodes which makes its implementation more difficult. The recurrent PNN usually feature sparse connectivity, so their training is faster and less demanding on memory.

The use of the epochwise BPTT method that performs batch temporal training is reasonable when there is preliminary knowledge indicating that the series data to be modeled are stationary. When the training environment is nonstationary, the incremental methods (real-time BPTT and RTRL) should be preferred as they are less sensitive to the changing data trajectory. RTRL is especially attractive due to its inherent abilities to conduct stochastic search which can overcome the deteriorating effect of the fluctuations in the given data on learning.

Chapter 8

BAYESIAN INFERENCE TECHNIQUES

The previous chapters presented maximum likelihood (ML) approaches to learning the network weights. They find the weights using the particular training set by minimizing the sum of squared errors criterion. There are alternative, more general approaches that generate maximum a posteriori (MAP) weights following the theory of Bayesian inference [MacKay, 1992a, MacKay, 2003, Buntine and Weigend, 1991b, Neal, 1996, Bishop, 1995, Tipping, 2001, Doucet et al., 2001]. The MAP weights are averaged statistics of the weights distribution with respect to the data distribution; they are not obtained simply as point estimates from the provided training data. According to the Bayesian framework, the weights and model uncertainties are described with probability distributions, and inference is performed by applying probabilistic rules to them. The initial beliefs in the weights are encoded into corresponding priors. After seeing the data through their likelihood, the belief in the weights is updated using Bayes' theorem and thus the posterior probability density of the weights is obtained. Having the weight posterior, and more precisely its mean, the MAP weights vector, allows us to compute the predictive data distribution and to generate predictions for unseen inputs along with their confidence intervals.

Probabilistic reasoning enables us to handle simultaneously the weights and the structure of the networks. During training, the model accuracy is balanced automatically with the model complexity so as to improve generalization. This integration helps to mitigate the over-flexibility problem in neural networks that causes capturing of spurious information from the data which is deteriorating for their predictive performance. The Bayesian inference techniques applied to polynomial networks offer the following benefits [MacKay, 1992a, Bishop, 1995]: 1) they provide objective error functions and analytical training rules that implicitly account for the noise level; 2) they learn the weight parameters along with doing model selection; and 3) they yield probabilistic results without artificial data splitting for model validation. Their shortcoming is their sensitivity to the prior assumptions.

The Bayesian approaches to neural network modelling have been developed in two main directions: 1) derivation of training techniques based on a Gaussian approximation to the weight posterior distribution, elaborated with the evidence framework [MacKay, 1992a, MacKay, 1992b]; and 2) derivation of techniques based on Monte Carlo sampling of the weights [Neal, 1996, Doucet et al., 2001]. The evidence framework assumes that the weight posterior is Gaussian in order to obtain the priors on the weights, and reevaluates them in an alternating manner to adapt the model to the data. Applying the evidence procedure to polynomial neural networks allows us to achieve: 1) inference of the most probable weight parameters at the mean of their posterior distribution, with proper handling of the noise; 2) adaptive learning of global and local regularization parameters for model smoothing; 3) neural network complexity tuning by pruning due to the adaptive regularization; the adaptive regularization eliminates implausible weights, which involves automatic relevance determination of the necessary input variables and discarding of irrelevant connections; and 4) estimation of confidence and prediction intervals of the network outputs. The Monte Carlo approach helps to design alternative algorithms for neural network training in relaxed conditions like non-Gaussianity. Most popular is the Markov Chain Monte Carlo (MCMC) algorithm based on sampling.

This chapter offers specialized techniques for Bayesian PNN learning. These probabilistic techniques are iterative in the sense that they repeatedly carry out computations with the training data until the network structure and its weights become optimally adjusted. Algorithms have been developed for finding local, individual regularization parameters for each polynomial term weight, and for pruning polynomial terms from the network architecture. Computing the predictive density and performing prediction using this data distribution is explained. Sparse Bayesian learning is investigated using the Expectation-Maximization (EM) algorithm. Next, a recursive algorithm for sequential Bayesian learning is given. This algorithm is especially suitable to apply when modelling time series. Finally, a Monte Carlo sampling algorithm made for training polynomial networks is illustrated. Bayesian prediction intervals for PNN are later discussed in Chapter 9. The specific application details concerning linear PNN models and nonlinear multilayer PNN are discussed separately.

8.1 Bayesian Error Function

The problem of inductive learning with neural networks is to find the most probable weights from the data. This learning problem usually has to deal with noisy targets, so overfitting avoidance is an essential objective. Avoidance of overfitting with the data can be pursued adopting the principles of Bayesian inference theory. Bayesian methods use probabilities to represent uncertainties, and doing inference with them involves solving integrals; that is, finding averaged statistics.

Traditionally, neural network training aims at minimization of the sum-of-squares error function estimated with the data (6.2):

$$E_D(\mathbf{w}) = \frac{1}{2}\sum_{n=1}^{N}(y_n - P(\mathbf{x}_n, \mathbf{w}))^2 \tag{8.1}$$

where y_n are the targets, and $P(\mathbf{x}_n, \mathbf{w})$ are the network outputs produced with the n-th input vector $\mathbf{x}_n$ using the weights $\mathbf{w}$. The relationship between the targets and the model is: $y_n = P(\mathbf{x}_n, \mathbf{w}) + \epsilon_n$, where ϵ_n is independent Gaussian noise with zero mean and variance σ_y^2, which is usually denoted by $\epsilon_n = \mathcal{N}(0, \sigma_y^2)$.

Bayes' theorem helps to find that the degree of data fitting is not sufficient as a single learning criterion because it may lead to data sensitive models. It is necessary to impose structural constraints to the network in order to make it smooth enough to attain good generalization. This factor is subjective because the characteristics of the model that best describes the data are not known in advance. The model generalization can be improved by adding to the error complexity penalties that favor simpler, sparse models with small weights. This is achieved by regularizing the accuracy $E_D(\mathbf{w})$ (8.1) with a complexity factor $E_W(\mathbf{w})$ factor, and so making a *Bayesian error function*:

$$E_R(\mathbf{w}) = \beta E_D(\mathbf{w}) + E_W(\mathbf{w}) \tag{8.2}$$

where the hyperparameters α enter the factor $E_W(\mathbf{w})$.

A popular complexity factor in the neural network community is the *weight decay regularization*, defined by the following equation:

$$E_W(\mathbf{w}) = \frac{1}{2}\mathbf{w}^T\mathbf{A}\mathbf{w} \tag{8.3}$$

where $\mathbf{A}$ is a diagonal matrix with the prior hyperparameters $\mathbf{A} = diag(\alpha_0, \alpha_1, \alpha_2, ..., \alpha_W)$. In the general case, there is a separate, local hyperparameter α_i that controls each particular weight w_i, $1 \leq i \leq W$. The number W of hyperparameters is equal to the number of weights. The hyperparameters only take positive values.

The effect of this complexity factor can be explained from two points of view. First, viewing this complexity factor (8.3) as a formula dependent on the number of weights in the network implies that too many weights should be penalized. This is because a complex model approximates the data very closely, including even their uncertainties, and thus it leads to overfitting. Less complex, sparse networks should be favored because they are more likely to describe the data smoothly, and so they are more likely to have good generalization potential. Secondly, viewing this complexity factor (8.3) as dependent on the weights implies that small weight values should be tolerated while large weights should not be preferred as they imply fluctuating mappings.

8.2 Bayesian Neural Network Inference

The learning of neural networks using the above cost function (8.2) may be envisioned as a process of Bayesian inference of the posterior distribution of the weights given the data. The weight posterior can be described using the *Bayes' theorem*:

$$\Pr(\mathbf{w}|\mathbf{y}, X, \boldsymbol{\alpha}, \beta^{-1}) = \frac{\Pr(\mathbf{y}|X, \mathbf{w}, \beta^{-1}) \Pr(\mathbf{w}|\boldsymbol{\alpha})}{\Pr(\mathbf{y}|X, \boldsymbol{\alpha}, \beta^{-1})} \tag{8.4}$$

where the given training data $D = \{(\mathbf{x}_n, y_n)\}_{n=1}^N$ are assumed to be independent. Here, for notational convenience, the inputs are taken in rows as a matrix X, and the outputs are a column vector $\mathbf{y}$.

According to Bayes' rule (8.4), the weight posterior is obtained as a normalized product of the data probability $\Pr(\mathbf{y}|X, \mathbf{w}, \beta^{-1})$ and the weight prior probability $\Pr(\mathbf{w}|\boldsymbol{\alpha})$ divided by the evidence for the adopted network model $\Pr(\mathbf{y}|X, \boldsymbol{\alpha}, \beta^{-1})$ [MacKay, 1992a]. Since the normalizer $\Pr(\mathbf{y}|X, \boldsymbol{\alpha}, \beta^{-1})$ is a sum of Gaussians, the weight posterior distribution also becomes Gaussian $\Pr(\mathbf{w}|\mathbf{y}, X, \boldsymbol{\alpha}, \beta^{-1}) = \mathcal{N}(\mathbf{w}|\boldsymbol{\mu}, \boldsymbol{\Sigma})$ with mean $\boldsymbol{\mu}$ and covariance matrix $\boldsymbol{\Sigma}$.

In this probabilistic network model (8.4), the quantity in the numerator $\Pr(\mathbf{y}|X, \mathbf{w}, \beta^{-1})$ is the *likelihood of the data.* This likelihood accounts for the neural network accuracy on the training set. It is actually a distribution with variance σ_y^2, which taken inversely is denoted as a special *output noise hyperparameter* $\beta = \sigma_y^{-2}$. Assuming a zero-mean normally distributed noise, the likelihood of the data can be written as:

$$\Pr(\mathbf{y}|X, \mathbf{w}, \beta^{-1}) = \frac{1}{Z_D(\beta^{-1})} \exp\left(-\beta E_D(\mathbf{w})\right) \tag{8.5}$$

where the normalizing constant $Z_D(\beta)$ is given by the expression:

$$Z_D(\beta^{-1}) = \left(2\pi\beta^{-1}\right)^{N/2} \tag{8.6}$$

The second quantity in the numerator $\Pr(\mathbf{w}|\boldsymbol{\alpha})$ is the *prior probability of the weights*. This weight prior accounts for the assumptions concerning the correlations between the weights and the shape of the functional network mapping. The treatment of this prior follows modern Bayesian analysis which provides ideas for proper assignment of subjective beliefs in the inductive learning process [MacKay, 1992a]. More precisely, Bayesian analysis using weight priors gives formulae that show how and where we may include our initial knowledge about the relative model complexity with respect to the data.

Two kinds of priors can be assigned: a global prior, which is a common regularization hyperparameter, or local individual priors for each weight. Both kinds of *prior hyperparameters* can be expressed with the notation: $\boldsymbol{\alpha} = [\alpha_1, ..., \alpha_W]$. In the case of a global prior, we have: $\alpha_1 = \alpha_2 = ... = \alpha_W$. Imposing local Gaussian priors on the weights is described by the following zero-mean factorized prior:

$$\Pr(\mathbf{w}|\boldsymbol{\alpha}) = \frac{1}{\prod_{i=1}^{W} Z_W(\alpha_i)} \exp\left(-\frac{1}{2}\sum_{i=1}^{W} \alpha_i w_i^2\right) \tag{8.7}$$

where the hyperparameters are independent, and the normalizer is:

$$Z_W(\alpha_i) = \left(\frac{2\pi}{\alpha_i}\right)^{W/2} \tag{8.8}$$

which involves the weight variances written inversely as: $\alpha_i = \sigma_{w_i}^{-2}$.

The quantity $\Pr(\mathbf{y}|X, \boldsymbol{\alpha}, \beta^{-1})$ in the denominator of the Bayesian network model (8.4) is the joint distribution of the hyperparameters. This distribution is constant, does not depend on the network weights, and is called *evidence* [MacKay, 1992a]. The calculation of the evidence for the hyperparameters enables us to determine the level of regularization with which the maximum posteriori weights are obtained. The evidence plays another special role in the Bayesian paradigm, namely it helps to rank the networks and to carry out objective model selection. It is useful to compute this evidence for PNN because they are extremely flexible models that often tend to overfit, so the ability to distinguish the optimal models among them is important for successful learning.

The conventional backpropagation algorithms attempt to find the weights $\mathbf{w}$ by maximizing the likelihood $\Pr(\mathbf{y}|X, \mathbf{w}, \beta^{-1})$, thus trying to maximize the posterior probability $\Pr(\mathbf{w}|\mathbf{y}, X, \boldsymbol{\alpha}, \beta^{-1})$ relying on a fixed network architecture. What the Bayesian approach changes in this strategy is providing means for adaptation of the model complexity with respect to the data distribution, in other words, for dealing properly with alternative models. The *evidence procedure* [MacKay, 1992b] shows that this idea can be implemented by estimating the hyperparameters $\boldsymbol{\alpha}$ and β iteratively, in order to approach the maximum of the weight posterior and to produce a plausible neural network model. Since the weight posterior is sensitive to the changes of $\boldsymbol{\alpha}$ and β, they are called hyperparameters. Tuning these hyperparameters impacts the computation of the weight posterior distribution.

A picture of the probabilistic PNN learning process is demonstrated here using the Hermite polynomial: $1.0 + ((1.0 - t + 3t^2) * exp(-t^2))$, where the argument t is: $-5 < t < 5$. The generated data were additionally contaminated by random noise of variance 0.01. The targets to be modelled are the next values in the series: x_t. In order to investigate the development of the probabilistic inductive process, an initial PNN architecture was designed using two input variables: x_{t-1}, x_{t-2}, all second-order polynomial terms, and all third-order terms. This PNN was evaluated with random initial weights, and next sparse Bayesian learning (Subsection 8.4) was performed to obtain a parsimonious PNN model with maximum a posteriori (MAP) weights.

The effects from Bayesian inference of the weights and the PNN mapping are illustrated in Figure 8.1. The upper parts of this figure show: a) the projection of the weight prior distribution made with two randomly drawn weights from $\Pr(w_1, w_2)$, where the two-dimensional grid dimensions indicate that the weight values are taken from the interval $[-1; 1]$; and b) the ellipsoidal projection of the inferred peaked weight posterior distribution $\Pr(w_1, w_2|\mathbf{y}, X, \boldsymbol{\alpha}, \beta^{-1})$ computed with the same weights w_1 and w_2, plotted together with the initial prior contours. It can be seen in Figure 8.1a that the Bayesian training process starts with an almost flat prior over the weights. At the end of the network training process the weights converge to a posterior distribution which is peaked around the most probable weight vector. This most probable weight vector is plotted in Figure 8.1b with a bold ellipse which is the contour of the peaked distribution projected onto the weight space.

The lower parts of Figure 8.1 show: c) PNN functions generated using the randomly drawn weights from Figure 8.1a; and d) the final PNN approximation estimated with the inferred MAP weights vector from Figure 8.1b. In Figure 8.1c it can be observed that when the initial weights arbitrarily sampled from their prior distribution are used in the PNN network model, the network produces varying curves that do not pass exactly through the given data. When the learned MAP weight vector is used in the neural network architecture, it leads to curves that closely approximate the data. Figure 8.1d demonstrates the outputs of this PNN model having MAP weights.

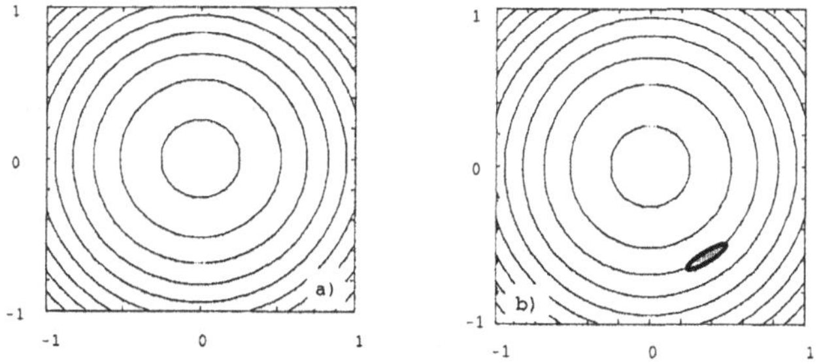

Figure 8.1. Demonstration of Bayesian inference with a polynomial network model: a) Contours of the flat weights prior distribution $\Pr(w_1, w_2)$; b) inferred weights posterior distribution $\Pr(w_1, w_2|\mathbf{y}, X, \alpha, \beta)$ whose peak contour is a bold ellipse.

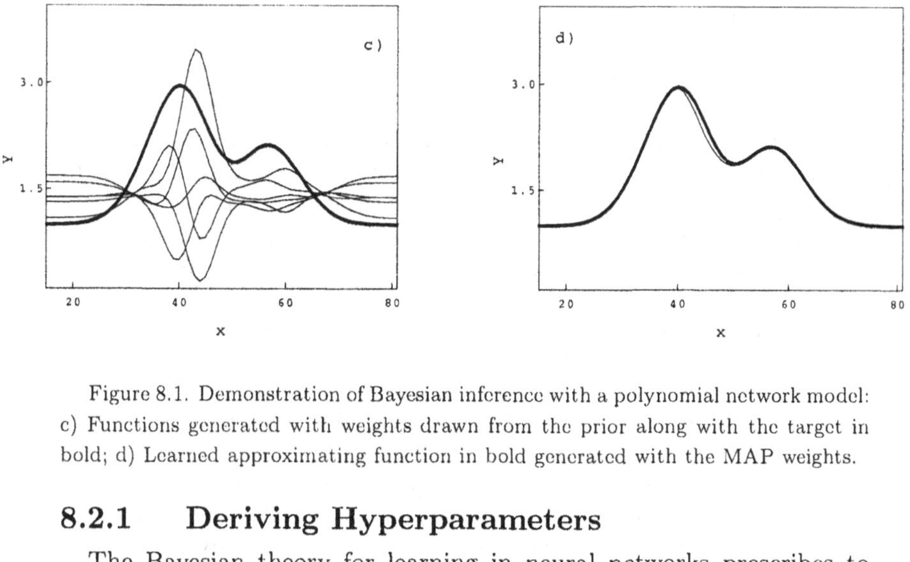

Figure 8.1. Demonstration of Bayesian inference with a polynomial network model: c) Functions generated with weights drawn from the prior along with the target in bold; d) Learned approximating function in bold generated with the MAP weights.

8.2.1 Deriving Hyperparameters

The Bayesian theory for learning in neural networks prescribes to first calculate the weight posterior $\Pr(\mathbf{w}|\mathbf{y}, X, \boldsymbol{\alpha}, \beta^{-1})$ and next to use it for computing the probability density of the data. The probability of the data is necessary for deriving the values of the hyperparameters and for prediction. The weight posterior, however, cannot be evaluated directly. The reason is that its normalizer Z' cannot be obtained analytically: $\Pr(\mathbf{w}|\mathbf{y}, X, \boldsymbol{\alpha}, \beta^{-1}) = (1/Z')\exp(-\beta E_D(\mathbf{w}) - E_W(\mathbf{w}))$. This is why, the total regularized error (8.2) is substituted by its quadratic Taylor expansion in the vicinity of a significant minimum to facilitate tractable probabilistic reasoning. The weight posterior distribution in this case tends to a single Gaussian [MacKay, 1992a].

The Gaussian weight posterior expressed around the extremum arising from weight vector $\mathbf{w}_{MP}$ is:

$$\Pr(\mathbf{w}|\mathbf{y}, X, \boldsymbol{\alpha}, \beta^{-1}) \simeq \frac{1}{Z_E} \exp\left(-E_R(\mathbf{w}_{MP}) - \frac{1}{2}(\mathbf{w} - \mathbf{w}_{MP})^T \mathbf{H}(\mathbf{w} - \mathbf{w}_{MP})\right) \tag{8.9}$$

where $\mathbf{H}$ is the Hessian matrix of second-order derivatives of the regularized error $E_R(\mathbf{w}_{MP})$ (8.2) evaluated at this extremum: $\mathbf{H} = \nabla\nabla E_R(\mathbf{w}_{MP})$, $\mathbf{H} = \beta\nabla\nabla E_D(\mathbf{w}_{MP}) + \mathbf{A}$. Since the posterior tends to a single Gaussian, its normalizing constant is:

$$Z_E(\boldsymbol{\alpha}, \beta^{-1}) = (2\pi)^{W/2} |\mathbf{H}|^{-1/2} \exp\left(-E_R(\mathbf{w}_{MP})\right) \tag{8.10}$$

where $|\mathbf{H}|$ stands for the determinant of the Hessian matrix (6.39,6.40). The following notational relationship between the Hessian and the inverted covariance matrix holds: $\mathbf{H} = \boldsymbol{\Sigma}^{-1}$.

Although it is not clear whether a sufficiently good minimum on the error surface has been located after training of the neural network until reaching the weight vector $\mathbf{w}_{MP}$, this Gaussian posterior approximation (8.9) is very useful. If polynomial networks are evolved by genetic programming, a large number of networks are sampled during each run, so it can be expected that a good minima on the error surface is attained and the weight vector is nearly optimal. For the sake of precision, the best network from a number of runs may be taken. The rigorous approach is to apply the Bayesian techniques to polynomial networks after their identification by genetic programming, however this does not preclude their application to manually crafted PNN.

Finding proper hyperparameter values is important for successful polynomial network learning as they determine the model complexity through the calculation of the regularizers. The Bayesian inference aims at maximization of the weight posterior with plausible hyperparameter. The most probable values of the hyperparameters are those which maximize the evidence. This reasoning comes from hierarchical analysis at a second level (supposing that the first level studies the distribution of the weights), which reveals that the maximization of the likelihood of the hyperparameters $\Pr(\mathbf{y}|X, \boldsymbol{\alpha}, \beta^{-1})$ helps to obtain their maximum posterior values. Substituting the likelihood (8.5), the prior (8.7), and the approximated posterior weight distribution (8.9) in the Bayes' theorem (8.4), gives the *evidence for the hyperparameters*:

$$\Pr(\mathbf{y}|X, \boldsymbol{\alpha}, \beta^{-1}) = \frac{\int \exp\left(-E_R(\mathbf{w})\right) d\mathbf{w}}{Z_D(\beta^{-1}) Z_W(\boldsymbol{\alpha})} \tag{8.11}$$

where the integral in the numerator evaluates to $Z_E(\boldsymbol{\alpha}, \beta^{-1})$ (8.10).

Taking the logarithms of both sides of the above probability yields the *log of the evidence criterion:*

$$\log \Pr(\mathbf{y}|X, \boldsymbol{\alpha}, \beta^{-1}) = -\beta E_D - E_W - \frac{1}{2}\left[\log|\mathbf{H}| - \log|\mathbf{A}| - c\right] \quad (8.12)$$

where the constant is $c = N \log \beta + N \log(2\pi)$.

The evidence procedure maximizes the log of the evidence criterion (8.12) searching for the most probable posterior values for the output noise variance β and the prior hyperparameters $\boldsymbol{\alpha}$. The optimization is carried out by calculating the derivatives of the log-evidence $\log \Pr(\mathbf{y}|X, \boldsymbol{\alpha}, \beta^{-1})$ with respect to each of these hyperparameters, equating these derivatives to zero, and next solving for α and β. The following updating formula for the *hyperpriors* α is obtained:

$$\alpha = \frac{\gamma}{2\mathbf{w}^T\mathbf{w}} \quad (8.13)$$

where γ is the effective number of network parameters (8.18, 8.19).

Taking the derivative of the log of the evidence criterion with respect to β gives the learning rule for the *hyperparameter* β:

$$\beta = \frac{N - \gamma}{2\mathbf{e}^T\mathbf{e}} \quad (8.14)$$

where N is the number of the available training data.

Seeking to maximize the log-evidence (8.12) of the hyperparameters so as to minimize the Bayesian error function, these formulae (8.13) and (8.14) are reevaluated repeatedly until an acceptably low error is attained or until the improvement is less than a selected threshold. The values of the hyperparameters are then plugged in as regularizers to compute the network weights. The network weights are trained iteration by iteration, so they are sensitive to the level of regularization.

8.2.2 Local vs. Global Regularization

There are two cases to consider: using a global regularization parameter for all weights, and using individual regularization parameters for each weight. A global, common hyperprior α for all weights in the vector is made by defining $\boldsymbol{\alpha} = [\alpha, \alpha, ..., \alpha]$, while local hyperpriors α_i for each network weight are defined with the vector $\boldsymbol{\alpha} = [\alpha_1, \alpha_2, .., \alpha_W]$. The regularized error criterion (8.2) can be rewritten in matrix notation to capture such regularization effects as follows: $E_R(\mathbf{w}) = 0.5\left(\mathbf{e}^T\mathbf{e} + \mathbf{w}^T\mathbf{L}\mathbf{w}\right)$, where $\mathbf{e} = [e_1, e_2, ..., e_N]$ is the error vector of elements $e_n = y_n - P(\mathbf{x}_n, \mathbf{w})$, $1 \leq n \leq N$, and $\mathbf{w}$ is the weight vector.

Bayesian regularization of the network weights is often implemented using the fraction between the regularization constants $\boldsymbol{\alpha}$ and the noise variance β to achieve stability in the computations. The global regularization uses a diagonal matrix $\mathbf{L} = diag(\lambda, \lambda, \lambda, ..., \lambda)$ of size $(W + 1) \times (W + 1)$. The common *global regularization parameter* λ allocated on the diagonal of this matrix is:

$$\lambda = \frac{\alpha}{\beta} = \left(\frac{\gamma}{N - \gamma}\right) \frac{\mathbf{e}^T\mathbf{e}}{\mathbf{w}^T\mathbf{w}} \tag{8.15}$$

where γ is the number of effective network parameters.

The goal of PNN modeling is to properly learn the model regions of both low and high nonlinearities in the data. The overfitting, however, may vary in the different regions of the model. Since each term contributes a different curvature to the overall model, there is a need to manipulate each term separately in order to adjust the polynomial smoothness. Adapting the weights through local regularization helps to achieve: 1) accurate quantification of the impact of each polynomial term on the overall output, and 2) local control over the particular term nonlinearities and adaptation of the model curvature to the data.

Local regularization is accomplished using a diagonal matrix $\mathbf{L} = diag(\lambda_0, \lambda_1, \lambda_2, ..., \lambda_W)$ whose *local regularization parameters* are defined with the equation:

$$\lambda_i = \left(\frac{\gamma}{N - \gamma}\right) \frac{\mathbf{e}^T\mathbf{e}}{w_i^2} \tag{8.16}$$

where w_i is the weight shrinked by its corresponding regularizer λ_i.

The number of well-determined parameters γ is computed in different ways in the two cases of linear-in-the-weights PNN models and inherently nonlinear multilayer PNN. This is because in these cases the Hessian matrix is evaluated with different techniques.

8.2.3 Evidence Procedure for PNN Models

Evidence for Linear-in-the-weights PNN. The evidence framework [MacKay, 1992a] enables automatic adjustment of the level of regularization, and thus it helps to enhance the model generalization performance. This framework was originally developed for linear networks like the linear-in-the-weights PNN. Training these networks by least squares techniques leads to maximally likely (ML) weights that are optimal in the mean squared error sense. However, these techniques cause overfitting because they tend to fit the data too closely. The Bayesian techniques help us to obtain *maximum a posteriori* (MAP) weights which overcome such problems. They infer the mean of the weight posterior distribution, not simply point estimates.

Bayesian regularization is performed by adding the individual regularizers $\mathbf{L} = diag(\lambda_0, \lambda_1, \lambda_2, ..., \lambda_W)$ to the diagonal of the inverse covariance matrix $\mathbf{\Phi}^T\mathbf{\Phi}$, which impacts the least-squares estimation of the network weights in the following way:

$$\mathbf{w} = (\mathbf{\Phi}^T\mathbf{\Phi} + \mathbf{L})^{-1}\mathbf{\Phi}^T\mathbf{y} \tag{8.17}$$

where $\mathbf{w}$ is the column weight vector $\mathbf{w} = [w_0, w_1, ..., w_i]^T$, $\mathbf{\Phi}$ is the design matrix (1.8), and $\mathbf{y}$ is the output vector.

The number of *well-defined parameters* γ in linear-in-the-weights polynomial networks are computed by the formula:

$$\gamma = W - \sum_{i=0}^{W} \lambda_i \left[(\mathbf{\Phi}^T\mathbf{\Phi})^{-1}\right]_{ii} \tag{8.18}$$

where $\mathbf{\Phi}^T\mathbf{\Phi}$ is the inverse covariance matrix of the polynomial model, and the index ii enumerates its diagonal elements. These parameters γ are also called effective parameters (4.6).

The algorithm for computing individual Bayesian regularization parameters for linear PNN is illustrated in Table 8.1.

Table 8.1. Algorithm for calculating local regularization parameters for linear-in-the-weights PNN according to the Bayesian evidence procedure.

Computing Bayesian Regularizers for Linear PNN

step	*Algorithmic sequence*
1. Initialization	Data $\mathcal{D} = \{(\mathbf{x}_n, y_n)\}_{n=1}^{N}$ and learning rate $\eta = 0.1$. A PNN architecture with W weights initial hyperparameters: $\alpha = 1.0/W$, and $\beta = 1.0/stdy$.
2. Reevaluate the hyperparameters	Repeat a predefined number of times: a) Make local regularizers: $\mathbf{L} = diag(\lambda_0, \lambda_1, ..., \lambda_W)$ $\lambda_i = \alpha_i/\beta$, $0 \leq i \leq W$. b) Reestimate the weights by OLS fitting $\mathbf{w} = (\mathbf{\Phi}^T\mathbf{\Phi} + \mathbf{L})^{-1}\mathbf{\Phi}^T y$. c) Compute the effective number of parameters $\gamma = W - \sum_{i=0}^{W} \lambda_i \left[(\mathbf{\Phi}^T\mathbf{\Phi})^{-1}\right]_{ii}$ and the hyperparameters $\alpha_i = \gamma/w_i^2$ $\beta = (N-\gamma)/\mathbf{e}^T\mathbf{e}$. d) Calculate the Bayesian error $E_R(\mathbf{w}) = \mathbf{e}^T\mathbf{e} + \mathbf{w}^T\mathbf{L}\mathbf{w}$ until minimum of the log-evidence criterion is reached. $\log \Pr(\mathbf{y}\mid X, \alpha, \beta) = -\mathbf{e}^T\mathbf{e} - \mathbf{w}^T\mathbf{L}\mathbf{w} - \frac{1}{2}\left[\log\lvert\mathbf{H}\rvert - \log\lvert\mathbf{A}\rvert\right]$.

Evidence for Nonlinear Multilayer PNN. The computation of the hyperparameters according to the Bayesian evidence procedure is more involved when processing nonlinear PNN models, because in such cases the Hessian (6.39, 6.40) has to be computed in a special way using the $\mathcal{R}$-propagation algorithm [Pearlmutter, 1994].

Consider a nonlinear multilayer PNN model trained with the BP algorithm to minimize the Bayesian cost function (8.2). The algorithm is made to perform updating of the weights using local regularization with the following gradient-descent training rule: $w_i = (1 - \eta\lambda_i)^T w_i + \Delta w_i$ (6.34). Next, the $\mathcal{R}$-propagation algorithm (Section 6.3.1) is applied to evaluate the Hessian matrix. Then, the number of the *well-determined parameters* γ in nonlinear PNN is obtained as follows:

$$\gamma = W - \sum_{i=0}^{W} \lambda_i \left[\mathbf{H}^{-1}\right]_{ii} \tag{8.19}$$

where $\left[\mathbf{H}^{-1}\right]_{ii}$ are the diagonal elements of the inverse Hessian.

Table 8.2 gives the algorithm for finding Bayesian regularizers for multilayer PNN using the $\mathcal{R}$-propagation algorithm for the Hessian.

Table 8.2. Algorithm for calculating local regularization parameters for inherently nonlinear PNN according to the Bayesian evidence procedure.

Computing Bayesian Regularizers for Nonlinear PNN

step	*Algorithmic sequence*
1. Initialization	Data $\mathcal{D} = \{(\mathbf{x}_n, y_n)\}_{n=1}^{N}$, PNN with W weights hyperparameters: $\alpha_i = 1.0/W$, and $\beta = 1.0/stdy$.
2. Reevaluate the hyperparameters	Repeat a predefined number of times: a) Make local regularizers: $\mathbf{L} = diag(\lambda_0, \lambda_1, ..., \lambda_W)$ $\lambda_i = \alpha_i/\beta$, $0 \le i \le W$. b) Re-train the weights by BP with local regularization $\mathbf{w} = (1 - \eta\mathbf{L})^T\mathbf{w} + \Delta\mathbf{w}$. c) Calculate by $\mathcal{R}$-propagation the dot product $\mathbf{v}^T\mathbf{H} = \mathbf{v}^{T2}E_R$, and extract the Hessian $\mathbf{H}$. d) Compute the effective number of parameters $\gamma = W - \sum_{i=0}^{W} \lambda_i \left[\mathbf{H}^{-1}\right]_{ii}$ and the hyperparameters $\alpha_i = \gamma/w_i^2$, and $\beta = (N - \gamma)/\mathbf{e}^T\mathbf{e}$. e) Calculate the Bayesian error $E_R(\mathbf{w}) = \mathbf{e}^T\mathbf{e} + \mathbf{w}^T\mathbf{L}\mathbf{w}$ until minimum of the log-evidence criterion is reached. $\log \Pr(\mathbf{y}|X, \alpha, \beta) = -\mathbf{e}^T\mathbf{e} - \mathbf{w}^T\mathbf{L}\mathbf{w} - \frac{1}{2}\left[\log|\mathbf{H}| - \log|\mathbf{A}|\right]$.

8.2.4 Predictive Data Distribution

Neural network learning involves finding the weights, and then evaluating the predictive data distribution. The predictive distribution is taken to generate model outputs from future unseen inputs. The data distribution provides an estimate of the uncertainty about the network outputs and enables us to make probabilistic predictions. The predictive distribution of the model outputs is:

$$\Pr(y_*|\mathbf{x}_*, \mathbf{y}, X, \boldsymbol{\theta}) = \int \Pr(y_*|\mathbf{x}_*, \mathbf{y}, X, \mathbf{w}, \boldsymbol{\theta}) \Pr(\mathbf{w}|\mathbf{y}, X, \boldsymbol{\theta}) d\mathbf{w} \quad (8.20)$$

where y_* is the prediction, $\mathbf{x}_*$ is the unseen input, and $\boldsymbol{\theta} = [\boldsymbol{\alpha}, \beta^{-1}]$.

Although this probability cannot be directly computed as the integral is intractable, in practice its Gaussian approximation is considered. In this case, predictions can be calculated using the mean $y_* \equiv P(\mathbf{x}_*)$ of the distribution $\Pr(y_*|\mathbf{x}_*, \mathbf{y}, X, \boldsymbol{\alpha}, \beta^{-1})$ [Nabney, 2002], while its variance β_* may be used to produce prediction intervals (Section 9.6).

Let's consider the particular case of a linear PNN model. Plugging the inferred hyperparameters $\boldsymbol{\alpha}$ and β into the normal equation yields maximum a posteriori weights. These weights are representative of the mean of their posterior distribution with which probabilistic predictions could be made. Given an unseen, test input vector $\mathbf{x}_*$, the polynomial network generates a forecast y_* with probability $\Pr(y_*|\mathbf{x}_*, \mathbf{y}, X, \boldsymbol{\alpha}, \beta^{-1})$. This forecast y_* is the mean of the predictive distribution with variance β_*^{-1}, computable as follows:

$$y_* = \mathbf{w}^T \boldsymbol{\phi}(\mathbf{x}_*) \quad (8.21)$$

$$\beta_*^{-1} = \beta^{-1} + \boldsymbol{\phi}^T(\mathbf{x}_*)\mathbf{H}^{-1}\boldsymbol{\phi}(\mathbf{x}_*) \quad (8.22)$$

where $\mathbf{w}$ are the weights, and $\boldsymbol{\phi}(\mathbf{x}_*)$ is the basis vector (1.9).

8.2.5 Choosing a Weight Prior

A crucial problem in applying the Bayesian evidence framework to neural networks and to polynomial networks in particular is what prior probability density to choose for the weights. There are various strategies for assigning priors to linear and to nonlinear models, however there is still no general recipe that can robustly decide which prior is best for the concrete model. This is why different priors may be considered for different models. The previous sections presented the Gaussian prior (8.3) which is most suitable for linear networks. Other priors have been developed, especially for multilayer networks like the nonlinear multilayer PNN. These are the Laplace and the Cauchy priors [Williams, 1995], obtained assuming different weight distributions.

The weights in multilayer PNN may be symmetric within the network, so equivalent mappings may occur by exchanging the signs of the weights on the same connections. There may even be symmetry groups of weights whose permuting within the same network may cause identical mappings. In order to capture such symmetries, the Laplacian distribution may be used. It leads to a weight penalty that is sensitive to the absolute magnitudes of the weights. The regularization that sets a *Laplacian prior* over the weights is [Williams, 1995]:

$$E_W(\mathbf{w}) = \sum_{i=1}^{W} \alpha_i |w_i| \tag{8.23}$$

where $|w_i|$ denotes the absolute value of weight w_i.

Research into neural network models conducted with the intention to prune them effectively has suggested use of the Cauchy distribution [Weigend et al., 1992]. The Cauchy distribution can be incorporated through a correcting complexity factor which is a logarithmic function of the squared weights. It is similar to the Gaussian penalty in the sense that the square of the weights influences the error, and differs in that it discourages too many small weights. The following regularization factor imposes a *Cauchy prior* over the weights [Williams, 1995]:

$$E_W(\mathbf{w}) = \sum_{i=1}^{W} \frac{1}{\alpha_i} \log\left(1 + \alpha_i^2 w_i^2\right) \tag{8.24}$$

which still remains steep in the interval $-1.0 \leq w \leq 1.0$.

8.3 Bayesian Network Pruning

The evidence framework provides a tool for *automatic relevance determination* (ARD) that can be used for network pruning of very small weights. This is possible as the fast increase of some local hyperparameters shrinks the corresponding weights toward zero. The advantage of ARD is that it evaluates the significance of all weights in the model together, thus pointing out that they are irrelevant in the context of the model as a whole. The evidence procedure can also be used in an incremental manner to prune weights similarly to the other backprop pruning techniques (Sections 6.6.1 and 6.6.2).

The alternative *Bayesian incremental pruning* strategy is to discard weights from the initially fully connected network one-by-one by freezing those with extremely small magnitudes. This is made by setting the small weights to zero and computing the effect of this on the overall model performance. In the course of retraining, the weights with values close to zero are discarded until the difference between log-evidences of the model and its version with a weight removed becomes positive.

Let the joint data distribution with the network be $\Pr(\mathbf{y}|X, \boldsymbol{\alpha}, \beta^{-1})$, and assume that after deleting one weight from this model it becomes $\Pr(\mathbf{y}|X, \boldsymbol{\alpha}', \beta^{-1\prime})$. The *change in log-evidence* criterion for model comparison can be calculated with the equation [MacKay, 1995]:

$$\log \Pr(\mathbf{y}|X, \boldsymbol{\alpha}, \beta^{-1}) - \log \Pr(\mathbf{y}|X, \boldsymbol{\alpha}', \beta^{-1\prime}) = \frac{w_i^2}{2\left[\mathbf{H}^{-1}\right]_{ii}} + \log \sqrt{\alpha_i \left[\mathbf{H}^{-1}\right]_{ii}} \tag{8.25}$$

which should be considered to examine eventual removal of a weight w_i using its diagonal entry in the inverse Hessian matrix $[\mathbf{H}^{-1}]_{ii}$, and its hyperparameter α_i. It should be noted that this pruning technique can be applied to handle several weights at a time; that is, it can be modified for direct removal of subsets of network weights.

The smoothing effect from Bayesian incremental pruning of a polynomial network is illustrated with the plots in Figure 8.2. The plots have been made using a randomly designed PNN for learning a model from a data set produced with a simple third-order function: $0.2 - 1.6x_1 - 0.1x_1^2 - 0.4x_1x_2 + 0.5x_1x_2^2 + 0.9x_1^3$. There were generated 50 data points and Gaussian noise was added from the interval: $[0, 0.1]$. An initial multilayer PNN was constructed with 3 hidden nodes having $3 \times 6 = 18$ weights. The overall polynomial generated by this network was: $P(\mathbf{x}) = p_8(x_1, p_8(x_1, p_8(x_1, x_2)))$. The initial hyperparameters were: $\alpha = 0.001$, and $\beta = 10$.

The PNN was trained and pruned incrementally, after which the following polynomial remained: $0.1972 - 1.6256x_1 + 0.998x_1(-0.1224x_1 + 0.8546x_1^2 - 0.4217x_2(0.987 + 0.952x_2))$. A close inspection of this polynomial reveals that it is very similar to the original one, and it contains 8 weights. If it is extracted from this network representation, and next simplified by dropping the parentheses, exactly a polynomial model similar to the original with 6 coefficients will be produced.

What is interesting to note in Figure 8.2 is that the curve of the initial complex polynomial, to which the incremental Bayesian pruning procedure has been applied, seems to overfit the noise in the data since it attempts to pass irregularly through the given points, while it does not capture the hidden data regularities well. One can see that the curve of the initial large PNN overfits the data, obviously mislead by the MSE cost function. After pruning of the superfluous weights, due to their shrinking by the adjusted local regularization parameters, the remaining pruned polynomial becomes considerably smoother and approaches the original target function curvature quite closely.

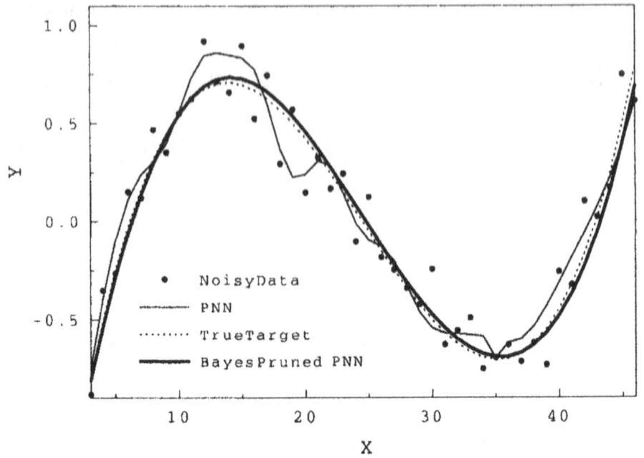

Figure 8.2. Smoothing of a polynomial neural network mapping by Bayesian incremental pruning. The initial network has 18 weights, while the remaining simplified, pruned polynomial network has 8 weights.

A common issue in both Bayesian pruning approaches, the ARD procedure and the incremental pruning procedure, is the concern that they involve computation of the Hessian matrix which sometimes faces numerical computation difficulties. Another concern is that if reasonably many weights cannot be removed from the network model, computation time may be wasted.

8.4 Sparse Bayesian Learning

The evidence framework applied to PNN brings four essential advantages that help to enhance their generalization potential: 1) it performs Bayesian inference with training formula obtained using proper probabilistic treatment of the inductive process, which involves the data and the noise; 2) it automatically determines the neural network complexity; 3) it is not necessary to completely determine and fix the noise parameters in advance, rather they are adapted during training, and 4) it does not carry out repetitive validations using statistical approaches that are time-consuming. These advantages can be achieved following the *sparse Bayesian learning* [Tipping, 2001] approach. It is applied here for learning parsimonious and well-generalizing PNN models.

The evidence procedure however does not tell us how many times the training cycle has to be repeated; its convergence properties are not established. This is why our attention is directed toward a principled approach that ensures convergence while doing probabilistic inference, which is the Expectation-Maximization (EM) approach [Dempster et al.,

1977]. It is suitable for offline PNN learning of sparse Bayesian models [Quiñonero-Candela, 2004]. The EM algorithm is taken to find the maximum of the log marginal likelihood $\log \Pr(\mathbf{t}|\boldsymbol{\alpha}, \beta^{-1})$, and thus to infer optimal hyperparameters $\boldsymbol{\alpha}$ and β. The approach seeks to determine the mode of $\log \Pr(\mathbf{t}|\boldsymbol{\alpha}, \beta^{-1})$ by alternating between two steps E-step and M-step, whose successive application guarantees an increase of the likelihood at each cycle.

The idea for dividing the maximal likelihood maximization process into two steps is to facilitate separate tuning of the weight parameters, and their hyperparameters. The idea is to attempt to directly solve the integral: $\log \Pr(\mathbf{t}|\boldsymbol{\alpha}, \beta^{-1}) = \log \int \Pr(\mathbf{t}, \mathbf{w}|\boldsymbol{\alpha}, \beta^{-1}) d\mathbf{w}$, rather than: $\log \Pr(\mathbf{t}|\boldsymbol{\alpha}, \beta^{-1}) = \log \int \Pr(\mathbf{t}|\mathbf{w}, \boldsymbol{\alpha}, \beta^{-1}) \Pr(\mathbf{w}|\boldsymbol{\alpha}, \beta^{-1}) d\mathbf{w}$. Then, the influence of the weights and the hyperparameters can be distinguished after applying Jensens' inequality [Bishop, 1995]:

$$
\begin{aligned}
\log \int \Pr(\mathbf{t}, \mathbf{w}|\boldsymbol{\alpha}, \beta^{-1}) d\mathbf{w} &= \log \int q(\mathbf{w}) \frac{\Pr(\mathbf{t}, \mathbf{w}|\boldsymbol{\alpha}, \beta^{-1})}{q(\mathbf{w})} d\mathbf{w} \\
&\geq \log \int q(\mathbf{w}) \log \frac{\Pr(\mathbf{t}, \mathbf{w}|\boldsymbol{\alpha}, \beta^{-1})}{q(\mathbf{w})} d\mathbf{w} - \mathcal{Q}(\mathbf{w}) \\
&= \mathcal{F}(q, \boldsymbol{\alpha}, \beta^{-1}) \qquad (8.26)
\end{aligned}
$$

where the quantity on the second line is $\mathcal{Q}(\mathbf{w}) = \int q(\mathbf{w}) \log q(\mathbf{w}) d\mathbf{w}$.

Therefore, a good approximation of the likelihood $\Pr(\mathbf{t}, \mathbf{w}|\boldsymbol{\alpha}, \beta^{-1})$ can be obtained by maximizing the lower bound $\mathcal{F}(q, \boldsymbol{\alpha}, \beta^{-1})$ in this inequality separately: 1) with respect to the arbitrary distribution $q(\mathbf{w})$, called *expectation* E-step, and 2) with respect to the prior $\boldsymbol{\alpha}$ and output noise β hyperparameters, called *maximization* M-step. When performing the expectation step $\arg\max_q \mathcal{F}(q, \boldsymbol{\alpha}, \beta^{-1})$, the hyperparameters $\boldsymbol{\alpha}$ and β are kept fixed and the maximum of the distribution $q(\mathbf{w})$ is achieved using the weight posterior $\Pr(\mathbf{w}|\mathbf{t}, \boldsymbol{\alpha}, \beta^{-1})$. The posterior weights are found by least squares fitting, in the case of linear PNN, and by gradient-descent techniques like the BPA, in the case of nonlinear PNN.

When performing the maximization step: $\arg\max_{\boldsymbol{\alpha}, \beta^{-1}} \mathcal{F}(q, \boldsymbol{\alpha}, \beta^{-1})$, the weights are fixed and only the first component in $\mathcal{F}(q, \boldsymbol{\alpha}, \beta^{-1})$ (8.26) is considered. The expectation of the data likelihood $\log \Pr(\mathbf{t}, \mathbf{w}|\boldsymbol{\alpha}, \beta^{-1})$ is maximized as follows [Quiñonero-Candela, 2004]:

$$
\begin{aligned}
\left[\boldsymbol{\alpha}, \beta^{-1}\right] &= \arg\max_{\boldsymbol{\alpha}, \beta^{-1}} \left\langle \log \Pr(\mathbf{t}, \mathbf{w}|\boldsymbol{\alpha}, \beta^{-1}) \right\rangle \\
&= \arg\max_{\boldsymbol{\alpha}, \beta^{-1}} \left\langle -\beta E_D - E_W - \frac{1}{2} \left[c - \log |\mathbf{A}|\right] \right\rangle \qquad (8.27)
\end{aligned}
$$

where the numerator $q(\mathbf{w})$ is omitted as it does not change at this step, and the constant is $c = N \log \beta$.

The maximum is attained by differentiation with respect to the hyperparameters. Taking the derivatives of this expectation $\langle \log \Pr(\mathbf{t}, \mathbf{w}|\boldsymbol{\alpha}, \beta) \rangle$, equating to zero, and solving respectively for $\boldsymbol{\alpha}$ and β yields corresponding formulae for their updates. The modification rule for the *individual hyperpriors* α_i is:

$$\alpha_i = \frac{1.0}{w_i^2 + [\mathbf{H}^{-1}]_{ii}} \tag{8.28}$$

where w_i is the network weight affected by this α_i.

Taking the derivative of the log of the evidence criterion with respect to β, leads to the learning rule for the *output noise hyperparameter* β:

$$\beta = \frac{N}{\mathbf{e}^T\mathbf{e} + \beta \sum_{i=1}^{W} \gamma_i} \tag{8.29}$$

where γ_i is the local efficient parameter number $\gamma_i = 1.0 - \alpha_i \left[\mathbf{H}^{-1}\right]_{ii}$.

The E-step evaluates the likelihood of the complete data using the available hyperparameters. After that, this evidence is used in the M-step to judge as to what degree the belief in the weights parameter density is correct with respect to the training data. Next, the hyperparameters are adjusted with the above formulae (8.28) and (8.29) aiming at improvement of the overall model performance. Theoretically, the repetitive execution of this procedure converges to a stationary point because the second step always increases the quantity $\mathcal{F}(q, \boldsymbol{\alpha}, \beta^{-1})$, thus approaching the likelihood of the complete data. When training linear-in-the-weights PNN, the error function has a unique minimum and the expectation step has an exact solution. In nonlinear multilayer PNN, however, the solution is approximate, as there are many local as well as local minima on the error surface, and it depends how good the located weight vector is by the training algorithm. A problem arising in multilayer PNN is the need to compute the Hessian, which is often computationally unstable and may cause computational difficulties.

Another possibility for doing sparse Bayesian learning is to directly maximize the log marginal $\log \Pr(\mathbf{t}|\boldsymbol{\alpha}, \beta^{-1})$, but this approach does not guarantee local optimization of the lower bound $\mathcal{F}(q, \boldsymbol{\alpha}, \beta^{-1})$. The hyperparameter update formulae for such a strategy are presented in Section 8.5 and applied for incremental tuning of the prior and output noise hyperparameters while doing recursive PNN training. Although this direct approach may not be strictly optimal, it has been found that it sometimes makes faster steps on the search landscape [Tipping, 2001].

Table 8.3 presents the EM algorithm for sparse Bayesian learning of linear-in-the-weights polynomial networks.

Table 8.3. Expectation-Maximization algorithm for marginal likelihood maximization and learning sparse Bayesian linear PNN models.

Sparse Bayesian Learning of PNN

step	*Algorithmic sequence*
1. Initialization	Data $\mathcal{D} = \{(\mathbf{x}_n, y_n)\}_{n=1}^{N}$, PNN with W weights hyperparameters: $\alpha = 1.0/W$, and $\beta = 1.0/stdy$.
2. Reevaluate the hyperparameters	Repeat a predefined number of times: a) Perform the expectation E-step Estimate the weight posterior mean $\mathbf{w} = (\mathbf{\Phi}^T\mathbf{\Phi} + \mathbf{L})^{-1}\mathbf{\Phi}^T y$, where: $\lambda_i = \alpha_i/\beta$, $0 \leq i \leq W$. b) Perform the maximization M-step i) Update the prior hyperparameter $\alpha_i = 1.0/\left(w_i^2 + \left[\mathbf{H}^{-1}\right]_{ii}\right)$, where: $\mathbf{H}^{-1} = (\mathbf{\Phi}^T\mathbf{\Phi} + \mathbf{L})^{-1}$. ii) Update the output noise variance $\beta = N/\left(\mathbf{e}^T\mathbf{e} + \beta\sum_{i=1}^{W}\gamma_i\right)$, where: $\gamma_i = 1.0 - \alpha_i\left[\mathbf{H}^{-1}\right]_{ii}$ until reaching the minimum of the criterion. $\log\Pr(\mathbf{y}\vert X, \alpha, \beta) = -\mathbf{e}^T\mathbf{e} - \mathbf{w}^T\mathbf{L}\mathbf{w} - \frac{1}{2}\left[c - \log\vert\mathbf{A}\vert\right]$.

The capacity of the sparse Bayesian learning approach to infer parsimonious PNN can be examined using plots of the curves generated by its polynomial terms. As an example, a time series of 100 points were generated using the Hermite polynomial: $1.0 + ((1.0 - t + 3t^2) * exp(-t^2))$, where $-5 < t < 5$. Next, random noise of variance 0.01 was added. The experiments were conducted using three input variables: x_{t-1}, x_{t-2}, x_{t-3}, second-order polynomial terms: $x_{t-1}x_{t-2}$, $x_{t-1}x_{t-3}$, $x_{t-2}x_{t-3}$, x_{t-1}^2, x_{t-2}^2, x_{t-3}^2, and third-order terms: $x_{t-1}^2x_{t-2}$, $x_{t-1}^2x_{t-3}$, $x_{t-2}^2x_{t-3}$, $x_{t-1}x_{t-2}^2$, $x_{t-1}x_{t-3}^2$, $x_{t-2}x_{t-3}^2$, x_{t-1}^3, x_{t-2}^3, and x_{t-3}^3.

Figure 8.3 illustrates with a bold curve the approximated Hermite polynomial by an overfitting PNN, along with the curves of the particular term components extracted from the network. The PNN was learned after doing only 2 iterations. The polynomial contained 9 terms, which were used to produce the curves by multiplying these terms with their weights. An additional experiment was performed to train the same initial PNN using all the above first-order, second-order, and third-order terms, but this time 5 iterations of the algorithm were performed. After five iterations, a parsimonious PNN of 5 terms remained: x_{t-1}, x_{t-2}, x_{t-3}, $x_{t-1}x_{t-3}$, and $x_{t-2}x_{t-3}^2$. The curves produced by multiplying these terms by their weights are given in Figure 8.4.

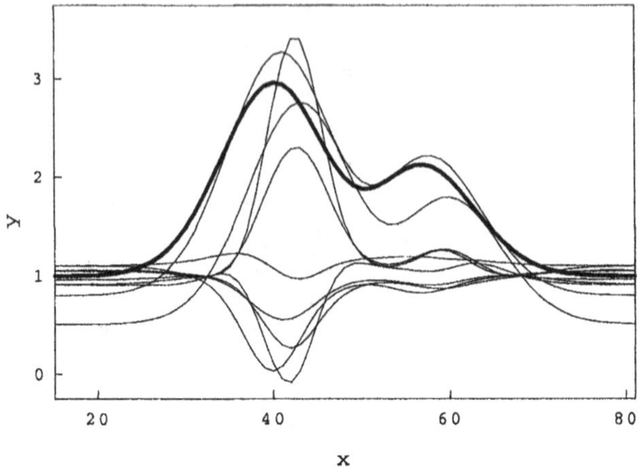

Figure 8.3. Overfitting of the Hermite polynomial by a nonparsimonious PNN model with 9 (linear and nonlinear) terms identified using sparse Bayesian learning.

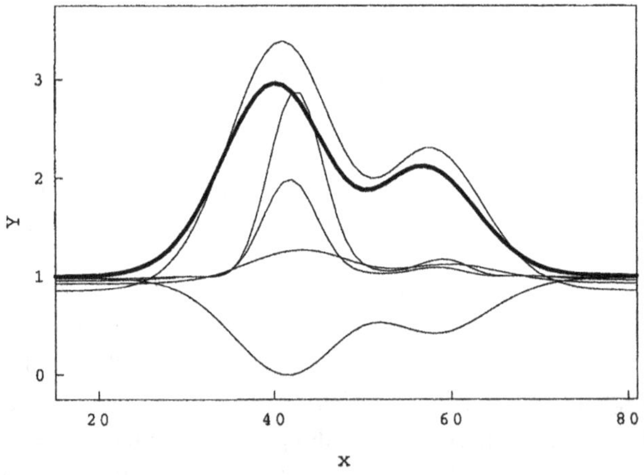

Figure 8.4. Parsimonious PNN having only 5 terms learned from the Hermite polynomial data series using sparse Bayesian learning with the EM algorithm.

The polynomial term curves in Figure 8.4 fluctuate much less which is an indication for their general character, so this sparse PNN has greater generalization capacity. One can note in these figures that the approximating potential of both PNN models, learned after 2 and after 5 iterations, are quite similar. That is, both PNN feature good fitting accuracy but they have different extrapolation potential.

8.5 Recursive Bayesian Learning

In practice, the training data may be given not only as a batch, but they may also be provided sequentially. There are recursive Bayesian learning approaches that operate on sequentially arriving data [de Freitas et al., 2000b, Nikolaev and Tino, 2005a]. Such an approach is elaborated here for weight training, stabilized computation of local regularization parameters, and automatic relevance determination of terms.

The sequential methods overcome the main disadvantages of the batch approaches arising from their offline character. The first disadvantage, especially of the linear training techniques, is that they rely on analytical formulae which sometimes cannot be evaluated safely due to numerical computation problems. Second, the reestimation of the hyperparameters after processing all data often yields large values, thus causing instabilities in the algorithm performance [Chen et al., 2004]. Third, such batch algorithms need special adjustments of the predictive mean and variance in order to be successful in iterative forecasting [Quiñonero-Candela, 2004]. These problems can be avoided by recursive evaluation of the weight posterior using one data example at a time.

A Bayesian version of the Recursive Levenberg-Marquardt (RLM) algorithm [Ljung and Södeström, 1983, Ngia and Sjöberg, 2000] is made in this section for sequential training of polynomial networks. Starting with the complete model of all terms, the algorithm gradually evolves the weight posterior $\Pr(\mathbf{w}|D, \boldsymbol{\alpha}, \beta^{-1})$ while cycling over the data, and prunes irrelevant terms. The developments include: 1) derivation of a regularized equation for sequential estimation of the weights; 2) formulation of a general technique for sequential computation of the inverted regularized dynamic Hessian matrix which avoids the problematic direct matrix inversion; and 3) implementation of incremental gradient-descent training rules for the prior hyperparameters.

8.5.1 Sequential Weight Estimation

The key idea for making a recursive Bayesian RLM is to carry out partial sequential regularization while doing weight estimation. The implementation of this idea adopts a technique for augmentation of the dynamic Hessian matrix only by the fractions of the total regularization. This is necessary because when the data arrive one at a time, the total regularization effect has to be distributed in parts after each training example. This technique is generalized here in a Bayesian setting using individual regularization hyperparameters. Performing incremental regularization impacts the development of both the weight learning and the dynamic estimation of the Hessian matrix.

Let's adopt the following notation: the weight vector modified up to moment (arrival of data point $\mathbf{x}_t$) t is $\mathbf{w}_t$, the basis vector from the t-th current data point is $\boldsymbol{\phi}(\mathbf{x}_t) = [\phi(\mathbf{x}_t, \mathbf{x}_1), \phi(\mathbf{x}_t, \mathbf{x}_2), ..., \phi(\mathbf{x}_t, \mathbf{x}_M)]^T$, and the design matrix includes the relevant M basis functions evaluated with all arrived training points $\mathbf{x}_i$ that is $\mathbf{\Phi}_t = \{\phi(\mathbf{x}_i, \mathbf{x}_j)\}$ where: $1 \leq i \leq t$, $1 \leq j \leq M$. Let the *dynamic Hessian* be: $\mathbf{H}_t = \beta \nabla\nabla E_D(\mathbf{w}_t) + \mathbf{A}_t$, and the dynamic output error derivatives at this time instant are given by the *Jacobian*: $\mathbf{j}_t = \partial P(t)/\partial \mathbf{w}|_{\mathbf{w}=\mathbf{w}_{t-1}}$ (Section 6.3.1).

Sequential Bayesian regularization can be accomplished by augmenting the dynamic Hessian successively by fractions $\alpha_i \mathbf{Z}$ of the i-th hyperparameter α_i, $0 \leq i \leq M$, added one at a time: $\mathbf{H}_t = \mathbf{H}_{t-1} + \beta \mathbf{j}_t \mathbf{j}_t^T + \alpha_i \mathbf{Z}$. The index of the next hyperparameter to add α_i, $1 \leq i \leq M$, changes from iteration to iteration according to the equation $i = t$ mod M. The hyperparameter α_i is scaled by a special matrix $\mathbf{Z}$ which is fixed in advance. The matrix $\mathbf{Z}$ (of size $M \times M$) contains zeroes everywhere except its selecting diagonal element $[\mathbf{Z}]_{ii}$ at position i which has a value $[\mathbf{Z}]_{ii} = 1.0/z_i$. The denominator z_i is a constant: $z_i = N$ div M if $t < M * (N$ div $M)$ or otherwise a very large number $z_i = 1.0e10$.

The recursive weight update rule is derived so as to modify the maximum a posteriori weight vector $\mathbf{w}_t$ after seeing the next training pair $(\mathbf{x}_t, y_t)$ using the information at the previous step $t-1$. The following *recursive weight training rule* is obtained [Nikolaev and Tino, 2005a]:

$$\mathbf{w}_t = \mathbf{w}_{t-1} + \beta \mathbf{H}_t^{-1} \mathbf{j}_t e_t - \alpha_i \mathbf{H}_t^{-1} \mathbf{Z} \mathbf{w}_{t-1} \tag{8.30}$$

where $\mathbf{w}_{t-1}$ is the weight vector at iteration $t-1$, and α_i has index: $i = t$ mod M. The degree of impact on the hyperparameter α_i is determined by the i-th non-zero diagonal element of the matrix $\mathbf{Z}$.

Recursive Bayesian RLM training involves repeated iteration of formula (8.30). The second term in this formula $\beta \mathbf{H}_t^{-1} \mathbf{j}_t e_t$ is actually the incremental update of the weight vector. The third term $\alpha_i \mathbf{H}_t^{-1} \mathbf{Z} \mathbf{w}_{t-1}$ accounts for the regularization which is applied partially until the number of training examples reaches the boundary $M * (N$ div $M)$.

8.5.2 Sequential Dynamic Hessian Estimation

The recursive computation of the inverted Hessian matrix $\mathbf{H}_t^{-1}$ from $\mathbf{H}_{t-1}^{-1}$ depends on the local hyperparameters. When the dynamic covariance matrix is reevaluated, the regularization effect of each local hyperparameter is evenly allocated among the recursive steps. Using individual prior hyperparameters for the weights is a more general case compared to the use of a common single regularizer as in RLM [Ljung and Södeström, 1983]. This general case enables us to more accurately tune the model and enhances its generalization.

Taking into account the individual hyperparameters through partial factors $\alpha_i \mathbf{Z}$, the sequential modification of the dynamic Hessian matrix: $\mathbf{H}_t = \mathbf{H}_{t-1} + \beta \mathbf{j}_t \mathbf{j}_t^T + \alpha_i \mathbf{Z}$ is further reformulated in such a way as to facilitate the application of the matrix inversion lemma. The update $\beta \mathbf{j}_t \mathbf{j}_t^T + \alpha_i \mathbf{Z}$ is represented as a product of three matrices that yields the exact same modification of the regularized dynamic Hessian matrix by one training vector at a time in the following way:

$$\mathbf{H}_t = \mathbf{H}_{t-1} + \beta \mathbf{j}_t^* \mathbf{\Lambda}_t^{-1} \mathbf{j}_t^{*T} \tag{8.31}$$

where $\mathbf{j}_t^*$ is the matrix: $\mathbf{j}_t^* = \begin{bmatrix} & & \mathbf{j}_t^T & & \\ 0 & \dots & 1 & \dots & 0 \end{bmatrix}$, and the regularization matrix is $\mathbf{\Lambda}_t^{-1} = \begin{bmatrix} 1 & 0 \\ 0 & \alpha_i / z_i \end{bmatrix}$ with hyperparameter index $i = t \bmod M$.

Then, applying the matrix inversion lemma: $(A + BCD)^{-1} = A^{-1} - (A^{-1}BDA^{-1})/(DA^{-1}B + C^{-1})$ [Mardia et al., 1979], yields the following *sequential modification formula* for the inverted Hessian:

$$\mathbf{H}_t^{-1} = \mathbf{H}_{t-1}^{-1} - \frac{\beta \mathbf{H}_{t-1}^{-1} \mathbf{j}_t^* \mathbf{j}_t^{*T} \mathbf{H}_{t-1}^{-1}}{\beta \mathbf{j}_t^{*T} \mathbf{H}_{t-1}^{-1} \mathbf{j}_t^* + \mathbf{\Lambda}_t} \tag{8.32}$$

where $\mathbf{\Lambda}_t$ is the inverted regularization matrix $\left(\mathbf{\Lambda}_t^{-1}\right)^{-1}$. The scaling constant z included in the matrix $\mathbf{\Lambda}_t$ allows increments to the regularization effect by fractions $(\alpha_i/(N \text{ div } M))^{-1}$. Such increments continue up to iteration $t = M * (N \text{ div } M)$, after which the constant z_i does not influence the results as it becomes a very large number.

Since the quantity in the denominator of equation (8.32) is a two-dimensional square matrix, it can be inverted without problems. Let's adopt the notation:

$$\mathbf{S}_t = \beta \mathbf{j}_t^{*T} \mathbf{H}_{t-1}^{-1} \mathbf{j}_t^* + \mathbf{\Lambda}_t = \begin{bmatrix} s_{11} & s_{12} \\ s_{21} & s_{22} \end{bmatrix} \tag{8.33}$$

Then the inversion can be computed as follows [Mardia et al., 1979]:

$$\mathbf{S}_t^{-1} = \begin{bmatrix} cs_{22} & -cs_{12} \\ -cs_{21} & cs_{11} \end{bmatrix}, \text{ where: } c = \frac{1}{s_{11}s_{22} - s_{12}s_{21}} \tag{8.34}$$

which is fast and not sensitive to numerical instabilities.

It is well-known that such recursive computations depend on the initial values of the dynamic Hessian matrix. Fortunately, a lot of research has been done on this problem in the signal processing literature [Haykin, 1999], so we know that the initial matrix can be selected with recommended large diagonal elements $\left[\mathbf{H}_{t-1}^{-1}\right]_{ii} = 1.0e6$.

8.5.3 Sequential Hyperparameter Estimation

Pursuing implementation of a stable recursive Bayesian RLM training process needs modification of the hyperparameters after each training example, which should be carried out after the adjustment of the weights (8.30). Such incremental hyperprior updating will reflect the change in the belief in the corresponding weights. Otherwise, it has been found that when the hyperpriors are reestimated after training with the whole batch of data, the iterative training process may become unstable [Chen et al., 2004]. The problem is that, in this case, some hyperparameters tend to grow extremely fast to very large values, and their weights cannot adapt properly to the data so as to balance the degree of fitting with the model complexity. Reliable convergence of the Bayesian RLM learning process is achieved by reevaluating the output noise hyperparameter with formula (8.14) at the end of each training cycle.

Stable marginal likelihood maximization can be performed with sequential gradient-descent hyperparameter adaptation. Implementing such a technique requires taking the instantaneous derivatives of the marginal log likelihood function $\mathcal{L}(\boldsymbol{\alpha})$ with respect to the hyperparameters $\partial\mathcal{L}/\partial\alpha$ [Tipping, 2001]. For clarity, let a hyperparameter α at time step t be denoted by α_t. Then, the following gradient-descent prior hyperparameter training rule is obtained [Nikolaev and Tino, 2005a]:

$$\alpha_t = \alpha_{t-1} + \eta\left({\alpha_{t-1}}^{-1} - \left[\mathbf{H}_{t-1}^{-1}\right]_{ii} - w_{t-1}^2\right) \tag{8.35}$$

where η is a positive learning rate constant.

The meta-parameter η is common for all hyperparameters α_i, $1 \leq i \leq M$. Here, $\left[\mathbf{H}_{t-1}^{-1}\right]_{ii}$ denotes the i-th diagonal element of the inverted dynamic Hessian $\mathbf{H}_{t-1}^{-1}$, and all diagonal elements are available (8.32) as calculated for tuning the weights. The initial values α_0 are selected to be small numbers so as to allow them to grow up to reasonable magnitudes.

During iterative training, while doing sequential hyperparameter estimation some hyperpriors will increase while other decrease in magnitude. This means that some weights will shrink toward zero and can be removed from the model. Automatic model selection can be achieved after each cycle with all training examples by removing those weights whose priors exceed the selected threshold. The probabilistic RLM training algorithm for PNN is given in Table 8.4.

The presented recursive Bayesian approach to training PNN has four distinctive advantages: 1) it features a numerically reliable computational performance; 2) it is an incremental probabilistic algorithm with rapid convergence due to the use of second-order information from the covariance matrix to direct the weight search process; 3) it carries out stabilized hyperparameter learning; and 4) it has the capacity to learn well from time series. In particular, this method can learn well from time-varying data and noisy environments.

Table 8.4. Algorithm for recursive probabilistic training of PNN models based on the regularized Levenberg-Marquardt optimization approach.

Recursive Bayesian Learning of PNN

step	*Algorithmic sequence*
1. Initialization	Data $\mathcal{D} = \{(\mathbf{x}_t, y_t)\}_{t=1}^{N}$, initial w_0,
	covariance matrix $[\mathbf{H}^{-1}(0)]_{ii} = 1.0e6$, α_{MAX},
	hyperparameters $\alpha_0 = 1.0e^{-3}/(Nw_0^2)$, and $\beta = 1.0/stdy$.
2. Perform iterative network training	Repeat a number of iterations
	a) For each time instant $t, 1 \leq t \leq N$, do
	i) Forward propagate: the input $\mathbf{x}_t$ and compute $e_t = y_t - P(\mathbf{x}_t, \mathbf{w})$.
	ii) Backward pass: during tree traversal do
	- compute the dynamic derivatives
	$\mathbf{j}_t = \partial P_t / \partial \mathbf{w}_{kj}$ (at the output node)
	$\mathbf{j}_t = [\partial P_t / \partial p_j][\partial p_j / \partial \mathbf{w}_{ji}]$ (at the hidden nodes).
	- update the dynamic Hessian matrix
	$\mathbf{H}_t^{-1} = \mathbf{H}_{t-1}^{-1} - \beta \mathbf{H}_{t-1}^{-1} \mathbf{j}_t^* \mathbf{j}_t^{*T} \mathbf{H}_{t-1}^{-1} / d_t$
	where: $d_t = \beta \mathbf{j}_t^{*T} \mathbf{H}_{t-1}^{-1} \mathbf{j}_t^* + \mathbf{\Lambda}_t$
	$[\mathbf{\Lambda}_t]_{00} = 1.0$, $[\mathbf{\Lambda}_t]_{11} = z_i/\alpha_i$,
	$[\mathbf{\Lambda}_t]_{01} = [\mathbf{\Lambda}_t]_{10} = 0.0$.
	- update the weights at this network node
	$\mathbf{w}_t = \mathbf{w}_{t-1} + \beta \mathbf{H}_t^{-1} \mathbf{j}_t e_t - \alpha_i \mathbf{H}_t^{-1} \mathbf{Z} \mathbf{w}_{t-1}$.
	b) Re-estimate the hyperparameters
	i) Incrementally train the priors
	$\alpha_t = \alpha_{t-1} + \eta \left(\alpha_{t-1}{}^{-1} - \left[\mathbf{H}_{t-1}^{-1}\right]_{ii} - w_{t-1}^2 \right)$.
	ii) Compute the output noise variance
	$\beta = (N - \gamma) / \left(2\mathbf{e}^T \mathbf{e}\right)$, $\gamma = W - \sum_{i=0}^{W} \alpha_i \left[\mathbf{H}^{-1}\right]_{ii}$.
	c) Prune irrelevant weights w_i whose $\alpha_i > \alpha_{MAX}$.

The performance of the Bayesian RLM when training PNN is illustrated below using a time series of 445 points ($1 \leq t \leq 445$) generated using the following equation: $y(t) = \sin(0.0125t) + 0.2\sin(0.2t)$, which is a sinusoidal wave with added sinusoidal fluctuations on a smaller scale. The series was contaminated with random noise of variance 0.01. The first 380 points were used for training, and the remaining points were used for testing. Figure 8.5 shows the prediction of this series using a linear PNN trained by the regularized RLM. The curvature of the PNN forecast is very close the curvature of the generated series.

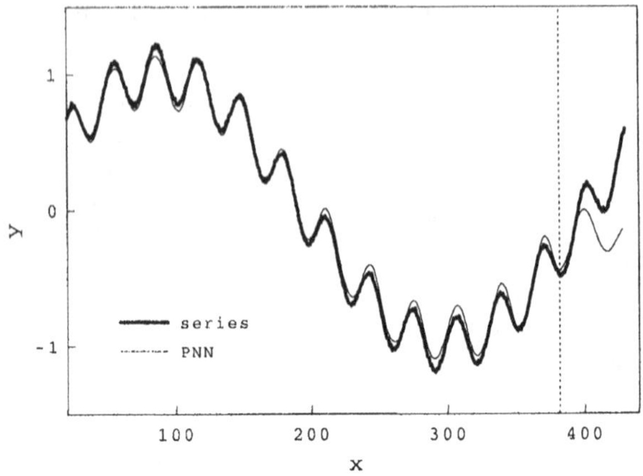

Figure 8.5. Approximation of the first 380 data points and multistep (50 steps) ahead forecasting of the time series with varying mean by the Bayesian RLM.

8.6 Monte Carlo Training

The PNN learning problem viewed from a Bayesian perspective is to find the weight posterior: $\Pr(\mathbf{w}|\mathbf{y}, X, \boldsymbol{\alpha}, \beta^{-1})$, which involves evaluation of the usually intractable integral of the joint data distribution $\int \Pr(\mathbf{t}|\mathbf{w}, X, \boldsymbol{\alpha}, \beta^{-1}) \Pr(\mathbf{w}|\boldsymbol{\alpha}) d\mathbf{w}$. The intractability of this integral can be alleviated using either approaches that exploit a *Gaussian approximation to the weight posterior* [MacKay, 1992a], or *Markov Chain Monte Carlo sampling* [Neal, 1996]. Although using the Gaussian approximation to the weight density allows easy implementations, as demonstrated in the previous subsections of this chapter, the true weight density in the general case may not be normal. If the assumption for normality is violated this approach may lead to poor results. That is why researchers have proposed to realize the intractable integrals by summations according to Monte Carlo sampling theory. Sampling methods help to deal with high-dimensional integrals, but it should be noted that they take a long time to reach accurate enough solutions. Monte Carlo methods for Bayesian training in relaxed circumstances, like non-Gaussianity and non-stationarity, are currently under investigation [Doucet et al., 2001].

This section presents a hybrid approach to Monte Carlo simulation of the summary statistics: $I = (1/N) \sum_{n=1}^{N} P(\mathbf{w}) + v$, for approximating the integral $I \approx \langle P(\mathbf{w})|\mathbf{t}\rangle = \int P(\mathbf{w}) \Pr(\mathbf{w}|\mathbf{t}) d\mathbf{w}$ with independently sampled weight vectors $\mathbf{w}$, where v is the sample variance defined as: $v = (1/N)\sqrt{\langle P(\mathbf{w})^2\rangle - \langle P(\mathbf{w})\rangle^2}$ with $\langle P(\mathbf{w})\rangle = (1/N) \sum_{n=1}^{N} P(\mathbf{w})$. The simulation allows us to obtain empirically the mean output and also the weight posterior mean $\widehat{\Pr}(\mathbf{w}|\mathbf{t})$. The empirical estimates are produced by averaging over a population of weight vectors. The averaging is performed using importance ratios associated with each population member. The importance ratios play a major role in this approach as they help to achieve asymptotic convergence of the learning process. The population is continuously modified by making sampling and resampling steps, and such steps are alternated many times to achieve sufficient accuracy. Each candidate weight vector from the population is sampled by random perturbation using the chosen prior distribution. The resampling of promising weight vectors is based on their importances.

In order to further improve the accuracy of the method, so as to avoid wandering on the search landscape, the sampled weights can additionally be optimized [de Freitas et al., 2000b] with a suitable algorithm. Such a hybrid sampling importance resampling technique using gradient-descent training is demonstrated below.

8.6.1 Markov Chain Monte Carlo

The Monte Carlo technique can be applied for neural network training by sampling weights from their predefined prior distribution, next evaluating the likelihood, and finally computing the importance ratios. One strategy is to generate a Markov Chain of sampled weight vectors such that in the limit, when a large number of samples are drawn, it approaches their unknown probability distribution. Independent from the choice of the initial sample, if the sampling is possible and performed properly, the Markov Chain tends to a fixed approximation. Such an approximation is probabilistic in the sense that its components occur with a transition probability (that is not with certainty), and depend only on the recent components from the previous discrete time step. This inspires us to use the Markov Chain Monte Carlo (MCMC) strategy for implementing Bayesian learning algorithms for PNN.

Specialized MCMC algorithms for training neural networks have been made using *importance sampling* [de Freitas et al., 2000b]. According to this method, an importance, also called proposal, distribution $\pi(\mathbf{w}|\mathbf{t})$ is selected which can be easily sampled and with which integration by means of summation can be implemented. Then an approximation to the integral of the joint data distribution can be computed simply by summation over the ratio: $\Pr(\mathbf{w}|\mathbf{t})/\pi(\mathbf{w}|\mathbf{t})$, with respect to the chosen proposal distribution. In this way, the difficulty of drawing samples directly from the posterior distribution is alleviated by drawing samples from the proposal distribution instead.

This allows us to approximate the integral as follows:

$$I \approx \langle P(\mathbf{w})|\mathbf{t}\rangle = \int P(\mathbf{w}) \frac{\Pr(\mathbf{w}|\mathbf{t})}{\pi(\mathbf{w}|\mathbf{t})} \pi(\mathbf{w}|\mathbf{t}) d\mathbf{w} \quad (8.36)$$

using summation instead of attempting to solve it directly.

The MCMC training algorithm begins with random generation of a set of initial weight vectors from their selected prior. The training proceeds by perturbing these weights with uniformly drawn noise from the proposal distribution; that is, corrections are made in the search directions using the proposal density. The perturbed weights are considered in the context of the adopted PNN model to produce outputs by propagating the inputs through the network in a feed-forward manner. In the limit with the increase in the number of sampled weight vectors, the expectation of the data can be approximated by the following sum:

$$I = \frac{\sum_{s=1}^{S} P(\mathbf{w}_s) q(\mathbf{w}_s)}{\sum_{s=1}^{S} q(\mathbf{w}_s)} \quad (8.37)$$

where q is a substituion for the normalized *importance ratios*:

$$q(\mathbf{w}) = \frac{\Pr(\mathbf{t}|\mathbf{w}) \Pr(\mathbf{w})}{\pi(\mathbf{w}|\mathbf{t})} \quad (8.38)$$

which contains the likelihood $\Pr(\mathbf{t}|\mathbf{w})$ and the weight prior $\Pr(\mathbf{w})$.

The approximate *Monte Carlo estimate of the weight posterior* distribution $\widehat{\Pr}(\mathbf{w}|\mathbf{t})$ in this setting can be obtained by summation:

$$\widehat{\Pr}(\mathbf{w}|\mathbf{t}) = \sum_{s=1}^{S} \frac{q(\mathbf{w}_s)}{\sum_{s=1}^{S} q(\mathbf{w}_s)} \delta(\mathbf{w} - \mathbf{w}_s) \quad (8.39)$$

where δ is the Dirac delta function.

The accuracy of this technique depends on whether using the proposal distribution $\pi(\mathbf{w}|\mathbf{t})$ weights $\mathbf{w}$ that are representative enough for the distribution $\Pr(\mathbf{w}|\mathbf{t})$ can be drawn, or whether sampling from such regions in which the probability $\Pr(\mathbf{w}|\mathbf{t})$ is large can be accomplished. This is the motivation to model the proposal distribution by the transition distribution of a Markov Chain $\pi(\mathbf{w}_k|\mathbf{w}_{k-1}, \mathbf{t}_k) = \Pr(\mathbf{w}_k|\mathbf{w}_{k-1})$. Such a simulation of a Markov process guarantees asymptotic convergence to the target posterior density. The Markov Chain is a sequence in which each sample is produced from the previous one by a stochastic update drawn independently according to the transition function: $\mathbf{w}_k = \mathbf{w}_{k-1} + \varepsilon$, where: $\varepsilon \in \pi(\mathbf{w}|\mathbf{t})$. The transition distribution function is typically chosen proportional to the variance of successive weight vectors, that is to the difference between the most recent vectors.

Taking these details into consideration makes the above formula for the importance ratios (8.38) sequentially computable as follows:

$$\begin{aligned} q_k(\mathbf{w}_{k,s}) &= q_{k-1}(\mathbf{w}_{k,s})\frac{\Pr(\mathbf{t}_k|\mathbf{w}_{k,s})\Pr(\mathbf{w}_{k,s}|\mathbf{w}_{k-1,s})}{\pi(\mathbf{w}_{k,s}|\mathbf{w}_{k-1,s},\mathbf{t}_k)} \\ &= q_{k-1}(\mathbf{w}_{k,s})\Pr(\mathbf{t}_k|\mathbf{w}_{k,s}) \end{aligned} \tag{8.40}$$

where $\Pr(\mathbf{t}_{k,s}|\mathbf{w}_{k,s}) \approx \exp(-\beta E_D(\mathbf{w}_{k,s}))$. Here s ranges over the weight vectors and k enumerates the iterative steps of the algorithm.

8.6.2 Importance Resampling

The approximation quality of this approach strongly depends on the choice of the proposal density. It is suggested here to model it with the transition distribution of the Markov Chain, but other choices are also possible. There are two main requirements for the proposal distribution: 1) it should make drawing of random samples computationally easy; and 2) it should be as close as possible to the unknown posterior. Only when $\pi(\mathbf{w}|\mathbf{t})$ is similar enough to $\Pr(\mathbf{w}|\mathbf{t})$, good results can be expected. A proposal distribution function which almost attains equivalence: $\Pr(\mathbf{w}|\mathbf{t})/\pi(\mathbf{w}|\mathbf{t}) \approx 1$ is often feasible.

The analysis of this importance ratio leads to the idea of resampling. After the weights have been sampled with the chosen probability, they are resampled to retain the most promising among them. Since the population vectors determine the search directions, this means that the resampling contributes to focusing the search into plausible areas on the error landscape. *Importance resampling* is performed by selecting weights with high importance ratios and discarding weights with low importance ratios. This efficient algorithm is called MCMC with Sampling Importance Resampling (SIR) [de Freitas et al., 2000b].

8.6.3 Hybrid Sampling Resampling

In practice the Sampling Importance Resampling technique may take a very large number of iterations to converge to a solution of acceptable accuracy. For this reason the MCMC algorithm may additionally be focused so as to push it faster on the search landscape toward promising regions for exploration instead of leaving it to wander, which is a promising search direction. This can be achieved by using a proper weight training algorithm applied to each weight vector after random sampling [de Freitas et al., 2000b]. Such a *Hybrid Sampling Importance Resampling* technique is specialized for PNN using the RLM algorithm (Section 8.5) for weight focusing in Table 8.5.

Table 8.5. A Bayesian Markov Chain Monte Carlo algorithm for PNN based on Hybrid Sampling Importance Resampling with RLM optimization.

MCMC Training of PNN

step	*Algorithmic sequence*
1. Initialization	Data $\mathcal{D} = \{(\mathbf{x}_t, y_t)\}_{t=1}^{N}$, PNN architecture, sample size $1 \leq s \leq S$, weight variance $\alpha_i = \sigma_{W_i}^{-2}$, output noise variance $\beta = 1.0/stdy$, threshold Z proposal distribution $\pi(\mathbf{w}\|\mathbf{t}) = \mathcal{N}(0, \sigma_W^2)$.
2. Sample weights	Sample a weight vector $\mathbf{w}_0$ from the prior $\pi(\mathbf{w}\|\mathbf{t})$
3. Perform sampling importance resampling	Repeat a number of iterations k, $1 \leq k \leq K$ a) Sample a weight vector from the prior $\mathbf{w}_{k+1,s} = \mathbf{w}_{k,s} + \varepsilon$, where: $\varepsilon \in \pi(\mathbf{w}\|\mathbf{t})$. b) Optimize $\mathbf{w}_{k+1,s}$ according to the gradient by executing one RLM cycle. c) Compute the unnormalized importances $e_i = y_i - P(\mathbf{x}_i, \mathbf{w}_{k+1,s})$ $q_{k+1}(\mathbf{w}_{k+1,s}) = q_k(\mathbf{w}_{k+1,s}) \exp\left(-0.5\beta \sum_{i=1}^{N} e_i^2\right)$ and next normalize them $q'_{k+1}(\mathbf{w}_{k+1,s}) = q_{k+1}(\mathbf{w}_{k+1,s}) / \sum_{s=1}^{S} q_{k+1}(\mathbf{w}_{k+1,s})$. d) Resample promising weights among these with $1.0/\sum_{s=1}^{S}\left(q'_{k+1}(\mathbf{w}_{k+1,s})\right)^2 < Z$ by selecting weights with high importance ratios and assign importances $q_{k+1}(\mathbf{w}_{k+1,s}) = 1.0/S$.
5. Estimate the mean weight	Compute the average weight vector $\mathbf{w} = \sum_{s=1}^{S} q'(\mathbf{w}_s)\delta(\mathbf{w} - \mathbf{w}_s)$.

The behavior of the MCMC algorithm from Table 8.5 was applied to train a PNN using the same Hermite polynomial from Section 8.4: $1.0 + ((1.0 - t + 3t^2) * exp(-t^2))$, where the argument t is taken from the interval: $-5 < t < 5$. One hundred points were generated and then random noise of variance 0.01 was added. In order to produce meaningful and illustrative results the PNN was trained for five iterations, and the remaining parsimonious PNN of 5 terms: x_{t-1}, x_{t-2}, x_{t-3}, $x_{t-1}x_{t-3}$, and $x_{t-2}x_{t-3}^2$ was taken. After that, the Hybrid SIR was run on this network and the weights were perturbed assuming proposal distribution with weight variance 0.01. The population size was 50 for fast computation. During Hybrid SIR for selection of promising weight vectors, among those generated by random perturbation, 16 samples were taken out of all 50 in the population. Among these 16 weight vectors, half of them were from those discarded by Hybrid SIR and the other half from those kept to the end of the algorithm.

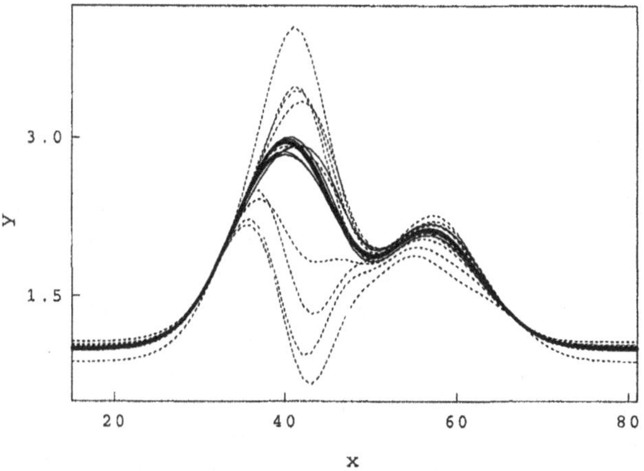

Figure 8.6. Markov Chain Monte Carlo training of a PNN using the Sampling Importance Resampling technique and the Hermite polynomial data.

Figure 8.6 illustrates the 16 polynomials generated by evaluation of the PNN with these sampled weight vectors. The dashed curves are the polynomials produced by the weight vectors that were discarded, while the straight line curves are the functions retained in the population. The bold curve is the average of the 8 good polynomials made from the promising weight vectors. The resulted bold curve is the empirically generated PNN approximation to the Hermite polynomial.

There are two design issues that arise when implementing this hybrid MCMC training algorithm: 1) how to select initial starting values; and 2) how many runs to perform. The second issue depends on the possibility to find out whether the chain has converged sufficiently close to an accurate solution. This criterion can be measured by conducting a number of runs, starting from distant initial vectors, and evaluating the inter sequence and between sequences variances. If they are close, then it can be assumed that the algorithm converges [Nabney, 2002].

8.7 Chapter Summary

This section presented Bayesian techniques for learning with polynomial networks. PNN algorithms that implement the two main Bayesian approaches were demonstrated: the evidence approach [MacKay, 1992a], and the sampling approach [Neal, 1996]. The evidence approach suggests to approximate the integration over the hyperparameters in order to determine the values that maximize their joint probability. These hyperparameters are taken as fixed to carry out weight posterior maximization. Although this evidence approach is not exact, it has been found that it produces superior results than those generated by integration over the hyperparameters [Buntine and Weigend, 1991b].

An essential advantage of the Bayesian regularization and pruning techniques developed according to the evidence framework is that they are general and applicable to polynomial networks with various activation functions; that is, these techniques can be considered to improve the generalization of all of the presented models in Section 3. These Bayesian techniques provide a reliable means to tune further the best discovered models for example by IGP, in order to achieve parsimonious models. In addition to this, the Bayesian error function can be used as a fitness function for guiding the evolutionary search process toward better polynomial network structures, as it is objective and utilizes all the data without the need to split them artificially.

There are several distinctive features of this chapter: 1) it offers an approach to Sparse Bayesian Learning with proper treatment of the weight variances and output variances during training, which is implemented using the reliable EM algorithm; 2) it provides an innovative algorithm for Recursive Bayesian training which is a robust tool for sequential learning from time series; 3) it offers a Markov Chain Monte Carlo algorithm for weights training based on a hybrid sampling-resampling technique.

Chapter 9

STATISTICAL MODEL DIAGNOSTICS

The goal of polynomial identification is to discover faithful models of the given data. That is why it is important to quantify the reliability of the learned models so as to obtain evidence of their usefulness. There are two main factors that cause deviations in PNN: the data uncertainty and the model uncertainty. Central notions for the analysis of such learning problems are the standard error, the total error, and the confidence and prediction intervals. The total error reflects the model accuracy over the entire data distribution (not only over the training data sample), and allows us to make decisions about the correctness of the models. Both the data and the model discrepancies can be examined by estimating the intervals which with high degree of belief contain the model. These are the confidence and prediction intervals, also called error bars.

This chapter investigates the factors that impact the generation of faithful PNN models and provides means for their statistical diagnosis. The standard error is traditionally estimated by data resampling and model reevaluation. The direct estimation of the total error is difficult practically but mitigated by decomposing it into bias and variance components. The integrated bias and variance components of the total error are evaluated separately by a resampling technique. There are two groups of approaches to measuring error bars for neural network models: analytical and empirical. Confidence intervals can be obtained by the analytical delta method and the empirical bootstrapping method. Prediction intervals can be estimated by an analytical method for nonlinear models, and empirically by extending the network architecture to learn the output error variance as a function of the inputs. Another possibility to assess the model reliability is to compute Bayesian intervals, also by corresponding analytical and empirical methods.

The analytical methods for error bar estimation rely on several assumptions. First, the given training data set is of fixed size. Second, the data are contaminated by noise ε which is independent, normally distributed with zero mean and variance σ_y^2, thus the targets are noisy samples: $y = P(\mathbf{x}, \mathbf{w}) + \varepsilon$, where $P(\mathbf{x}, \mathbf{w})$ is the PNN model. Third, the training cost function is continuous and it allows us to calculate its first-order and second-order error derivatives. Fourth, the network has been trained until convergence to a global minimum of the error surface. There are no clear criteria that tell how to satisfy the fourth assumption when doing network training. However, the PNN evolved by IGP and further trained by BP and Bayesian techniques may be envisioned as nearly optimal (virtually the best solution of the task), and hence it can be assumed that the tests are statistically valid. The empirical methods are less demanding; they usually consider that the network structure and weights are sufficiently good models of the data.

The statistical diagnosis tools have to be applied in order to examine the inferred PNN models and to judge whether successful induction from the given data has been performed. The presented plots in this chapter demonstrate that different approaches produce different error bands. Which of them will be used as most plausible depends on the current task and the desired accuracy from the inferred model. Finally, we present statistical validation tests for detecting residual correlations suitable for PNN models.

9.1 Deviations of PNN Models

There are many reasons in practice that hinder the inductive learning process and cause deviations of the model from the true regression function $\tilde{P}(\mathbf{x}) = E[y|\mathbf{x}]$. When inferring nonlinear PNN models from data, the main sources for difference from the unknown true regressor are: a) uncertainties in the data, and b) uncertainties in the model, which concern the model complexity and weight accuracy.

Impacts from the Data. First, there are inherent inaccuracies in the data, like noise, omitted data, outliers, and measurement errors, which influence the model identification. Second, it depends from which region of the true function the given data sample has been taken, because the true data may have different densities in different regions and they may not be sufficiently represented in the provided training sample. The learning algorithms are unfortunately sensitive to the sampling variations of the data. An effect from the data sample when flexible models are learned is that they have high variance, while if the learned models are restricted they tend to exhibit less variance.

Impacts from the Model. First, the relevant input variables in the model, their number, and which they should be, may not have been selected properly. Second, the number of terms and the maximal order (degree) of the polynomial model may not have been determined correctly. Such model complexity problems may arise due to inefficient evolutionary search by the mechanisms of IGP as well as improper Bayesian tuning. Third, the pruning techniques may introduce model misspecification due to overpruning or underpruning of the network. Overall, the imposed particular functional form of the model to be learned introduces another bias component to the total error.

Even if the model complexity is relatively good, the weights may have not been learned accurately. This happens because often the multilayer network training process may be unable to converge to a good weight vector. There are many inferior local optima on the error surface, and a lot of them usually do not possess the desired fitting characteristics. This is why the presented inductive learning methodology in this book recommends to use additional retraining of the best evolved models by IGP using backpropagation techniques or Bayesian training techniques, or both, for attaining optimal results.

9.2 Residual Bootstrap Sampling

There are two main groups of methods for statistical model diagnosis: sampling methods and splitting methods. The sampling methods for error evaluation are advantageous over splitting methods as they are less sensitive to the specific data divisions and often produce more reliable results. Especially suitable for regression tasks is the *residual bootstrap sampling* method [Tibshirani, 1996]. It prescribes to create artificial data distributions by randomly adding the errors of the model to the given data. Such sampling of noise is performed repeatedly for a reasonable number of times and the studied model is estimated. This approach is usually applied for measuring the standard error and helps to get a statistical picture of the model uncertainty.

Residual bootstrap sampling suggests generating a number B of different models $P(\mathbf{x}, \mathbf{w}^b)$ from a particular studied one $P(\mathbf{x}, \mathbf{w})$ by estimating it with replicates of the given data sample $D = \{(\mathbf{x}_n, y_n)\}_{n=1}^N$. Every model $P(\mathbf{x}, \mathbf{w}^b)$, $1 \leq b \leq B$, is made by reestimating the studied $P(\mathbf{x}, \mathbf{w})$ with its output deliberately contaminated by a randomly drawn residual error: $P(\mathbf{x}_n, \mathbf{w}^b) = P(\mathbf{x}_n, \mathbf{w}) + e_n^b$, $1 \leq n \leq N$, where e_n^b is the n-th residual from the b-th error series: $\mathbf{e}^b = [e_1^b, e_2^b, ..., e_N^b]$, $1 \leq b \leq B$. In order to derive the different models $P(\mathbf{x}, \mathbf{w}^b)$, an error series $\mathbf{e}^b$ is produced by resampling the residuals $[e_1, e_2, ..., e_N]$ independently from the studied model: $e_n = y_n - P(\mathbf{x}_n, \mathbf{w})$. The *standard error* at a data point $\mathbf{x}$ may be computed using residual bootstrap sampling as follows:

$$\hat{se}_{boot}(P(\mathbf{x},\mathbf{w})) = \sqrt{\frac{1}{B-1}\sum_{b=1}^{B}\left(P(\mathbf{x},\mathbf{w}^b) - \bar{P}\,(\mathbf{x},\mathbf{w})\right)^2} \tag{9.1}$$

where $\bar{P}\,(\mathbf{x},\mathbf{w})$ is the average from the reevaluated B models using the resampled data: $\bar{P}\,(\mathbf{x},\mathbf{w}) = (1/(B-1))\sum_{b=1}^{B} P(\mathbf{x},\mathbf{w}^b)$.

Although the residual bootstrap is a computationally intensive procedure, it is useful not only for measuring the standard error, but also for evaluating the bias and variance components of the total error, as well as for finding confidence intervals.

9.3 The Bias/Variance Dilemma

9.3.1 Statistical Bias and Variance

The model variation in performance over the training and over the unseen data can be investigated with the total error, also called generalization error. It evaluates the capacity of the model to generalize beyond the provided data set. When learning from a fixed data set it is not enough to use only the residual error as inductive criterion in pursuit of generalization. This is because real data are often not completely reliable due to noise, omitted data, and other defects. There is a need to obtain evidence for the total error over the entire set of training and unseen testing data as well.

The *total squared error* $(P(\mathbf{x})-E[y|\mathbf{x}])^2$ explains how well the solution $P(\mathbf{x})$ approximates the true regression function $\tilde{P}(\mathbf{x}) = E[y|\mathbf{x}]$. Such evidence can be acquired by decomposing the total error in two separate components [Geman et al., 1992]:

$$E_D[(P(\mathbf{x})-E[y|\mathbf{x}])^2] = (E_D[P(\mathbf{x})]-E[y|\mathbf{x}])^2 + E_D[(P(\mathbf{x})-E_D[P(\mathbf{x})])^2] \tag{9.2}$$

which are called statistical bias $BIAS^2(P(\mathbf{x}))$, and statistical variance $VAR(P(\mathbf{x}))$:

$$BIAS^2(P(\mathbf{x})) = (E_D[P(\mathbf{x})] - E[y|\mathbf{x}])^2 \tag{9.3}$$

$$VAR(P(\mathbf{x})) = E_D[(P(\mathbf{x}) - E_D[P(\mathbf{x})])^2] \tag{9.4}$$

where the index D means with respect to the available training data $D = \{(\mathbf{x}_n, y_n)\}_{n=1}^N$.

The total error shows how well the model agrees with a randomly drawn data sample from the true function distribution. When the sample size increases to infinity, the total error diminishes to zero. Since in practice we are always given finite data samples, the measurements of the total error are approximate.

The *statistical bias* is an error estimate that shows to what degree the model structure is adequate to the data, in the sense of whether it is complex enough to be a close approximation to the true function. For example, the statistical bias may reveal whether the selected representation and learning algorithm have adjusted the model structure to the data well. When the bias is relaxed the accuracy of interpolation improves but the extrapolation of unseen data becomes worse. This is because a very low bias means that the model is too sophisticated and overfits the specificities of the data. At the other extreme, a very high bias indicates that the model is not sufficiently complex to describe the regularities in the data. The model components that affect the bias are the selected inputs, the maximal order (degree) of the polynomial model, and the network architecture. Thus by changing these components the bias can be modified so as to impact on the level of generalization. These effects can be examined with measurements of the fitting accuracy.

The *statistical variance* is an error estimate that accounts mainly for the generalization capacity of the model, that is whether the model fits the data without regard to the particularities of the provided data sample. The statistical variance shows the model sensitivity to training with different samples of the same underlying function. A large variance indicates that the model does not capture well the general properties of the unknown data source. Such data properties that affect learning are: the noise in the data, omitted data, outliers, and measurement errors. The learning algorithms are equipped with mechanisms for control over the variance aiming at reduction of the model deviation from one data sample to another. In order to increase the predictability the variance should be reduced, but then the fitting accuracy becomes worse and the results may not be satisfactory. This is why the bias and variance should be properly balanced in order to achieve identification of optimal models with very low total error.

The practical question is how to calculate the statistical bias and variance with the available knowledge for the model and the data.

9.3.2 Measuring Bias and Variance

Research into the statistical characteristics of neural networks shows that one can measure the *integrated bias and variance* [Geman et al., 1992], which are estimates of the statistical bias and the statistical variance. While the statistical bias and variance cannot be directly computed, as the true function that generates the data is usually not known in practice, the integrated bias and variance can be evaluated with concrete formulae by performing data resampling. Resampling is necessary to obtain information for the possible deviation of the data; that is, to distinguish the essential characteristics of the studied model from the specificities of the given training sample.

The *integrated bias* can be calculated using the provided training sample, using the following formula:

$$BIAS^2 = \frac{1}{N}\sum_{n=1}^{N}\left(\bar{P}\ (\mathbf{x}_n, \mathbf{w}) - P(\mathbf{x}_n, \mathbf{w})\right)^2 \tag{9.5}$$

where $\bar{P}\ (\mathbf{x}_n, \mathbf{w})$ is the average from the generated B polynomials by the selected sampling method: $\bar{P}\ (\mathbf{x}_n, \mathbf{w}) = (1/B)\sum_{b=1}^{B} P(\mathbf{x}_n, \mathbf{w}^b)$, estimated with the n-th data vector $\mathbf{x}_n$. The same average $\bar{P}\ (\mathbf{x}_n, \mathbf{w})$ is also necessary to compute estimates of the integrated variance.

The *integrated variance* can be calculated as follows:

$$VAR = \frac{1}{N}\sum_{n=1}^{N}\left(\frac{1}{B}\sum_{b=1}^{B}\left(P(\mathbf{x}_n, \mathbf{w}^b) - \bar{P}\ (\mathbf{x}_n, \mathbf{w})\right)^2\right) \tag{9.6}$$

where b enumerates the sampled polynomials $P(\mathbf{x}_n, \mathbf{w}^1)$,...,$P(\mathbf{x}_n, \mathbf{w}^B)$.

It should be clarified that the above formulae for measuring the integrated bias (9.5) and the integrated variance (9.6) can be used with different resampling methods. The residual bootstrap sampling, given in subsection 9.2, is recommended for addressing real-world regression and time series modeling tasks.

Figures 9.1 and 9.2. provide separate plots of the integrated $BIAS^2$ (9.5) and VAR (9.6) components of the total error, made as the average of several PNN, estimated using the residual bootstrap resampling method using a benchmark time series. The IGP was run using the Mackey-Glass series [Mackey and Glass, 1977] and the best evolved PNN model was taken without further improvement, by retraining it. Such runs were repeated 50 times to diminish effects from resampling. Next an averaged solution from the generated best 50 polynomials was made. The integrated $BIAS^2$ and VAR of the averaged solution was computed as a function of the regularization parameter λ. The impact of the regularization parameter λ on the model accuracy was changed by increasing its values from 0.0001 to 0.09 by 0.0005.

The curves in Figures 9.1 and 9.2 demonstrate that using larger values of the regularizer λ makes smoother polynomials. As a result of this, the bias becomes stronger while the variance diminishes. The overall effect as λ is increased is initially a decrease in total error followed by an increase in error after λ passes a certain optimal value. The most appropriate regularization value is the one with which the total error reaches its minimum.

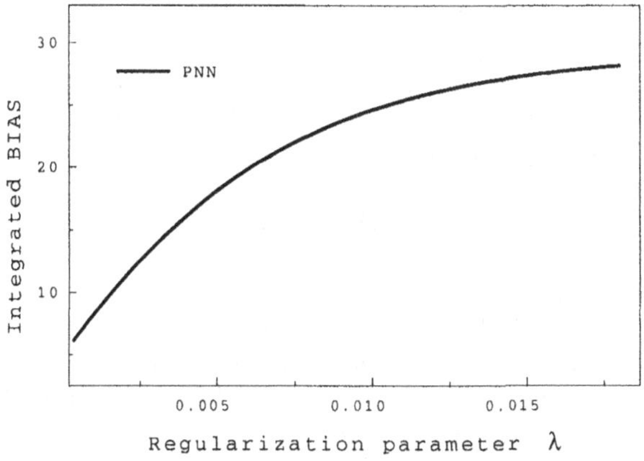

Figure 9.1. Integrated $BIAS^2$ of fitting the Mackey-Glass series by a PNN evolved using IGP, averaged over 50 runs to diminish effects from randomness due to resampling. Each curve point is produced after residual bootstrapping of 100 PNN.

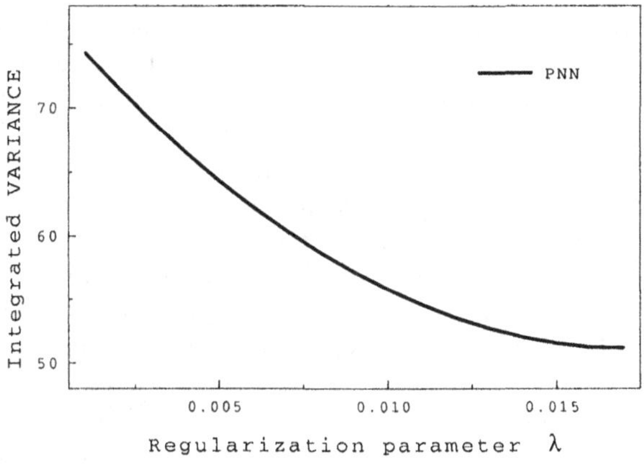

Figure 9.2. Integrated $VARiance$ of fitting the Mackey-Glass series by a PNN evolved using IGP, averaged over 50 runs to diminish effects from randomness due to resampling. Each point is produced after residual bootstrapping of 100 PNN.

9.4 Confidence Intervals

When inferring models from experimental data it is important to quantify the belief in them in order to become certain of their usefulness. Confidence intervals, also called error bars, are statistical means for evaluating the uncertainty of models learned from concrete data. They reveal the expected fluctuation of the standard error.

The reliability of a model, here a PNN, is defined by the probability with which this model contains the true regression function. In statistical parlance the task of measuring the model uncertainty is to find the confidence interval in which one has $(1-\alpha)\%$ (i.e. 95%) belief that randomly drawn data will be described correctly by the model. *Confidence interval* for a population mean like the regressor function $\tilde{P}(\mathbf{x}) = E[y|\mathbf{x}]$ consists of two limits: from above and from below, which with a certain probability contains this value $\tilde{P}(\mathbf{x})$.

Confidence intervals for multilayer PNN models, like the error bars proposed for neural networks [Hwang and Ding, 1997, De Veaux et al., 1998, Rivals and Personnaz, 2000, Tibshirani, 1996], can be estimated with two different analytical and empirical approaches. The analytical approaches are inherited from the theory of nonlinear regression models. Such an analytical approach can be implemented using the delta method [Efron and Tibshirani, 1989]. The delta method requires the first-order and second-order error derivatives with respect to the weights. There are two cases to consider: estimating confidence intervals in linear PNN and in nonlinear PNN. While the Hessian in linear PNN is available from the weight learning process, the Hessian in nonlinear PNN has to be calculated additionally using $\mathcal{R}$-propagation. The Hessian contains the second-order error derivatives, and in the case of neural networks it plays the same role as the covariance matrix in traditional nonlinear models. A popular empirical approach to constructing confidence intervals is the one based on the residual bootstrap method [Tibshirani, 1996].

9.4.1 Interval Estimation by the Delta Method

The *delta method* [Efron and Tibshirani, 1989] provides an estimate of the standard error through the maximum likelihood theory. It suggests to measure the standard error of the model as follows:

$$\hat{se}_{delta}(P(\mathbf{x}, \mathbf{w})) = \sqrt{\sigma_y^2 \mathbf{g}^T \mathbf{H}^{-1} \mathbf{g}} \qquad (9.7)$$

where σ_y^2 is the variance of the noise ε, $\mathbf{g}$ is the gradient vector (6.36) with the first-order error derivatives with respect to the weights, and $\mathbf{H}$ is the Hessian matrix (6.39) with the second-order derivatives of the error function with respect to the weights. All first-order and second-order error derivatives are evaluated at the learned weight vector. Strictly speaking, the above formula (9.7) assumes that the PNN model is nearly the best solution from a global perspective.

The standard error in (9.7) may be approximated using the traditional average mean squared error: $\hat{\sigma}_y^2 = (1/(N-\gamma))\sum_{n=1}^{N}(y_n - P(\mathbf{x}_n, \mathbf{w}))^2$, where N is the number of the training data and γ is the effective number of network parameters (which is typically less than the number of all neural network weights). A practical concern is to take into account the weight decay regularization, which is usually applied when training polynomial networks with the intention of achieving stable numerical performance and good generalization. The impact of regularization should be included by adding the individual regularization factors λ_i to the diagonal elements of the Hessian before doing inversion.

The empirical *confidence interval of a PNN model* according to the Delta method can be obtained using the formula:

$$P(\mathbf{x}, \mathbf{w}) \pm z_{.025}\sigma_y^2\sqrt{\mathbf{g}^T(\mathbf{H}+\mathbf{L})^{-1}\mathbf{g}} \qquad (9.8)$$

where $z_{.025}$ is the critical value of the normal distribution, and $\mathbf{L}$ is the diagonal matrix with the local regularizers λ_i, $1 \leq i \leq W$.

Formula (9.8) for evaluating the confidence intervals of linear models directly takes the inverted Hessian matrix: $\mathbf{H}^{-1} = (\mathbf{\Phi}^T\mathbf{\Phi} + \mathbf{L})^{-1}$, which is available after learning the network weights by least squares fitting, which saves computation time and makes the implementation easy. When trying to evaluate confidence intervals in nonlinear PNN models formula (9.8) can be implemented in two different ways: 1) using the full Hessian (6.39, 6.40), and 2) using a diagonal approximation of the Hessian with elements $[\mathbf{H}]_{ij} = (\partial P(\mathbf{x}, \mathbf{w})/\partial w_i)(\partial P(\mathbf{x}, \mathbf{w})/\partial w_j)$.

The second version for measuring confidence intervals using the diagonal approximation of the Hessian matrix can be derived using a linear Taylor expansion of the nonlinear model output [Rivals and Personnaz, 2000]. This is a simplified version which leads to less accurate intervals because using only a diagonal approximation of the Hessian means that some precision contributed by the off-diagonal matrix elements is lost. Since there are very precise techniques available for evaluating the full Hessian matrix, e.g. the $\mathcal{R}$-propagation algorithm [Pearlmutter, 1994] for example, these should be preferred as they quantify the statistical significance of the models more accurately.

Error bars of PNN can be estimated using the backpropagation algorithm (Section 6.2) to compute the gradient vector $\mathbf{g}$, and the $\mathcal{R}$-propagation algorithm (Section 6.3.1) to compute the Hessian matrix $\mathbf{H}$. The application of formula (9.8) has to be adjusted in practice because PNN are identified as models of the normalized series.

PNNs are usually trained over the normalized data; they do not directly describe the given data at their original magnitude. In order to produce error bounds at their original magnitude, formula (9.8) should be modified to reflect the fact that the input and output data are normalized. More precisely, realistic confidence intervals can be obtained by multiplying the square root by $z_{.025}\hat{\sigma}^* y_{std}$, where $\hat{\sigma}^*$ is the mean squared error of the normalized model, and y_{std} is the standard deviation of the original outputs y [Rivals and Personnaz, 2000].

The confidence intervals measured with PNN learned from normalized data can be restored to their original magnitude in the following way:

$$P(\mathbf{x}, \mathbf{w}) \pm z_{.025}\hat{\sigma}^* y_{std}\sqrt{\mathbf{g}^T(\mathbf{H}+\mathbf{L})^{-1}\mathbf{g}} \tag{9.9}$$

where the Hessian **H** and the gradient **g** are calculated with the normalized data, and the standard deviation of the original outputs is: $y_{std} = \sqrt{(1/(N-\gamma))\sum_{n=1}^{N}(y_n - \bar{y})^2}$.

As an example, these algorithms were used to calculate the confidence intervals of the best PNN evolved on the benchmark Mackey-Glass series [Mackey and Glass, 1977]. Figure 9.3 illustrates the confidence intervals produced by the delta method according to formula (9.9) using the full Hessian matrix. Figure 9.4 displays the confidence intervals derived by the delta method again according to formula (9.9) but using the diagonal approximation of the Hessian. Both figures 9.3 and 9.4 show clearly that the two implementations of the delta method lead to slightly different error bars. One is inclined to think that using the diagonal elements of the Hessian matrix without taking into account the off-diagonal elements seem to give overly optimistic evidence for the possible error deviations. Confidence intervals generated by this method with the use of the full Hessian matrix seem to be more realistic. Similar observations are made after bootstrapping of confidence intervals of the same polynomial network model shown later in the following Figure 9.5.

It should be clarified that the plots in Figures 9.3 and 9.4 have been produced by evaluating the PNN model with the Mackey-Glass data series prenormalized into the interval [0, 1]. The IGP system, as well as the neural network algorithm, learn and train PNN models using normalized input data which helps to avoid numerical problems arising when computing the weights and when attempting to invert the Hessian matrix. That is, the PNN model is inferred in the normalized space, not in the space of the original data magnitude.

The algorithm for finding the confidence intervals of PNN models according to the modified delta method is summarized in Table 9.1.

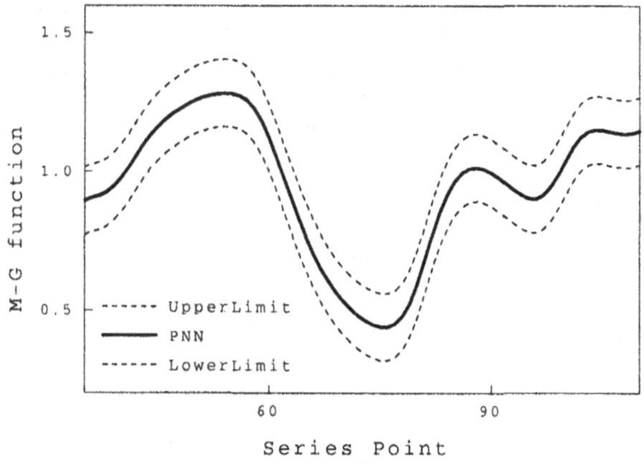

Figure 9.3. Confidence intervals of PNN made with the Mackey-Glass series according to the Delta method using the full Hessian matrix ($\lambda = 0.001$).

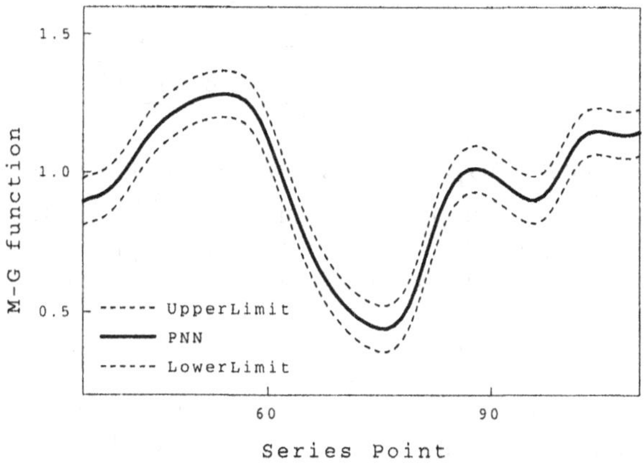

Figure 9.4. Confidence intervals of PNN made with the Mackey-Glass series according to the Delta method using a diagonal Hessian approximation ($\lambda = 0.001$).

Table 9.1. Algorithm for estimating the analytical confidence intervals of PNN.

Estimating Confidence Intervals of PNN using the Delta Method

step	*Algorithmic sequence*
1. Initialization	Normalized model $P^*(\mathbf{x}^*, \mathbf{w})$, *normalized* training data: $D = \{(\mathbf{x}^*_n, y^*_n)\}_{n=1}^N$ $\mathbf{L}$ regularization matrix, effective parameters γ $z_{.025}$ critical value of the normal distribution.
2. Calculate the gradient vector	Evaluate the elements of the gradient with each input data vector $\mathbf{x}^*_n, 1 \leq n \leq N$ $g_i = \partial E(\mathbf{x}^*_n, \mathbf{w})/\partial w_i, g_i \in \mathbf{g}, 1 \leq i \leq W$.
3. Calculate the Hessian matrix	Evaluate the elements of the Hessian: with each input data vector $\mathbf{x}^*_n, 1 \leq n \leq N$ $[\mathbf{H}]_{ij} = \partial^2 E^*(\mathbf{x}^*_n, \mathbf{w})/\partial w_i \partial w_j, 1 \leq i, j \leq W$.
4. Estimate the confidence intervals	a) Evaluate the normalized error $\hat{\sigma}^{*2}$ between the normalized targets y^* and the normalized output $P^*(\mathbf{x}^*_n, \mathbf{w})$ $\hat{\sigma}^{*2} = (1/(N-\gamma)) \sum_{n=1}^N (y^*_n - P^*(\mathbf{x}^*_n, \mathbf{w}))^2$. b) Evaluate standard deviation y_{std} of the targets $y_{std} = \sqrt{(1/(N-1)) \sum_{n=1}^N (y_n - \bar{y})^2}$. c) Compute the confidence intervals $P(\mathbf{x}, \mathbf{w}) \pm z_{.025} \hat{\sigma}^* y_{std} \sqrt{\mathbf{g}^T (\mathbf{H} + \mathbf{L})^{-1} \mathbf{g}}$.

9.4.2 Bootstrapping Confidence Intervals

Residual bootstrap sampling [Tibshirani, 1996] is a method that can be used to find empirical confidence intervals of nonlinear models. The *confidence interval* of a PNN estimated by residual bootstrapping is:

$$P(\mathbf{x}, \mathbf{w}) \pm t_{.025[B]} \hat{se}_{boot}(P(\mathbf{x}, \mathbf{w})) \tag{9.10}$$

where $\hat{se}_{boot}(P(\mathbf{x}, \mathbf{w}))$ is the bootstrapped standard error (9.1) of the network model $P(\mathbf{x}, \mathbf{w})$, and $t_{.025[B]}$ is the critical value of the Student's t-distribution with B degrees of freedom.

The residual bootstrap is a model-based approach which requires a good enough model with a proper structure; that is, a model whose complexity is relevant to the data. Since the evolved PNN feature nearly optimal structure and weights inferred from the data [Nikolaev and Iba, 2001a, Nikolaev and Iba, 2003], the bootstrap method is suitable for analyzing them. The same reasoning holds even if the PNN is improved by backpropagation and Bayesian techniques.

The same best polynomial network evolved by IGP during previous experiments with the benchmark Mackey-Glass time series [Mackey and

Glass, 1977] is taken, and its confidence intervals were computed by residual bootstrapping. The error bands generated are plotted in Figure 9.5. A comparison with the confidence intervals of the same PNN model computed by the delta method (Figures 9.3 and 9.4) indicates that the bootstrapped intervals seem quite reliable.

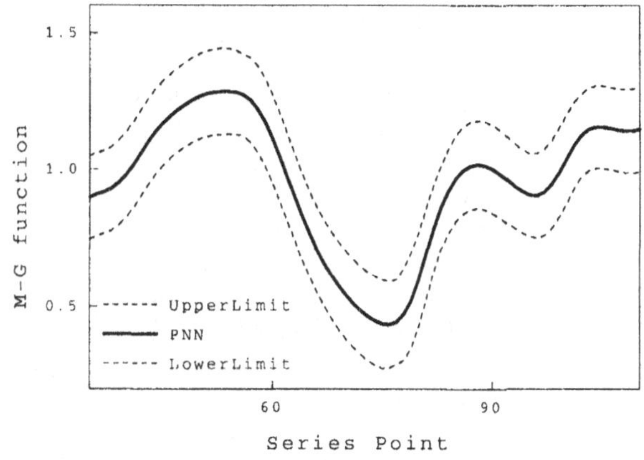

Figure 9.5. Confidence intervals of PNN estimated by residual bootstrapping of 100 PNN sampled using the Mackey-Glass series ($\lambda = 0.001$).

The problem that arises again is how to produce the error bars in their realistic original magnitude. The implementation of the bootstrap method requires us to initially compute the errors $\mathbf{e} = [e_1, e_2, ..., e_N]$ using the original outputs y and the estimated model output in its realistic magnitude $P(\mathbf{x}, \mathbf{w})$. Next, it has to be transformed into a normalized error vector $\mathbf{e}^* = [e_1^*, e_2^*, ..., e_N^*]$ in order to generate the normalized error series $\mathbf{e}^{*b}$ necessary for the estimation of the bootstrap sample models $P^*(\mathbf{x}_n^*, \mathbf{w}^b)$. The sampled models have to be made using the normalized input data. Finally, the realistic differences $P(\mathbf{x}, \mathbf{w}^b) - \bar{P}\ (\mathbf{x}, \mathbf{w})$ are produced using the outputs restored to their original magnitude $P(\mathbf{x}, \mathbf{w}^b)$ and the mean output $\bar{P}\ (\mathbf{x}, \mathbf{w})$. All these transitions from one kind of model to another are necessary since the PNN model is learned from the normalized data, and its weights are determined in the normalized space. The PNN structure is valid in the normalized space and there is no guarantee that its complexity characteristics will be retained by direct estimation of the same model in the original space.

The algorithm for computing realistic confidence intervals of PNNs by the residual bootstrapping method is given in Table 9.2.

Table 9.2. Algorithm for finding the empirical confidence intervals of PNN.

Bootstrapping Confidence Intervals of PNN

step	*Algorithmic sequence*
1. Initialization	Normalized model $P^*(\mathbf{x}^*, \mathbf{w})$ *normalized* training data: $D = \{(\mathbf{x}_n^*, y_n^*)\}_{n=1}^{N}$ $t_{.025[B]}$ is the critical value of the Student's t-distribution with B degrees of freedom.
2. Sample bootstrap models	a) Calculate the original errors $\mathbf{e} = (e_1, e_2, ..., e_N)$ $\hat{e}_n = y_n - P(\mathbf{x}_n, \mathbf{w}), 1 \leq n \leq N$. b) Normalize the errors to become $\mathbf{e}^* = (e_1^*, ..., e_N^*)$ $\hat{e}_n^* = (\hat{e}_n - \bar{x})/x_{std}, 1 \leq n \leq N$. c) Make a number b of normalized error series by random sampling $\hat{\mathbf{e}}^{*b} = (\hat{e}_1^{*b}, \hat{e}_2^{*b}, ..., \hat{e}_N^{*b}), 1 \leq b \leq B$. d) Reestimate the model with outputs contaminated by the errors $P^*(\mathbf{x}_n^*, \mathbf{w}^b) = P(\mathbf{x}_n^*, \mathbf{w}) + e_n^{*b}, 1 \leq n \leq N$.
3. Calculate the standard error	Compute the standard error by returning the outputs $P^*(\mathbf{x}_n^*, \mathbf{w}^b)$ to their magnitute $P(\mathbf{x}, \mathbf{w}^b)$ $d_b = P(\mathbf{x}, \mathbf{w}^b) - \bar{P}(\mathbf{x}, \mathbf{w})$ $\hat{se}_{boot}(P(\mathbf{x}, \mathbf{w})) = \sqrt{(1/(B-1)) \sum_{b=1}^{B} d_b^2}$.
4. Estimate the error bars	Produce the confidence intervals $P(\mathbf{x}, \mathbf{w}) \pm t_{.025[B]} \hat{se}_{boot}(P(\mathbf{x}, \mathbf{w}))$.

9.5 Prediction Intervals

Statistical model diagnosis also involves evaluation of the uncertainty in their prediction. Although PNN describe the mean of the data distribution, whose variation from one sample to another can be estimated by confidence intervals, it is also important to quantify the belief that a future PNN output will belong to the distribution inferred by the given sample. The task of measuring the model reliability is to find the prediction interval in which one has $(1-\alpha)\%$ (i.e. 95%) belief that the model output will belong to this interval.

Prediction interval for a randomly drawn value are two limits: from above and from below, which with a certain probability contain this unseen value. While the confidence intervals account for the variance due to improper model components, the prediction intervals account for the model variance from the data. The prediction bars are estimates of the input dependent target noise, and they should be expected to be wider than the confidence error bars.

The prediction intervals for PNN are determined according to the hypothesis that their output error varies as a function of the inputs:

$$P(\mathbf{x}, \mathbf{w}) \pm z_{.025}\sigma_y^2(\mathbf{x}) \tag{9.11}$$

where $\sigma_y^2(\mathbf{x})$ denotes the variance of the noise distribution.

9.5.1 Analytical Prediction Intervals

Asymptotic prediction bands can be estimated following nonlinear regression theory in a similar way as the confidence bands using the delta method. The modification of the delta method, discussed in Section 8.4.1, however, often leads to suspiciously wide intervals. This happens because the preliminary assumptions are often violated, more precisely: 1) neural networks are often trained with the early stopping strategy, not exactly until convergence; that is, there is no guarantee that the obtained weight vector is sufficiently close to the optimal one; and 2) the provided data sets are of small size (not large enough), so they may not carry enough information. In such cases of violated assumptions, the intervals are found to be unreliable because the variance is unstable to compute. These observations inspired the development of more accurate analytical formula for evaluating prediction error bars.

Analytical prediction intervals that take into account the effect of weight regularization can be estimated in the case of PNN with the following formula [De Veaux et al., 1998]:

$$P(\mathbf{x}, \mathbf{w}) \pm z_{.025}\hat{\sigma}^* y_{std}\sqrt{1 + \mathbf{g}^T(\mathbf{H}+\mathbf{L})^{-1}\mathbf{J}^T\mathbf{J}(\mathbf{H}+\mathbf{L})^{-1}\mathbf{g}} \tag{9.12}$$

where $\mathbf{g}$ is the gradient vector, $\mathbf{H}$ is the Hessian matrix (6.39), $\mathbf{J}$ is the Jacobian with the output derivatives with respect to the weights (6.43), $\mathbf{L}$ is a matrix with the local regularization parameters, $\hat{\sigma}^*$ is the mean squared error of the normalized model, and y_{std} is the standard deviation of the targets. The Jacobian $\mathbf{J}$ is made during BP training in nonlinear PNN, while its generation for linear PNN is straightforward.

The error variance under the square root is derived especially for weight decay regularization of the kind $\sum_{i=1}^{W} w_i^2$, so if another kind of regularization is considered, another formula has to be rederived. Because of this specific derivation it is clear that the quantity under the square root is actually proportional to the squared quantity: $\mathbf{g}^T(\mathbf{H}+\mathbf{L})^{-1}\mathbf{g}$ used for estimating confidence intervals according to the Delta method (9.9). This is reasonable because the weight decay regularization impacts the learning of the weights inversely proportional to their squared magnitudes, therefore this fact should be taken into account when making forecasts in order to explain more precisely what can be expected from such types of neural network models.

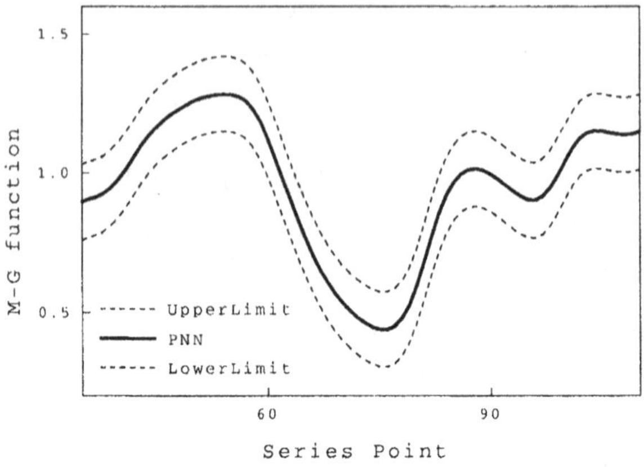

Figure 9.6. Analytical prediction intervals of a PNN model obtained by estimation with the benchmark Mackey-Glass series ($\lambda = 0.001$).

This formula (9.12) is elaborated to generate prediction bars restored in their original magnitude. This restoration is necessary because the PNN are usually evolved by IGP and trained by BP using the normalized input data in order to avoid computational instabilities and inaccuracies. The computer algorithm for finding the prediction intervals of PNN looks similar to the one given in Table 9.1 and differs only in that formula (9.8) is replaced by formula (9.12) to measure the prediction intervals.

Prediction bands of a PNN estimated using this analytical approach of using the selected time series data are plotted in Figure 9.6.

9.5.2 Empirical Learning of Prediction Bars

The unknown noise variance function can be found empirically by a neural network method derived from a maximum likelihood perspective [Nix and Weigend, 1995]. This method provides the idea of extending the polynomial neural network so that it learns not only the mean of the data distribution, but also the variance of this mean around the desired targets. While the conventional PNN output produces the mean $P(\mathbf{x}) \simeq E[y|\mathbf{x}]$, another output node is installed to produce the noise variance $\hat{\sigma}^2(\mathbf{x})$ assuming that it is not constant but dependent on the inputs. Thus, the conditional probability density of the outputs is inferred as a function of the input data.

In order to capture the characteristics of the analyzed PNN architecture, it is extended so that the the second output node accepts signals from all hidden (functional) and input (terminal) PNN nodes through a separate layer. An additional separate hidden layer whose nodes have incoming connections from all input and hidden nodes of the original PNN is installed. The extension features full connectivity; every input and hidden node output is passed along a corresponding link to every node in the additional hidden layer, whose outputs are next passed to the second output node. The number of nodes in the additional hidden layer is determined by the number of functional PNN nodes.

The expanded topology keeps the same binary bivariate polynomials in the original PNN part, while the nodes in the extended part consider different transfer functions. The second output node transforms the weighted summation of the outputs from the extended hidden nodes by the exponential function:

$$\hat{\sigma}^2(\mathbf{x}) = \exp\left(\sum_{j=1}^{J} v_{kj}u_j + v_{k0}\right) \tag{9.13}$$

where v_{kj} are the weights on connections feeding the second output node, v_{k0} is a bias term, and u_j are the outputs of the J additional hidden nodes. The exponent function is a suitable choice to guarantee production of only positive values.

The additional hidden layer uses sigmoidal activation functions to filter out the weighted summations of the incoming signals:

$$u_j = sig\left(\sum_{i=1}^{I} v_{ji}x_i + v_{j0}\right) \tag{9.14}$$

where x_i are the outputs from the activation polynomials in the PNN part of the extended network, v_{ji} are the weights on connections from the PNN nodes to the extended hidden nodes, v_{j0} is a bias term, and sig is the sigmoid function: $sig(z) = 1/(1 + \exp(-z))$.

The secondary network is a Multilayer Perceptron (MLP) with universal approximation capacity so its use is theoretically motivated. Although it is different (that is it has a different structure from the original polynomial network), it has sufficient power to obtain a good estimate of the noise variance of the provided data. The secondary MLP network learns the output uncertainty of the original network as it reflects its performance by accepting its inputs and hidden node outputs.

Figure 9.7 presents the extension of the PNN tree-like network topology previously demonstrated in Figure 6.1.

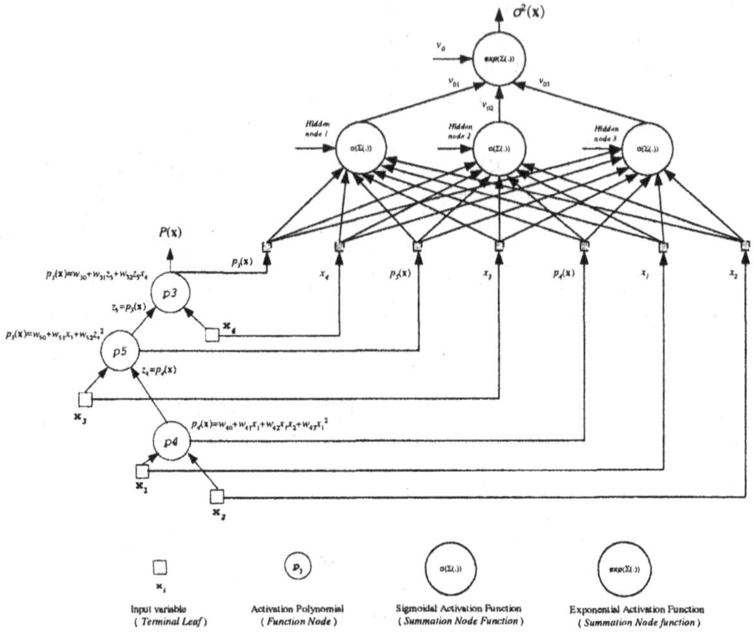

Figure 9.7. Expanded tree-structured PNN with additional hidden layer and second output node for learning the error variance.

Rules for PNN Learning of Error Variance. The development of the PNN training algorithm for error variance learning, according to the ML principle, relies on two assumptions [Nix and Weigend, 1995]: 1) that the noise in the data obeys the Gaussian distribution, and 2) that the errors are statistically independent. This enables us to introduce the following negative log likelihood criterion for coherent training of both the first and the second output network nodes:

$$C = \frac{1}{2} \sum_{n=1}^{N} \left(\frac{[y_n - P(\mathbf{x}_n, \mathbf{w})]^2}{\hat{\sigma}^2(\mathbf{x}_n)} + \ln(\hat{\sigma}^2(\mathbf{x}_n)) \right) \tag{9.15}$$

where y_n is the target, $P(\mathbf{x}_n, \mathbf{w})$ is the network output, and $\hat{\sigma}^2(\mathbf{x}_n)$ is the sensitivity of the error variance to the n-th input.

The weight update rules for training the extended PNN are obtained by seeking the minimum of this criterion function (9.15); that is, by differentiating it with respect to the weights, equating the resulted expression to zero, and solving it for the free variables. This is performed for both the first PNN output producing the mean, as well as for the second output producing the variance as they are mutually dependent.

Delta Rule for the Second Output Node Weights. Let the second output network node that models the variance $\hat{\sigma}^2(\mathbf{x})$ be indexed by k and the hidden nodes whose outgoing connections feed this node be indexed by j. The *delta rule for training the second output node* is:

$$\Delta v_{kj} = \eta \left(\frac{[y_n - P(\mathbf{x}_n, \mathbf{w})]^2 - \hat{\sigma}^2(\mathbf{x}_n)}{2\hat{\sigma}^2(\mathbf{x}_n)} \right) u_j \tag{9.16}$$

where η is the learning rate, v_{kj} are the hidden to output weights that enter the second output node, and the signals on their connections from the additional hidden nodes are u_j. Note that this rule uses the squared error $(y_n - P(\mathbf{x}_n, \mathbf{w}))^2$ generated at the output of the first node when the original PNN is estimated with the same n-th input.

Delta Rule for the First Output Node Weights. Let the first PNN output network node modelling the mean of the data distribution $P(\mathbf{x}) \simeq E[y|\mathbf{x}]$ be indexed by k, let its children nodes be at level j, and the weights on the links between them be specified by w_{kj}. The *delta rule for training the first output node* that prescribes how to modify the weights associated with its incoming connections is:

$$\Delta w_{kj} = \eta \delta'_k x'_{kj} = \eta \left(\frac{[y_n - P(\mathbf{x}_n, \mathbf{w})]^2}{\hat{\sigma}^2(\mathbf{x}_n)} \right) x'_{kj} \tag{9.17}$$

where w_{kj} are the hidden to first output weights, and x'_{kj} are the derivatives of the output activation polynomial with respect to its weights (Section 6.2). Here, it should be noted that this rule uses the variance $\hat{\sigma}^2(\mathbf{x}_n)$ emitted from the second output node.

The remaining weights below the roots are updated as follows: 1) the network weights in the original PNN part are adjusted according to the backpropagation learning rules for multilayer polynomial networks given in section 6.2; and 2) the weights on links to the nodes in the additional hidden layer are adjusted according to the standard delta rules for gradient descent search in multilayer perceptron neural networks using sigmoidal activation functions.

Delta Rule for the Extended Hidden Node Weights. Let the hidden nodes in the extended layer be indexed by j as above and the PNN nodes that feed them be indexed by i. Taking into account that the additional hidden nodes after weighted summation of their input signals transform the sum by the sigmoidal function, the *delta rule for the additional hidden nodes* becomes:

$$\Delta v_{ji} = \eta [u_j (1 - u_j)(-\delta'_k) w_{kj}] x_i \tag{9.18}$$

where the input signals x_i are either direct inputs or outputs from the activation polynomials in the PNN network, u_j are the outputs from the hidden nodes in the additional layer, and δ'_k is the error backpropagated down from the second output node (9.17).

Training Extended PNN. The extended PNN can be trained with a version of the BPA made to conduct gradient descent search in the weight space with the above learning rules (9.16, 9.17, 9.18). The secondary network however is a nonlinear MLP which suffers from the problem of entrapment into inferior solutions. That is, the neural network training process may lead to a weight vector which causes an error that is not optimal, rather it is an unacceptably high local minima. In addition to this, it could be noted that the learning rules for the hidden to output node connections in both parts of the extended network are mutually dependent. Because of these reasons, in order to avoid early entrapment at suboptimal local optima on the error landscape, the weight training process is divided into three consecutive phases.

During the first phase, the original PNN is trained aiming at minimization of the mean squared error $E_D = (1/N) \sum_{n=1}^{N} (y_n - P(\mathbf{x}_n, \mathbf{w}))^2$, using some backpropagation technique for high-order neural networks with polynomial activation functions (Section 6). In this phase, the extended secondary part of the network is not trained; its weight parameters are kept fixed. This stage should be performed with only a subset of the given data so as to avoid eventual overfitting.

The second phase uses a different subset of the data for training just the extended MLP part of the network, also aiming at minimization of the mean squared error. This is implemented using the backpropagation algorithm with the learning rule for the second output node (9.16) without dividing it by $2\hat{\sigma}^2(\mathbf{x}_n)$, and the delta learning rules for the hidden nodes in the additional layer (9.18). In the second phase the weights in the original PNN part remain frozen, and they are not changed.

The aim of training in the third phase is to minimize the log likelihood criterion (9.15). During this third phase the hidden to root node weights in the original PNN part are tuned according to the novel learning rule (9.17), while the remaining weights below are tuned with the learning rules for high-order networks with activation polynomials (Section 6.2). The weights in the second extended MLP part of the network are adjusted using the learning rule for the second output node weights (9.16), and the weights on connections by the learning rules for the hidden nodes in the additional layer (9.18). The training proceeds until reaching the minimum of the log likelihood criterion; that is, until attaining a satisfactory low error. PNN prediction intervals computed following this empirical method using the benchmark Mackey-Glass series for training are plotted in Figure 9.8.

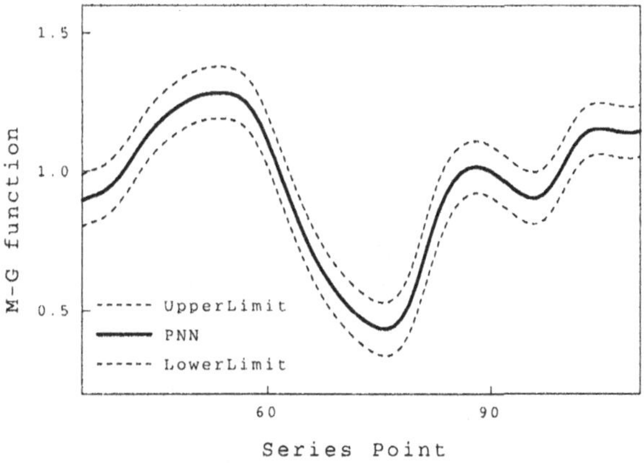

Figure 9.8. Prediction intervals of a PNN model obtained with the benchmark Mackey-Glass series ($\lambda = 0.001$).

The incremental version of the backprop algorithm for training the extended PNN to learn prediction intervals is summarized in the following Table 9.3. It should be noted that for training the original PNN part in this algorithmic framework, the backpropagation training rules given in Section 6.2 have to be substituted.

Training of the extended PNN to learn the output error distribution can unfortunately lead to under-estimated error bars. Such overoptimistic estimates of the prediction intervals can be unrealistic and misleading. The main reason for the unrealistic results is the fact that this approach to learning prediction bands with extended PNN is derived from a maximum likelihood perspective. According to the maximum likelihood approach the mean is directly estimated from the data, so it also captures the noise in them and the mean becomes biased. The effect of the noise contaminated mean is inferring biased output variance, whose expectation is not exactly equal to the true error variance [Bishop and Qazaz, 1997].

A remedy for overcoming these problems is to perform modeling of the error variance following the Bayesian perspective. The empirical prediction bands obtained by training the extended PNN using rules derived from the maximum likelihood perspective can be compared and related to the Bayesian intervals generated from the same PNN models. Having different prediction bands allows us to reason more precisely about the quality of the PNN models.

Table 9.3. Incremental algorithm for error variance learning by tree-like PNN extended by a traditional MLP network.

Training Algorithm for PNN Learning of Error Bars

step	*Algorithmic sequence*
1. Initialization	Data $\mathcal{D} = \{(\mathbf{x}_n, y_n)\}_{n=1}^{N}$ and learning rate $\eta = 0.1$.
2. First Phase	Perform BP training of the original PNN using the learning rules from Section 6.2.
3. Second Phase	Perform BP training of the extended part of the network a) For each training example $(\mathbf{x}_n, y_n)$, $1 \leq n \leq N$, do i) forward pass, and backward pass using the rules: $\Delta v_{kj} = \eta([y_n - P(\mathbf{x}_n, \mathbf{w})]^2 - \hat{\sigma}^2(\mathbf{x}_n))u_j$ $\Delta v_{ji} = \eta[u_j(1-u_j)(-\delta'_k)w_{kj}]x_i.$ ii) Update the extended network weights.
4. Third Phase	Simultaneously train the PNN and the extended part a) For each training example $(\mathbf{x}_n, y_n)$, $1 \leq n \leq N$, do i) Forward pass through PNN to produce $P(\mathbf{x}_n)$ and forward pass through the MLP to produce $\hat{\sigma}^2(\mathbf{x}_n)$. ii) Backward pass through PNN - compute the hidden to output deltas $\Delta w_{kj} = \eta([y_n - P(\mathbf{x}_n, \mathbf{w})]^2/\hat{\sigma}^2(\mathbf{x}_n))x'_{kj}$. - compute the remaining node deltas using the rules from Section 6.2. - update the PNN weights. iii) Backward pass through the extended network - compute the hidden to output deltas $\Delta v_{kj} = \eta([y_n - P(\mathbf{x}_n, \mathbf{w})]^2 - \hat{\sigma}^2(\mathbf{x}_n))u_j/2\hat{\sigma}^2(\mathbf{x}_n).$ - compute backwards the hidden node deltas $\Delta v_{ji} = \eta[u_j(1-u_j)(-\delta'_k)w_{kj}]x_i.$ - update the weights of the extended network
	Until termination condition is satisfied.

9.6 Bayesian Intervals

Recent research provides analytical and empirical approaches to measuring error bars from a Bayesian viewpoint [MacKay, 1992a]. Such error bars are called Bayesian intervals. These contemporary approaches produce estimates that quantify the degree of belief in the models depending on both the uncertainties in the model weights, and the uncertainties in the training data. The commonality in them is that they capture variance due to inaccuracies of the weights, but differ in the way they capture the output error variance.

A *Bayesian prediction interval* is such that there is a $(1-\alpha)\%$ (i.e. 95%) belief that the model output will belong to this interval according to the posterior distribution of the population mean. The output that models the mean of the data distribution is regarded as a random variable associated with its own distribution. Such Bayesian error bars for regression models are derived from the probabilistic posterior distribution of the weights. It is reasoned that if the prior opinion on the weights is high but they do not fit the data well, then they seem less plausible. The basic assumption is that the posterior weight distribution, which determines the output distribution, is Gaussian. The parameters of the normal weight distribution can be determined analytically or empirically by training a complementary network.

Both analytical and empirical approaches are developed algorithmically in this section. The analytical Bayesian intervals involve constant output noise level, while the empirical Bayesian intervals feature by learned input-dependent noise level.

9.6.1 Analytical Bayesian Intervals

The analytical approach suggests optimizing the weight posterior distribution by iterative adjustment of its hyperparameters [Nabney, 2002]. The optimal values of these hyperparameters can be found using the evidence procedure [MacKay, 1992a]. The evidence procedure is an incremental technique to reestimate the hyperparameters after the neural network has been trained to some error minima.

Bayesian prediction intervals for PNN models are defined as follows:

$$P(\mathbf{x}, \mathbf{w}) \pm z_{.025}\sigma_{MP} \tag{9.19}$$

where σ_{MP} denotes the variance of the most probable model conditioned on the data. It can be evaluated after training the network model until a minimum on the error surface is reached. Since the presented inductive PNN learning methodology involves IGP search as its first step, it is assumed that the best evolved PNN network is an acceptably good solution so it is reasonable to apply the suggested equation derived using Bayesian inference [Nabney, 2002]:

$$\sigma_{MP} = \sqrt{\sigma_y^2 + \hat{se}^2(P(\mathbf{x}, \mathbf{w}))} = \sqrt{\frac{1}{\beta} + \mathbf{g}^T\mathbf{H}^{-1}\mathbf{g}} \tag{9.20}$$

where σ_y^2 is the noise variance component which is represented by the hyperparameter β, $\hat{se}^2(P(\mathbf{x}, \mathbf{w}))$ is the standard error of the network model, $\mathbf{g}$ is the gradient vector (6.36, 6.37), and $\mathbf{H}$ is the regularized version of the Hessian matrix (6.39, 6.40).

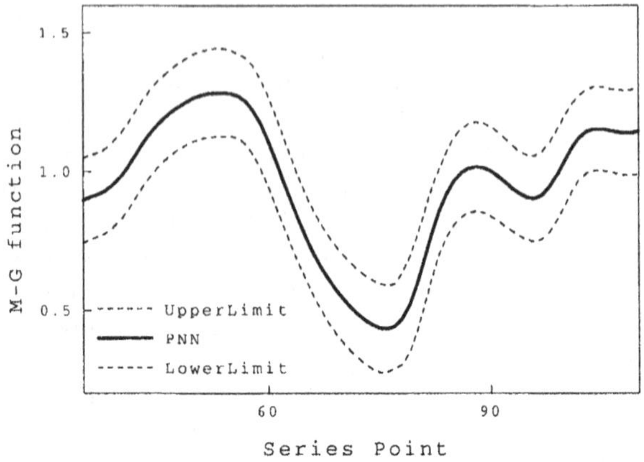

Figure 9.9. Bayesian intervals of a PNN model obtained with the benchmark Mackey-Glass series ($\lambda = 0.001$).

Working with this evidence procedure is efficient because it does not require performing repetitive model reestimations like the empirical bootstrapping. However, the application of the evidence procedure can be problematic in practice because it requires construction and invertion of the Hessian matrix in run time. As previously studied, one remedy for avoiding numerical computation instabilities during the inversion of the Hessian matrix is to augment its diagonal elements by a regularization factor. Another possibility is to use incremental or iterative least squares fitting techniques for reliable computation of the Hessian.

Figure 9.9 offers a plot of the Bayesian prediction bands of a PNN obtained using the computational algorithm given in Table 9.4. Again, the benchmark Mackey-Glass time series was used, as well as a common global regularization parameter to facilitate comparisons.

The Bayesian error bars in Figure 9.9 are slightly broader than those of the analytically estimated prediction intervals given in Figure 9.6 because they include probable discrepancies due to the noise in the input data as well as due to the uncertainties in the identified network weights. The Bayesian and analytical prediction intervals are larger than the learned empirical intervals by training the extended PNN following the maximum likelihood approach. In this sense, they seem to be more realistic estimates of the expected output error.

Table 9.4. Algorithm for evaluating Bayesian error bars of tree-like PNN.

Computing Bayesian Intervals of PNN

step	*Algorithmic sequence*
1. Initialization	Data $\mathcal{D} = \{(\mathbf{x}_n, y_n)\}_{n=1}^{N}$, learning rate $\eta = 0.1$.
	Take the most probable PNN found by IGP
2. Reevaluate the hyperparameters	Repeat a sufficiently large number of times:
	a) Reestimate the weights by OLS fitting $\mathbf{w} = (\mathbf{\Phi}^T\mathbf{\Phi} + \mathbf{L})^{-1}\mathbf{\Phi}^T y$.
	b) Calculate the regularized Hessian $\mathbf{H} = \mathbf{\Phi}^T\mathbf{\Phi} + \mathbf{L}$.
	c) Compute the effective parameters $\gamma = W - \alpha trace(\mathbf{H})^{-1}$ and the hyperparameters $\alpha = \gamma/(2\mathbf{w}^T\mathbf{w})$ $\beta = (N - \gamma)/(2\mathbf{e}^T\mathbf{e})$.
	d) Calculate the Bayesian error $E_B = \beta E_D + E_W$
	until reaching the minimum of the log evidence -$\ln(D\|\alpha, \beta) = E_B + \frac{1}{2}(\ln\|\mathbf{A}\| - W\ln\alpha - N\ln\beta)$.
3. Estimate the Bayesian Intervals	Compute the model variance $\sigma_{MP} = \sqrt{\frac{1}{\beta} + \mathbf{g}^T\mathbf{A}^{-1}\mathbf{g}}$.
	Produce the intervals using the formula $P(\mathbf{x}, \mathbf{w}) \pm z_{.025}\sigma_{MP}$.

9.6.2 Empirical Bayesian Intervals

The weight posterior distribution can be learned empirically by training another secondary network complementary to the original one [Bishop and Qazaz, 1997]. For the purpose of finding the output error as a function of the input, the original network is extended with a hidden layer and a second output as illustrated in Figure 9.7. A secondary layer of sigmoidal neurons fully connected both to the training inputs and to the activation polynomial outcomes from the original PNN is added. Training of the expanded network is performed using the learning rules obtained by Bayesian analysis in pursuit of unbiased estimation of the noise variance. Bayesian prediction intervals for PNN regression models are constructed using the equation:

$$P(\mathbf{x}, \mathbf{w}) \pm z_{.025}\hat{\sigma}(\mathbf{x}) \tag{9.21}$$

where $\hat{\sigma}(\mathbf{x})$ denotes the input-dependent noise variance.

This conditional output error distribution can be learned by training the secondary network, attached to the original one, to minimize the following Bayesian cost function:

$$C_B = \frac{1}{2}\sum_{n=1}^{N}\left(\frac{[y_n - P(\mathbf{x}_n, \mathbf{w})]^2}{\hat{\sigma}^2(\mathbf{x}_n)} + \ln(\hat{\sigma}^2(\mathbf{x}_n))\right) + \alpha\sum_{i=1}^{V} v_i^2 + \ln|\mathbf{H}| \quad (9.22)$$

where the correction involves two terms: the regularization $\alpha \sum_{i=1}^{W} w_i^2$, and the logarithm of the determinant $|\mathbf{H}|$ of the regularized Hessian.

Two corresponding delta rules for the second output node weights and for the first output node weights are derived, seeking for the minimum of this criterion. The second output node that infers the error variance is trained by the following delta rule:

$$\Delta v_{kj} = \eta\left(\frac{[y_n - P(\mathbf{x}_n, \mathbf{w})]^2 - \hat{\sigma}^2(\mathbf{x}_n)}{2\hat{\sigma}^2(\mathbf{x}_n)} + 2\alpha v_{kj}\right) u_j \quad (9.23)$$

where η is the learning rate, v_{kj} are the hidden to output weights that enter the second output node, and u_j are the signals on them.

The first output node of the original network is trained according to another delta rule:

$$\Delta w_{kj} = \eta\left(\frac{[y_n - P(\mathbf{x}_n, \mathbf{w})]^2}{\hat{\sigma}^2(\mathbf{x}_n)}\right) x'_{kj} \quad (9.24)$$

where w_{kj} are the hidden to first output weights, and x'_{kj} are the derivatives of the output activation polynomial with respect to its weights (Section 6.2). Here it can be observed that this rule uses the variance $\hat{\sigma}^2(\mathbf{x}_n)$ emitted from the second output node.

This empirical approach to making Bayesian intervals uses fixed hyperparameters and learns the weights in the secondary network that infer the conditional noise distribution, while the analytical approach uses adaptive hyperparameters. Another characteristic of the empirical Bayesian approach is that it applies regularization to both networks: to the original one that produces the conditional mean, and to the additional network that models the conditional variance of the output error.

The incremental version of the backprop algorithm for training the extended PNN to learn Bayesian prediction bars is given in Table 9.5. It involves training of both the original PNN part of the network and the extended MLP part of the network. In order to implement it completely, the available backpropagation training rules for PNN models from Section 6.2 have to be substituted in step 2 (first training phase).

Table 9.5. Algorithm for Bayesian error variance learning by tree-like PNN extended by a traditional MLP network.

Training Algorithm for PNN Learning of Bayesian Prediction Bars

step	*Algorithmic sequence*
1. Initialization	Data $\mathcal{D} = \{(\mathbf{x}_n, y_n)\}_{n=1}^{N}$ and learning rate $\eta = 0.1$.
2. First phase	BP training of the original PNN (rules from Section 6.2)
3. Second phase	Carry out BP training of the extended network a) For each training example $(\mathbf{x}_n, y_n)$, $1 \leq n \leq N$, do i) forward pass, and then backward pass: $\Delta v_{kj} = \eta([y_n - P(\mathbf{x}_n, \mathbf{w})]^2 - \hat{\sigma}^2(\mathbf{x}_n) + 2\alpha v_{kj})u_j$ $\Delta v_{ji} = \eta[u_j(1 - u_j)(-\delta'_k)w_{kj}]x_i$. ii) Update the extended network weights.
4. Third phase	Train simultaneously the PNN and the extended part a) For each training example $(\mathbf{x}_n, y_n)$, $1 \leq n \leq N$, do i) Forward pass through PNN to produce $P(\mathbf{x}_n)$ forward pass through the MLP part for $\hat{\sigma}^2(\mathbf{x}_n)$. ii) Backward pass through PNN - compute the hidden to output deltas $\Delta w_{kj} = \eta([y_n - P(\mathbf{x}_n, \mathbf{w})]^2 / \hat{\sigma}^2(\mathbf{x}_n))x'_{kj}$. - compute the remaining hidden node deltas using the learning rules from Section 6.2. - update the PNN weights. iii) Backward pass through the extended network - compute the hidden to output deltas $e_n = y_n - P(\mathbf{x}_n, \mathbf{w})$ $\Delta v_{kj} = \eta((e_n^2 - \hat{\sigma}^2(\mathbf{x}_n))/2\hat{\sigma}^2(\mathbf{x}_n) + 2\alpha v_{kj})u_j$. - compute backwards the hidden node deltas $\Delta v_{ji} = \eta[u_j(1 - u_j)(-\delta'_k)w_{kj}]x_i$. - update the weights of the extended network
	Until the termination condition is satisfied.

9.7 Model Validation Tests

The tests for statistical model validation, especially when processing time series, involve examination of the residuals. A model is considered correct when its residuals are random, which means that the model exhibits unpredictable errors. In order to find out whether the residuals make a random sequence, specific correlation functions of the residuals are defined and estimated. If the past residuals are correlated with the future residuals, this is an indication that the model does not capture the data characteristics well. In other words, it must be investigated whether the model residuals carry information from the past, which means that the model is not reliable. When there is dependence between the residuals, this indicates that the model fails to describe some intrinsic component from the data.

The model validation tests exploit the relationship between the model input and the model errors committed by the analyzed polynomial network model over the training data. These tests include three steps [Billings and Zhu, 1995]: 1) determination of an acceptable domain for the decision values by establishing confidence intervals, usually $-1.96\sqrt{N} < \Phi(\tau) < 1.96\sqrt{N}$, for the statistics $\Phi(\tau)$ to be computed next; 2) measuring the model residuals on the available training data; and 3) making a decision to accept or reject the model.

When validating models it should be understood that the tests for linear models are not appropriate for nonlinear models because they may produce misleading results, as they fail to diagnose nonlinear terms. Working with PNN models requires the application of *nonlinear residual autocorrelation tests* [Billings and Zhu, 1995]. Learning PNN however, may produce only linear polynomial networks, for example when there are only linear activation functions in the hidden nodes. That is why linear as well as nonlinear tests should be available to perform testing of both kinds of polynomial neural networks.

Several correlation functions are given below. These are sample correlation functions whose distribution approaches the normal Gaussian distribution with the increase of data. The linear correlation function of the residuals and the cross-correlation function between the input and the residuals are [Billings and Zhu, 1995]:

$$\Phi_{ee}(\tau) = \frac{\sum_{t=1}^{N}[e_t - \bar{e}][e_{t-\tau} - \bar{e}]}{\sum_{t=1}^{N}[e_t - \bar{e}]^2} = \begin{cases} 1, & \tau = 0 \\ 0, & \text{otherwise} \end{cases} \tag{9.25}$$

$$\Phi_{xe}(\tau) = \frac{\sum_{t=1}^{N}[x_t - \bar{x}][e_{t-\tau} - \bar{e}]}{\sqrt{\left(\sum_{t=1}^{N}[x_t - \bar{x}]^2\right)\left(\sum_{t=1}^{N}[e_t - \bar{e}]^2\right)}} = 0, \forall\tau \tag{9.26}$$

where τ is the lag, x are the model inputs, and e are the errors.

Nonlinear cross-correlation functions increase the statistical power of the existent tests providing more discriminatory evidence as follows [Billings and Zhu, 1995]:

$$\Phi_{x^2e}(\tau) = \frac{\sum_{t=1}^{N}\left[x_t^2 - \bar{x}^2\right][e_{t-\tau} - \bar{e}]}{\sqrt{\left(\sum_{t=1}^{N}\left[x^2(t) - \bar{x}^2\right]^2\right)\left(\sum_{t=1}^{N}[e_t - \bar{e}]^2\right)}} = 0 \tag{9.27}$$

$$\Phi_{x^2e^2}(\tau) = \frac{\sum_{t=1}^{N}\left[x_t^2-\bar{x}^2\right]\left[e_{t-\tau}^2-\bar{e}^2\right]}{\sqrt{\left(\sum_{t=1}^{N}\left[x_t^2-\bar{x}^2\right]^2\right)\left(\sum_{t=1}^{N}\left[e_t^2-\bar{e}^2\right]^2\right)}} = 0 \quad (9.28)$$

$$\Phi_{\vartheta e^2}(\tau) = \frac{\sum_{t=1}^{N}\left[\vartheta_{t-\tau}-\bar{\vartheta}\right]\left[e_{t-\tau}^2-\bar{e}^2\right]}{\sqrt{\left(\sum_{t=1}^{N}\left[\vartheta_t-\bar{\vartheta}\right]^2\right)\left(\sum_{t=1}^{N}\left[e_t^2-\bar{e}^2\right]^2\right)}} = \left\{ \begin{array}{c} k \\ 0 \end{array} \right. \quad (9.29)$$

$$\Phi_{\vartheta x^2}(\tau) = \frac{\sum_{t=1}^{N}\left[\vartheta_{t-\tau}-\bar{\vartheta}\right]\left[x_{t-\tau}^2-\bar{x}^2\right]}{\sqrt{\left(\sum_{t=1}^{N}\left[\vartheta_t-\bar{\vartheta}\right]^2\right)\left(\sum_{t=1}^{N}\left[x_t^2-\bar{x}^2\right]^2\right)}} = 0, \forall\tau \quad (9.30)$$

where τ is the lag, $\bar{e}$, $\bar{x}$, and $\bar{\vartheta}$ denote averages over the interval $[1, N]$. The substitution for ϑ expresses the cross-dependence between the network output and the error, which is introduced for clarity:

$$\vartheta_t = P(t, \mathbf{w})e_t \quad (9.31)$$

assuming that $P(t, \mathbf{w})$ is the PNN output determined by weight vector $\mathbf{w}$, and e_t is its error on the available data.

The remaining constant in the above correlations k is defined as follows:

$$k = \frac{\sqrt{\sum_{t=1}^{N}\left[e_t^2-\bar{e}^2\right]}}{\sqrt{\sum_{t=1}^{N}\left[\vartheta_t-\bar{\vartheta}\right]^2}} \quad (9.32)$$

These formula allow us to test whether for lags in the interval $\tau \in [-20, 20]$, the autocorrelations fall in the corresponding predefined confidence intervals. This will indicate that there are no predictable terms in the error sequence produced by the model, and therefore the inferred model can be considered as a good solution to the task.

Figures 9.10 and 9.11 present plots with high-order correlations obtained using two of the formula described above. These plots show that the model errors do not contain information from the past; that is, the correlation functions have not detected any deviation from normality. Therefore, it may be concluded that no cross variable terms are missing from the polynomial network models, otherwise the curves would have been outside of the suggested confidence intervals with dotted lines.

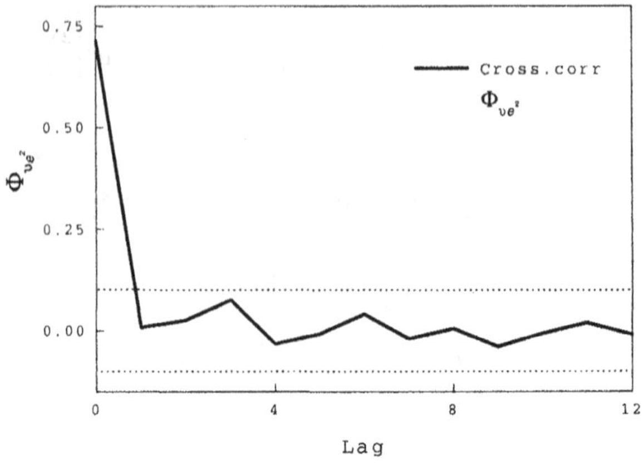

Figure 9.10. Nonlinear correlation function between the output-error pair and the quadratic error of a PNN evolved using IGP using the Mackey-Glass series.

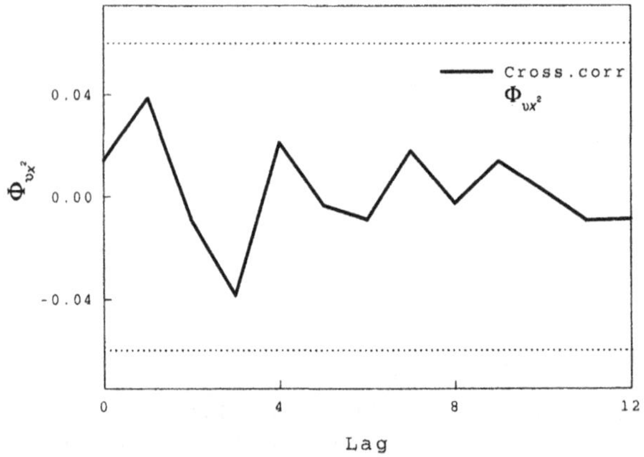

Figure 9.11. Nonlinear correlation function between the output-error pair and the quadratic inputs of a PNN evolved using IGP using the Mackey-Glass series.

9.8 Chapter Summary

This chapter presented the basic algorithms for statistical diagnosis and validation of PNN. The benefit of having them is that the reliability of PNN is increased when supported by such means for statistical analysis. The algorithms for measuring confidence, prediction, and Bayesian intervals are found to produce satisfactory results, in the sense that they generate intervals of similar size with slight differences in shape. The intervals are likely to possess similar characteristics when they are obtained under the same conditions: sufficiently large number of data, clean enough data, and model training by efficient learning algorithms. The shape and size of the error bars made with the studied algorithms depend on the changes of these circumstances in the following ways: 1) when more training data are available the intervals will be narrower; 2) when the data are cleaner and contain less noise the intervals will also be narrower; 3) when the network model is trained by early stopping the intervals will be broader; and 4) when the model structure and the input variables are irrelevant, the intervals will be different in different data regions; they will be very large in sparse data areas, and they will be very small in dense data areas.

Many other implementations of these statistical tools are possible [Efron and Tibshirani, 1989], for example other sampling and bootstrapping methods are available [Efron and Tibshirani, 1989]. Other methods, however, cannot be expected to yield significantly different results, so those investigated here may be considered sufficient for reliable PNN testing. The standard error is often applied to carry out model selection [Zapranis and Refenes, 1999], that is, to compare the adequacy of alternative PNN and to judge which of them is best. The integrated bias and variance estimates of PNN can be used to prevent overfitting in several ways: 1) by changing the model representation, for example by reducing the number of variables, the number of terms, or the model degree; 2) by improving the network weight learning algorithm with techniques like regularization, early stopping, or training with noise; and 3) by making additional decorrelating data transformations or collecting more data for the same underlying function.

The confidence intervals can be used for evaluating the significance of the PNN structure. More precisely, analysis could be performed on the PNN sensitivity to removal of polynomial terms and variables [Zapranis and Refenes, 1999]. When the polynomial structure of cascaded terms and variables is changed its approximation capacity changes, and this could be observed in the plots of the confidence bands. If the PNN modification leads to better models, the error band will shrink in comparison to that of the initial model.

The studied approaches to statistical PNN diagnosis differ in computational speed and implementation effort. Most complex to develop are the Bayesian intervals. The analytical methods are difficult to encode because they require the evaluation of the Hessian. The empirical methods, like the one for making confidence intervals by residual sampling and learning the error variance, seem easier to make but are relatively more time consuming because they require repetitive computations, usually with large amount of data. Which of these methods and how to apply in practice should be judged by a careful design decision.

The recommendation is to perform all the types of statistical model validation tests presented with the discovered models in order to be sure that they satisfy the theoretical requirements.

Chapter 10

TIME SERIES MODELLING

This chapter relates PNN to linear and nonlinear models generated by alternative inductive approaches. Time series modelling is the context in which the strengths and weaknesses of PNN, as well as its similarities to and differences from the other approaches are discussed. The models investigated include linear autoregressive moving average models, genetically programmed functions, statistical learning networks, neural networks, kernel models, and recurrent neural networks. The belief in PNN is increased in relation to the other approaches and models because they have been studied extensively and it is well-known how to apply them with respect to the circumstances of the given task.

Strictly speaking modelling of discretely sampled time series should be carried out according to the following sequence of steps: 1) examination of the series characteristics using statistical tests; 2) preprocessing of the data with suitable transformation formulae; 3) learning of PNN by IGP, BP, and Bayesian techniques including network pruning; and 4) diagnosis and validation of PNN with statistical tools.

Before processing a time series it is reasonable to inquire whether it is potentially predictable. The predictability of a time series can be studied from a static perspective using statistical tests such as: 1) tests for autoregressive behavior; 2) tests for nonstationarity; 3) tests for random walk behavior; and 4) tests for nonlinearity. Applying autocorrelation tests to the given time series helps to realize whether the future series data depend on the past, that is such tests provide statistically significant evidence that the series can be predicted. Popular autocorrelation tests are the Box-Pierce Q-statistic [Box and Pierce, 1970] and the Ljung-Box Q-statistics [Ljung and Box, 1978]. The tests for nonstationarity allow us to detect whether the series contains a mean-reversion component which is difficult to model. Whether there is a nonstationary component in a series can be determined using unit root tests such as the Dickey-Fuller test [Dickey and Fuller, 1981]. In order to find out if a series is uncorrelated, measurements can be made to see whether the series contains increments that are random or not. Random behavior in a time series can be examined using variance-ratio tests for deviations from random walk [Lo and MacKinley, 1988]. Motivation for discarding linear models can be obtained by tests for nonlinearity that check whether the data contain evidence for nonlinear signal dependence. This can be done using the Brock-Dechert-Sheinkman test [Brock et al., 1996].

The predictability of a time series can also be investigated from a dynamical system perspective using invariant series properties, such as the Lyapunov spectrum and the correlation dimension [Abarbanel, 1996]. These dynamic properties characterize the sensitivity of the series to the initial conditions and they quantify the uncertainty about the future series behavior. Positive Lyapunov exponents and noninteger correlation dimension indicate that the series is chaotic. When the time series is chaotic it is difficult to infer stable forecast from different starting points. All these statistical and dynamic tests for time series are available from general-purpose and specialized software tools.

This chapter presents empirical investigations into time series modelling by PNN models evolved by IGP, and also some of their improved versions using backpropagation and Bayesian techniques. These PNN are selected after conducting a large number of runs. The experimental scenario is as follows: 1) the given time series is split into training and testing subseries; 2) a number of runs, approximately 100, are carried out with IGP to find the best PNN on the training series; 3) the best PNN from each run is improved by backpropagation and Bayesian retraining; 4) a number (usually 5%) of all best PNN are taken to decide which of them to accept by carrying out statistical examination. The best PNN is taken for comparisons with the alternative approaches.

10.1 Time Series Modelling

Time-series modelling may be regarded as an inductive learning problem. The task is to identify the regularities among a given series of points: $..., x(t), x(t+1), x(t+2), ...$, sampled at discrete time intervals. The goal is to find out how future points depend on points from the past. In the ideal case the behavior of the data generator can be described by differential equations, but in practice knowledge for such mathematical modelling is not available. This is why efforts to discover plausible descriptions of the unknown data source are made using model search. Here, this description is assumed to be a PNN model.

The empirical investigations in this chapter use input vectors $\mathbf{x}(t)$ created from the given observations assuming embedding dimension d, and delay time τ:

$$\mathbf{x}(t) = [x(t), x(t-\tau), x(t-2\tau), ..., x(t-(d-1)\tau)] \qquad (10.1)$$

that is lagged, sliding window vectors from $d\tau$ nearest previous points starting at a point t. The delay time is a positive number $\tau > 0$, here in all experiments $\tau = 1$ is used. The dependant variable is the immediate neighboring point to the start point $y = x(t+1)$.

The justification for this idea to use delay window vectors for predicting the future series values is given by Takens' theorem [Takens, 1981]. Takens' theorem states that delay window vectors of past time series data contain sufficient information to reconstruct the behavior of the unknown system mapping which is smooth and invertible. The lagged vector components can be envisioned as independent degrees of freedom of the dynamic system that has generated the series. These coordinates determine an equivalent to the original state space from which the system can be recovered unambiguously. Therefore, the orbits of state transitions of the system can be modelled by nonlinear functions of delay vectors. The point in the original state space toward which the system trajectory tends to converge is called the attractor. Each delay window vector is a different unfolding of the attractor point from its projection on the time series. In order to capture the behavior of the attractor a proper number of delay vector components should be selected, which is the embedding dimension.

Takens' theorem leaves the question of exactly how to determine the embedding dimension unanswered. Obviously each lagged vector should include components that convey different information to the model. Their separating delay time should be such that instabilities and measurement noise can be avoided, yet they should capture well the evolution of the series over time. What Takens' theorem suggests is a bound on the global embedding dimension, but it may be too large while smaller dimensions may be sufficient for accurate data modelling. There are algorithms for calculating the embedding dimension of time series, for example the global embedding dimension can be computed using the global false nearest neighbors algorithm [Abarbanel, 1996], while the minimal active embedding dimension can be computed using the local false nearest neighbor algorithm [Abarbanel, 1996].

The next question arising in time series modelling is what kind of model to use. Linear models can produce misleading results because they may require high-dimensionality even if it is possible to restore the system that has generated the data with a low dimensional nonlinear model. Linear models can be deceived by the strange attractors in the state-space. True linear data sources have fixed points, or simple attractors. Real-world time series, however, often exhibit strange attractors. This occurs as the system trajectory wanders along nonlinear manifolds of complex forms. Although exhibiting unstable trajectories, a system may have purely deterministic dynamics that produce quite irregular, nontrivial series. The dynamics of such systems may be reconstructed with nonlinear models. Measuring the correlation dimension of the attractor [Grassberger and Procaccia, 1983] can provide evidence for the need of nonlinearities. A brief discussion on a linear and several nonlinear time series models is offered below, and they are related to PNN.

Applying delayed input vectors to nonlinear models is a promising strategy for time series modelling but it guarantees reliable forecasts for only a limited number of steps ahead, depending on the embedding dimension. Long time ahead reliable predictions are not guaranteed because the true dynamics of the unknown data source cannot always be found, for example when the unknown generator is chaotic, and changes in the starting value may lead to different trajectories. The prediction horizon can be derived theoretically as inversely proportional to the maximum Lyapunov exponent of the series [Abarbanel, 1996].

10.2 Data Preprocessing

Data preparation for learning is performed using three main preprocessing techniques: 1) filtering redundant components from the series; 2) removing outliers from the series; and 3) scaling, or normalization, of the data. Our concern here is mainly normalization of the time series. Practical data collected from observations of natural phenomena differ significantly in magnitude. Such real data have to be rescaled for avoidance of computational instabilities and rounding errors due to the floating point format. A convenient technique for scaling the data, subject to next polynomial modelling, is normalization to zero mean and unit variance. This kind of scaling is especially suitable for PNN. Such a *normalization* is given by the matrix formula:

$$\mathbf{U} = \mathbf{\Theta}^{-1/2}(\mathbf{X} - \mathbf{1}\,\bar{\mathbf{x}}^T) \tag{10.2}$$

where $\mathbf{X}$ is the given $N \times d$ input data matrix, $\mathbf{1}$ is an identity $N \times 1$ vector of ones, $\bar{\mathbf{x}}$ is a $d \times 1$ vector of means $\bar{\mathbf{x}}= (1/N)\sum_{n=1}^{N} \mathbf{x}_n$, $\mathbf{\Theta}$ is a $d \times d$ diagonal variance matrix $\mathbf{\Theta} = (1/(N-1))(\mathbf{X} - \mathbf{1}\,\bar{\mathbf{x}}^T)^T(\mathbf{X} - \mathbf{1}\,\bar{\mathbf{x}}^T)$, and $\mathbf{U}$ is the transformed matrix. The columns of the matrix $\mathbf{U}$ become the input variables to be passed to the model. Here, it is assumed that the columns of the matrix $\mathbf{U}$ are used to build the design matrix for the weights of the activation polynomials in PNN.

All the experiments presented in this chapter have been conducted using this normalization, which is also called *standardization* due to the division by the standard deviation of the data.

10.3 PNN vs. Linear ARMA Models

Linear models are widely used for time series modelling due to the sound theory that explains them [Box and Jenkins, 1970]. Although nonlinear models can also produce linear models, they usually outperform the linear models in the presence of nonlinearities, and especially sustained oscillations, as well as in the presence of stochastic disturbances. Simpler linear models such as exponential smoothing and linear regressions may be used if there is no clear evidence of more complex nonlinearity in the data. The linear models often need specific manipulation with techniques for elimination of trends and seasonal patterns for example, which require additional knowledge.

A comparison of an evolved PNN model with a linear AutoRegressive Moving Average (ARMA) model was made recently [de Menezes and Nikolaev, 2006]. The PNN resemble ARMA models in that the activation polynomials are treated as linear regressors. The weights of the PNN activation polynomials are learned by efficient least squares fitting as are the weights of the linear ARMA models. This provides the advantage of reaching the optimal weights due to the unique global minimum on the error surface in case of linear models.

The benchmark *Airline series* [Faraway and Chatfield, 1998], popular in the statistical community, is chosen here for performing experimental comparisons. The series contains 144 observations, which are monthly totals of international airline passengers. The initial 132 points are taken for training through input vectors $\mathbf{x}(t) = [x(t), x(t-1), ..., x(t-11)]$. Following the standard methodology of Box and Jenkins (1970), a seasonal ARMA model is developed and it is fit to the logarithm of the observed values: $\log x_t \sim ARMA(0,1,1) \times (0,1,1)_{12}$. Next, a PNN model is evolved using IGP by performing 50 runs using fitness proportional selection, both crossover and mutation operators, population of size 100, common regularization parameter for all weights $\lambda = 0.001$ and selection threshold for pruning $z = 0.01$.

The $ARMA$ model shows accuracy of fitting the series $MSE_{ARMA} = 90.53$, which is better than the PNN accuracy $MSE_{PNN} = 152.12$. The prediction performance of the $ARMA$ model is much worse showing one-step-ahead forecasting error $MSE^f_{ARMA} = 356.75$, while the PNN shows $MSE^f_{PNN} = 185.27$. The fitting accuracy and the prediction of the examined PNN model are illustrated in Figures 10.1 and 10.2.

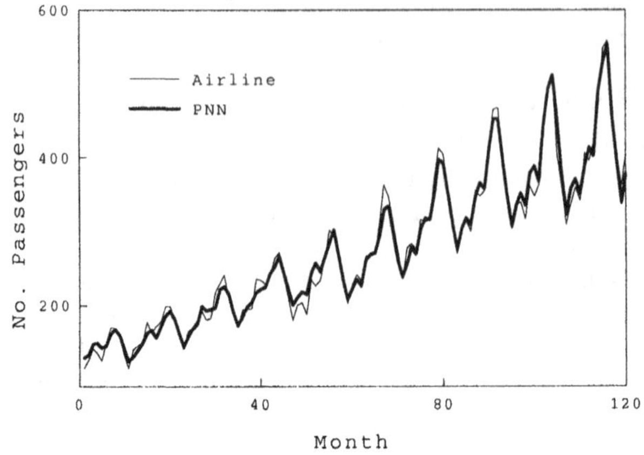

Figure 10.1. Fitting of the Airline series by a PNN model evolved by IGP.

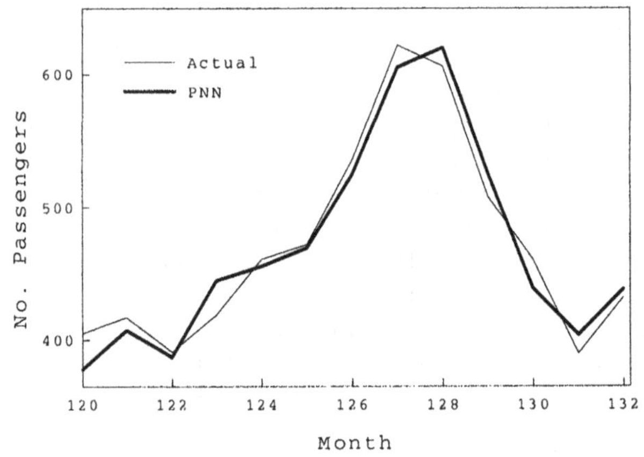

Figure 10.2. Forecasting (single-step-ahead prediction) of the Airline series by a PNN model evolved by IGP.

This brief study allows us to make several observations that are indicative of the advantages of genetically programmed PNN over linear ARMA models for time series modelling: 1) the use of PNN eliminates the need to perform data transformations before learning, so the need to decide whether and how to preprocess the given data is avoided; 2) the IGP of PNN are able to find polynomials that capture the time series characteristics well and predict well in the short-term; 3) the IGP of

PNN can help to discover the relevant input variables for learning, and thus they help to understand the lag dependencies in time series; and 4) the PNN structure as a hierarchical composition of simple polynomials is a factor that affects the forecasting performance.

10.4 PNN vs. Genetically Programmed Functions

The construction of PNN as tree-like topologies is especially suitable for GP style processing and can easily be extended to accommodate various components, such as harmonics, Gaussians, etc.. Recent research [Nikolaev and Iba, 2001a] shows that when evolved by the mechanisms of GP, these PNN usually outperform the traditional symbolic expression models composed of inhomogeneous primitive functions when evolved by Koza-style genetic programming.

The IGP with PNN models is compared here to the traditional Koza-style GP [Koza, 1992], which manipulates symbolic regression models of elementary functions such as: $+$, $=$, $*$, $/$, sin, cos, exp, etc., The traditional GP is made with the same micromechanisms as IGP: steady state reproduction of 50% from the population, fitness proportional selection, crossover by cut and splice, and context-preserving mutation. These evolutionary micromechanisms offer potential for doing powerful global, as well as local, search in high-dimensional spaces, which is a widely claimed strength of the GP paradigm.

Both IGP and GP systems are evaluated with the same fitness function using the benchmark *Mackey-Glass series* [Mackey and Glass, 1977]. The series is produced by generating 200 points with the Mackey-Glass differential equation for simulating blood flow using parameters: $a = 0.2, b = 0.1$, and differential $\Delta = 17$. The first 100 points are used for training, and the remaining for testing. The considered embedding dimension is $d = 6$. IGP uses $MaxTreeDepth = 4$, regularization $\lambda = 0.001$, selection threshold $z = 0.001$. Both systems use mutation probability $p_m = 0.01$ and crossover probability $p_c = 1.5$. Fifty runs are conducted with each system using populations of size 100 and maximum tree limit size 40 nodes (functionals+terminals). The best PNN found has 9 nodes with 14 coefficients, while the best GP composite function has 11 nodes with 19 coefficients.

The PNN model fits the series with accuracy $MSE_{PNN} = 0.000238$, which is better than the accuracy of the GP function $MSE_{GP} = 0.000341$. The prediction performance of PNN is also better demonstrating one-step-ahead forecasting error $MSE^f_{PNN} = 0.000104$, while the GP function exhibits $MSE^f_{GP} = 0.000202$. The fitting accuracy and the prediction of the the PNN model are plotted in Figures 10.3 and 10.4.

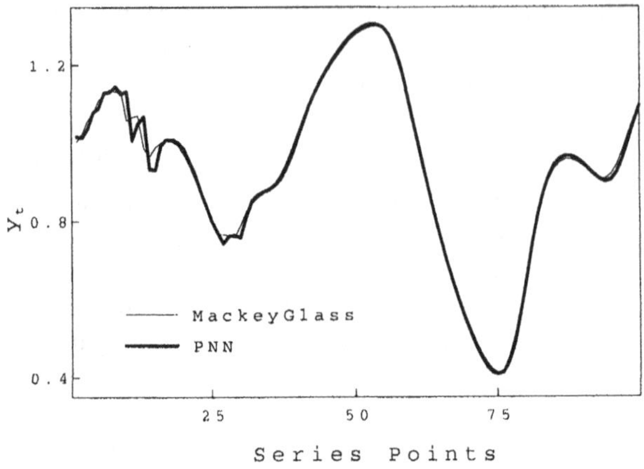

Figure 10.3. Fitting of the Mackey-Glass series by a PNN model evolved by IGP.

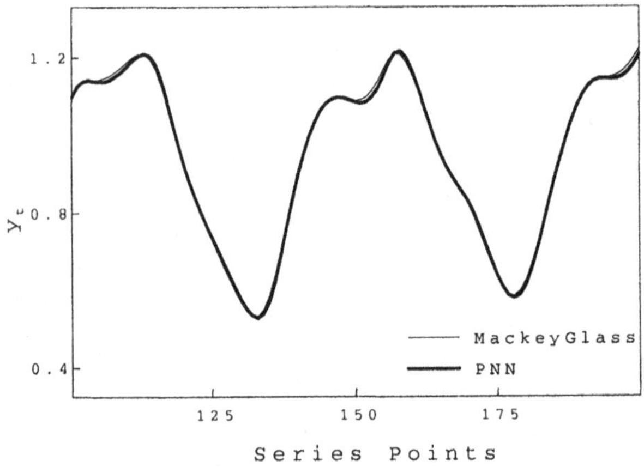

Figure 10.4. Forecasting (single-step-ahead prediction) of the Mackey-Glass series by a PNN model evolved by IGP.

Learning PNN models by IGP entails several advantages compared to Koza-style GP with functions. First, the IGP efficiently computes the PNN coefficients/weights by least squares fitting so there is no need for the IGP system to conduct search for coefficient values as in traditional GP. Second, the IGP evolves universally approximating PNN with reliable descriptive characteristics, while traditional GP usually tries to find arbitrary compositions of arbitrarily selected basis functions. Using bivariate polynomials in PNN entails three main benefits: 1) it leads to smaller spaces for the IGP to search; 2) it requires less sophisticated mutation and crossover operators; and 3) it allows us to conduct evolutionary search with populations of smaller size.

10.5 PNN vs. Statistical Learning Networks

PNNs are closely related to statistical learning networks [Barron, 1988], and more precisely they construct similar polynomials as the classical Group Method of Data Handling (GMDH) [Ivakhnenko, 1971, Madala and Ivakhnenko, 1994, Farlow, 1984, Müller and Lemke, 2000, Elder and Brown, 2000], and the Multivariate Adaptive Polynomial Splines (MAPS) algorithm [Barron and Xiao, 1991].

IGP infers polynomial network representations similar to those built by Multilayer GMDH [Ivakhnenko, 1971]. Multilayer GMDH synthesizes a polynomial network layer by layer conducting a heuristic search for pairs of variables to feed the next node so as to decrease the residual outcome error. This, however, constrains the feeding of higher layers since they depend on previously learned lower nodes that may not be optimal. GMDH makes strictly layered networks having a large number of internode connections because there are links radiating from every internal node to every node in the next layer. The tree-structured PNNs evolved by IGP feature a lower complexity, which improves their accuracy of fit and forecasting potential.

Experiments are performed to find out whether a genetically programmed PNN can outperform the Multilayer GMDH on the benchmark *Sunspot series* [Weigend et al., 1992]. 255 points are taken and divided into two subsets: the data from years 1700 – 1920 for training, and those from 1921 – 1955 for testing. The embedding dimension is $d = 9$. Fifty runs are conducted with IGP using: $MaxTreeSize = 40$, $MaxTreeDepth = 5$, mutation probability $p_m = 0.01$, crossover probability $p_c = 1.5$, regularization $\lambda = 0.0015$, and selection threshold $z = 0.01$. The GMDH network has been designed with 4 layers, 8 nodes in each layer using the complete bivariate activation polynomial, and also using regularization $\lambda = 0.0015$.

The trained *GMDH* displays accuracy $MSE_{GMDH} = 0.00469$ which is worse than the PNN accuracy $MSE_{PNN} = 0.00372$. The *GMDH* model also shows worse one-step-ahead forecasting error $MSE^f_{GMDH} = 0.0247$, while the PNN displays $MSE^f_{PNN} = 0.01138$. The best polynomial has 11 nodes with 18 coefficients, while the GMDH network has 32 with 192 coefficients. The fitting accuracy and the prediction of the PNN on the Sunspots are illustrated in Figures 10.5 and 10.6.

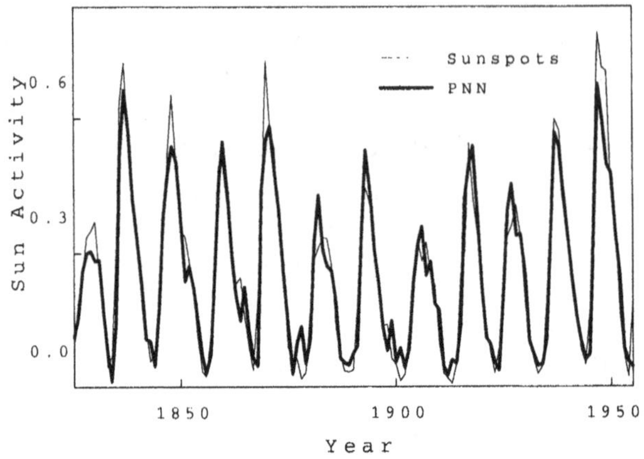

Figure 10.5. Fitting of the Sunspots series by a PNN model evolved by IGP.

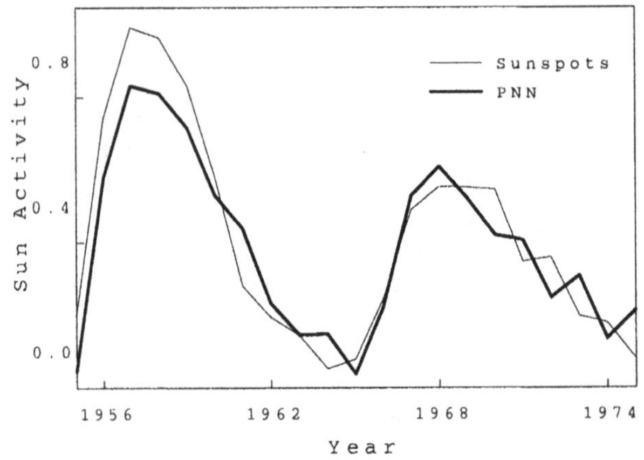

Figure 10.6. Forecasting (single-step-ahead prediction) of the Sunspots series by a PNN model evolved by IGP.

A principle distinction from GMDH [Ivakhnenko, 1971, Madala and Ivakhnenko, 1994, Farlow, 1984, Elder and Brown, 2000] and MAPS [Barron and Xiao, 1991] is that IGP performs search in the space of whole polynomials, while the others grow a single polynomial iteratively. GMDH and MAPS build one polynomial network in such a way that the formation of the next layer is guided by the partial fitnesses from previous levels. Such a hill-climbing constructive approach makes these statistical learning algorithms susceptible to entrapment at local optima. IGP conducts more powerful search as it performs global exploration as well as local exploitation of the landscape.

10.6 PNN vs. Neural Network Models

The PNN generated by the IGP system belong to the category of feed-forward MLP networks [Rumelhart et al., 1986, Hertz et al., 1991, Haykin, 1999]. Both kinds of networks, MLP and PNN, implement nonlinear functions as hierarchical compositions. The practical problem of MLP is that the proper number of layers and the number of nodes usually must be found experimentally. A distinctive feature of PNN is that their model structure and variables can be found automatically using the evolutionary micromechanisms of IGP.

PNN and MLP both use adaptive learning by backpropagation techniques for gradient descent search in the weight space. In this sense, PNN benefit from the efficacy, simplicity, and power of the backprop techniques. At the same time, both PNN and MLP suffer from the need to identify suitable values for the parameters of the algorithm such as the learning rate, the momentum, the regularization parameter, and the termination criterion. There are approaches to finding suitable parameter values that can be applied directly to PNN such as those based on the Bayesian evidence procedure [MacKay, 1995]. PNN also assume the strategies for improving the generalization performance developed for MLP such as network pruning and early stopping [Bishop, 1995].

A PNN evolved by IGP and improved after that by BP is compared to an MLP network on the benchmark *Far-Infrared-Laser* series [Hübner et al., 1994]. This Laser series contains fluctuations of a physical laser recorded in a chaotic state during a laboratory experiment with an oscilloscope. The objective is to learn the description of a far-infrared NH_3 laser given its intensity pulsations. The initial 900 points are taken for training, and the next 100 points for testing as in the other research. The embedding dimension is $d = 10$. Approximately fifty runs are conducted with IGP using populations of size 100, $MaxTreeSize = 40$, and $MaxTreeDepth = 6$. The IGP system uses parameters: mutation probability $p_m = 0.01$, crossover probability $p_c = 1.5$, regularization $\lambda = 0.001$, and selection threshold $z = 0.01$.

The BP training algorithm is run to perform 150 epochs with parameters: learning rate $\eta = 0.001$ and momentum $\alpha = 0.01$. The MLP network is manually designed with one hidden layer of 10 sigmoidal activation functions and a summation output node. Training of the MLP by the backpropagation algorithm is made using a fixed learning rate $\eta_{MLP} = 0.01$ and momentum $\alpha_{MLP} = 0.02$.

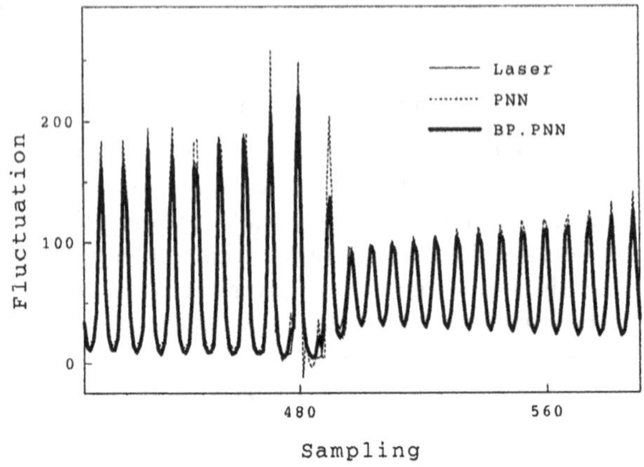

Figure 10.7. Fitting the Laser series by an evolved PNN model retrained by BP.

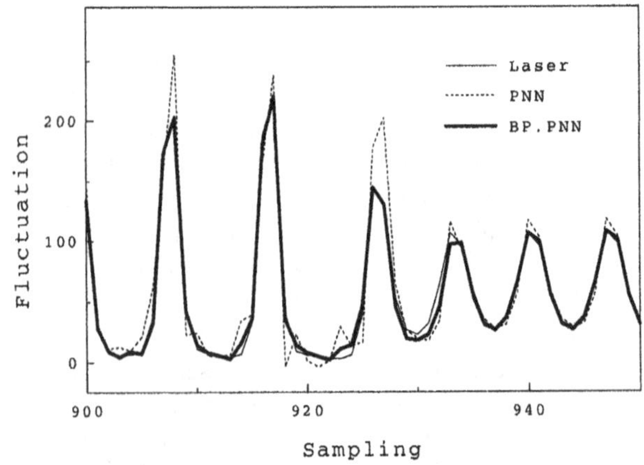

Figure 10.8. Forecasting (single-step-ahead prediction) of the Laser series by a PNN model evolved by IGP and retrained by BP.

The fitting accuracy and the prediction capacity of the best discovered PNN model are given in Figures 10.7 and 10.8. The evolved PNN has 15 nodes with 34 coefficients, while the MLP is fully connected with 10 hidden nodes. The PNN model shows accuracy on fitting the series $MSE_{PNN} = 32.45$, which is better than accuracy of the MLP $MSE_{MLP} = 48.62$. The prediction performance of PNN is also better demonstrating one-step-ahead forecasting error $MSE^f_{PNN} = 55.67$ while the MLP shows $MSE^f_{MLP} = 80.07$.

MLP can benefit from using the input variables from the best PNN found by IGP, and this helps to achieve neural networks with improved forecasting performance. The IGP system, however, has similar computational disadvantages to the MLP; their algorithms require tuning many free parameters and there are random initializations that can affect their operation. While the MLP uses randomly initialized weights and derivatives to start the learning process, the IGP uses a random initialization of the initial population of PNN, fitness proportional randomized selection, and random selection of transformation nodes for the learning crossover and mutation operators. All of these random effects require a large number of runs in order to acquire convincing results.

The benefit of evolving PNN by IGP is that polynomials of almost unlimited order could be discovered due to the hierarchical polynomial network construction inherited from the multilayer GMDH algorithm. The identification of the higher-order term weights is made efficiently by cascading low-order activation polynomials whose weights are estimated without serious computational problems. This is an advantage over traditional multilayer feed-forward neural networks trained by backpropagation which are limited in modelling very high-order functions by the computer capacity to calculate higher-order weights [Wray and Green, 1994]. The precision of linear polynomial networks [Wray and Green, 1994] is also sensitive to the computational limitations of the BP training algorithm.

10.7 PNN vs. Kernel Models

PNN, as well as kernel models, are suitable tools for time-series modelling [Müller et al., 1999, Quiñonero-Candela, 2004]. In developing kernel models such as PNN models, one has to decide which kernel functions should enter the model and how to find their coefficients. That is, PNN and kernel models both face the problem of which should be the basis set, and how to combine the selected elementary basis functions. Research in kernel models generally utilizes local-basis functions such as Gaussians, splines, or multiquadratics. While the problem of PNN model structure selection can be addressed by evolutionary style search using the IGP paradigm, the structure identification problem in kernel modelling has considered mainly greedy hill-climbing structural search algorithms and Bayesian techniques. A linear PNN trained by Bayesian techniques is presented here to illustrate the advantage of using these probabilistic techniques for addressing difficult modelling tasks.

The capacity of linear PNN with polynomial kernels to learn from time series is related here to a model with Gaussian kernels trained by the Sparse Bayesian Learning [Tipping, 2001] algorithm on a real-world *financial exchange rates series.* A series of 280 cross-currency exchange rates between the dollar USD and the Japanese yen sampled every minute, is taken without any kind of preprocessing; only normalization was applied. The initial 265 points were used for training and the remaining 15 for testing. The embedding dimension was $d = 15$.

The IGP program was run 50 times using typical system parameters: $PopulationSize = 100$, $MaxTreeSize = 40$, $MaxTreeDepth = 7$, mutation probability $p_m = 0.01$, crossover probability $p_c = 1.5$, regularization $\lambda = 0.001$, and selection threshold $z = 0.01$. The SBL algorithm [Tipping, 2001] has been designed using Gaussian kernels with spread (width) $s^{-2} = 0.1$. SBM was made using the EM principle (Subsection 8.4). The best evolved PNN was retrained with the recursive Bayesian version of the Levenberg-Marquardt algorithm (BRLM) (Subsection 8.5). Both the BRLM and SBL were implemented with the same initial noise hyperparameter $\beta = 1.0/std(y)$. However, they used different initial prior hyperparameters: SBL was made with $\alpha = 1e^{-3}$, while the BRLM was made with a very small $\alpha = 1e^{-3}/(Nw^2)$ since it performs hyperparameter training. The hyperparameter learning rate in BRLM was set to $\eta = 1e^{-3}/N$. Both training algorithms were iterated 10 times, and they pruned weights when their corresponding alphas exceeded the predefined threshold value $\alpha_{MAX} = 1.0$.

The PNN and SBL models show very close training accuracy with $MSE_{SBL} = 0.00326$ and $MSE_{PNN} = 0.00352$. In addition, both kernel models are examined on multi-step-ahead forecasting which is a challenging task. While the SBL model demonstrates prediction with error $MSE^f_{SBL} = 0.0228$, the PNN with polynomial kernels predicts with much smaller error $MSE^f_{PNN} = 0.0176$. It should be noted that both models are of quite similar complexity. The best PNN contained 52 kernels (with 52 weights) and the SBL model had 58 kernels (coefficients), which indicates that the Bayesian approach provides potential to generate sparse and good forecasting models. The observation that both models produce similar results is due to their similar representation capacity: they are both kernel models. Illustrations of the PNN performance are provided in Figures 10.9 and 10.10.

What is interesting to note in Figure 10.9 is that the PNN can exhibit good interpolation and extrapolation performance on such time series with quite irregular characteristics. Figure 10.10 illustrates the multi-step-ahead prediction from the PNN which is informative about its abilities to generate long-lasting forecasts.

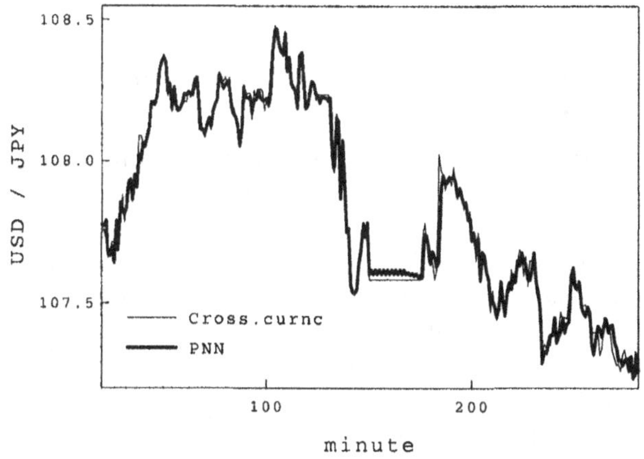

Figure 10.9. Fitting of the cross-currency exchange rates series by a PNN model evolved by IGP and retrained by recursive Bayesian learning.

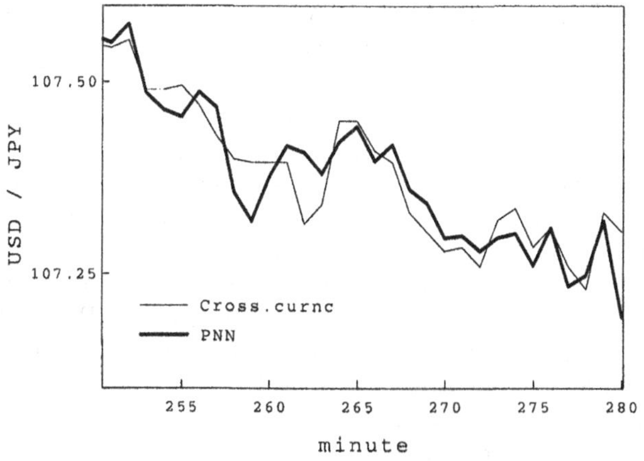

Figure 10.10. Forecasting (multi-step-ahead prediction) of the cross-currency exchange rates series by a PNN model evolved by IGP and retrained by recursive Bayesian learning.

The SBL taken alone offers the advantage of faster training compared to the PNN is initially evolved by IGP. However, BRLM can be applied directly to PNN without model selection by IGP. The efficiency of doing probabilistic training is in the proper adjustment of the weight parameters to the noise with respect to the assumption for its distribution.

Kernel models are sensitive to the characteristics of the training data, and their spreads should be well-tuned before learning.

10.8 Recurrent PNN vs. Recurrent Neural Networks

Recurrent PNN, such as the recurrent MLP, are nonlinear models that use memory to model time-dependant sequences of data. Encoding of memory by means of hidden network nodes and recurrent feedback connections enables us to achieve sensitivity to the order of presentation of the data, thus it contributes to capturing dynamic characteristics especially when dealing with time series.

A recurrent PNN is related here to an Elman-type [Elman, 1990] recurrent neural network (RNN) using real-world *electricity load series.* This series contains 5850 electricity load measurements in megawatts from a certain area recorded every day at 12:30. The initial 4900 data are considered for training and the remaining for testing. The embedding dimension is $d = 12$. A dynamic PNN is evolved by IGP and further retrained using the RTRL algorithm specialized for PNN (Subsection 7.3). The IGP system was run 50 times using parameters: $PopulationSize = 100$, $MaxTreeSize = 40$, $MaxTreeDepth = 7$, mutation probability $p_m = 0.01$, crossover probability $p_c = 1.5$, regularization $\lambda = 0.001$, and selection threshold $z = 0.01$.

The best PNN model found by IGP has 6 hidden nodes, and 7 input terminal leaves including those feeding back outputs. The RNN has been designed with 1 layer of 6 hidden nodes and feedback connections from each hidden node to all hidden nodes. The hidden nodes are made with sigmoidal activations, while the output node simply used summation. The weights of this RNN are also trained using RTRL. Both RTRL implementations are made to perform 1000 epochs. The approximation abilities of the best recurrent PNN evolved by IGP and improved by RTRL are illustrated in Figures 10.11 and 10.12.

The Elman-type RNN model demonstrates a better fitting accuracy on the training data $MSE_{Elman} = 1.02e6$ than the PNN accuracy $MSE_{PNN} = 1.13e6$. The prediction performance of the RNN is worse, however, showing one-step-ahead forecasting error $MSE^f_{Elman} = 2.04e6$ while the PNN shows $MSE^f_{PNN} = 1.93e6$. These results show that the Elman-type RNN may achieve better approximation of the given training data, but it tends to exhibit worse forecasting performance than PNN. The main reason for the superior forecasting is again the evolution of a parsimonious model by IGP which has not only a small number of inputs, but also features sparse connectivity.

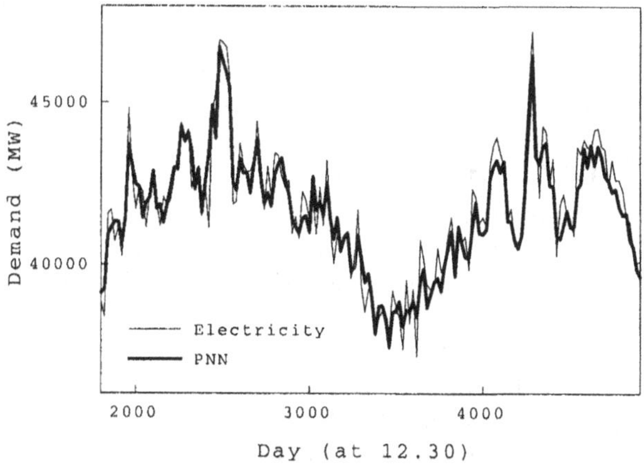

Figure 10.11. Fitting of the *COMPLEX series* by a recurrent PNN model evolved by IGP and retrained by RTRL.

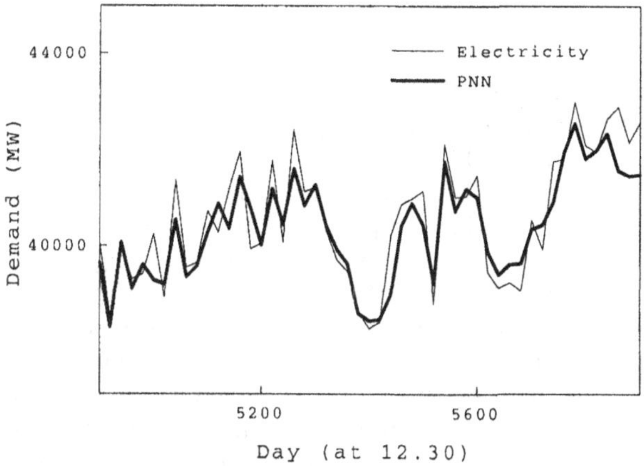

Figure 10.12. Forecasting (single-step-ahead prediction) of the COMPLEX series by a recurrent PNN model evolved by IGP and retrained by RTRL.

It has been found that on average the temporal training of recurrent PNN converges reliably to nearly optimal solutions once a parsimonious network architecture has been discovered by IGP. One reason for this learning behavior is that the training process starts not with arbitrarily generated weights but with good weights determined during the structural PNN search process by the mechanisms of the IGP system, in particular using least squares fitting. Another condition for achieving good asypmtotic stability when training recurrent PNN is the replacement of the squashing sigmoid function with activation polynomials in the hidden network nodes. Investigations showed that the sigmoid function tends to attenuate the temporal signals too fast.

10.9 Chapter Summary

This section demonstrated results on modelling benchmark and real-world time series by PNN learned adaptively using IGP, backpropagation, and Bayesian techniques. The performances of the best discovered PNN have been related to other popular approaches to time series modelling in order to understand whether they can be superior for such regression tasks. It has been found that the presented methodology provides computational mechanisms that infer PNN which are more consistent models than genetically programmed regression functions, statistical learning networks, feed-forward MLP neural networks, kernel models, and recurrent neural networks on the same data.

The experimental results reported in this chapter have been produced using the basic tree-like PNN representation as proposed in Section 2.1.2. This has been done in order to provide understanding about the average expected performance of all remaining models given in Chapter 3. The remaining tree-like PNN representations may exhibit only slightly better or slightly worse performance depending on the characteristics of the provided data. There could be arguments for and against each particular PNN model because each concrete model could be superior on data with corresponding properties. The presented models have been given normalized data, but various other preprocessing techniques could also be applied. For example, there could be made integral data transformations, differential transformations, rational transformations, etc..

What this chapter also suggests is that in practice it may be useful to try inductive learning of alternative nonlinear models because in some situations they may show better approximation qualities, for example if the researcher has much more experience in them. The decision of which precise model to use for the given training sample can be made after performing statistical model diagnostics and validation tests. It should also be noted that whatever model is considered it always has to be processed using smoothness constraints (for example using regularization), because time series modelling is an ill-posed problem.

Chapter 11

CONCLUSIONS

This book is inspired by the thought that nature has created the most perfect mechanisms, and if we want to attain the efficacy of nature we may try to simulate, and mimic its mechanisms at least to the degree to which we know them. Studies into biology, human genetics, and neuroscience not only enhance our understanding of the surrounding world, but also provide us principles of evolution and operation. These principles can be used to develop efficient computer algorithms for solving difficult practical problems in a similar manner to which nature deals with them.

Biologically inspired inductive computation is a multidiscipline that unifies invaluable theoretical achievements from many areas. When unified these theoretical findings become complementary and enhance their importance and reliability. In particular, the presented methodology for adaptive learning polynomial networks from data offers a common view of evolutionary and neural computation. Integrated together the evolutionary, neural, and probabilistic computation are a coherent paradigm for inductive problem solving. This methodology is a symbiosis of findings from various fields including computer science, mathematics and statistics, as well as biology. Seemingly different ideas, methods, strategies, representations, and models from these well-established areas of science are generalized in a common framework for inductive computation. The reasons for collecting this knowledge come from the understanding that their resources actually serve for addressing similar tasks known under different names such as approximation, regression, nonlinear modelling, and time series forecasting, to name a few.

The results obtained according to the presented methodology allow us to draw three main conclusions: first, genetic programming helps us to alleviate to a large extent the basic difficulties in model selection; second, neural network techniques allow us to improve evolved models; and three, more accurate tuning of inferred models can be performed using Bayesian techniques. Inductive genetic programming provides powerful algorithmic means for tackling some problems that neural network and even probabilistic approaches are unable to resolven namely: 1) identification of the model structure and selection of the input variables; 2) deciding which is the best function format in the sense of which kind of activation functions in which nodes to use them; and 3) how to interpret the learned model. Genetic programming offers possibilities to carry out global as well as local search that progressively adapts the model structure to the data.

This book adopts neural network representations as a model description language for evolutionary computation. The rationale is that the hybridization of the two paradigms enables us to apply reliable backpropagation training techniques for gradient descent weight search. Relieved of the need to specify the network architecture and the inputs in advance, assuming that they have been found by genetic programming, the connectionist training offers several advantages: 1) reliable weight learning algorithms that deal well with uncertain data; and 2) facilities for control over the generalization during learning.

Many practical data can be modelled robustly only after the application of Bayesian techniques. There are practical data contaminated with different noise characteristics, outliers, and omitted values which can only be modelled reliably in a probabilistic setting. This book demonstrates that the Bayesian inference helps to extend the capability of polynomial networks and makes them promising learning tools for practical data. Polynomial networks equipped with probabilistic training algorithms can capture the regularities in the data better because they assume adaptation of the model with respect to the adopted data distribution. Based on the evidence presented in this book, we are inclined to think that the inductive genetic programming, neural network and Bayesian paradigms combine together their strengths and enables us to implement promising tools for nonlinear modelling.

The motivation for developing this adaptive computation methodology for computational induction of polynomials is the idea to bind together the advantages of the three paradigms. In order to achieve gradual adaptation of the model structure to the data, attention is directed toward using the principles of natural selection, crossover, mutation, and their computer realizations suggested by genetic programming. In order to achieve fine-tuning of the model coefficients, attention is directed toward gradient descent search methods designed for neural networks. In order to adjust the model properly to the general features in the data without capturing the hidden noise, Bayesian learning is performed. In this sense the three paradigms, genetic programming, neural networks and probabilistic inference, provide algorithms for adaptive inductive learning of models from data.

This book demonstrated successful results on nonlinear modelling of time series by polynomial networks. It was shown that genetically programmed polynomial networks outperform traditional statistical autoregressive moving average models, neural networks, statistical learning networks, kernel models, and recurrent networks on benchmark time series. The presented empirical results may serve as arguments to employ polynomial networks for solving real-world tasks from practice. The decision to use them for time series processing should follow the prescribed sequence of steps, in accordance with which the final decision should be taken after careful validation of the model using statistical diagnostics. Even if the polynomial model discovered from the data may seem adequate from visual inspection of its output, it should not be considered without a thorough examination of its residuals. Passing the statistical diagnosis tests is a sound evidence for the quality of the model.

Research on polynomial networks has two main aspects: theoretical and practical. The first group of theoretical research concerns elaboration of a more rigorous formalism describing the evolutionary search process conducted by genetic programming. Further investigations should be oriented toward making a more precise Markov model of genetic programming that can give a better probabilistic explanation of how it works and how its population evolves generation by generation. Such a model can help to perform more careful convergence analysis and can give guidelines on how to design more robust evolutionary search control. The second group of theoretical research concerns investigation of the convergence of the polynomial network training process. Special attention has to be made to study the convergence of recurrent polynomial networks.

The practical research on polynomial networks is oriented toward implementing easy to use algorithms for fine-tuning of the genetic programming parameters and the neural network parameters. The genetic programming parameters should be improved in order to enable better adjustment of the model structure to the given data. These parameters include initialization of the mutation and crossover probabilities, selection of crossover and mutation points, the parameters of the selection mechanism, etc.. The parameters of the neural network training algorithm should be improved to adjust the model nonlinearity better and to increase the generalization. This mainly concerns the learning rate parameter. In order to achieve efficient Bayesian learning, the initial hyperpriors and the noise hyperparameter have to be carefully selected.

The developments on polynomial networks offered here can be used separately and can be applied in practice in different ways depending on what is the purpose of the implementation: is it required to learn models very fast from the provided data, to find extremely accurate models, to produce sparse models, to provide forecasts online, etc.. Several guidelines can be given on possible uses of the models and algorithms offered in this book:

- the tree-structured PNN representations can be learned using only IGP without further training; when the main objective is discovery of parsimonious models there is no need to finely tune the coefficients, in such case using only IGP is sufficient and fast enough as it takes less time than one neural network training cycle of thousands of epochs;

- alternative PNN models, using kernels, harmonics, local basis functions, splines, sigmoids, Gaussians, etc., can be grown layer-by-layer as cascaded hierarchical polynomial networks using constructive algorithms like the Multilayer GMDH or Combinatorial GMDH for example, which is facilitated by the corresponding weight learning techniques provided for each particular network model;

- PNN architectures can be manually designed by fixing their topologies in advance using some heuristics, and next trained by a suitable backpropagation or Bayesian technique for the relevant model.

This book is a product of long research into model-free computational induction. It proposes a methodology for adaptive learning of polynomials represented as neural networks. These polynomial networks provide uniform treatment for different kinds of nonlinear function models and their important characteristic is that they are easy to understand and interpret. PNNs are open-box models and this is another reason to promote them as promising tools for successful real-world applications to tasks such as system identification, signal processing, adaptive control, forecasting, etc..

References

[Abarbanel, 1996] Abarbanel, H.D.I. (1996). *Analysis of Observed Chaotic Data*, Springer-Verlag, Berlin.

[Ackley, 1987] Ackley, D.H. (1987). *A Connectionist Machine for Genetic Hillclimbing*, Kluwer Academic, Boston, MA.

[Akaike, 1970] Akaike,H. (1970). Statistical Predictor Identification, *Annals Inst. Stat. Math.*, vol.22, 203-217.

[Akaike, 1973] Akaike, H. (1973). A New Look at the Statistical Model Identification, *IEEE Trans. Automatic Control*, vol.19, 716-723.

[Altenberg, 1994a] Altenberg, L. (1994). Emergent Phenomena in Genetic Programming, In: Sebald, A.V. and L.J. Fogel (Eds.), *Proc. Third Annual Conference on Evolutionary Programming*, World Scientific, Singapore, 233-241.

[Altenberg, 1994b] Altenberg, L. (1994). The Evolution of Evolvability in Genetic Programming, In: Kinnear Jr., K. (Ed.), *Advances in Genetic Programming*, The MIT Press, Cambridge, MA, pp.47-74.

[Angeline, 1994] Angeline, P.J. (1994). Genetic Programming and Emerging Intelligence, In: Kinnear Jr., K. (Ed.), *Advances in Genetic Programming*, The MIT Press, Cambridge, MA, 75-98.

[Anthony and Holden, 1994] Anthony, M. and S.B. Holden (1994). Quantifying Generalization in Linearly Weighted Networks, *Complex Systems*, vol.8, 91-114.

[Atkeson et al., 1997] Atkeson, C.G., A.W. Moore and S. Schaal (1997). Locally Weighted Learning, *Artificial Intelligence Review*, vol.11, 11-73.

[Bäck, 1996] Bäck, T. (1996). *Evolutionary Algorithms in Theory and Practice*, Oxford University Press, New York, NY.

[Bäck and Hoffmeister, 1991] Bäck, T. and F. Hoffmeister (1991). Extended Selection Mechanisms in Genetic Algorithms, In: Belew, R.K. and L.B. Booker (Eds.), *Proc. Fourth Int. Conf. on Genetic Algorithms*, Morgan Kaufmann, San Mateo, CA, 92-99.

[Bäck et al., 2000] Back, T., D.B. Fogel and Z. Michalewicz (2000). *Evolutionary Computation 1: Basic Algorithms and Operators*, IOP Publ., Bristol, UK.

[Baker, 1987] Baker, J.E. (1987). Reducing Bias and Inefficiency in the Selection Algorithm, In: Grefenstette, J.J. (Ed.), *Proc. Second Int. Conf. on Genetic Algorithms and their Applications*, Lawrence Erlbaum Assoc., Hillsdale, NJ, 14-21.

[Banzhaf et al., 1998] Banzhaf, W., P. Nordin,P., R.E. Keller and F.D. Francone (1998). *Genetic Programming: An Introduction. On the Automatic Evolution of Computer Programs and Its Applications*, Morgan Kaufmann, San Francisco, CA.

[Barron, 1988] Barron, A.R. and R.L. Barron (1988). Statistical Learning Networks: A Unifying View, In: Fraser, M.D. (Ed.), *Proc. 20th Symposium on the Interface: Computing Science and Statistics*, 192-203.

[Barron and Xiao, 1991] Barron, A.R. and X. Xiao (1991). Discussion on MARS, *Annals of Statistics*, vol.19, 67-82.

[Bastert et al., 2001] Bastert, O., D. Rockmore, P.F. Stadler and G. Tinhofer (2001). Landscapes on Spaces of Trees, Working Paper SFWP 01-01-006, Santa Fe Institute, NM.

[Battiti, 1989] Battiti, R. (1989). Accelerated Backpropagation Learning: Two Optimization Methods, *Complex Systems*, vol.3, 331-342.

[Becker and LeCun, 1989] Becker, S. and Y. LeCun (1989). Improving the Convergence of Back-Propagation Learning with Second-Order Methods, In: Touretzky, D., G. Hinton and T. Sejnowski (Eds.), *Proc. 1988 Connectionist Models Summer School*, Morgan Kaufmann, San Mateo, CA, 29-37.

[Bengio et al., 1994] Bengio, Y., P. Simard and P. Frasconi (1994). Learning Long-Term Dependencies with Gradient Descent is Difficult, *IEEE Trans. on Neural Networks*, vol.5, N:2, 157-166.

[Bersini and Varela, 1991] Bersini, H. and F. Varela (1991). Hints for Adaptive Problem Solving Gleaned from Immune Networks. In: Schwefel, H.-P. and H.M. Mühlenbein (Eds.), *Proc. First Int. Conf. Parallel Problem Solving from Nature PPSN I*, Springer, Berlin, 343-354.

[Billings and Zhu, 1991] Billings,S.A. and Zhu,Q.M. (1991). Rational Model Identification using an Extended Least Squares Algorithm, *International Journal of Control*, vol.54, N:3, pp.529-546.

[Billings and Zhu, 1995] Billings, S.A. and Q.M. Zhu (1995). Model Validation Tests for Multivariable Nonlinear Models Including Neural Networks, *Int. Journal of Control*, vol.62, 749-766.

[Bishop, 1995] Bishop, C. (1995). *Neural Networks for Pattern Recognition*, Oxford University Press, Oxford, UK.

[Bishop and Qazaz, 1997] Bishop, C.M. and C.Z. Qazaz (1997). Regression with Input-Dependent Noise: A Bayesian Treatment, In: Touretzky, D.S., M.C. Mozer and M.E. Hasselmo (Eds.), *Advances in Neural Information Processing Systems 9*, The MIT Press, Cambridge, MA, 347-353.

[Blickle and Thiele, 1997] Blickle, T. and L. Thiele (1997). A Comparison of Selection Schemes used in Evolutionary Algorithms, *Evolutionary Computation*, vol.4, N:4, 361-394.

[Böhm and Geyer-Schulz, 1996] Böhm, W. and A. Geyer-Schulz (1996). Exact Uniform Initialization For Genetic Programming, In: Belew, R.K. and M.D. Vose (Eds.), *Foundations of Genetic Algorithms FOGA-4*, Morgan Kaufmann, San Mateo, CA, 379-407.

[Box and Jenkins, 1970] Box, G.E.P. and G.M. Jenkins (1970). *Time Series Analysis Forecasting and Control*, Holden-Day, San Francisco, CA.

[Box and Pierce, 1970] Box, G.E.P. and D.A. Pierce (1970). Distribution of Residual Correlations in Autoregressive-Integrated Moving Average Time Series Models, *Journal of the American Statistical Association*, vol.65, 1509-1526.

[Braess, 1986] Braess, D. (1986). *Nonlinear Approximation Theory*, Springer-Verlag, Berlin.

[Brock et al., 1996] Brock, W.A., W.D. Dechert, J.A. Sheinkman and B. LeBaron (1996). A Test for Independence Based on the Correlation Dimension, *Econometric Reviews*, vol.15, N:3, 197-235.

[Buntine and Weigend, 1991a] Buntine, W.L. and A.S. Weigend (1991). Computing Second Order Derivatives in Feed-forward Networks- A review, *IEEE Trans. on Neural Networks*, vol.5, N:3, 480-488.

[Buntine and Weigend, 1991b] Buntine, W.L. and A.S. Weigend (1991). Bayesian Back-propagation, *Complex Systems*, vol.5, 603-643.

[Catfolis, 1993] Catfolis, T. (1993). A Method for Improving the Real-Time Recurrent Learning Algorithm, *Neural Networks*, vol.6, N:6, 807-822.

[Chakraborty et al., 1996] Chakraborty, U.K., K. Deb, and M. Chakraborty (1996). Analysis of Selection Algorithms: A Markov Chain Approach, *Evolutionary Computation*, vol4, N:2, 133-167.

[Chen and Manry, 1993] Chen, M.S. and M.T. Manry (1993). Conventional Modelling of the Multi-Layer Perceptron Using Polynomial Basis Functions, *IEEE Trans. on Neural Networks*, vol.4, N:1, 164-166.

[ShuChen, 2002] Chen, S.-H. (Ed.) (2002). *Genetic Algorithms and Genetic Programming in Computational Finance*, Kluwer Academic Publ., Boston, MA.

[Chen et al., 1990] Chen, S., S.A. Billings and P.M. Grant (1990). Non-linear Systems Identification using Neural Networks, *Int. J. Control*, vol.51, N:6, 1191-1214.

[Chen et al., 2004] Chen, S., X. Hong, C.J. Harris and P.M. Sharkey (2004). Sparse Modelling using Orthogonal Forward Regression with PRESS Statistic and Regularization, *IEEE Trans. Systems, Man and Cybernetics*, B, vol.34, N:2, 898-911.

[Cherkassky et al., 1999] Cherkassky, V., X. Shao, F.M. Mulier and V. Vapnik (1999). Model Complexity Control for Regression Using VC Generalization Bounds, *IEEE Trans. on Neural Networks*, vol.10, N:5, 1075-1088.

[Cotter, 1990] Cotter, N.E. (1990). The Stone-Weierstrass Theorem and its Application to Neural Networks, *IEEE Trans. on Neural Networks*, vol.1, N:4, 290-295.

[Cramer, 1985] Cramer, N.L. (1985). A Representation for the Adaptive Generation of Simple Sequential Programs, In: Grefenstette, J.J. (Ed.), *Proc. First Int. Conf. on Genetic Algorithms and their Applications*, Lawrence Erlbaum Assoc., Hillsdale, NJ, 183-187.

[Craven and Wahba, 1979] Craven, P. and G. Wahba. (1979). Smoothing Noisy Data with Spline Functions: Estimating the Correct Degree of Smoothing by the Method of Generalized Cross-Validation, *Numerishe Math.*, vol.31, 377-403.

[Cristiani and Shawe-Taylor, 2000] Cristiani, N. and J. Shawe-Taylor (2000). *An Introduction to Support Vector Machines and other kernel-based learning methods*, Cambridge University Press, Cambridge, UK.

[Cybenko, 1989] Cybenko, G. (1989). Approximations by Superpositions of a Sigmoidal Function, *Mathematics of Control, Signals and Systems*, vol.2, 303-314.

[Darken and Moody, 1990] Darken, C. and J. Moody (1990). Note on Learning Rate Schedules for Stochastic Optimization, In: Touretzky, D.S. (Ed.), *Advances in Neural Inf. Processing Systems NIPS-2*, Morgan Kauffman, CA, 832-838.

[Davis, 1975] Davis, P.J. (1975). *Interpolation and Approximation*, Dover, New York.

[Davis and Principe, 1993] Davis, T. and J. Principe (1993). A Markov Framework for the Simple Genetic Algorithm, *Evolutionary Computation*, vol.1, N:3, 269-288.

[DeBoer and Hogeweg, 1989] DeBoer, R.G. and P. Hogeweg (1989). Idiotypic Networks Incorporating T-B Cell Cooperation. The Condition for Percolation, *Journal of Theoretical Biology*, vol.139, 17-38.

[de Freitas et al., 2000b] de Freitas, N., M. Niranjan, A. Gee and A. Doucet (2000). Sequential Monte Carlo Methods to Train Neural Network Models, *Neural Computation*, vol.12, N:4, 933-953.

[De Jong and Sarma, 1992] De Jong, K.A. and J. Sarma (1992). Generation Gaps Revisited. In: Whitley, D. (Ed.), *Foundations of Genetic Algorithms FOGA-2*, Morgan Kaufmann, San Mateo, CA, 19-28.

[de Menezes and Nikolaev, 2006] de Menezes, L. and N. Nikolaev (2006). Forecasting with Genetically Programmed Polynomial Neural Networks, *Int. J. of Forecasting*, vol.22, N:2, 2006.

[Dempster et al., 1977] Dempster, A.P., N.M. Laird and D.B. Rubin (1977). Maximum Likelihood from Incomplete Data via the EM Algorithm, *Journal of the Royal Statistical Society* B, vol.39, N:1, 1-38.

[De Veaux et al., 1998] De Veaux, R.D., J. Schumi, J. Schweinsberg and H.U. Lyle (1998). Prediction Intervals for Neural Networks via Nonlinear Regression, *Technometrics*, vol.40, N:4, 273-282.

[Dickey and Fuller, 1981] Dickey, D. and W. Fuller (1981). Likelihood Ratio Statistics for Autoregressive Time Series with a Unit Root, *Econometrica*, vol.49, 1057-1072.

[Doucet et al., 2001] Doucet, A., N. de Freitas and N. Gordon (2001). *Sequential Monte Carlo Methods in Practice*, Springer-Verlag, Berlin.

[Ebner, 1999] Ebner, M. (1999). On the Search Space of Genetic Programming and its Relation to Nature's Search Space, In: *Proc. 1999 Congress on Evolutionary Computation CEC-1999*, IEEE Press, Piscataway, NJ, 1357-1361.

[Efron and Tibshirani, 1989] Efron, B. and R.J. Tibshirani (1989). *An Introduction to the Bootstrap*, Chapman and Hall, New York, NY.

[Eiben and Smith, 2003] Eiben, A.E. and J.E. Smith (2003). Introduction to Evolutionary Computing, Springer-Verlag, Berlin.

[Elder and Pregibon, 1996] Elder IV, J.F. and D. Pregibon (1996). A Statistical Perspective on Knowledge Discovery in Databases, In: Fayyad, U.M., G. Piatetsky-Shapiro, P. Smyth and R. Uthurusamy (Eds.), *Advances in Knowledge Discovery and Data Mining*, The AAAI Press/The MIT Press, Chapter 4, 83-113.

[Elder and Brown, 2000] Elder IV, J.F. and D.E. Brown (2000). Induction and Polynomial Networks, In: Fraser, M.D. (Ed.), *Network Models for Control and Processing*, Intellect Books, Exeter, UK, 143-198.

[Elman, 1990] Elman, J.L. (1990). Finding Structure in Time, *Cognitive Science*, vol.14, 179-211.

[Fadeev and Fadeeva, 1963] Fadeev, D.K. and V.N. Fadeeva (1963). *Computational Methods of Linear Algebra*, W.H.Freeman, San Francisco, CA.

[Faraway and Chatfield, 1998] Faraway, J. and C. Chatfield (1998). Time Series Forecasting with Neural Networks: A Comparative Study using the Airline Data, *Applied Statistics*, vol.47, N:2, 231-250.

[Farlow, 1984] Farlow ,S.J. (Ed.) (1984). *Self-Organizing Methods in Modeling. GMDH Type Algorithms*, Marcel Dekker, New York, NY.

[Farmer et al., 1986] Farmer, J.D., N.H. Packard and A.S. Perelson (1986). The Immune System, Adaptation and Machine Learning. *Physica* 22D, 187-204.

[Farmer, 1990] Farmer, J.D. (1990). A Rosetta Stone for Connectionism, *Physica* 42D, 153-187.

[Finnoff et al., 1992] Finnoff, W., F. Hergert and H.G. Zimmermann (1992). Improving Generalization Performance by Nonconvergent Model Selection Methods, In: Aleksander, I. and J. Taylor (Eds.), *Neural Networks 2: Proc. of the Int. Conf. on Artificial Neural Networks ICANN-92*, 233-236.

[Fletcher, 1987] Fletcher, R. (1987). *Practical Methods of Optimization*, (2nd ed.), John Wiley and Sons, New York.

[Fogel et al., 1966] Fogel, L.J, A.J. Owens and M.J. Walsh (1966). *Artificial Intelligence through Simulated Evolution*, Wiley, New York, NY.

[Fogel, 1995] Fogel, D.B. (1995). Phenotypes, Genotypes, and Operators in Evolutionary Computation, In: *Proc. of the 1995 IEEE Int. Conf. on Evolutionary Computation ICEC'95*, IEEE Press, Piscataway, NJ, 193-198.

[Fogel, 1999] Fogel, D.B. (1999). *Evolutionary Computation: Toward a New Philosophy of Machine Intelligence*, IEEE Press, Piscataway, NJ.

[Gabor et al., 1961] Gabor, D., W. Wildes and R. Woodcock (1961). A Universal Nonlinear Filter, Predictor and Simulator which Optimizes Itself by a Learning Process, *Proceedings IEE*, vol.108B, 422-438.

[Geman et al., 1992] Geman, S, E. Bienenstock and R. Doursat (1992). Neural Networks and the Bias/Variance Dilemma, *Neural Computation*, vol.4, N:1, 1-58.

[Glover, 1989] Glover, F. (1989). Tabu Search, *ORSA Journal on Computing*, vol.1, N:3, 190-206.

[Goldberg, 1989] Goldberg, D.E. (1989). *Genetic Algorithms in Search, Optimization and Machine Learning*, Addison-Wesley Pub., Reading, MA.

[Goldberg et al., 1989] Goldberg, D.E., B. Korb and K. Deb (1989). Messy Genetic Algorithms: Motivation, Analysis and First Results, *Complex Systems*, vol.3, 493-530.

[Goldberg and Deb, 1991] Goldberg, D.E. and K. Deb (1991). A Comparative Analysis of Selection Schemes used in Genetic Algorithms, In: Rawlins, G. (Ed.), *Foundations of Genetic Algorithms FOGA-1*, Morgan Kaufmann, CA, 69-93.

[Gómez-Ramírez et al, 1999] Gómez-Ramírez, A. Poznyak, A. González-Yunes and M. Avila-Alvarez (1999). Adaptive Archictecture of Polynomial Artificial Neural Network to Forecast Nonlinear Time Series, In: *Proc. of 1999 Congress on Evolutionary Computation CEC-99*, IEEE Press, Piscataway, NJ, vol.1, 317-324.

[Gosh and Shin, 1992] Gosh, J. and Y. Shin (1992). Efficient Higher Order Neural Networks for Classification and Function Approximation, *Int. Journal of Neural Systems*, vol.3, N:4, 323-350.

[Grassberger and Procaccia, 1983] Grassberger, P. and I. Procaccia (1983). Characterization of Strange Attractors, *Physical Review Letters*, vol.50, N:5, 346-349.

[Green et al, 1988] Green, D.G., R.E. Reichelt and R.H. Bradbury (1988). Statistical Behaviour of the GMDH Algorithm, *Biometrics*, vol.44, 49-69.

[Grefenstette and Baker, 1989] Grefenstette, J.J. and J.E. Baker (1989). How Genetic Algorithms Work: A Critical Look at Implicit Parallelism, In: Schaffer, J.D. (Ed.), *Proc. Third Int. Conf. on Genetic Algorithms and their Applications*, Morgan Kaufmann, San Mateo, CA, 20-27.

[Ham and Kostanic, 2000] Ham, F.M. and I. Kostanic (2000). *Principles of Neurocomputing for Science and Engineering*, McGraw-Hill Co., New York, NY.

[Hammer, 2001] Hammer, B. (2001). Generalization Ability of Folding Networks, *IEEE Trans. on Knowledge and Data Engineering*, vol.13, N:2, 196-206.

[Hassibi and Stork, 1993] Hassibi, B. and D.G. Stork (1993). Second Order Derivatives for Network Pruning: Optimal Brain Surgeon, In: Hanson, J, J. Cowan and C. Lee Giles (Eds.), *Advances in Neural Inf. Processing Systems NIPS-5*, Morgan Kauffman, San Mateo, CA, 164-171.

[Haykin, 1999] Haykin, S. (1999). *Neural Networks. A Comprehensive Foundation*, 2nd edition, Prentice Hall, Upper Saddle River, NJ.

[Haykin, 2001] Haykin, S. (Ed.) (2001). *Kalman Filtering and Neural Networks*, John Wiley and Sons, New York, NY.

[Hertz et al., 1991] Hertz, J., A. Krough and R.G. Palmer (1991). *Introduction to the Theory of Neural Computation*, Addison-Wesley, Redwood City, CA.

[Heywood and Noakes, 1996] Heywood, M. and P. Noakes (1996). A Framework for Improved Training of Sigma-Pi Networks, *IEEE Trans. on Neural Networks*, vol.6, N:4, 893-903.

[Hildebrand, 1987] Hildebrand, F.B. (1987). *Introduction to Numerical Analysis*, Dover Publ., New York, NY.

[Holden and Rayner, 1992] Holden, S.B. and P.J.W. Rayner (1992). Generalization and Learning in Volterra and Radial Basis Function Networks: A Theoretical Analysis, In: *Proc. IEEE Int. Conf. on Acoustics, Speech and Signal Processing*, vol.2, II-273-II-276.

[Holland, 1975] Holland. J. (1975). *Adaptation in Natural and Artificial Systems*, The University of Michigan Press, Ann Arbor, MI.

[Hordijk, 1996] Hordijk, W. (1996). A Measure of Landscapes, *Evolutionary Computation*, vol.4, N:4, 335-360.

[Hornik et al., 1989] Hornik, K., M. Stinchcombe and H. White (1989). Multilayer Feedforward Networks are Universal Approximators, *Neural Networks*, vol.2, N:5, 359-366.

[Hübner et al., 1994] Hübner, U., C.-O. Weiss, N.B. Abraham and D. Tang (1994). Lorenz-Like Chaos in NH3-FIR Lasers, In: Weigend, A.S. and N.A.Gershenfeld (Eds.), *Time Series Prediction: Forecasting the Future and Understanding the Past*, Reading, MA: Addison-Wesley, 73-104.

[Hwang and Ding, 1997] Hwang, J.T.G. and A.A. Ding (1997). Prediction intervals for artificial neural networks, *Journal of the American Statistical Association*, vol.92, N:438, 748-757.

[Iba and Sato, 1992] Iba, H. and T. Sato (1992). Meta-level Strategy for Genetic Algorithms based on Structured Representations, In: *Proc. 2nd Pacific Rim Int. Conf. on Artificial Intelligence*, 548-554.

[Iba et al,1993] Iba, H., T. Kurita, H. deGaris and T. Sato (1993). System Identification using Structured Genetic Algorithms, In: *Proc. of 5th Int. Joint Conf. on Genetic Algorithms ICGA'93*, San Mateo, CA: Morgan Kaufmann, 279-286.

[Iba, 1994] Iba, H. (1994). Random Tree Generation for Genetic Programming, In: Voigt, H.-M., W. Ebeling, I. Rechenberg, and H.-P. Schwefel (Eds.), *Parallel Problem Solving from Nature PPSN-IV*, LNCS 1141, Springer-Verlag, Berlin, 144-153.

[Iba and de Garis, 1994] Iba, H. and H. de Garis (1994). Genetic Programming Using the Minimum Description Length Principle. In: Kinnear Jr., K. (Eds.), *Advances in Genetic Programming*, The MIT Press, Cambridge, MA, 265-284.

[Iba et.al, 1995] Iba, H., H. de Garis and T. Sato (1995). Temporal Data Processing using Genetic Programming, In: Eshelman, L. (Ed.), *Proc. 6th Int. Conf. on Genetic Algorithms ICGA-95*, San Mateo, CA: Morgan Kaufmann, 279-286.

[Iba et.al, 1996] Iba, H., H. de Garis and T. Sato (1996). Numerical Approach to Genetic Programming for System Identification, *Evolutionary Computation*, vol.3, N:4, 417-452.

[Iba et.al, 1996b] Iba, H., H. deGaris and T. Sato (1996). Extending Genetic Programming with Recombinative Guidance, In: Angeline, P. and K. Kinnear (Eds.), *Advances in Genetic Programming 2*, The MIT Press, Cambridge, MA, 69-88.

[Igel, 1998] Igel, C. (1998). Causality of Hierarchical Variable Length Representations, In: *Proc. 1998 IEEE Int. Conf. on Evolutionary Computation*, 324-329.

[Ivakhnenko, 1971] Ivakhnenko, A.G. (1971). Polynomial Theory of Complex Systems, *IEEE Trans. on Systems, Man, and Cybernetics*, vol.1, N:4, 364-378.

[Jacobs, 1988] Jacobs, R.A. (1988). Increased Rates of Convergence through Learning Rate Adaptation, *Neural Networks*, vol.1, 295-307.

[Jolliffe, 1986] Jolliffe, I.T. (1986). *Principal Component Analysis*, Springer-Verlag, New York, NY.

[Jones and Forrest, 1995] Jones, T.C. and S. Forrest (1995). Fitness Distance Correlation as a Measure of Problem Difficulty for Genetic Algorithms, In: Eshelman, L.J. (Ed.), *Proc Sixth Int. Conf. on Genetic Algorithms ICGA-95*, Morgan Kaufmann, San Mateo, CA, 184-192.

[Jones, 1995] Jones, T.C. (1995). Evolutionary Algorithms, Fitness Landscapes and Search, PhD dissertation, The University of New Mexico, Albuquerque, NM.

[Jordan, 1986] Jordan, M.I. (1986). Attractor Dynamics and Parallelism in a Connectionist Sequential Machine, In: *Proc. of the Eighth Conference of the Cognitive Science Society*, Lawrence Erlbaum, 531-546.

[Judd, 1990] Judd, J.S. (1990). *Neural Network Design and the Complexity of Learning*, The MIT Press, Cambridge, MA.

[Kargupta and Smith, 1991] Kargupta, H. and R.E. Smith (1991). System Identification with Evolving Polynomial Networks, In: Belew, R.K. and L.B. Booker (Eds.), *Proc. 4th Int. Conf. Genetic Algorithms*, San Mateo, CA: Morgan Kaufmann, 370-376.

[Kasabov, 2002] Kasabov, N. (2002). *Evolving connectionist systems: Methods and applications in bioinformatics, brain study and intelligent machines*, Springer-Verlag, London.

[Kauffman, 1989] Kauffman, S.A. (1989). Adaptation on Rugged Fitness Landscapes, In: Stein, D.L. (Ed.), *Lectures in the Science of Complexity*, vol.1, Addison-Wesley Longman, 527-618.

[Keith and Martin, 1994] Keith, M.J. and M.C. Martin (1994). Genetic Programming in C++: Implementation Issues, In: Kinnear Jr., K.E. (Ed.), *Advances in Genetic Programming*, The MIT Press, Cambridge, MA, 285-310.

[Kendall and Ord, 1983] Kendall, M. and J.K. Ord (1983). *Time Series*, 3rd ed., Edward Arnold, Kent, UK.

[Kinnear, 1994] Kinnear, K.E. (1994). Fitness Landscapes and Difficulty in Genetic Programming, In: *Proc. 1994 IEEE World Conference on Computational Intelligence*, IEEE Press, Piscataway, NJ, vol.1, 142-147.

[Kirkpatrick et al., 1983] Kirkpatrick, S., C.D. Gelatt Jr. and M.P. Vecchi (1983). Optimization by Simulated Annealing, *Science*, vol.220, 671-680.

[Kolmogorov, 1957] Kolmogorov, A.N. (1957). On the Representation of Continuous Functions of Several Variables by Superpositions of Continuous Functions of One Variable and Addition, *Dokl. Akad. Nauk. SSSR*, vol.114, N:5, 953-956.

[Kolmogorov and Fomin, 1999] Kolmogorov, A.N. and S.V. Fomin (1999). *Elements of the Theory of Functions and Functional Analysis*, Dover Publ., New York, NY.

[Koza, 1992] Koza, J.R. (1992). *Genetic Programming: On the Programming of Computers by Means of Natural Selection*, The MIT Press, Cambridge, MA.

[Koza, 1994] Koza, J.R. (1994). *Genetic Programming II: Automatic Discovery of Reusable Programs*, The MIT Press, Cambridge, MA.

[Koza et al., 1999] Koza, J.R., F.H. Bennett, D. Andre and M.A. Keane (1999). *Genetic Programming III: Darwinian Invention and Problem Solving*, Morgan Kaufmann, San Mateo, CA.

[Koza et al., 2003] Koza,J.R., Keane,M.A., Streeter,M.J., Mydlowec,W., Yu,J. and Lanza,G. (2003). *Genetic Programming IV: Routine Human-Competitive Machine Intelligence*, Kluwer Academic Publishers, Boston, MA.

[Lanczos, 1957] Lanczos, C. (1957). *Applied Analysis*, Prentice-Hall, London, UK.

[Lang et al., 1990] Lang, K.J., A.H. Waibel and G. Hinton (1990). A Time-delay Neural Network Architecture for Isolated Word Recognition, *Neural Networks*, vol.3, 23-44.

[Langdon and Poli, 2002] Langdon, W.B. and R. Poli (2002). *Foundations of Genetic Programming*, Springer-Verlag, Heidelberg.

[LeCun et al., 1990] LeCun, Y., J. Denker, S. Solla, R.E. Howard and L.D. Jackel (1990). Optimal Brain Damage, In: Touretzky, D.S. (Ed.), *Advances in Neural Inf. Processing Systems NIPS-2*, Morgan Kauffman, San Mateo, CA, 598-605.

[Lee and Jeng, 1997] Lee, T.-T. and J.-T. Jeng (1997). Chebyshev Polynomials Based (CPB) Unified Model Neural Networks for Function Approximation, In: Rogers, S.K. and D.W. Ruck (Eds.), *Proc. SPIE: Applications and Science of Artificial Neural Networks III*, vol.3077, 372-381.

[Leung and Haykin, 1993] Leung, H. and S. Haykin (1993). Rational Function Neural Network, *Neural Computation*, vol.5, N:6, 928-938.

[Levenberg, 1944] Levenberg, K. (1944). A Method for the Solution of Certain Non-linear Problems in Least Squares, *Quarterly Journal of Applied Mathematics*, vol.II, N:2, 164-168.

[Liu et al., 1998] Liu, G.P., V. Kadirkamanathan and S.A. Billings (1998). On-line Identification of Nonlinear Systems using Volterra Polynomial Basis Function Neural Networks, *Neural Networks*, vol.11, N:9, 1645-1657.

[Ljung and Box, 1978] Ljung, G.M. and G.E.P. Box (1978). On a Measure of Lack of Fit in Time Series Models, *Biometrika*, vol.65, 553-564.

[Ljung and Södeström, 1983] Ljung, L. and T. Södeström (1983). *Theory and Practice of Recursive Identification*, The MIT Press, Cambridge, MA.

[Lo and MacKinley, 1988] Lo, A.W., and A.C. MacKinley (1988). Stock Market Prices Do Not Follow Random Walks: Evidence from a Simple Specification Test, *Review of Financial Studies*, vol.1, N:1, 41-66.

[Luke, 2000] Luke, S. (2000). Two Fast Tree-Creation Algorithms for Genetic Programmimg, *IEEE Trans. on Evolutionary Computation*, vol.4, N:3, 274-283.

[Mackey and Glass, 1977] Mackey, M.C. and L. Glass (1977). Oscillation and Chaos in Physiological Control Systems, *Science*, vol.197, 287-289.

[MacKay, 1992a] MacKay, D.J.C. (1992). Bayesian Interpolation, *Neural Computation*, vol.4, N:3, 415-447.

[MacKay, 1992b] MacKay, D.J.C. (1992). A Practical Bayesian Framework for Backprop Networks, *Neural Computation*, vol.4, N:3, 448-472.

[MacKay, 1995] MacKay, D.J.C. (1995). Probable Networks and Plausible Predictions- A Review of Practical Bayesian Methods for Supervised Neural Networks, *Network: Computation in Neural Systems*, vol.6, N:3, 469-505.

[MacKay, 2003] MacKay, D.J.C. (2003). *Information Theory, Inference and Learning Algorithms*, Cambridge University Press, Cambridge, UK.

[Madala and Ivakhnenko, 1994] Madala, H.R. and A.G. Ivakhnenko (1994). *Inductive Learning Algorithms for Complex Systems Modeling*, CRC Press, Boca Raton, FL.

[Mallows, 1973] Mallows, C.L. (1973). Some Comments on Cp, *Technometrics*, vol.15, 661-676.

[Manderick et al., 1991] Manderick, B., M. deWeger and P. Spiessens (1991). The Genetic Algorithm and the Structure of the Fitness Landscape. In: Belew, R.K. and L.B. Booker (Eds.), *Proc. Fourth Int. Conf. on Genetic Algorithms ICGA-91*, Morgan Kaufmann, San Mateo, CA, 143-150.

[Mardia et al., 1979] Mardia, K.V., J.T. Kent and J.M. Bibby (1979). *Multivariate Analysis*, Academic Press, London.

[Marin and Sole, 1999] Marin, J. and R.V. Sole (1999). Macroevolutionary Algorithms: A New Optimization Method on Fitness Landscapes, *IEEE Trans. on Evolutionary Computation*, vol.3, N:4, 272-286.

[Marmarelis, 1994] Marmarelis, V.Z. (1994). Three Conjectures on Neural Network Implementations of Volterra Models, In: Marmarelis, V.Z. (Ed.), *Advanced Methods of Physiological System Modeling*, vol.3, Plenum Press, NY, 261-267.

[Marmarelis and Zhao, 1997] Marmarelis, V.Z. and X. Zhao (1997), Volterra Models and Threee-Layer Perceptrons, *IEEE Trans. on Neural Networks*, vol.8, N:6, 1421-1433.

[Marquardt, 1963] Marquardt, D.W. (1963). An Algorithm for Least-squares Estimation of Non-linear Parameters, *Journal of the Society of Industrial and Applied Mathematics*, vol.11, N:2, 431-441.

[Matthews and Moschytz, 1994] Matthews, M.B. and G.S. Moschytz (1994). The Identification of Nonlinear Discrete-time Fading-memory Systems using Neural Network Models, *IEEE Trans. on Circuits and Systems-II*, vol.41, 740-751.

[Merz and Freisleben, 2000] Merz, P. and B. Freisleben (2000). Fitness Landscapes, Memetic Algorithms and Greedy Operators for Graph Bi-Partitioning, *Evolutionary Computation*, vol.8, no.1, 61-91.

[Michalewics, 1992] Michalewics, Z. (1992). *Genetic Algorithms+Data Structures=Evolution Programs*, Springer-Verlag, New York, NY.

[Mitchell, 1997] Mitchell, T. (1997). *Machine Learning*, McGraw Hill, New York, NY.

[Moody, 1992] Moody, J. (1992). The Effective Number of Parameters: An Analysis of Generalization and Regularization in Nonlinear Learning Systems, In: Moody, J.E., S.J. Hanson, and R.P. Lippmann (Eds.), *Advances in Neural Information Processing Systems 4*, Morgan Kaufmann, San Mateo, CA, 847-854.

[Moscato and Norman, 1992] Moscato, P. and M.G. Norman (1992). A Memetic Approach for the Traveling Salesman Problem:, In: Valero, M., E. Onate, M. Jane, J.L. Larriba and B. Suarez (Eds.), *Parallel Computing and Transputer Applications*, IOS Press, Amsterdam, 187-194.

[Müller et al., 1999] Müller, K.-R., A.J. Smola, G. Rätsch, B. Schölkopf, J. Kohlmorgen and V. Vapnik (1999). Predicting Time Series with Support Vector Machines, In: Schölkopf, B., C.J.C. Burges and A.J. Smola (Eds.), *Advances in Kernel Methods- Support Vector Learning*, Cambridge, MA: MIT Press, 243-254.

[Müller and Lemke, 2000] Müller, J.-A. and F. Lemke (2000). *Self-Organising Data Mining*, Trafford Publ., Canada.

[Mühlenbein and Schlierkamp-Voosen, 1995] Mühlenbein, H. and D. Schlierkamp-Voosen (1995). Predictive Models for the Breeder Genetic Algorithm: I, *Evolutionary Computation*, vol.1, N:1, 25-49.

[Myers, 1990] Myers, R.H. (1990). *Classical and Modern Regression with Applications*, Duxbury Press, PWS-KENT Publ., CA.

[Nabney, 2002] Nabney, I.T. (2002). *Netlab: Algorithms for Pattern Recognition*, Springer-Verlag, London, UK.

[Namatame and Ueda, 1992] Namatame, A. and N. Ueda (1992). Pattern Classification with Chebychev Neural Networks, *Int. J. of Neural Networks*, vol.3, N:1, 23-31.

[Narendra and Parthasarathy, 1990] Narendra, K.S. and K. Parthasarathy (1990). Identification and Control of Dynamical Systemns Using Neural Networks, *IEEE Trans. on Neural Networks*, vol.1, N:1, 4-27.

[Neal, 1996] Neal, R.M. (1996). *Bayesian Learning for Neural Networks*, Lecture Notes in Statistics No.118, Springer-Verlag, New York.

[Neuneier and Zimmermann, 1998] Neuneier, R. and H.G. Zimmermann (1998). How to Train Neural Networks, In: Orr, G.B. and K.-R. Müller (Eds.), *Neural Networks: Tricks of the Trade*, LNCS-1524, Springer-Verlag, Berlin, 373-423.

[Ng and Lippmann, 1991] Ng, K. and R.P. Lippmann (1991). A Comparative Study of the Practical Characteristics of Neural Network and Conventional Pattern Classifiers, In: Lippmann, R.P., J. Moody and D.S. Touretzky (Eds.), *Advances in Neural Inf. Proc. Systems 3*, San Mateo, CA: Morgan Kaufmann, 1991, 970-976.

[Ngia and Sjöberg, 2000] Ngia, L.S.H. and J. Sjöberg (2000). Efficient Training of Neural Nets for Nonlinear Adaptive Filtering using a Recursive Levenberg-Marquardt Algorithm, *IEEE Tr. on Signal Processing*, vol.48, N:7, 1915-1927.

[Nikolaev and Slavov, 1998] Nikolaev, N.Y. and V. Slavov (1998). The Dynamics of Biased Inductive Genetic Programming, In: Koza, J. et al. (Eds.) *Proc. Third Annual Conf. on Genetic Programming, GP-98*, Morgan Kaufmann, CA, 260-268.

[Nikolaev et al., 1999] Nikolaev, N., H. Iba and V. Slavov (1999). Inductive Genetic Programming with Immune Network Dynamics, In: Spector, L., W.B. Langdon, U.-M. O'Reilly and P.J. Angeline (Eds.), *Advances In Genetic Programming 3*, Chapter 15, MIT Press, Cambridge, MA, 355-376.

[Nikolaev and Iba, 2001a] Nikolaev, N.Y. and H. Iba (2001). Regularization Approach to Inductive Genetic Programmimg, *IEEE Trans. on Evolutionary Computation*, vol.5, N:4, 359-375.

[Nikolaev and Iba, 2001b] Nikolaev, N.Y. and H. Iba (2001). Accelerated Genetic Programming of Polynomials, *Genetic Programming and Evolvable Machines*, Kluwer Academic Publ., vol.2, N:3, 231-257.

[Nikolaev and Iba, 2001c] Nikolaev, N.Y. and H. Iba (2001). Genetic Programming of Polynomial Harmonic Networks using the Discrete Fourier Transform, *Int. Journal of Neural Systems*, vol.12, N:5, 399-410.

[Nikolaev and Iba, 2001d] Nikolaev, N.Y. and H. Iba (2001). Genetic Programming using Chebishev Polynomials, In: Spector, L., E.D. Goodman, A. Wu, W.B. Langdon, H.-M. Voigt, M. Gen, S. Sen, M. Dorigo, S. Pezeshk, M.H. Garzon, and E. Burke (Eds.), *Proc. of the Genetic and Evolutionary Computation Conference GECCO-2001*, Morgan Kaufmann Publ., San Francisco, CA, 89-96.

[Nikolaev and Iba, 2003] Nikolaev, N.Y. and H. Iba (2003). Learning Polynomial Feedforward Neural Networks by Genetic Programming and Backpropagation, *IEEE Trans. on Neural Networks*, vol.14, N:2, 337-350.

[Nikolaev and Tino, 2005a] Nikolaev, N.Y. and P. Tino (2005). A Recursive Relevance Vector Machine for Sequential Bayesian Learning, Tech Report TR 29-05-2005, Goldsmiths College, University of London, London.

[Nilsson, 1980] Nilsson, N.J. (1980). *Principles of Artificial Intelligence*, Tioga Publishing Company, Palo Alto, CA.

[Nix and Weigend, 1995] Nix, D.A. and A.S. Weigend (1995). Learning Local Error Bars for Nonlinear Regression, In: Tesauro, G., D.S. Touretzky, and T.K. Leen (Eds.), *Advances in Neural Inf. Processing Systems NIPS-7*, MIT Press, Cambridge, MA, 489-496.

[O'Reilly, 1995] O'Reilly, U.-M. (1995). An Analysis of Genetic Programming, PhD Dissertation, Carleton University, Ottawa, Canada.

[Pao, 1989] Pao, Y.H. (1989). *Adaptive Pattern Recognition and Neural Networks*, Addison-Wesley, Reading, MA.

[Paton, 1997] Paton, R.C. (1997). Principles of Genetics, In: Back, T., D.B. Fogel, and Z. Michalewicz (Eds.), *Handbook of Evolutionary Computation*, IOP Publ. and Oxford University Press, Oxford, UK, A2.2:1-2:9.

[Pearlmutter, 1994] Pearlmutter, B.A. (1994). Fast Exact Multiplication by the Hessian, *Neural Computation*, vol.6, N:2, 147-160.

[Pedersen and Hansen, 1995] Pedersen, M.W. and L.K. Hansen (1995). Recurrent Networks: Second Order Properties and Pruning, In: Tesauro,G., D. Touretzky and T. Leen (Eds.), *Advances in Neural Information Processing Systems NIPS-7*, The MIT Press, Cambridge, MA, 673-680.

[Pham and Liu, 1995] Pham, D.T. and X. Liu (1995). *Neural Networks for Prediction, Identification and Control*, London, UK: Springer-Verlag.

[Polak, 1971] Polak, E. (1971). *Computational Methods in Optimization: A Unified Approach*, Academic Press, New York.

[Poli and Langdon, 1998] Poli, R. and W.B. Langdon (1998). Schema Theory for Genetic Programming with One-point Crossover and Point Mutation, *Evolutionary Computation*, vol.6, N:3, 231-252.

[Press et al., 1992] Press, W.H. B.P. Flannery, S.A. Teukolski and W.T. Vetterling (1992). *Numerical Recipes in C: The Art of Scientific Computing*, 2nd ed., Cambridge University Press, Cambridge, England.

[Puskorius and Felkamp, 1994] Puskorius, G.V. and L.A. Felkamp (1994). Neurocontrol of nonlinear dynamical systems with Kalman Filter-trained recurrent networks, *IEEE Trans. on Neural Networks*, vol.5, N:2, 279-297.

[Quiñonero-Candela, 2004] Quiñonero-Candela, C.E. (2004). *Learning with Uncertainty-Gaussian Processes and Relevance Vector Machines*, PhD thesis IMM-PHD-2004-135, Technical University of Denmark.

[Rayner and Lynch, 1989] Rayner, P.J.W. and M.R. Lynch (1989). A New Connectionist Model Based on a Non-linear Adaptive Filter, In: *Proc. IEEE Int. Conf. Acoustics, Speech and Signal Processing*, 1191-1194.

[Riolo and Worzel, 2003] Riolo, R.L. and B. Worzel (Eds.) (2003). *Genetic Programming Theory and Practice*, Kluwer Academic Publ., Boston, MA.

[Rissanen, 1989] Rissanen, J. (1989). *Stochastic Complexity in Statistical Inquiry*, World Scientific Publishing, Singapore.

[Rivals and Personnaz, 2000] Rivals, I. and L. Personnaz (2000). Construction of Confidence Intervals for Neural Networks Based on Least Squares Estimation, *Neural Networks*, vol.13, 463-484.

[Rodriguez-Vazquez, 1999] Rodriguez-Vazquez, K. (1999). *Multiobjective Evolutionary Algorithms in Non-Linear System Identification*, PhD Thesis, Dept. of Automatic Control and Systems Engineering, University of Sheffield, UK.

[Rodriguez-Vazquez and Fleming, 2000] Rodriguez-Vazquez, K. and P.J. Fleming (2000). Use of Genetic Programming in the Identification of Rational Model Structures, In: Poli, R., W. Banzhaf, W.B. Langdon, J.F. Miller, P. Nordin and T.C. Fogarty (Eds.), *Genetic Programming, Proc. of EuroGP'2000*, LNCS 1802, Springer-Verlag, Berlin, 181-192.

[Rosca and Ballard, 1995a] Rosca, J.P. and D.H. Ballard (1995). Causality in Genetic Programming, In: Eshelman, L.J. (Ed.), *Proc. Sixth Int. Conf. Genetic Algorithms*, Morgan Kaufmann, San Francisco, CA, 256-263.

[Rosca and Ballard, 1995b] Rosca, J.P. and D.H. Ballard (1995). Discovery of Subroutines in Genetic Programming, In: Angeline, P.J. and K. Kinnear Jr. (Eds.), *Advances in Genetic Programming II*, The MIT Press, Cambridge, MA, 177-202.

[Rosca and Ballard, 1999] Rosca, J.P. and D.H. Ballard (1999). Rooted-Tree Schemata in Genetic Programming, In: Spector, L., W.B. Langdon, U.-M. O'Reilly and P.J. Angeline (Eds.), *Advances In Genetic Programming 3*, Chapter 11, MIT Press, Cambridge, MA, 243-271.

[Rumelhart et al., 1986] Rumelhart, D.E., G.E. Hinton and R.J. Williams (1986). Learning Internal Representations by Error Propagation, In: *Parallel Distributed Processing: Explorations in the Microstructure of Cognition*, vol.1, Rumelhart, D.E., et al. (Eds.), The MIT Press, Cambridge, MA, 318-362.

[Salustowicz and Schmidhuber, 1997] Salustowicz, R. and J. Schmidhuber (1997). Probabilistic Incremental Program Evolution, *Evolutionary Computation*, vol.5, N:2, 123-141.

[Schetzen, 1980] Schetzen,M. (1980). *The Volterra and Wiener Theories of Nonlinear Systems*, Wiley, New York.

[Schölkopf and Smola, 2002] Schölkopf, B. and A. Smola (2002). *Learning with Kernels*, The MIT Press, Cambridge, MA.

[Schwartz, 1978] Schwartz, G. (1978). Estimating the Dimension of a Model, *Annals of Statistics*, vol.6, 461-464.

[Schwefel, 1995] Schwefel, H.P. (1995). *Evolution and Optimum Seeking*, John Wiley and Sons, New York, NY.

[Sendhoff et al., 1997] Sendhoff, B., M. Kreutz and W. Seelen (1997). A Condition for the Genotype-Phenotype Mapping: Causality, In: T.Bäck (Ed.), *Proc. Seventh Int. Conf. on Genetic Algorithms ICGA-97*, Morgan Kaufman, CA, 73-80.

[Shin and Ghosh, 1995] Shin, Y. and J. Ghosh (1995). Ridge Polynomial Networks, *IEEE Trans. on Neural Networks*, vol.6, N:3, 610-622.

[Slavov and Nikolaev, 1997] Slavov, V. and N. Nikolaev (1997). Inductive Genetic Programming and the Superposition of Fitness Landscapes, In: Bäck, T. (Ed.), *Proc. Seventh Int. Conf. on Genetic Algorithms ICGA-97*, Morgan Kaufmann, San Mateo, CA, 97-104.

[Shah et al., 1992] Shah, S., E. Palmieri and M. Datum (1992). Optimal Filtering Algorithms for Fast Learning in Feedforward Neural Networks, *Neural Networks*, vol.5, N:5, 779-787.

[Shepherd, 1997] Shepherd, A.J. (1997). *Second-Order Methods for Neural Networks: Fast and Reliable Training Methods for Multi-Layer Perceptrons*, Springer-Verlag, London.

[Smirnov, 2001] Smirnov, E.N. (2001). *Conjunctive and Disjunctive Version Spaces with Instance-based Boundary Sets*, Shaker Publ., Maastricht, The Netherlands.

[Smith and Vavak, 1998] Smith, J.E. and F. Vavak (1998). Replacement Strategies in Steady State Genetic Algorithms: Static Environments, In: Banzhaf, W. and C. Reeves (Eds.), *Foundations of Genetic Algorithms FOGA-V*, Morgan Kaufmann, San Francisco, CA, 219-234.

[Sontag, 1992] Sontag, E.D. (1992). Feedback Stabilization Using Two-Hidden Layer Nets, *IEEE Trans. on Neural Networks*, vol.3, N:6, 981-990.

[Stadler, 1996] Stadler, P. (1996). Landscapes and their Correlation Functions, *Journal of Mathematical Chemistry*, vol.20, 1-45.

[Syswerda, 1991] Syswerda, G. (1991). A study of Reproduction in Generational SteadyState Genetic Algorithms, In: Rawlings, G.J.E. (Ed.), *Foundations of Genetic Algorithms FOGA-1*, Morgan Kaufmann, San Mateo, CA, 94-101.

[Tackett and Carmi, 1994] Tackett, W.A. and A. Carmi (1994). The Donut Problem: Scalability and Generalization in Genetic Programming, In: Kinnear, K. (Ed.), *Advances in Genetic Programming*, The MIT Press, Cambridge, MA, 143-176.

[Takens, 1981] Takens, F. (1981). Detecting Strange Attractors in Turbulence. In: Rand, D.A. and L.-S. Young (Eds), *Dynamical Systems and Turbulence*, Lecture Notes in Mathematics, 898, Springer-Verlag, Berlin, 366-381.

[Tai, 1979] Tai, K.-C. (1979). The Tree-to-Tree Correction Problem, *Journal of the ACM*, vol.26, N:3, 422-433.

[Teller and Veloso, 1996] Teller, A. and M. Veloso (1996). PADO: A New Learning Architecture for Object Recognition, In: Ikeuchi, K. and M. Veloso (Eds.), *Symbolic Visual Learning*, Oxford University Press, Oxford, UK, 81-116.

[Tenorio and Lee, 1990] Tenorio, M.F. and W.-T. Lee (1990). Self-Organizing Network for Optimum Supervised Learning, *IEEE Trans. on Neural Networks*, vol.1, 100-110.

[Tibshirani, 1996] Tibshirani, R. (1996). A Comparison of Some Error Estimates for Neural Network Models, *Neural Computation*, vol.8, N:1, 152-163.

[Tipping, 2001] Tipping, M.E. (2001). Sparse Bayesian Learning and the Relevance Vector Machine, *Journal of Machine Learning Research*, vol.1, N:1, 211-244.

[Tsoi and Back, 1994] Tsoi, A.C. and A. Back (1994). Locally Recurrent Globally Feedforward Networks: A Critical Review, *IEEE Trans. on Neural Networks*, vol.5, N:2, 229-239.

[Vapnik and Chervonenkis, 1971] Vapnik, V.N. and A.Y. Chervonenkis (1971). On the Uniform Convergence of Relative Frequences of Events to their Probabiliries, *Theory of Probability and its Applications*, vol.17, N:2, 264-280.

[Vapnik, 1992] Vapnik, V. (1992) Principles of Risk Minimisation for Learning Theory, In: Moody,J., Hanson,S., Lippmann,R. (Eds.), *Advances in Neural Information Processing Systems 4*, Morgan Kaufmann, San Mateo, CA, 831-838.

[Vapnik, 1995] Vapnik, V. (1995). *The Nature of Statistical Learning Theory*, Springer Verlag, New York.

[Vapnik, 1998] Vapnik, V. (1998). *Statistical Learning Theory*, Wiley and Sons, New York.

[Vassilev et al., 2000] Vassilev, V.K., T.C. Fogarty and J.F. Miller (2000). Information Characteristics and the Structure of Landscapes, *Evolutionary Computation*, vol.8, N:1, 31-60.

[Volterra, 1959] Volterra, V. (1959). *Theory of Functionals*, Dover Publ., New York.

[Vose, 1999] Vose, M.D. (1999). *The Simple Genetic Algorithm: Foundations and Theory*, The MIT Press, Cambridge, MA.

[Wahba, 1990] Wahba, G. (1990). *Spline Models for Observational Data*, CBMS-NSF Regional Conf. Series 59, Society for Industrial and Applied Mathematics, Philadelphia, Pennsylvania.

[Weigend et al., 1992] Weigend, A.S., B.A. Huberman and D.E. Rumelhart (1992). Predicting Sunspots and Exchange Rates with Connectionist Networks, In: Eubank, S. and M. Casdagli (Eds.), *Nonlinear Modeling and Forecasting*, Addison-Wesley, Redwood City, CA, 395-432.

[Weinberger, 1990] Weinberger, E.D. (1990). Correlated and Uncorrelated Fitness Landscapes and How to Tell the Difference, *Biological Cybernetics*, vol.63, 325-336.

[Werbos, 1974] Werbos, P.J. (1974). *Beyond Regression: New Tools for Prediction and Analysis in the Behavioral Sciences*, PhD thesis, Harvard University.

[Whitley, 1989] Whitley, D. (1989). The GENITOR Algorithm and Selection Pressure: Why Rank-based Allocation of Reproduction Trials is Best, In: Schaffer, J.D. (Ed.), *Proc. Third Int. Conf. on Genetic Algorithms and their Applications*, Morgan Kaufmann, San Mateo, CA, 116-121.

[Williams, 1995] Williams, P.M. (1995). Bayesian Regularisation and Pruning Using a Laplace Prior, *Neural Computation*, vol.7, N:1, 117-143.

[Williams and Zipser, 1989] Williams, R.J. and D. Zipser (1989). A Learning Algorithm for Continually Running Fully Recurrent Neural Networks, *Neural Computation*, vol.1, 270-280.

[Williams and Zipser, 1995] Williams, R.J. and D. Zipser (1995). Gradient-based Learning Algorithms for Recurrent Networks and their Computational Complexity, In: Chauvin, Y. and D.E. Rumelhart (Eds.), *Back-propagation: Theory, Architectures and Applications*, Lawrence Erlbaum, Hillsdale, NJ, 433-486.

[Wray and Green, 1994] Wray, J. and Green, G.G.R. (1994). Calculation of the Volterra Kernels of Non-linear Dynamic Systems using an Artificial Neural Networks, *Biological Cybernetics*, vol.71, N:3, 187-195.

[Wright, 1932] Wright, S. (1932). The Roles of Mutation, Inbreeding, Crossbreeding and Selection in Evolution, In: Jones, D.F. (Ed.), *Proc. of the Sixth Int. Congress on Genetics*, vol.1, 356-366 (also in: Provine, W.B. (Ed.), *Sewall Wright Evolution. Selected Papers*, University of Chicago Press, Chicago, IL, 1986).

[Yang et al., 1996] Yang, A.S., C. Sun and C. Hsu (1996). Energy, Matter, and Entropy in Evolutionary Computation. In: *Proc. Third IEEE Int. Conf. on Evolutionary Computation ICEC-96*, IEEE Press, Piscataway, NJ, 196-200.

[Yao, 1999] Yao, X. (Ed.) (1999). *Evolutionary Computation: Theory and Applications*, World Scientific, Singapore.

[Zapranis and Refenes, 1999] Zapranis, A.D. and A.-P. Refenes (1999). *Principles of Neural Model Selection, Identification and Adequacy: With Applications to Financial Econometrics*, Springer-Verlag, London, UK.

[Zhang and Mühlenbein, 1995] Zhang, B.-T. and H. Mühlenbein (1995). Balancing Accuracy and Parsimony in Genetic Programming, *Evolutionary Computation*, vol.3, N:1, 17-38.

[Zhang et al., 1997] Zhang, B.-T., P. Ohm and H. Mühlenbein (1997). Evolutionary Induction of Sparse Neural Trees, *Evolutionary Computation*, vol.5, N:2, 213-236.

[Zhu, 2003] Zhu, Q.M. (2003). A Back Propagation Algorithm to Estimate the Parameters of Non-linear Dynamic Models, *Applied Mathematical Modelling*, vol.27, N:3, 169-187.

Index